Teacher's Edition

Learning for Earning

Your Route to Success

Sixth Edition

Teaching strategies written by

Colleen J. Angel

Instructor and Tech Prep Student Services Coordinator
Luzerne County Community College
Nanticoke, Pennsylvania

Publisher

The Goodheart-Willcox Company, Inc.
Tinley Park, Illinois
www.g-w.com

Manufactured in the United States of America.

ISBN: 978-1-59070-947-4
2 3 4 5 6 7 8 9 – 09 – 13 12 11 10 09

Contents

Learning for Earning

Prepare your students for the challenges of making the transition from school to work. Topics include

- exploring the world of work
- exploring career options
- making plans for career success
- acquiring workplace skills
- developing personal skills for job success
- managing your money
- growing toward independence

The Building Blocks of the Package

A complete package of materials is available to help your students learn and to help you teach effectively.

For Students

Student Text

Colorful headings, readable typeface, and logical organization facilitate reading comprehension and learning.

Interactive Student Edition

This powerful CD contains the content of the printed text to allow easy viewing of pages. Also includes Web links and a search feature for checking individual chapters or the entire text.

Student Workbook

Includes various activities to help students review and apply chapter concepts.

For Students and Teachers

A Companion Web Site

Motivates and engages students beyond the classroom with online flash cards, interactive quizzes, animated activities, and more. Provides answers in a secure site for teachers.

For Teachers

Teacher's Edition

The text provides a variety of teaching aids in the page margins to help you review and reinforce chapter content. Answer keys appear next to review questions.

Teacher's Annotated Workbook

Designed for presenting answers to workbook activities right where you need them.

Teacher's Resource Guide

Contains learning strategies, reproducible masters, black line transparencies, and chapter tests.

Teacher's Resource Portfolio

Conveniently groups the content of the *Teacher's Resource Guide* into an easy-to-use binder! Includes color transparencies.

Teacher's Resource CD

Allows you to easily access the content of the portfolio and the Teacher's Edition of the text, plus show color transparencies in PowerPoint® and create daily lesson plans.

Exam*View*® Assessment Suite

This test generator CD lets you quickly and easily create and print tests from a test bank of hundreds of questions.

Teacher's PowerPoint® Presentations

Includes presentations for each chapter to reinforce key concepts and terms.

Learning for Earning is designed to introduce students to the skills they will need to succeed in school, on the job, and on their own.

Strategies for Successful Teaching

You can make the *Learning for Earning* subject matter exciting and relevant for your students by using a variety of teaching strategies. Many suggestions for planning classroom activities are given in the various teaching supplements that accompany this text. As you plan your lessons, you might also want to keep the following points in mind.

Helping Your Students Develop Critical-Thinking Skills

As today's students leave their classrooms behind, they will face a world of complexity and change. They are likely to work in several career areas and hold many different jobs. Young people must develop a base of knowledge and be prepared to solve complex problems, make difficult decisions, and assess ethical implications. In other words, students must be able to use critical-thinking skills. These skills are often referred to as the higher-order thinking skills. Benjamin Bloom listed these as

- analysis—breaking down material into its component parts so that its organizational structure may be understood
- synthesis—putting parts together to form a new whole
- evaluation—judging the value of material for a given purpose

In a broader perspective, students must be able to use reflective thinking in order to decide what to believe and do. According to Robert Ennis, students should be able to

- define and clarify problems, issues, conclusions, reasons, and assumptions.
- judge the credibility, relevance, and consistency of information.
- infer or solve problems and draw reasonable conclusions.

Critical thinking goes beyond memorizing or recalling information. Critical thinking cannot occur in a vacuum; it requires individuals to apply what they know about the subject matter. It requires students to use their common sense and experience. It may involve controversy, too.

Critical thinking also requires *creative thinking* to construct all the reasonable alternatives, consequences, influencing factors, and supporting arguments. Unusual ideas are valued and perspectives outside the obvious are sought.

Finally, the teaching of critical thinking does not require exotic and highly unusual classroom approaches. Complex thought processes can be incorporated in ordinary, basic activities, such as reading, writing, and listening, if the activities are carefully planned and skillfully executed.

Help your students develop their analytical and judgment skills and to go beyond what they see on the surface. Rather than allowing students to blindly accept what they read or hear, encourage them to examine ideas in ways that show respect for others' opinions and different perspectives. Encourage students to think about points raised by others. Ask them to evaluate how new ideas relate to their attitudes about various subjects.

Debate is an excellent way to explore opposite sides of an issue. You may want to divide the class into two groups, each to take an opposing side of the issue. You can also ask students to work in smaller groups and explore opposing sides of different issues. Each group can select students from the group to present the points for their side.

Problem-Solving and Decision-Making Skills

An important aspect in the development of critical thinking skills is learning how to solve problems and make decisions. Some very important decisions lie ahead for your students, particularly those related to their future education and career choices.

Simulation games and role-plays allow students to practice solving problems and making decisions under nonthreatening circumstances. Role-playing allows students to examine others' feelings as well as their own. It can help them learn effective ways to react or cope when confronted with similar situations in real life.

Using Cooperative Learning

Because of the new emphasis on teamwork in the workplace, the use of cooperative learning groups in your classroom will give students an opportunity to practice teamwork skills. During cooperative learning, students learn interpersonal and small-group skills that will allow them to function as part of a team. These skills include leadership, decision making, trust building, communication, and conflict management.

When planning for cooperative learning, you will have a particular goal or task in mind. You will first specify the objectives for the lesson. Small groups of learners are matched for the purpose of completing the task or goal, and each person in the group is assigned a role. The success of the group is measured not only in terms of outcome, but also in terms of the successful performance of each member in his or her role.

In cooperative learning groups, students learn to work together toward a group goal. Each member is dependent on others for the outcome. This interdependence is a basic component of any cooperative learning group. Students understand one person cannot succeed unless everyone succeeds. The value of each group member is affirmed as learners work toward their goal.

The success of the group depends on individual performance. Groups should be mixed in terms of abilities and talents so there are opportunities for the students to learn from one another. Also, as groups work together over time, the roles should be rotated so everyone has an opportunity to practice and develop different skills.

You will also need to monitor the effectiveness of the groups, intervening as necessary to provide task assistance or help with interpersonal and group skills. Finally, evaluate students' achievement and help them discuss how well they collaborated with each other.

Helping Students Recognize and Value Diversity

Your students will be entering a rapidly changing workplace—not only in matters pertaining to technology, but also in the diverse nature of its workforce. The majority of the new entrants to the workforce are women, minorities, and immigrants, all representing many different views and experiences. The workforce is aging, too, as the ranks of mature workers swell. Because of these trends, young workers must learn how to interact effectively with a variety of people who are considerably unlike them.

The appreciation and understanding of diversity is an ongoing process. The earlier and more frequently young people are exposed to diversity, the more quickly they can develop skills to bridge cultural differences. If your students are exposed to various cultures within your classroom, the process of understanding cultural differences can begin. This is the best preparation for success in a diverse society. In addition, teachers find the following strategies for teaching diversity helpful:

- Actively promote a spirit of openness, consideration, respect, and tolerance in the classroom.
- Use a variety of teaching styles and assessment strategies.
- Use cooperative learning activities whenever possible and make sure group roles are rotated so everyone has leadership opportunities.
- When grouping students, have each group's composition as diverse as possible with regard to gender, race, and nationality. If groups present information to the class, make sure all members have a speaking part.

- Make sure one group's opinions do not dominate class discussions. Seek out the unexpressed opinions of others, if necessary.
- If a student makes a sexist, racist, or similarly offensive comment, ask the student to rephrase the comment in a manner that it will not offend other class members. Remind students that offensive statements and behavior are inappropriate in the classroom.
- If a difficult classroom situation arises involving a diversity issue, ask for a time-out and have everyone write down his or her thoughts and opinions about the incident. This helps to calm the situation and allows you time to plan a response.
- Arrange for guest speakers who represent diversity in gender, race, and ethnicity, even though the topic does not relate to diversity.
- Have students change seats occasionally throughout the course and introduce themselves to their new "neighbors" so they become acquainted with all their classmates.
- Several times during the course, ask students to make anonymous, written evaluations of the class. Have them report any problems that may not be obvious.

Assessment Techniques

Various forms of assessment need to be used with students to evaluate their achievement. Written tests have traditionally been used to evaluate performance. This method of evaluation is good to use when assessing knowledge and comprehension. Other methods of assessment are preferable for measuring the achievement of the higher-level skills of application, analysis, synthesis, and evaluation.

Included in the *Learning for Earning* teacher supplements are objective tests for each chapter in the text. The "Reviewing Key Concepts" sections in the text can be used to evaluate students' recall of important chapter concepts. The activities suggested in each chapter's last page provide more opportunities for you to assess your students' abilities to use critical thinking, problem solving, and application.

Performance Assessment

When you assign students some of the projects described in the text, a different form of assessing mastery or achievement is required. One method that teachers have successfully used is a rubric. A *rubric* consists of a set of criteria that includes specific descriptors or standards that can be used to arrive at performance scores for students. A point value is given for each set of descriptors, leading to a range of possible points to be assigned, usually from 1 to 5. The criteria can also be weighted. This method of assessment reduces the guesswork involved in grading, leading to fair and consistent scoring. The standards clearly indicate to students the various levels of mastery of a task. Students are even able to assess their own achievement based on the criteria.

When using rubrics, students should see the criteria at the beginning of the assignment. Then they can focus their effort on what needs to be done to reach a certain level of performance or quality of project. They have a clear understanding of your expectations of achievement.

Though you will want to design many of your own rubrics, several generic ones are included in the front section of three *Learning for Earning* supplements: *Teacher's Resource Guide, Teacher's Resource Portfolio*, and *Teacher's Resource CD.* These are designed to assess the following:

- Individual Participation
- Individual Reports
- Group Participation

These rubrics allow you to assess a student's performance and arrive at a performance score. Students can see what levels they have surpassed and what levels they can still strive to reach.

Portfolios

Another type of performance assessment that is frequently used by teachers today is the portfolio. A *portfolio* consists of a selection of materials that students choose to document their performance over a period of time. Students select their best work samples to showcase their achievement. These items might provide evidence of employability skills as well as academic skills. The items appropriate for students to include in the portfolios they prepare for a job search are listed on pages 209–210.

The portfolio is assembled at the culmination of a course to provide evidence of learning. A self-assessment summary report should be included that explains what has been accomplished, what has been learned, what strengths the student has gained, and what areas need improvement, if any. The students may present portfolios to the class. The items in the portfolio can also be discussed with the teacher in light of educational goals and outcomes. Portfolios should remain the property of students when they leave the course.

Portfolio assessment is a powerful evaluation tool for both students and teachers. It encourages self-reflection and self-assessment of a broader nature. Traditional evaluation methods of tests, quizzes, and papers have their place in measuring the achievement of some course objectives, but other assessment tools should also be used to fairly assess the achievement of all desired outcomes.

Teaching the Learner with Special Needs

The students in your classroom will represent a wide range of ability levels and needs. Special needs students in your classes will require unique teaching strategies. The chart on the next page provides descriptions of several of the types of special needs students you may find in your classes, followed by some strategies and techniques to keep in mind as you work with these students. You will be asked to meet the needs of all your students in the same classroom setting. It is a challenge to adapt daily lessons to meet the demands of all your students.

Learning Disabled*

Description

Students with learning disabilities (LD) have neurological disorders that interfere with their ability to store, process, or produce information, creating a "gap" between ability and performance. These students are generally of average or above-average intelligence. Examples of learning disabilities or distractibility, spatial problems, and reading comprehension problems.

Teaching Strategies

- Assist students in getting organized.
- Give short oral directions.
- Use drill exercises.
- Give prompt cues during student performance.
- Let students with poor writing skills use a computer.
- Break assignments into small segments and assign only one segment at a time.
- Demonstrate skills and have students model them.
- Give prompt feedback.
- Use continuous assessment to mark students' daily progress.
- Prepare materials at varying levels of ability.
- Shorten the number of items on exercises, tests, and quizzes.
- Provide more hands-on activities.

Mentally Disabled*

Description

The mentally disabled student has subaverage general intellectual functioning that exists with deficits in adaptive behavior. These students are slower than others their age in using memory effectively, associating and classifying information, reasoning, and making judgments.

Teaching Strategies

- Use concrete examples to introduce concepts.
- Make learning activities consistent.
- Use repetition and drills spread over time.
- Provide work folders for daily assignments.
- Use behavior management techniques, such as behavior modification, in the area of adaptive behavior.
- Encourage students to function independently.
- Give students extra time to both ask and answer questions while giving hints to answers.
- Avoid doing much walking around while talking to MD students as this is distracting for them.
- Give simple directions and read them over with students.
- Use objective test items and hands-on activities because students generally have poor writing skills and difficulty with sentence structure and spelling.

Behaviorally Emotionally Disabled*

Description

These students exhibit undesirable behaviors or emotions that may, over time, adversely affect educational performance. Their inability to learn cannot be explained by intellectual, social, or health factors. They may be inattentive, withdrawn, timid, restless, defiant, impatient, unhappy, fearful, and unreflective; lack initiative; have negative feelings and actions; and blame others.

Teaching Strategies

- Call students' names or ask them questions when you see their attention wandering.
- Call on students randomly rather than in a predictable sequence.
- Move around the room frequently.
- Improve students' self-esteem by giving them tasks they can perform well, increasing the number of successful achievement experiences.
- Decrease the length of time for each activity.
- Use hands-on activities instead of using words and abstract symbols.
- Decrease the size of the group so each student can actively participate.
- Make verbal instructions clear, short, and to the point.

*We appreciate the assistance of Dr. Debra O. Parker, North Carolina Central University, with this section.

Academically Gifted	Limited English Proficiency	Physical Disabilities
Description		
Academically gifted students are capable of high performance as a result of general intellectual ability, specific academic aptitude, and/or creative or productive thinking. Such students have a vast fund of general knowledge and high levels of vocabulary, memory, abstract word knowledge, and abstract reasoning.	These students have a limited proficiency in the English language. English is generally their second language. Such students may be academically quite capable, but they lack the language skills needed to reason and comprehend abstract concepts.	Includes individuals who are orthopedically impaired, visually impaired, speech impaired, deaf, hard-of-hearing, hearing impaired, and health impaired (cystic fibrosis, epilepsy). Strategies will depend on the specific disability.
Teaching Strategies		
• Provide ample opportunities for creative behavior. • Make assignments that call for original work, independent learning, critical thinking, problem solving, and experimentation. • Show appreciation for creative efforts. • Respect unusual questions, ideas, and solutions these students provide. • Encourage students to test their ideas. • Provide opportunities and give credit for self-initiated learning. • Avoid overly detailed supervision and too much reliance on prescribed curricula. • Allow time for reflection. • Resist immediate and constant evaluation. This causes students to be afraid to use their creativity. • Avoid comparisons with other students, which applies subtle pressure to conform.	• Use a slow but natural rate of speech; speak clearly; use shorter sentences; repeat concepts in several ways. • Act out questions using gestures with hands, arms, and the whole body. Use demonstrations and pantomime. Ask questions that can be answered by a physical movement such as pointing, nodding, or manipulation of materials. • When possible, use pictures, photos, and charts. • Write key terms on the board. As they are used, point to them. • Corrections should be limited and appropriate. Do not correct grammar or usage errors in front of the class, causing embarrassment. • Give honest praise and positive feedback through your voice tones and visual articulation whenever possible. • Encourage students to use language to communicate, allowing them to use their native language to ask/answer questions when they are unable to do so in English. • Integrate students' cultural background into class discussions. • Use cooperative learning where students have opportunities to practice expressing ideas without risking language errors in front of the entire class.	• For visually and hearing-impaired students, seat them near the front of the classroom. Speak clearly and say out loud what you are writing on the board. • In lab settings, in order to reduce the risk of injury, ask students about any conditions that could affect their ability to learn or perform. • Rearrange lab equipment or the classroom and make modifications as needed to accommodate any special need. • Investigate assistive technology devices that can improve students' functional capabilities. • Discuss solutions or modifications with the student who has experience with overcoming his or her disability and may have suggestions you may not have considered. • Let the student know when classroom modifications are being made and allow him or her to test them out before class. • Ask advice from special education teachers, the school nurse, or physical therapist. • Plan field trips that can include all students.

Using Other Resources

The following list includes sources of information and materials that may be useful to you and your students. Please note that information provided here may have changed since publication.

Career-Related Sites

The following sites provide career exploration and planning tools, résumé-writing tips, job listings, workplace statistics, and career education information.

Career Builder
(866) 438-1485
careerbuilder.com

Career Magazine
(610) 878-2800
careermag.com

Career Resource Center
careers.org

CareerOneStop
(877) 348-0502
careeronestop.org

Mapping Your Future
mapping-your-future.org

Monster
(800) MONSTER
monster.com

My Future
myfuture.com

*O*NET Online*
online.onetcenter.org

Occupational Outlook Handbook
stats.bls.gov/oco

States' Career Clusters Initiative
careerclusters.org

U.S. Army: Partnership for Youth Success
goarmy.com

U.S. Bureau of Apprenticeship and Training
doleta.gov/OA/bat.cfm

U.S. Bureau of Labor Statistics
(202) 691-5200
stats.bls.gov

U.S. Department of Labor Employment and Training Administration
(800) US-2JOBS
doleta.gov

Trade and Professional Groups

These and other trade and professional organizations provide career information. Usually is is industry specific.

Air-Conditioning and Refrigeration Institute
(703) 524-8800
ari.org

American Association of Family and Consumer Sciences
(800) 424-8080
aafcs.org

American Bankers Association
(800) BANKERS
aba.com

American Bar Association
(800) 285-2221
abanet.org

American Chemistry Council
(703) 741-5000
plasticsinfo.org

American Culinary Federation
(800) 624-9458
acfchefs.org

American Design Drafting Association
(731) 627-0802
adda.org

American Dietetic Association
(800) 877-1600
eatright.org

American Medical Association
(800) 621-8335
ama-assn.org

American Society of Furniture Designers
(336) 617-3209
asfd.com

American Society of Interior Designers
(202) 546-3480
asid.org

Association for Career and Technical Education
(800) 826-9972
acteonline.org

Institute of Food Technologists
(800) IFT-FOOD
ift.org

International Association of Culinary Professionals
(800) 928-4227
iacp.com

International Association of Lighting Designers
iald.org

National Association for the Education of Young Children
(800) 424-2460
naeyc.org

National Association of Home Builders
(800) 368-5242
nahb.com

National Institute for Automotive Service Excellence
(888) ASE-TEST
asecert.org

National Research Center for Career and Technical Education
(800) 678-6011
nccte.org

National Restaurant Association
(800) 424-5156
restaurant.org

Small Business Administration
(800) 827-5722
sba.gov

General Information

These sites provide information that prepares students for gaining independence as they transition to their future roles in the workplace.

American Financial Services Association
(202) 296-5544
afsaonline.org

American Savings Education Council
(202) 659-0670
choosetosave.org

Credit Union National Association, Inc.
(800) 356-9655
cuna.org

Federal Deposit Insurance Corporation (FDIC)
(877) 275-3342
fdic.gov

Federal Trade Commission Bureau of Consumer Protection
(877) FTC-HELP
ftc.gov/bcp

Insurance Information Institute
(800) 331-9146
iii.org

Internet Fraud Watch
fraud.org

Jump$tart Coalition for Personal Financial Literacy
(888) 45-EDUCATE
jumpstart.org

National Council on Economic Education
(800) 338-1192
ncee.net

National Fraud Information Center
(800) 876-7060
fraud.org

Occupational Safety and Health Administration (OSHA)
(800) 321-OSHA
osha.gov

Securities and Exchange Commission (SEC)
(202) 942-8088
sec.gov

Students Against Destructive Decisions (SADD)
(877) SADD-INC
saddonline.com

Teen Consumer Scrapbook
atg.wa.gov/teenconsumer

Teenager's Guide to the Real World: Money Really Matters
(888) 294-7820
bygpub.com

U.S. Equal Employment Opportunity Commission
(800) 669-4000
eeoc.gov

Note: Phone numbers and Web addresses may have changed since publication. For some entries, reaching the correct Web site may require keying *www.* into the address.

Integrating Academics

No matter what career path a student chooses, academic skills will be critical to his or her success. The *No Child Left Behind Act of 2001* brought to national attention the importance of reading and mathematics to academic and personal success. The Act also instituted a program of accountability testing, placing high stakes on student achievement in key areas. The *No Child Left Behind Act* lists the following as core academic subjects in schools: English, reading, language arts, math, science, foreign languages, civics and government, economics, arts, history, and geography.

Because achieving in these areas is so important, many career and technical education teachers are asked to incorporate academic standards into their curriculum. A career education course can support the core subjects by including subject matter from these areas as appropriate. Co-curricular projects with core subject teachers can also support students' growth and achievement in these areas.

The *Learning for Earning* program supports student growth and achievement in key academic areas in several ways. Some subjects (reading, language arts, math, science, social studies, civics, and government) are covered as background information to career education concepts. To promote connection to academic areas, at least one cross-curricular activity appears on the last page of each chapter within the section titled "Building Academic Skills."

Reading, English, and Language Arts

The entire *Learning for Earning* student text is designed to encourage reading and understanding. Each chapter begins with a prereading question to engage student interest. The objectives, key terms, and key concepts are listed at the start of each chapter to focus on the information to come. Bold "Check Your Understanding" features appear throughout the chapters to pose questions that check student comprehension of the topics just read. Key terms are shown in red to draw attention to the reader and are defined in the margins for reinforcement. The *Student Activity Guide* and the *Teacher's Resources* provide more activities designed to develop skills in English/Language Arts.

Math

Mathematics is a tool necessary for success in the workplace as well as in managing personal finances. Unfortunately, some students have not learned the basics of arithmetic and using numbers. To strengthen these skills, various math activities appear in the student text, the *Student Workbook,* and the *Teacher's Resources* as chapter content dictates.

Social Studies

Social Studies is an important part of explaining the full meaning of work and the reasons for the changing workplace. Psychology is especially helpful in understanding self and the importance of recognizing personal interests when deciding on and preparing for a satisfying career. Appropriate activities are found in the student text on the last page of each chapter under "Building Career Knowledge and Skills" and "Building Workplace Skills." Additional activities appear in the *Student Workbook* and *Teacher's Resources.*

Civics and Government

Any discussion of career education must include a discussion of how laws and other government influences affect work, workers, and the workplace. As students learn to prepare for a career, teaching them to become responsible citizens is also important. To strengthen student skills in these areas, appropriate activities appear on the last page of each chapter under "Building Workplace Skills." Additional activities are in the *Student Workbook* and *Teacher's Resources* as chapter content dictates.

Incorporating Career and Technical Student Organizations

Career and Technical Student Organizations (CTSOs) have been a vital part of career and technical education since 1918. Currently, the U.S. Department of Education recognizes eight organizations.

CTSOs Officially Recognized by the U.S. Department of Education

Short Name	Full Name	Web Site
BPA	Business Professionals of America	www.bpa.org
DECA	DECA—An Association of Marketing Students	www.deca.org
FBLA/PBL	Future Business Leaders of America/Phi Beta Lambda	www.fbla-pbl.org
FCCLA	Family, Career and Community Leaders of America	www.fcclainc.org
FFA	National FFA Organization	www.ffa.org
HOSA	Health Occupations Students of America	www.hosa.org
SkillsUSA	Formerly VICA—Vocational Industrial Clubs of America	www.skillsusa.org
TSA	Technology Student Association	www.tsaweb.org

Federal career and technical education funds can be used to support activities of these CTSOs. Many states require that CTSOs be incorporated as a co-curricular activity in career and technical subjects. The CTSOs offer a wide variety of activities that can be adapted to almost any school and classroom situation. A brief introduction to CTSOs follows. If you would like more details, visit their Web sites.

Purpose

The purpose of CTSOs is to assist students in acquiring knowledge and skills in career and technical areas as well as leadership skills and experience. These organizations achieve these goals by enlisting teacher-advisors to organize and lead local chapters in their schools. Support for teacher-advisors and their chapters is often coordinated through each state's education department. The chapters elect officers and establish a program of work. This program of work can include a variety of activities, including community service, co-curricular projects, and competition preparation. Student achievement in specified areas is recognized with certificates and/or public acknowledgement through awards ceremonies. Competition is the most visible activity of CTSOs, but not the only one.

Competitive Events

Competitive events are a main feature of most CTSOs. The CTSO develops events that enable students to showcase how well they have mastered the learning of specific content and the use of decision-making, problem-solving, and leadership skills. The competitive events also give the winners the opportunity for public recognition of their achievements. Each CTSO has its own list of competitive events and activities. Members develop career and leadership skills even though they may not participate in or win competitions.

Scope and Sequence

A *Scope and Sequence Chart* is located at the end of the introduction. Since *Learning for Earning* focuses on career preparation, the organizing concepts are the 10 categories of knowledge and skills that are linked to the career clusters:

- academic foundations
- communications
- problem solving and critical thinking
- information technology applications
- systems
- safety, health, and environment
- leadership and teamwork
- ethics and legal responsibilities
- employability and career development
- technical skills

This special resource is provided to help you select for study those topics that meet your curriculum needs. Bold numbers indicate chapters in which concepts are found.

Marketing Your Program

Your class is likely to be the first career education class some of your students have taken. Many students and their parents may have preconceived ideas about what this curriculum includes. You need to identify these preconceptions and, if necessary, gently alter them to give students and their parents a more accurate idea of what your class entails.

To get your public relations campaign started, create a newsletter to inform parents about what their children will be studying in your class. You can also use copies of these promotionally to encourage students to enroll in your class. Post copies of flyers around your school or pass them out to students. You might ask some of your former students what they feel they have gained from taking your class and add some of their ideas to the flyer. (If you decide to use direct quotations, be sure to get permission from your students.)

Students and their parents are not likely to be the only ones who are not totally aware of the importance of career education classes. You can make people more aware through good public relations. It pays to make the student body, faculty, and community aware of your program. With good public relations, you can increase your enrollment, gain support from administrators and other teachers, and achieve recognition in the community. Following are some ways to market your program:

- Create visibility. It is important to let people know what is going on in your program. Ways to do this include announcements of projects and activities at faculty meetings and in school bulletins or newspapers, displays in school showcases or on bulletin boards, and articles and press releases in school and community newspapers. Talk up your program with administrators, other teachers, and students. Invite them to visit your classes.
- Interact with educators in other subject matter areas. Career education is related to many fields of learning. You can strengthen your program and contribute to other disciplines by cooperating with other teachers. You can coordinate the teaching of chapter material with other departments in your school that might be covering related information. The more interaction you can generate, the more you promote your class.
- Contribute to the education objectives of the school. If your school follows stated educational objectives and strives to strengthen specific skills, include these overall goals in your teaching. For example if students need special help in developing verbal or writing skills, select projects and assignments that will help them in these areas. Show administrators examples of work that indicate student improvement in needed skills.
- Serve as a resource center. Career education is of practical use and interest to almost everyone. You can sell your program by making your department a resources center of materials related to career exploration and job hunting. Invite faculty members, students, and parents to tap into the wealth of information available in your classroom.

- Generate involvement and activity in the community. You are teaching concepts that students can apply in their everyday life. You can involve students in community life and bring the community into your classroom through field trips, surveys, presentations from guest speakers, and interviews with businesspeople and community leaders. You may be able to set up cooperative projects between the school and community organizations around a variety of topics.
- Connect with parents. If you can get them involved, parents may be your best allies in teaching career education classes. Let parents know when their children have done good work. Moms and dads have had experiences related to many of the issues you discuss in class. Call on them to share individually or as part of a panel addressing a specific topic. Parents can be a rich source of real-life experience. Keep them informed about classroom activities and invite them to participate as they are able.
- Establish a student sales staff. Enthusiastic students will be your best salespeople. Encourage them to tell their parents and friends what they are learning. You might create bulletin boards or write letters to parents that focus on what students are studying in your classes. Ask students to put together a newsletter highlighting their experiences in your career education class. Students could write a column from your department for the school paper.

Goodheart-Willcox Welcomes Your Comments

We welcome your comments and suggestions regarding *Learning for Earning* and its supplements. Please send any comments you may have to the editor by visiting our Web site at www.g-w.com or writing to

Editorial Department
Goodheart-Willcox Publisher
18604 West Creek Drive
Tinley Park, IL 60477-6243

Scope and Sequence Chart

In planning your program, you may want to use this scope and sequence chart to identify the major concepts presented in each chapter of *Learning for Earning: Your Route to Success*. Concepts relate to the career cluster knowledge and skills. Refer to the chart to select topics that meet your curriculum needs. Bold numbers indicate chapters in which concepts are found.

Part One: Exploring the World of Work

Academic Foundations

1: Work requires knowledge and skills; Linking school to work; Developing a foundation; Developing transferable skills

Problem Solving and Critical Thinking

1: Work provides income; Work influences identity; Work influences lifestyle; Work provides satisfaction; Work requires knowledge and skills

2: Family first

3: Facing discrimination or sexual harassment; Action to take

Systems

1: Work keeps the economy strong

2: Changing workplace; Free enterprise system; Economic freedom; New directions for the workplace; Global perspective; Service and information economy; Commitment to quality; Factors affecting the labor market; Social change; Population shifts; Economy; World events; Government actions; Forces of competition on staff size

Safety, Health, and Environment

1: Work influences lifestyle

2: Family first

3: Barrier-free workplace

Leadership and Teamwork

2: Teamwork approach

Ethics and Legal Responsibilities

1: Work influences identity; Work influences lifestyle

2: Family first

3: Law in the workplace; What is discrimination? Equal opportunity; Equal work, equal pay; Barrier-free workplace; Age discrimination; What is sexual harassment?

Advances from authority figures; Hostile environment; Facing discrimination or sexual harassment; Action to take; Family and the workplace

Employability and Career Development

1: Importance of work; What is work? Job or a career; Work provides income; Work influences identity; Work influences lifestyle; Work provides satisfaction; Work keeps the economy strong; Work requires knowledge and skills; Linking school to work; Developing a foundation; Developing transferable skills

2: Changing workplace; New directions for the workplace; Global perspective; Service and information economy; Commitment to quality; Factors affecting the labor market; Social change; Population shifts; Economy; World events; Government actions; Forces of competition on staff size

Technical Skills

1: Work requires knowledge and skills; Linking school to work; Developing a foundation; Developing transferable skills

2: Technology revolution; New replaces old; Changing technology in the workplace; New world of work

Part Two: Exploring Career Options

Communications

4: Interviewing workers; Job shadowing; Career events and job fairs

Problem Solving and Critical Thinking

4: Job duties and responsibilities; Education, training, and skills; Salary and fringe benefits; Work location and environment; Obtaining career information

6: Do you want to be an entrepreneur? Planning a business; Financial considerations

Information Technology Applications

4: Obtaining career information; Department of labor references; Internet and your career; Research

Systems

4: Job duties and responsibilities; Advancement opportunities

5: Job growth

6: Types of business organizations; Sole proprietorship; Partnership; Corporation

Safety, Health, and Environment

4: Work location and environment

Employability and Career Development

4: Learning about careers; Basic job factors; Job duties and responsibilities; Job prospects; Education, training, and skills; Salary and fringe benefits; Advancement opportunities; Work location and environment; Obtaining career information; Department of Labor references; School counselors; Internet and your career; Additional ways to investigate careers; Research; Interviewing workers; Job shadowing; Community/service learning; Part-time jobs; Career events and job fairs

5: Exploring careers; Job growth; Agriculture, food, and natural resources; Architecture and construction; Arts, audio/video technology, and communications; Business, management, and administration; Education and training; Finance; Government and public administration; Health science; Hospitality and tourism; Human services; Information technology; Law, public safety, corrections, and security; Manufacturing; Marketing, sales, and service; Science, technology, engineering, and mathematics; Transportation, distribution, and logistics

6: A business of your own; Retail businesses; Service businesses; Do you want to be an entrepreneur? Planning a business; Financial considerations; Types of business organizations; Sole proprietorship; Partnership; Corporation

Technical Skills

4: Internet and your career

Part Three: Making Plans for Career Success

Problem Solving and Critical Thinking

7: Learning about yourself; Importance of knowing yourself; Examining the real you; Your personality; Your self-concept; Forming and changing your self-concept; How to evaluate yourself

8: Making decisions; Decision making—a daily task; Routine decisions; Impulse decisions; Thoughtful decisions and the decision-making process; Trade-offs; Personal decisions; Career decisions; Work decisions

9: Need for further training and education; Preparing for a career; Financing further training

10: Making a career plan; Importance of planning; Exploring your resources; Examining career interests; Setting career-related goals; Questions to consider

Information Technology Applications

10: Exploring your resources; Examining career interests; Developing a career plan

Systems

9: Career/technical training; Cooperative education; Apprenticeships; Company training programs; Community and junior colleges; Colleges and universities; Internships; Military training

Leadership and Teamwork

7: Three A's; Your attitude—positive or negative? Your aptitudes and abilities

Ethics and Legal Responsibilities

7: Your values; How to evaluate yourself

Employability and Career Development

7: Learning about yourself; Importance of knowing yourself; Examining the real you; Your personality; Your self-concept; Forming and changing your self-concept; Your interests; People; Data; Objects; Three A's; Your attitude—positive or negative? Your aptitudes and abilities; Your values; How to evaluate yourself

9: Options for education and training; Need for further training and education; Importance of foundation skills; Preparing for a career; Career/technical training; Cooperative education; Apprenticeships; Company training programs; Community and junior colleges; Colleges and universities; Internships; Military training; Financing further training

10: Making a career plan; Importance of planning; Exploring your resources; Your school; Your community; Examining career interests; Setting career-related goals; Taking steps to achieve career goals; Questions to consider; Developing a career plan

Part Four: Acquiring Workplace Skills

Communications

12: Telephone interviews; Personal interviews; Questions to answer; Questions to ask; Receiving a job offer

Problem Solving and Critical Thinking

12: Evaluate the job and the company; Receiving a job offer; Steps to follow if you do not get the job

16: Handling changes in job status; Changing from part-time to full-time work; Income; Fringe benefits; Lifestyle; Losing a job; Take positive action; Being promoted; Changing jobs; Leaving a job

Information Technology Applications

11: Sources of information about jobs; Internet; Electronic bulletin boards; Preparing your résumé; Portfolios

12: Write a follow-up letter

Safety, Health, and Environment

12: Be well groomed

15: Keeping safety first; Thinking and acting safely; Unsafe acts; Unsafe conditions; Proper safety attitude; Workplace safety; Safely using machinery, tools, and workplace items; Working with power tools and equipment; Proper use and care of hand tools; Lifting; Upkeep and organization; Using ladders safely; Fire protection; Health and first aid; OSHA; Employers' responsibilities; Employees' responsibilities; FLSA; Workers' compensation; Disability insurance

Leadership and Teamwork

13: Good employee skills; Winning at work; Consider your employer's expectations; Do your best as an employee; Use all your abilities; Watch for ways to improve; Be willing to learn; Accept responsibility for your work; Have a good attitude

14: Being a team player; Teamwork leads to success; Becoming an effective team member; Developing an effective team; Tips for new employees; Be friendly; Respect your coworkers; Present yourself as a likable person; Accept constructive criticism positively; Have a positive attitude; Keep a good sense of humor; Avoid the poor use of humor; Do not cause conflict; Do not cause arguments; Do not spread rumors; Avoid harassment; Avoid comparisons; Don't compare workloads; Don't compare salaries; Don't compare the treatment of coworkers

Ethics and Legal Responsibilities

15: OSHA; Employers' responsibilities; Employees' responsibilities; FLSA; Workers' compensation; Disability insurance

Employability and Career Development

11: Job search skills; Sources of information about jobs; Want ads; Networking; Internet; Employment agencies; Yellow pages; Community bulletin boards; Electronic bulletin boards; Résumés; Preparing your résumé; References; Portfolios; Job application forms; Gaps in employment

12: Interviewing skills; Most important step; Preparing for interviews; Telephone interviews; Personal interviews; Be well groomed; Be on time; Plan to go alone; Interviewing tips; After the interview; Evaluate the job and the company; Write a follow-up letter; Receiving a job offer; Steps to follow if you do not get the job

13: Good employee skills; Winning at work; Consider your employer's expectations; Do your best as an employee; Use all your abilities; Watch for ways to improve; Be willing to learn; Accept responsibility for your work; Have a good attitude

14: Be friendly; Respect your coworkers; Present yourself as a likable person; Accept constructive criticism positively; Have a positive attitude; Keep a good sense of humor; Avoid the poor use of humor; Do not cause conflict; Do not cause arguments; Do not spread rumors; Avoid harassment; Avoid comparisons; Don't compare workloads; Don't compare salaries; Don't compare the treatment of coworkers

16: Handling changes in job status; Changing from part-time to full-time work; Income; Fringe benefits; Lifestyle; Losing a job; Take positive action; Being promoted; Changing jobs; Leaving a job

Part Five: Developing Personal Skills for Job Success

Academic Foundations

17: Basic skills for job success; Starting point—basic skills; Reading skills; Writing skills; Math skills; Counting change; Measurements

18: Time management and study skills; Why is time management important? Time management; Computer and time management; IRS time; Study skills; Taking notes; Using a computer to study; Taking tests

19: Writing business communications; Writing letters; Writing memos; Creating reports; Sending e-mail

Communications

17: Reading skills; Writing skills

19: Communication skills; Methods of communication; Communication tools; Styles of communication; Passive communication; Aggressive communication; Assertive communication; Speaking; Improving your speech; Public speaking; Listening; Feedback; Multitasking; Using the telephone; Receiving calls; Making business calls; Placing orders; Making emergency calls; Accepting personal calls; Writing business communications; Writing letters; Writing memos; Creating reports; Sending e-mail; Nonverbal communication; Body language

Information Technology Applications

17: Using the computer; Computer skills

18: Computer and time management; Using the computer to study

19: Using the telephone; Receiving calls; Making business calls; Making emergency calls; Accepting personal calls; Writing business communications; Writing letters; Writing memos; Creating reports; Sending e-mail

Safety, Health, and Environment

19: Making emergency calls

20: Your appearance; Good grooming; Hair; Skin; Hands; Breath; Makeup; Fragrance; Wardrobe; Dress codes; Jewelry; Wardrobe planning; Avoiding fads; Shopping for quality; Laundry and ironing

21: Good health and job success; Staying healthy; Balance food and physical activity; Make smart food choices; Learn to handle stress; Ways to relax; Avoid tobacco use; How to quit smoking; Avoid drug use; Avoid alcohol use; Alcohol and other drug problems at work; Where to get help

Leadership and Teamwork

22: Developing leadership skills; Leadership; Leadership traits; Effective leadership at school and at work; School organizations create leaders; How student groups operate; Parliamentary procedure

Part Six: Managing Your Money

Problem Solving and Critical Thinking

24: Budgets; Need for money management; Sources of income; Types of expenses; How do you spend your money? Spending calendar; How do you want to spend your money? "Want" list; Planning a budget; Using personal finance software

25: Checking accounts; Convenience of checking; Checks; ATM cards; Debit cards; Where to open an account; Convenience; Services; Types of accounts; Fees; Opening a checking account; Making a deposit; Endorsing a check; Recording transactions; Online banking; Balancing your checkbook; Special types of checks; Certified checks; Cashier's checks; Money orders; Traveler's checks

26: Savings; Reasons for saving; Where to save; Will your savings be safe? Ways to save; Savings accounts; Savings clubs; Certificates of deposit; Money market accounts; U.S. Savings bonds; Mutual funds; Annuities; Retirement accounts; Avoiding investment fraud

27: Credit; Common uses of credit; Advantages of credit; Disadvantages of credit; When to use credit; Types of credit; Charge accounts; Credit cards; Installment credit; Loans; How to obtain credit; Creditors look for good credit risks; Getting a first loan; Credit applications; Credit bureaus and credit ratings; Examine all credit agreements; Identity theft

Information Technology Applications

24: Using personal finance software

25: Online banking

Ethics and Legal Responsibilities

23: Paychecks and taxes; Paychecks and paycheck deductions; W-4 form; W-2 form; Taxes; Income tax; Social Security tax; Filing an income tax return; State income tax; Tax penalties

26: Will your savings be safe? Avoiding investment fraud

27: Creditors look for good credit risks; Credit applications; Credit bureaus and credit ratings; Examine all credit agreements; Identity theft

28: Insurance; Financial protection; Automobile insurance; Health insurance; Life insurance; Disability insurance; Property insurance; Filing a claim

Employability and Career Development

23: Paychecks and taxes; Payday; Paychecks and paycheck deductions; W-4 form; W-2 form; Taxes; Income tax; Social Security tax; Filing an income tax return; State income tax; Tax penalties

Part Seven: Growing Toward Independence

Problem Solving and Critical Thinking

29: Place to live; Where will you live? Living at home; Living with a roommate; Living on your own; Looking for a place to live; Housing needs and costs; Furnishing your new home; Your legal responsibilities

Systems

30: Mass transportation; Schedules; Buses; Trains and subways; Airplanes

Safety, Health, and Environment

28: Insurance; Automobile insurance; Health insurance; Life insurance; Disability insurance; Property insurance

29: Place to live; Where will you live? Living at home; Living with a roommate; Living on your own; Looking for a place to live; Housing needs and costs; Furnishing your new home; Your legal responsibilities

30: Transportation; Self-powered transportation; Automobile transportation; Car pools; Mass transportation; Schedules; Buses; Trains and subways; Airplanes

31: Right to safety

Ethics and Legal Responsibilities

29: Your legal responsibilities

31: Being a responsible citizen; Being an active citizen; Right to vote; Laws of the land; How laws are made; Types of laws; When you may need a lawyer; Consumer rights and responsibilities; Right to information; Right to choose; Right to safety; Right to be heard

T 32

Learning for Earning

Your Route to Success

Sixth Edition

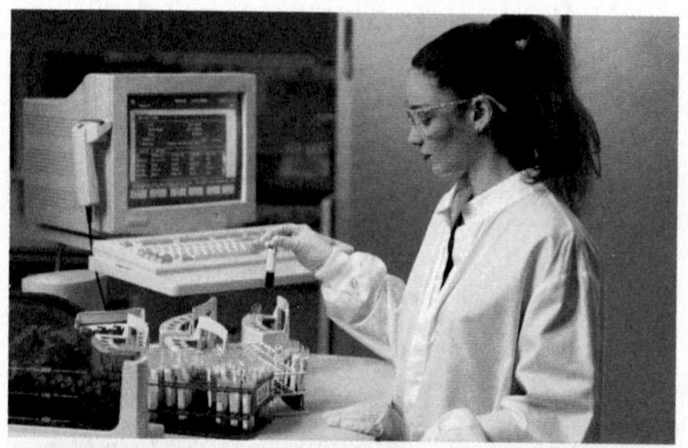

John A. Wanat
Consultant and Author on Occupational Education
Jackson, New Jersey

E. Weston Pfeiffer
Consultant on Technical and Vocational Training
Lambertville, New Jersey

Richard Van Gulik, PhD
Assistant Director—Curriculum
Withlacoochee Technical Institute
Inverness, Florida

Publisher
The Goodheart-Willcox Company, Inc.
Tinley Park, Illinois
www.g-w.com

Manufactured in the United States of America.

Library of Congress Catalog Card Number 2008013728
ISBN 978-1-59070-946-7
2 3 4 5 6 7 8 9 – 09 – 14 13 12 11 10 09

Library of Congress Cataloging-in-Publication Data

Wanat, John A.
Learning for earning : your route to success / John A. Wanat,
E. Weston Pfeiffer, Richard Van Gulik. --6th ed.
p. cm.
Includes index.
ISBN 987-1-59070-946-7
1. Vocational guidance. 2. Finance, Personal. 3. Students--Life skills
guides. I. Pfeiffer, E. Weston. II. Van Gulik, Richard. III. Title.
HF5381.W2135 2009
650.1--dc22

2008013728

About the Authors

John A. Wanat is executive director of the Monmouth County Division on Aging, Disabilities, and Veterans' Interment and author of numerous textbooks, articles, and audiovisual materials. Previously he managed several New Jersey State Department of Education bureaus and implemented a statewide program that found jobs for 10,000 high school graduates not bound for college. Wanat's career has included coordinating degree and nondegree programs for the Center for Occupational Education at Jersey City State College. He also has served as vice president of a security training institute, director of an adult learning center, and publisher/editor of two national education magazines.

E. Weston Pfeiffer provides consulting services to major corporations, the World Bank, and numerous education agencies. Pfeiffer began his career as a teacher, then joined the New Jersey Department of Education's Division of Vocational Education. There he was state supervisor of cooperative industrial education, lead program specialist for trade and industrial education, and state director for apprentice training. Recently Pfeiffer has served as advisor for the U.S. Department of Labor on technical and vocational training programs in Europe and the Middle East. He is a founding member of the Cooperative Work Experience Education Association.

Richard Van Gulik, PhD, is assistant director for curriculum at Withlacoochee Technical Institute. Previously he was superintendent of Hunterdon County Polytech and principal of Salem County Vocational School. While he was principal, Salem County Vocational School was recognized by the U.S. Department of Education as one of the top 10 vocational programs in the nation. Van Gulik also served as program specialist in trade and industrial education for New Jersey's Department of Education. He is a leader in initiating programs that address the employment needs of his county and in creating school-to-work and mentoring opportunities for students in vocational programs.

Welcome to the Student Edition of Learning for Earning

The Clear, Colorful Presentation Is Easy to Read

- Chapter titles preview the content for you.
- A key question stimulates your thinking.

Part Opener

- Key terms and learning objectives help you to see what you will learn.
- Key concepts summarize the main ideas you will find.

Chapter Opener

Complex Concepts Are Presented Simply

Colorful Margin Features
- Connect the chapter to your own life
- Stimulate you to think more

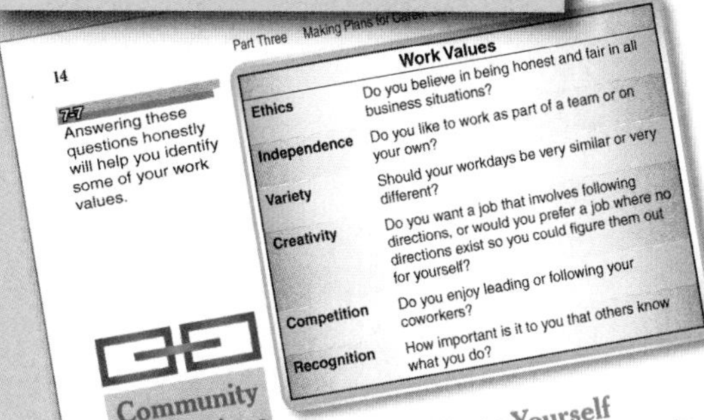
Part Three Making Plans for Career

14

7-7 Answering these questions honestly will help you identify some of your work values.

Work Values	
Ethics	Do you believe in being honest and fair in all business situations?
Independence	Do you like to work as part of a team or on your own?
Variety	Should your workdays be very similar or very different?
Creativity	Do you want a job that involves following directions, or would you prefer a job where no directions exist so you could figure them out for yourself?
Competition	Do you enjoy leading or following your coworkers?
Recognition	How important is it to you that others know what you do?

Community Connections

Ask three adults who know you well the following questions: What are my greatest skills? What future career can you see me pursuing? What is one thing I need to work on to be successful in that career? Write a summary of the

How to Evaluate Yourself

There are many ways to evaluate all the characteristics that make *you*. Your school may evaluate you to help you make choices and identify classes. Employers will evaluate you, too. They often use written tests to evaluate your personality, aptitudes, and abilities. They may also use interviews and supervisor reports to assist their evaluation.

You, too, can evaluate yourself. You can recognize your attitude and change it. Simple activities, such as listing your positive and negative attitudes, can be the first step. Deciding which attitude to change and how to do so are the next steps. Abilities can be changed in the same way. Your ability to ... can change with more practice. ...rself periodically is the best ... your family, teachers, and ... n you will also help. When ... ou, work to correct them.

12

Chapter 26 Savings

The Power of Compounding

$30,000 $25,000 $20,000 $15,000 $10,000 $5,000 $0
$50 $100 $150
$9,147 $18,295 $27,442
Year 5 Year 10

Note: The chart shows monthly contributions of $50, $100, and $150 with a return of 8% compounded monthly for 5-year and 10-year periods.

Source: The Ohio Tuition Trust Authority

26-7 Saving for retirement while working will allow your money to grow over time.

Companies may match employee contributions. A plan with matching contributions is a valuable benefit and helps your ... quickly. Many financial experts consider ... to be the best way to

Attractive Pictures, Charts, and Graphs
- Bring the content to life
- Make concepts clearer
- Help you relate to real workplace situations

fully understand ... you should seek advice from a ... similar expert. Depending on your investment ... savings may or may not be insured. Insured savings tend to grow at slower rates.

Community Connections
- Inspires you to apply learning to your own family or community

Part Four Acquiring Workplace Skills

14

Electronic Résumés for Internet Posting

The type of résumé shown in 11-6 should be used in general Internet job searches. It follows the same format as the electronic résumé to be sent to potential employers with one important difference. All personal information is deleted. Internet postings of personal information are sources for identity theft and Internet stalking.

Your posted résumé should only report your specific qualifications and work experience. This form may be posted on Internet job boards or Internet employment sources.

11-6 An electronic résumé for Internet posting should never include personal information, such as your name and address.

Sample Electronic Résumé for Internet Posting

JOB OBJECTIVE
Administrative Assistant

EMPLOYMENT
*Retail Sales Person: Assisted customers with selections; straightened merchandise displays; processed returns; closed sales. 2/20XX—present
*Counter Help: Filled customer orders; cleared tables; cashier. 11/20XX to 2/20XX

EDUCATION
*High School Graduate
*Major: Office Occupations Program, including classes in Microsoft Office, WordPerfect, Microsoft Word, Excel, and PowerPoint

ACTIVITIES AND HONORS
President, Business Professionals of America local chapter—20XX
Vice President, Student Council—20XX
Member, Ski Club
Member, Mercer County 4-H Club

SPECIAL SKILLS
*Keyboarding, word processing, microcomputer applications, and business mathematics
*Fluent in Spanish

REFERENCES
Available on request

REPLY TO: jqhenry@serviceprovider.com

Making a Difference

Check the local sections of the paper or any special newspaper sections that list volunteers needed. Check for any listings that might be from a community agency with which you could obtain work experience. You should include this work experience on your résumé.

Clearly Labeled Key Terms
- Shown in red to stand out in the text
- Defined in a glossary alongside each page reference

...portant Step

...the most important step in a job search. ...rience if you are prepared and know just

...a talk between an employer and a ...y also be described as a talk between ...an interviewee. An *interviewer* is an employer. In large companies, an interviewer may be a company representative who has the task of talking with job applicants. An *interviewee* is a person who is looking for a job. This person is also called a *job applicant*.

In large companies, the personnel department or the human resources department often conducts interviews. The function of these departments (or departments with similar names) is to find the right people to fill available positions.

An interview is usually your first chance to meet with an employer. Remember that first impressions are lasting impressions. Your interview is your chance to make a good first impression. See 12-1.

interviewer An employer who talks with a job applicant.

interviewee A job applicant who receives an interview.

Your Reading

Why are first impressions important?

Preparing for Interviews

Do a little homework to learn about the company. You should know what the company does. Does it make a product

Check Your Reading
- Helps you recall what you have read about each topic

Making a Difference
- Encourages your concern and involvement as a citizen

Reviews Enhance and Extend Learning

Summary
- Condenses the content into brief, concise paragraphs

Building Academic Skills
- Helps you improve your writing, speaking, reading, math, and science.

Building Career Knowledge and Skills
- Challenges you to do everything employers consider basic for career success.

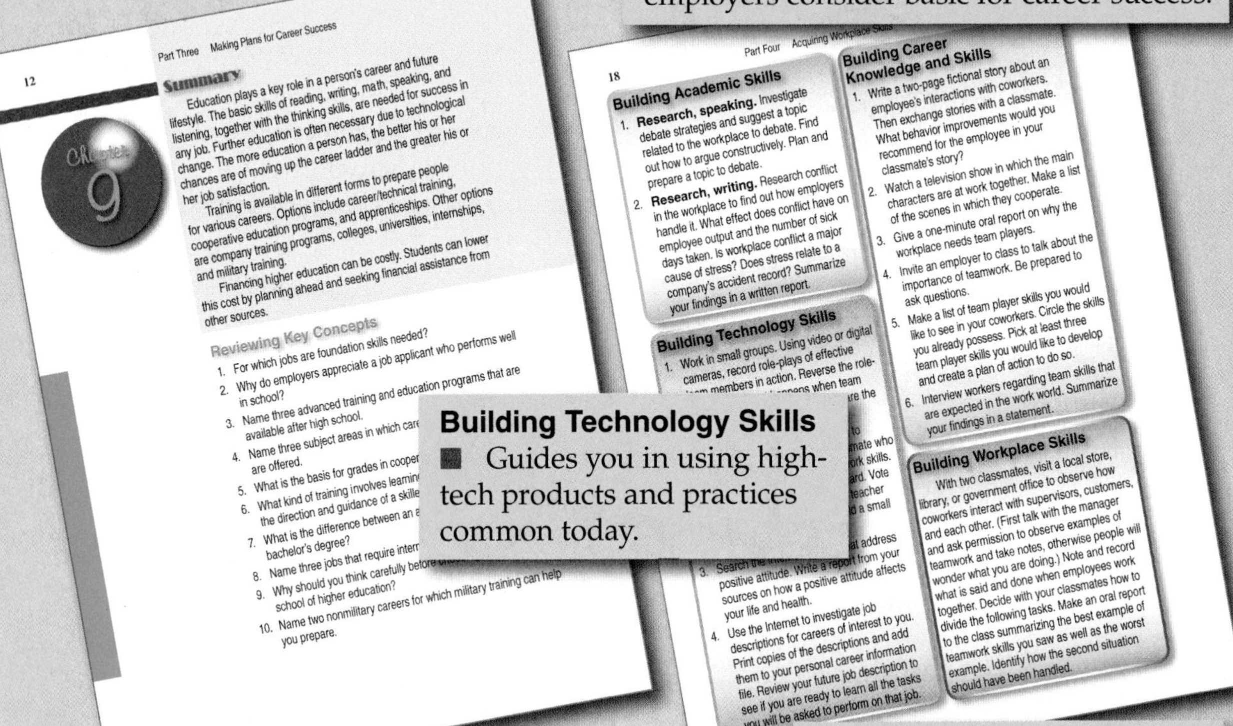

12 Part Three Making Plans for Career Success

Summary

Education plays a key role in a person's career and future lifestyle. The basic skills of reading, writing, math, speaking, and listening, together with the thinking skills, are needed for success in any job. Further education is often necessary due to technological change. The more education a person has, the better his or her chances are of moving up the career ladder and the greater his or her job satisfaction.

Training is available in different forms to prepare people for various careers. Options include career/technical training, cooperative education programs, and apprenticeships. Other options are company training programs, colleges, universities, internships, and military training.

Financing higher education can be costly. Students can lower this cost by planning ahead and seeking financial assistance from other sources.

Reviewing Key Concepts

1. For which jobs are foundation skills needed?
2. Why do employers appreciate a job applicant who performs well in school?
3. Name three advanced training and education programs that are available after high school.
4. Name three subject areas in which care[...] are offered.
5. What is the basis for grades in cooper[...]
6. What kind of training involves learnin[...] the direction and guidance of a skille[...]
7. What is the difference between an a[...] bachelor's degree?
8. Name three jobs that require intern[...]
9. Why should you think carefully before [...] school of higher education?
10. Name two nonmilitary careers for which military training can help you prepare.

18 Part Four Acquiring Workplace Skills

Building Academic Skills

1. **Research, speaking.** Investigate debate strategies and suggest a topic related to the workplace to debate. Find out how to argue constructively. Plan and prepare a topic to debate.
2. **Research, writing.** Research conflict in the workplace to find out how employers handle it. What effect does conflict have on employee output and the number of sick days taken. Is workplace conflict a major cause of stress? Does stress relate to a company's accident record? Summarize your findings in a written report.

Building Technology Skills

1. Work in small groups. Using video or digital cameras, record role-plays of effective team members in action. Reverse the role-[...]
3. Search the [...] positive attitude. Write a report from your sources on how a positive attitude affects your life and health.
4. Use the Internet to investigate job descriptions for careers of interest to you. Print copies of the descriptions and add them to your personal career information file. Review your future job description to see if you are ready to learn all the tasks you will be asked to perform on that job.

Building Career Knowledge and Skills

1. Write a two-page fictional story about an employee's interactions with coworkers. Then exchange stories with a classmate. What behavior improvements would you recommend for the employee in your classmate's story?
2. Watch a television show in which the main characters are at work together. Make a list of the scenes in which they cooperate.
3. Give a one-minute oral report on why the workplace needs team players.
4. Invite an employer to class to talk about the importance of teamwork. Be prepared to ask questions.
5. Make a list of team player skills you would like to see in your coworkers. Circle the skills you already possess. Pick at least three team player skills you would like to develop and create a plan of action to do so.
6. Interview workers regarding team skills that are expected in the work world. Summarize your findings in a statement.

Building Workplace Skills

With two classmates, visit a local store, library, or government office to observe how coworkers interact with supervisors, customers, and each other. (First talk with the manager and ask permission to observe examples of teamwork and take notes, otherwise people will wonder what you are doing.) Note and record what is said and done when employees work together. Decide with your classmates how to divide the following tasks. Make an oral report to the class summarizing the best example of teamwork skills you saw as well as the worst example. Identify how the second situation should have been handled.

Building Technology Skills
- Guides you in using high-tech products and practices common today.

Reviewing Key Concepts
- Ask you to recall the content

Building Workplace Skills
- Explores career-focused activities that simulate the workplace

Career Clusters Prepare Students for the Workplace

have refined school programs to better address career and workplace needs. As a result, students learn about career choices and the importance of career planning much earlier in their studies.

Linking School to Work

One of the best ways to study careers is by checking the *career clusters*. These are 16 broad groups of occupational and career specialties. See 1-6. Since all possible careers are

career clusters
The 16 broad groups of occupational and career specialties.

1-6 The career clusters connect students to careers and the knowledge and skills needed to achieve them.

The Sixteen Career Clusters

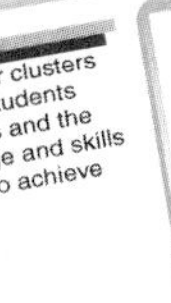

The Career Clusters icons are being used with permission of the States' Career

Chapter 1

- Gives you an introduction

Chapter 5

- Presents summaries of each of the 16 clusters
- Helps you understand the qualifications for jobs within each cluster
- Shows all the career pathways and several occupational options for each
- Brings the career clusters to life with photos of workplace settings

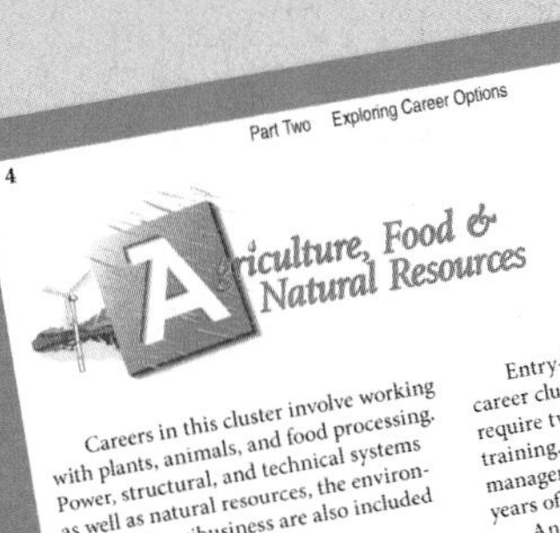

Agriculture, Food & Natural Resources

Careers in this cluster involve working with plants, animals, and food processing. Power, structural, and technical systems as well as natural resources, the environment, and agribusiness are also included in this cluster.

Farmers grow crops, and ranchers tend livestock. Food scientists and technologists discover new food sources, analyze food content, and develop ways to process, preserve, package, and store food. Foresters plan and supervise the growing and using of trees. Conservationists and environmentalists work on problems regarding the responsible use of air, land, and water. They also preserve marine life and wildlife. Animal scientists study genetics, nutrition, and reproduction.

Entry-level jobs are available in this career cluster. Many technical jobs require two or more years of advanced training. Engineers, scientists, and top managers need to complete at least four years of college.

An expanding population, globalization, and an increasing public focus on diet will result in more job opportunities in this career cluster. Many specialists work for the Environmental Protection Agency, the National Park Service, and the Fish and Wildlife Service. The federal government is one of the biggest employers in this career area. Other possible employers include landscape nurseries, golf courses, mining and logging operations, and oil exploration companies.

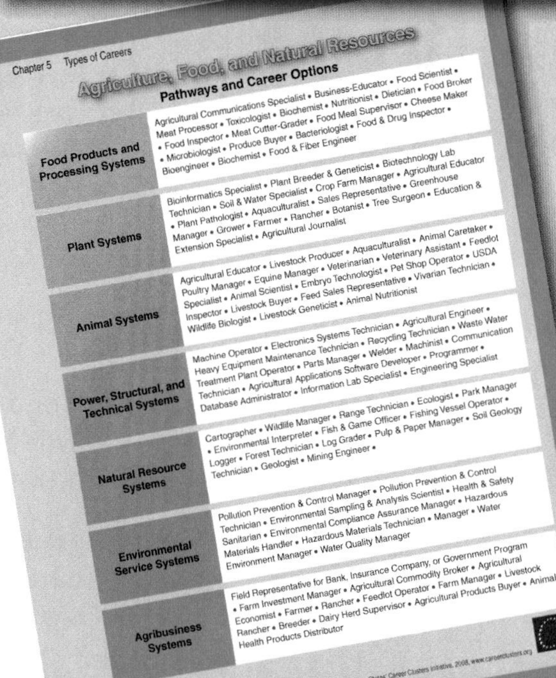

Agriculture, Food, and Natural Resources

	Pathways and Career Options
Food Products and Processing Systems	Agricultural Communications Specialist • Business-Educator • Food Scientist • Meat Processor • Toxicologist • Biochemist • Nutritionist • Dietician • Food Broker • Food Inspector • Meat Cutter-Grader • Food Meal Supervisor • Cheese Maker • Microbiologist • Produce Buyer • Bacteriologist • Food & Drug Inspector • Bioengineer • Biochemist • Food & Fiber Engineer
Plant Systems	Bioinformatics Specialist • Plant Breeder & Geneticist • Biotechnology Lab Technician • Soil & Water Specialist • Crop Farm Manager • Agricultural Educator • Plant Pathologist • Aquaculturalist • Sales Representative • Greenhouse Manager • Grower • Farmer • Rancher • Botanist • Tree Surgeon • Education & Extension Specialist • Agricultural Journalist
Animal Systems	Agricultural Educator • Livestock Producer • Aquaculturalist • Animal Caretaker • Poultry Manager • Equine Manager • Veterinarian • Veterinary Assistant • Feedlot Specialist • Animal Scientist • Embryo Technologist • Pet Shop Operator • USDA Inspector • Livestock Buyer • Feed Sales Representative • Vivarian Technician • Wildlife Biologist • Livestock Geneticist • Animal Nutritionist
Power, Structural, and Technical Systems	Machine Operator • Electronics Systems Technician • Agricultural Engineer • Heavy Equipment Maintenance Technician • Recycling Technician • Waste Water Treatment Plant Operator • Parts Manager • Welder • Machinist • Communication Technician • Agricultural Applications Software Developer • Programmer • Database Administrator • Information Lab Specialist • Engineering Specialist
Natural Resource Systems	Cartographer • Wildlife Manager • Range Technician • Ecologist • Park Manager • Environmental Interpreter • Fish & Game Officer • Fishing Vessel Operator • Logger • Forest Technician • Log Grader • Pulp & Paper Manager • Soil Geology Technician • Geologist • Mining Engineer •
Environmental Service Systems	Pollution Prevention & Control Manager • Pollution Prevention & Control Technician • Environmental Sampling & Analysis Scientist • Health & Safety Sanitarian • Environmental Compliance Assurance Manager • Hazardous Materials Handler • Hazardous Materials Technician • Manager • Water Environment Manager • Water Quality Manager
Agribusiness Systems	Field Representative for Bank, Insurance Company, or Government Program • Farm Investment Manager • Agricultural Commodity Broker • Agricultural Economist • Farmer • Rancher • Feedlot Operator • Farm Manager • Livestock Rancher • Breeder • Dairy Herd Supervisor • Agricultural Products Buyer • Animal Health Products Distributor

The Career Clusters icons are being used with permission of the: States' Career Clusters Initiative, 2008, www.careerclusters.org

Learning for Earning is designed to introduce you to the skills you will need to succeed in school, on the job, and on your own. It will serve as a guide as you prepare for a career and become a productive member of the workforce.

Success in a career begins with an understanding of the world of work. This text will explain the important changes taking place in the workplace and how they apply to you. It will cover the variety of careers available to you. Skills that are important in work and in your life will be identified as well as ways to acquire them.

Being a member of the workplace involves a whole new set of responsibilities as you strive to become an independent adult. Once you know what type of work you want, you are ready to begin exploring job options. You will learn how to find work suitable to your skills, personality, and values. You will also gain the knowledge needed to become successful at work and advance in your career.

Patti Jo DeVillers
Instructor
West De Pere Middle School
De Pere, Wisconsin

Vicky D. Keller
Instructor
Rochester Community and Technical College
Rochester, Minnesota

Diann Pilgrim
Teacher-Coordinator, Family and Consumer Sciences
Wenonah High School
Birmingham, Alabama

Janice Sullivan
Family and Consumer Sciences Instructor
Southington High School
Southington, Connecticut

Janet Thorley
Family and Consumer Sciences Department Head
Clinton Central School Corporation
Michigantown, Indiana

Contents in Brief

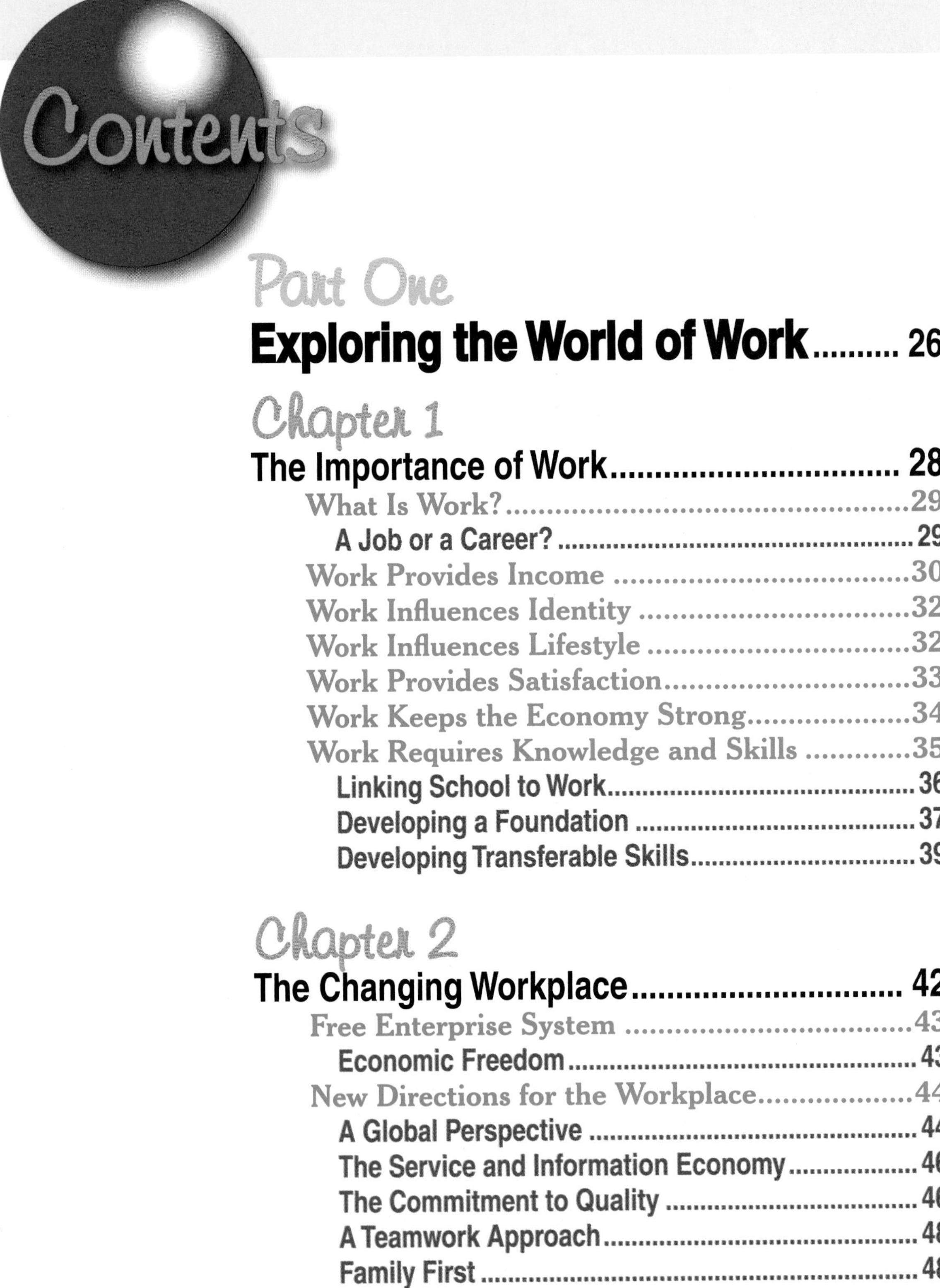

Contents

Chapter 5

Chapter 8

Chapter 9

Chapter 12

Chapter 13

Chapter 14

Chapter 19

Chapter 20

Chapter 21

Chapter 22

Chapter 25

Chapter 26

Chapter 27

Chapter 28

Part Seven

Chapter 29

Part One

Exploring the World of Work

Why is work important to me?

Chapter 1 The Importance of Work

Key Terms

work
job
occupation
career
career ladder
income
needs
wants
identity
lifestyle
self-esteem
economy
career clusters
transferable skills

Chapter Objectives

After studying this chapter, you will be able to

- **distinguish** the difference between a job and a career.
- **identify** three reasons for working.
- **explain** how work influences identity and lifestyle.
- **describe** ways in which work provides satisfaction.
- **discuss** how work keeps the economy strong.
- **explain** how to study careers.

Key Concepts

- School work prepares you for the workplace.
- Work provides income to meet needs and wants.
- Work influences your identity and lifestyle and provides satisfaction.
- Work affects the country's economy.
- Work requires career knowledge and skills.

What Is Work?

What is work? ***Work*** is defined as an activity done to produce or accomplish something. People work to gain something in return. As you go to school, you work. You do homework, read books, give reports, and study for tests. Students receive passing grades in return for doing their schoolwork well.

At this point in your life, schoolwork is very important. You are preparing yourself for your future work—your career.

A Job or a Career?

A ***job*** is the work done, usually to earn money. For example, delivering newspapers is a job. Some jobs are full-time, but many are temporary or part-time. You may take a job to earn extra money for a special occasion, such as a class trip, or to make a special purchase.

Jobs may involve as few as one task, but an occupation involves various tasks. An ***occupation*** is employment that requires related skills and experiences. However, an occupation is not a career. A ***career*** is a series of occupations, usually in the same or related fields, that help you advance in a chosen field of work.

A good way to display the steps of a career is with a career ladder. A ***career ladder*** shows a sequence of work in a career field, from entry to advanced levels. Each rung of the career ladder is another step in the progression to a better job. Each step in your career may require that you learn new and more-complex information and skills. Reaching your final career objective may take many years and require considerable education and training. See 1-1.

Careers require that many skills be learned to progress in a chosen area. No matter what career direction you choose, advancing will depend on learning more-complex information and skills. There is a direct link between how well you do in school now and your future in the work world. Prospective employers will consider your school records when they make hiring decisions. Apprenticeship programs, trade schools, and schools of higher education will consider academic success when processing applications for admission.

work
An activity done to produce or accomplish something.

job
The work a person does, usually to earn money.

occupation
Employment that requires related skills and experiences.

career
A series of occupations, usually in the same or related fields, that helps you advance in a chosen field of work.

career ladder
An illustration that shows a sequence of work in a career field, from entry to advanced levels.

Resource
Reinforcing Vocabulary, Activity A, WB. Students complete a vocabulary activity with the chapter's key terms.

Resource
Your Thoughts on Work, Activity B, WB. Students answer questions to determine how work will fit into their lives.

Your Reading

How does school prepare you for work?

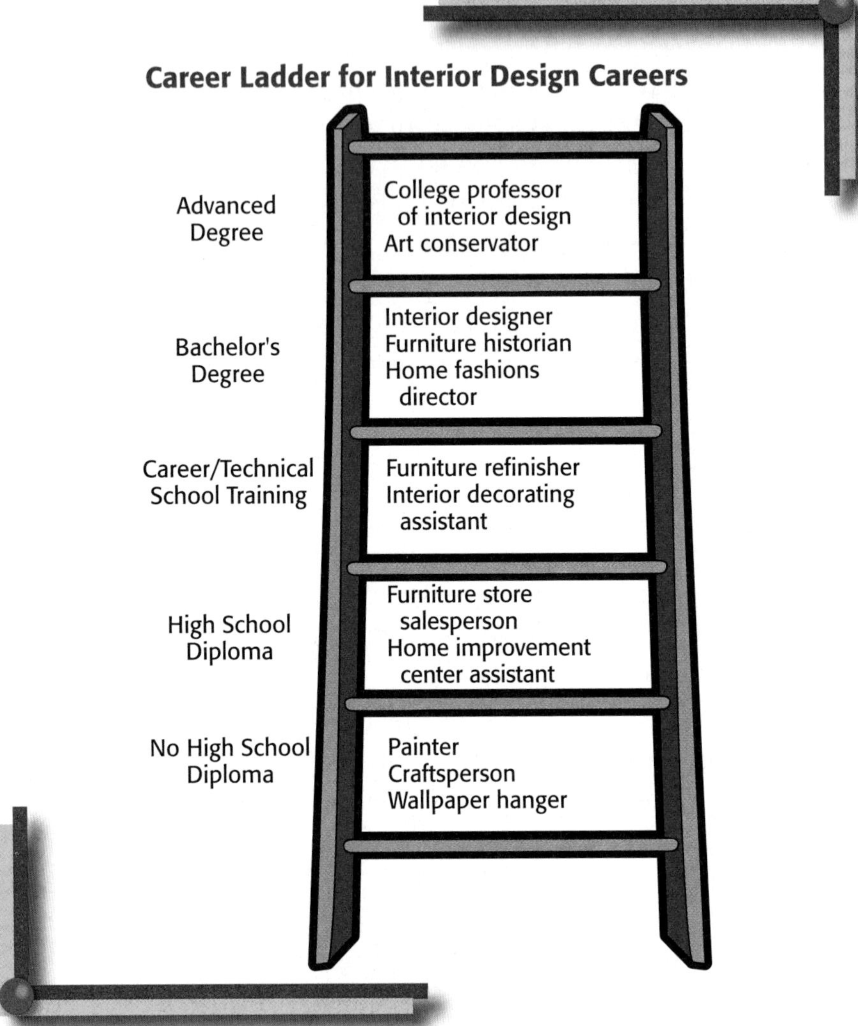

1-1
This career ladder shows different choices at each step that individuals can make to advance in the interior design field.

Activity
Arrange students in teams. Have the teams make a career ladder for each person in the group.

Discuss
What is the link between how well you do in school and how well you do on the job? Explain why each step on a career ladder will require you to learn more.

Activity
If students cannot see the progression of careers by following the example, create several career ladders as a class activity. Use popular career choices from student suggestions and work through the steps together.

Adapting the Lesson
Provide students who are low functioning with a list of jobs existing in the community that teenagers can hold. Have them circle the jobs that seem interesting and put a star beside the job they most prefer.

Activity
Write a paragraph on what type of career you want and how much yearly income you desire. In a second paragraph, describe the type of housing you would like.

income
The amount of money a person receives for doing a job.

That's why it is important to make every effort now to do well in school. See 1-2.

Work Provides Income

The purpose of work is to produce or accomplish something. That *something* could be job satisfaction or personal gain. Other reasons for working include a sense of obligation, commitment to a goal, or a sense of pride. The list could go on, but for most people, income is the key reason for working.

Income is the money a person receives for doing a job. With the money people earn from working, they buy things they need or want.

1-2
Success in school paves the way for future success in a career.

Vocabulary

Discuss the definitions of *income*, *needs*, and *wants*. Use each in a sentence to demonstrate understanding.

Adapting the Lesson

Provide students who are low functioning with a handout that lists the needs and wants teenagers usually record. Have students determine their top three needs and mark them *N1*, *N2*, and *N3*. Ask students to repeat the process for their wants, marking them *W1*, *W2*, and *W3*.

needs
The basics a person must have in order to live.

wants
The items a person would like to have, but are not needed to survive.

While you are still in school, you may have a part-time job. If so, it probably would allow you to earn spending money and save some money for the future. After you graduate from high school, you will probably find that you must have a full-time job to meet your needs. ***Needs*** are the basics you must have in order to live. You may need a car, a place to live, money for food, and tuition for further education. Eventually, you may need enough income to support a family. Satisfying greater needs usually requires income from a higher-paying job.

In addition to your needs, you also have wants. Wants go beyond actual needs. ***Wants*** include items you would like to have, but do not need to survive. For instance, while you may need a car, you may want a new sports car. You may also want a big apartment, stylish clothes, and fun vacations. Affording your needs and wants requires earning a living by working.

Your Reading

How is income related to needs and wants?

Work Influences Identity

Look around the community where you live. You will find many successful people in all types of occupations. Some people work for others. Some people work for themselves. Some of the businesses are big, while others are medium-size or small.

identity
The sum of traits that distinguishes a person as an individual.

The work you choose to do is likely to influence your identity. Your ***identity*** is the sum of traits that distinguish you as an individual. Your identity is two fold. It is how you see yourself. It also is how others see you. When you describe yourself, you are talking about your identity. For instance, you may say that you are a family member, student, and member of the swim team.

What does your work say about who you are?

As an adult, your job will be an important part of your identity. Your work will influence the way you think of yourself and the way others see you. It is important to choose work that will allow you to respect yourself and develop a positive identity.

Work Influences Lifestyle

Discuss
Explain how a person's career influences his or her lifestyle. What types of purchases can high-paying jobs afford that low-paying jobs cannot?

How do you spend your time? What activities do you enjoy? Where do you live? What is important to you? Your answers to these questions will help you describe your ***lifestyle***, or typical way of life.

lifestyle
A person's typical way of life.

The work you choose will affect your lifestyle in many ways. It will affect where you live. For instance, if you want to be a flight attendant, you should live near an airport.

Your work will also affect the people you meet and the time you have to spend with your family and friends, 1-3. Some jobs may require working nights and weekends. Others may involve overtime hours or out-of-town travel. Some work schedules are fixed—they are firmly set. Working hours and days do not change. Other work schedules are flexible, with work hours and workdays changing frequently.

What aspects of your lifestyle will your work influence?

Income is another factor that influences lifestyle. The more money you make, the more expensive your lifestyle may be. You may be able to afford a nice house, pricey clothes, and new cars. If you work too much, however, you may not have time to enjoy your purchases. How you balance your work and nonwork hours depends on your lifestyle decisions.

1-3
The amount of time you have to enjoy leisure activities will depend on your work schedule.

Resource

Working to Help Others, Activity C, WB. Students answer questions about people who have chosen to work in "helping" careers.

Work Provides Satisfaction

One of the most important reasons for working is to gain satisfaction. Doing a job well helps you build ***self-esteem***, which is confidence in yourself. When you have self-esteem, you feel good about yourself. You are proud of who you are and what you do.

self-esteem
The confidence a person has in himself or herself.

Work also provides a feeling of accomplishment. When you complete a job and do it well, you feel good about it. Others recognize excellent work and compliment you for it. That's why you should always put your best possible effort into any work you do.

Activity

Make a list of your noteworthy accomplishments in life so far. List what you accomplished in school and in extracurricular activities as well as outside school.

Another kind of satisfaction from work comes from being with other people. Most types of work allow occasional opportunities to socialize with others.

Resource

Careers That Meet Your Goals, Activity D, WB. Students identify their goals and list careers that would help meet them.

Work also provides the satisfaction of feeling useful. You can feel useful by earning money to support yourself. You can also feel useful by doing work that you believe is important. Work that provides a public service gives workers a strong sense of usefulness. Some examples include helping people in need, enforcing the law, fighting fires, and cleaning the environment.

Many people judge their success in terms of satisfaction rather than income. They do not feel they have to become wealthy to be successful. Many successful people have limited financial resources. They receive their rewards by seeing others helped. They take pride in their jobs and in their accomplishments.

Many of the most famous people in history dedicated their lives to helping society without expecting financial rewards. These people are regarded as society's heroes. See 1-4.

Your Reading

In what ways can work bring you satisfaction?

1-4
Volunteering at a library and sharing your love of reading with others is an example of work that improves the quality of life.

Reflect

When you work for pay, does the amount of money you earn relate to the satisfaction you feel for your job?

Resource

The Economic Cycle, color transparency CT-1, TR. Use this resource to inspire a class discussion on how a strong economy operates.

economy
The way goods and services are produced, distributed, and consumed in a society.

Community Connections

Work in groups to list the following: What does the local economy produce? What services does the community provide? Who are the major employers? What jobs do most residents hold?

Work Keeps the Economy Strong

When people go to work, they make products and perform services that others buy. They also earn money that allows them to buy whatever they need, such as cars, homes, clothes, and food. By making these purchases, people recycle their earnings back into the economy. A country's ***economy*** is its way of producing, distributing, and consuming goods and services. This process is one big cycle, 1-5. The income you earn from working goes back into the economy when you buy something.

When we purchase goods or services from another country, we are helping the economy of that country. The global marketplace has increased the way people, businesses, and countries all depend on one another.

Individuals and businesses in the United States depend on each other. Both must do their parts to keep the economy healthy. Businesses put goods into the marketplace and pay workers for their labor.

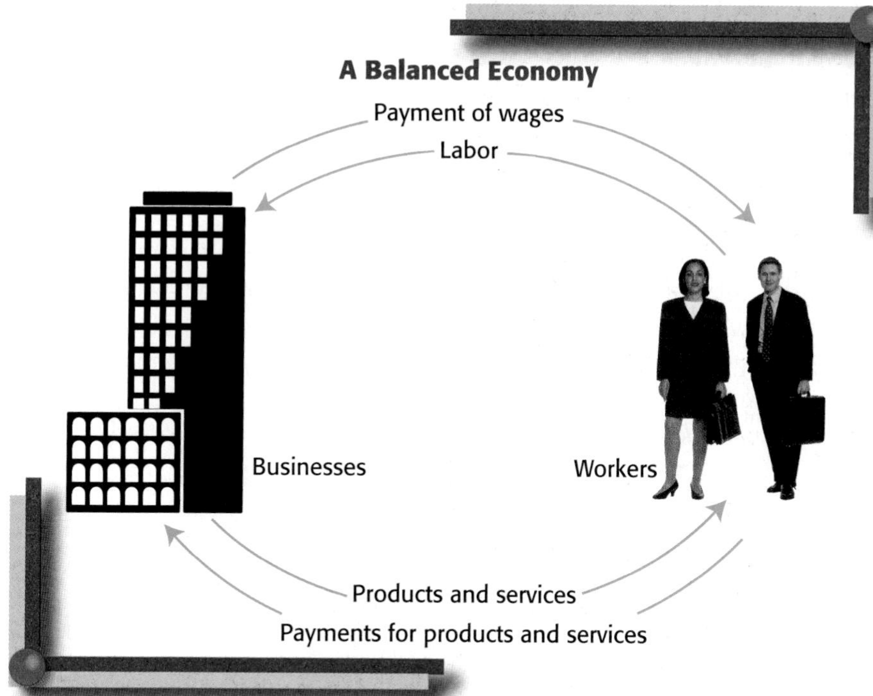

1-5
A strong economy depends on the balance between the production and consumption of goods and services.

Resource

Circular Flow of the American Economy, reproducible master 1-1, TR. Students provide an example from their own lives that shows how they are involved in the U.S. economic system.

Enthusiastic workers help keep the economy strong in two ways. They help businesses succeed by providing labor. They also buy goods and services in the marketplace when they shift from the role of worker to consumer.

You can do your part to keep the economy strong by taking your work role seriously. This will include performing your job correctly, being willing to learn, and having a good attitude. The jobs you will hold during your life will exist because customers are willing to purchase goods or services from your employer.

Your Reading

How do workers and businesses keep the economy healthy?

Work Requires Knowledge and Skills

Before you are hired, the employer will ask, "What can you do?" This short question requires much thought. The answer must convey all that you can bring to the workplace, such as special skills you have, your educational background, and previous work experiences.

Preparing yourself for the workplace is easier when you know what employers seek. To help students prepare for future success, experts in your state and across the nation

Discuss

What skills do you think employers seek in their workers?

Enrich

Invite a guest speaker from a local business to talk about what employers seek when hiring new employees. Have the speaker report what employers generally observe when screening résumés and cover letters.

have refined school programs to better address career and workplace needs. As a result, students learn about career choices and the importance of career planning much earlier in their studies.

Linking School to Work

career clusters
The 16 broad groups of occupational and career specialties.

One of the best ways to study careers is by checking the ***career clusters***. These are 16 broad groups of occupational and career specialties. See 1-6. Since all possible careers are

1-6 The career clusters connect students to careers and the knowledge and skills needed to achieve them.

Resource
Career Cluster Goals for Learners, transparency master 1-2, TR. Use this transparency to identify how career planning linked to a study of the career clusters helps learners successfully transition from school to a rewarding career.

Adapting the Lesson
Have students who are high functioning find the official Web site for *career clusters*. Ask them to report how their classmates could benefit from using the site.

Discuss
Name each of the 16 career clusters in Figure 1-6 as you poll the class. Determine how many students could picture themselves working in each cluster. Which is the most popular cluster? the least popular?

Note
The same job title may appear in more than one career cluster.

organized into just 16 groups, studying careers is easy with this method.

A key step in studying careers is recognizing your interests, talents, and abilities. They will determine the career areas that interest you. You may have no interest in many clusters, but some interest in others. After careful thought, one or two career areas will appeal to you more than others. (See Chapter 5, "Types of Careers," for more information on the career clusters.)

Each cluster includes several career directions, called *career pathways*. Within each pathway are various occupations ranging from entry-level to very challenging. All the career choices within a given pathway require a set of common knowledge and skills. This means the related careers require very similar programs of study. Being prepared for more than one career in a related field allows more flexibility when job hunting.

With the help of teachers and counselors, you will develop a study plan matched to your desired career. Compatible activities and learning experiences will be added as you refine your career choice. At least annually, you should review your study plan to see if it's still on target.

Through high school and further education, students will be asked to select courses based on their career plans. For many jobs, students must study to obtain licenses or certifications, too. For example, to practice hairstyling in a salon, a person must have a cosmetology license. Other licensed workers include a registered nurse, private detective, and insurance agent. See 1-7.

Many states offer certificates that are optional for some occupations. However, having one tells employers that you have successfully met the requirements. Examples of these include a certified public accountant, a certified home health aide, or an ASE (Automotive Service Excellence) certified automotive technician.

Developing a Foundation

Academic skills, thinking skills, and important personal qualities—these form a foundation on which workplace readiness can grow. Much of your work as a student is aimed at developing that foundation so you are prepared for the world of work.

Making a Difference

Brainstorm 10 volunteer jobs for teenagers. Make a list of the locations of these jobs in the community and identify contact information. Use the findings to make a poster to display in class. Discuss how these volunteer opportunities can relate to future careers.

Discuss

What are five jobs teenagers might have while in school? At what places of employment can you work when you are 14, 15, or 16 years old?

Discuss

List a career you would like to have and the yearly income you think a beginner would earn.

Reflect

What kinds of skills are needed in every career?

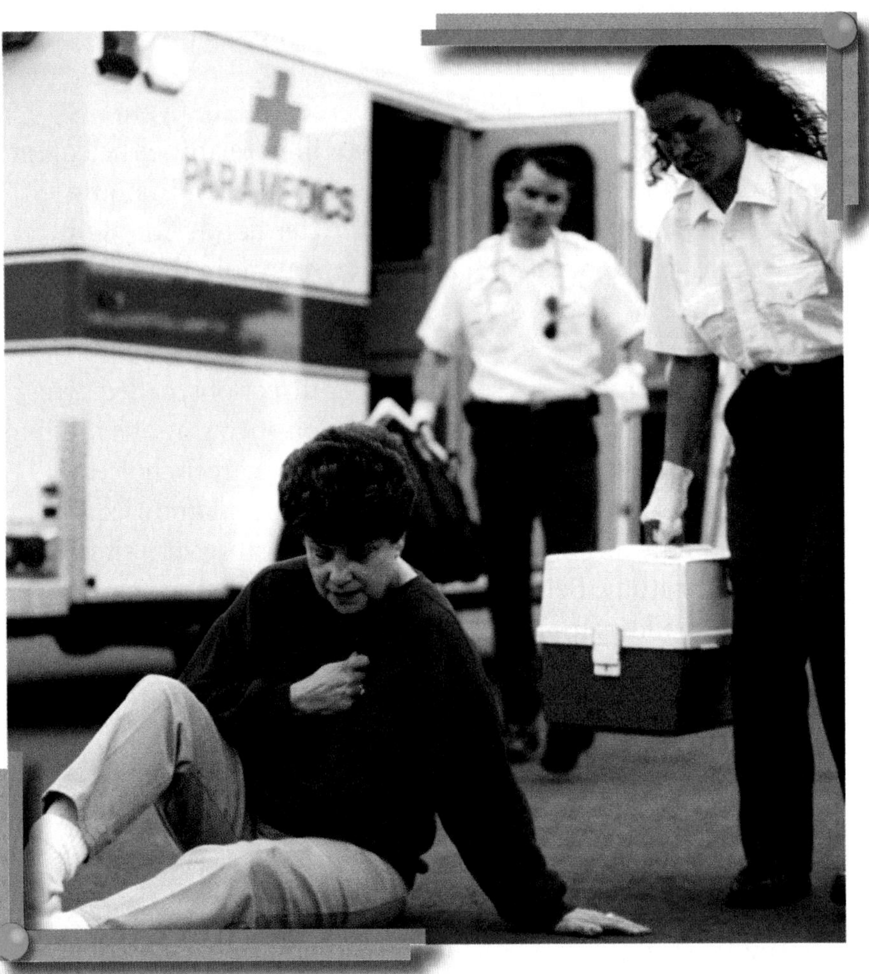

1-7
Emergency medical technicians (EMTs) must have one of several levels of certification to identify the specific types of emergency situations they can handle.

Activity
Divide the class into teams. Have students work together to list the academic skills taught in one of the following classes, foods, health education, or another choice. Discuss with the entire class how these skills build independence in young people, particularly when they begin living on their own.

Reflect
What can you do to sharpen your thinking skills?

Activity
Make a list of the personal qualities listed and put a star by the quality that best identifies you.

Resource
Thinking About Getting a Job, reproducible master 1-3, TR. Use the adapted worksheet to reinforce chapter concepts in students who are low functioning.

Discuss
What are examples of people you know who changed jobs and were able to transfer their skills from one career to another?

- *Academic skills* allow you to express your thoughts and communicate with coworkers. The key skills are reading, writing, speaking, listening, math, science, and basic computer skills.
- *Thinking skills* allow you to develop ideas and solve problems. The key skills are thinking creatively, visualizing ideas, making decisions, and thinking critically (analyzing, reasoning, and evaluating).
- *Personal qualities* shape the way you work and the kind of worker you are. The key qualities are positive attitude, self-esteem, sociability, flexibility, integrity, responsibility, leadership, and a "team" focus.

As a student preparing for the world of work, look for ways to develop these skills in yourself. Become involved in student council, school clubs, extracurricular activities, and community programs.

Workplace readiness is sometimes called *employability skills*. However, many believe that term is too limited because it implies a focus on just getting a job. Sometimes the term *career-success skills* is used. That term is a good substitute since having workplace skills yields lifelong success at work.

Developing Transferable Skills

Skills in one career that can be used in another are called ***transferable skills***. For example, the skills of a store cashier in working with money are the same skills needed by a teller in a bank. Usually academic skills and thinking skills are considered transferable skills. Specialized skills also are transferable, such as speaking a second language.

Having transferable skills is important to your future career success. That's because few jobs last forever. You are likely to switch jobs, and possibly career paths, several times during your life. Sometimes people tire of a career and desire something different. Often a person's interests and abilities expand, prompting a search for new opportunities.

Whatever the reason for a job change, examine which of your skills will carry over to a new position you desire. Consider a chef's artistic skills. Knowing how to apply the principles of design to make food attractive is a must. Similar artistic skills are used by advertising managers, interior decorators, and fashion designers. However, their focus is something other than food.

Another example of a transferable skill is the ability to persuade people. This is important to lawyers as they argue a case in court. Being persuasive is also important for salespeople as well as for doctors and nurses who deal with difficult patients.

Most people underestimate their skills. Be sure to take the time to identify all your skills in your search for a rewarding career.

Community Connections

Select someone employed in your community to interview. Document the worker's place of employment and skills needed for his or her job. Beside each skill, write down various school lessons and activities in which you are involved that might help you to learn these skills.

transferable skills
Skills used in one career that can be used in another.

Your Reading

Why do employers value the knowledge and skills of their employees?

Summary

In your lifetime, you will have many different jobs. A job may or may not be related to your career. A career requires that you learn increasingly more difficult jobs related to a chosen field. A career can be compared to a ladder. Each step is a progression toward a career objective.

Work is important for several reasons. It allows you to earn an income so you can buy things you need and want. It influences how you see yourself and others see you. Work also affects where you live, when you work, what you do, and whom you meet. Work provides a sense of purpose and direction for life.

One of the most important reasons for working is to gain satisfaction. Satisfaction from work comes in many different forms. The work satisfaction you seek may be different from the satisfaction others seek.

Work is needed to keep the country's economy strong. Every person who earns money and spends it plays a role in keeping the economy healthy. Workers who do their best on the job help make their employers successful. This makes the economy stronger.

Successful workers have the knowledge and skills their careers demand. They study career options and follow programs of study that match their choices. They develop the academic and thinking skills and personal qualities that employers seek. They link the demands of their future career to their schoolwork, extracurricular activities, and community involvement.

Reviewing Key Concepts

1. In your own words, define *job* and *career*.
2. Why is your schoolwork important at this point in your life?
3. For most people, what is the key reason for working?
4. Show the difference between needs and wants by listing three needs and three wants.
5. Describe three ways in which work influences lifestyle.
6. Explain how work can boost self-esteem.
7. Why should you always put your best possible effort into any work you do?
8. Satisfaction from work can come from ______.
   A. being with other people
   B. earning money
   C. doing work that helps others
   D. All of the above.
9. Explain how work keeps the economy strong.
10. True or false. Academic skills and thinking skills are considered transferable skills.

Answers to *Reviewing Key Concepts*

1. A job is something you do to earn money. A career is a series of jobs, usually in the same or related fields, that help you advance to higher levels in your chosen field of work.
2. Schoolwork helps a person prepare for a future career. Also, prospective employers will consider school records when they make hiring decisions. Apprenticeship programs, trade schools, and schools of higher education will consider academic success when processing applications for admission.
3. to earn income
4. (Student response.)
5. (Student response. Typical answers may refer to where people live, the new people they meet, the time they spend working, and the income they earn.)
6. You feel confident and good about yourself. You are proud of who you are and what you do.
7. Doing good work makes people see you in a positive way and gives you a good feeling of accomplishment.
8. D
9. Workers make products and perform services that are needed. They also earn money. When they spend their money to buy what they need and want, their money goes back into the economy.
10. true

Building Academic Skills

1. **Speaking, listening.** Prepare interview questions for your parents, grandparents, or other adult relatives regarding the type of jobs they held during their lifetime. Questions can cover what they liked most and least, and the skills they used on the job. Share with the class how satisfied you think the people you interviewed were with their career choices.
2. **Math.** Describe your desired career, income, and home. Estimate how long you must work at various careers to afford the lifestyle of your choice. Assume that 20 percent of your gross pay can be used to pursue your dream lifestyle, while 80 percent will go toward paying taxes and buying the basic necessities of food, clothing, transportation, and shelter.
3. **Reading, speaking.** Read a current magazine story about the role workers play in keeping the economy strong. Summarize the story in a brief, oral report.
4. **Writing.** Develop a list of at least 10 transferable skills you are learning in your various classes. Write a paragraph, summarizing how these skills will help you in a future career.

Building Technology Skills

1. Choose three careers. Estimate what the yearly income of a beginning worker in that career would be. Using a Web site, research average salaries for your career choices. Visit the *Occupational Outlook Handbook* Web site at **bls.gov/oco** to look up salaries. Was your prediction of yearly income for beginning workers accurate?
2. Use Internet resources to begin investigations into careers. Search **http//careers.yahoo.com** plus the following Web sites: **careerjournal.com**, and **bls.gov/oco**. Plot categories on a chart so you can easily compare several careers. Update this chart throughout the course. (You can refer to this chart in future chapters.)

Building Career Knowledge and Skills

1. Examine the classified section of a newspaper. Categorize the listings as jobs or occupations.
2. Ask three people in different careers how their work affects their lifestyles. Write a paper explaining what you learned. Also, identify the kind of lifestyle you prefer and the type of career that would allow you to achieve it.
3. Interview an individual approaching retirement regarding how his or her work and skills have changed over the years.

Building Workplace Skills

Work with two classmates to research career information and present it to the class. Select a career area and present a career ladder showing how a person can advance from one job to another. Decide as a team how to divide the work. Prepare a written plan outlining who will do each task. Find the following facts for each job listed on the career ladder: the predicted job growth or decline, the anticipated earnings, the skills and academic preparation needed, and whether a license or certificate is required. Present the findings to the class using charts, graphs, or pictures.

How is the world of work changing?

Chapter 2 The Changing Workplace

Key Terms

free enterprise system
profit
global economy
services
family-friendly programs
flextime
self-sufficient
demographics
diversity
outsourcing
technology
computer revolution
telecommuting
Internet
e-tailing
e-commerce
lifelong learning

Chapter Objectives

After studying this chapter, you will be able to

- **compare** and **contrast** employment opportunities in the free enterprise system with other world economic systems.
- **identify** five factors that are inspiring new ideas about the world of work.
- **describe** six factors that affect the labor market.
- **explain** the importance of technology to the workplace.
- **describe** what is expected of workers in today's workplace.

Key Concepts

- In a free enterprise system, individuals and businesses play a key role in making decisions.
- The workplace is constantly changing to make work faster and more efficient.
- Several factors shape the composition of the workforce and the types of jobs available.
- Technology is the cause of most ongoing change in the workplace.

Free Enterprise System

You live in a country that operates as a ***free enterprise system***. That term describes an economy in which individuals and businesses play a major role in making decisions. In a free enterprise system, people can operate any type of business they choose, provided it is lawful. Businesses sell goods and services to customers.

free enterprise system
An economy in which individuals and businesses play a major role in making decisions.

Note

The U.S. Congress acknowledges companies and products that meet established standards for quality. Congress established "The Baldrige Award" as one of the ways to recognize U.S. companies that meet standards of excellence.

Enrich

Find out how much profit is gained on *basic* versus *luxury* versions of clothes, cars, and so forth. Write a reaction to what you learned.

Resource

Reinforcing Vocabulary, Activity A, WB. Students match the chapter terms with their definitions.

Economic Freedom

How does a free enterprise system affect the people who live and work in it? The following are five effects, as demonstrated in the U.S. economy:

- People are free to be creative and choose where they work. They can choose to be their own boss or to work for someone else.
- People are free to own private property and buy whatever they want. Just think of all the choices available for any product you desire.
- The government allows people to buy or sell whatever they wish, so long as it doesn't harm others.
- Consumer *wants* and *needs* determine what products are desired in the marketplace.
- Businesses can compete against each other to make money. Those who sell successful products and services make a profit. A ***profit*** is the money left after all expenses are paid. Competition is good for consumers, too, because it promotes better products at lower prices.

profit
The money left in a business after all expenses are paid.

The freedom to own property and freely buy and sell goods began with the founders of this country. The free enterprise system is an outgrowth of their spirit of independence. This economic system is also called a *market economic system.*

The desire to make a profit and earn a good living is called the *profit motive.* See 2-1. In countries where the government (or a central authority) controls the production of goods, it also controls their prices and distribution. Under such a system, people must follow the government's dictates regarding how to work and live.

2-1
A child's lemonade stand is a simple example of the profit motive in action under the free enterprise system.

Community Connections

Interview at least four people who work full-time about changes in their various workplaces. (Parents, relatives, and neighbors may be included.) What are two examples of new equipment or tools used at each person's work? Have their employers made other changes, such as work methods or company size? If they are self-employed, what have they done to keep their business updated? Prepare a report about what you learn.

Resource

What's Happening in the Workplace? transparency master 2-1, TR. Use the transparency to introduce students to some key changes affecting today's workplace.

New Directions for the Workplace

The U.S. workplace is continually changing. New types of jobs are created each year. New tools are used to work faster and more efficiently. Companies have new ideas about how to find customers and how work should be done. Due to technology and more efficient methods of production, some jobs are replaced with other jobs.

The one thing you can count on in today's exciting workplace is *change*, and you will be a part of it. The question no longer is: Will change occur? Instead, it is: How will change occur? The following factors are inspiring new ideas that are changing the world of work.

A Global Perspective

Companies once reached no further than their neighborhoods to find customers. Then, companies searched for more customers beyond their towns and states. Today that search takes them beyond the nation's borders to every part of the world. Instant communications through phones, faxes, and computers makes this possible.

Customers are just one focus of the new global perspective. The other is labor. Companies constantly look to other nations for labor services. It generally costs less to make goods in another country because pay scales are much lower. Only a few countries in the world have wage rates that nearly match the rates here.

Cheaper labor in other countries has forced U.S. businesses to change their practices and manufacture many goods elsewhere. Once the United States was the manufacturing center of the world. Factories and production lines were a part of practically every U.S. worker's experience.

Nowadays, most manufacturing is done in various production centers in other countries. These centers fill orders placed by businesses located around the world. The centers make small items and parts for complex products. The parts are then sent to wherever the final product is assembled. This manufacturing process makes goods more affordable. See 2-2.

U.S. cars and other large items are often assembled in U.S. factories from parts made in other countries. Most small items are made entirely outside the country and shipped to a store near you. This is evidence of a global economy. A ***global economy*** is a financial interconnection among the countries of the world. It means that parts or entire products are created in one country for sale to customers in other countries.

The global economy has caused a major shift in the U.S. workforce. It has reduced the need for unskilled labor since a vast

Discuss
Does anyone know a family who moved for job-location reasons? How many times did the family move before? Was the latest move easy or hard on family members?

Reflect
How many items in your bedroom were made in other countries? How do you feel about buying products that were made in other countries because wages are lower?

Vocabulary
Discuss the definition of *global economy* and give examples.

global economy
Goods and services created by companies in one country are sold to customers in other countries.

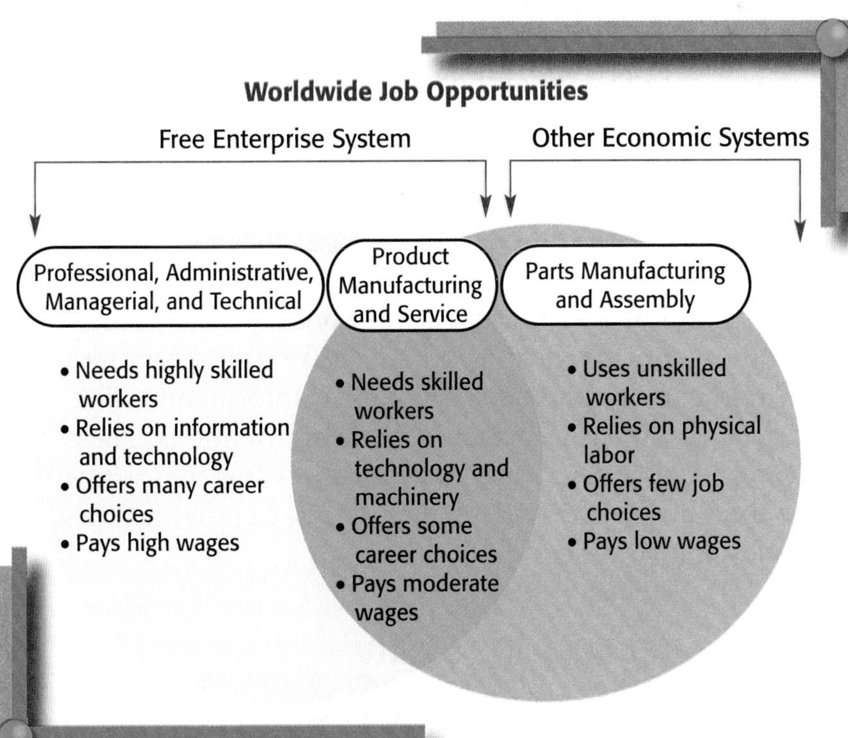

2-2
U.S. jobs generally call for skilled labor because work requiring unskilled labor is handled in other parts of the world.

Adapting the Lesson
As an enrichment project, have students who are high functioning research and write about companies and their global impact on labor conditions in other countries. While students research these companies, direct them to investigate job opportunities posted on each company's Web site.

Activity

Create a list of services provided by your community. Check the local telephone book to find additional services to add to your list.

Discuss

Why do you think people employed in U.S. occupations that provide services far outnumber those that produce goods?

supply exists in other parts of the world. Instead, skilled, well-educated U.S. workers are needed to plan, develop, and deliver the products and services of tomorrow. Skilled workers are also needed for assembling large, complex products such as cars.

Globalization is the integration of markets, technology, and resources between the economies of nations. Globalization involves the movement of money, material resources, and human resources between nations.

New technology in the workplace is speeding globalization of industries and businesses. This interdependence of the world's economies is impacting an ever-widening number of U.S. industries. Currently more than 130 U.S. industries rely on some form of globalization and are increasing their involvement. These industries represent a cross section of the U.S. economy—from vegetable farming to architectural services to office and financial services.

The Service and Information Economy

services
Nonmaterial assistance for which people are willing to pay.

The decline of the manufacturing sector paved the way for today's U.S. economy, which is based on services and information. ***Services*** are nonmaterial assistance for which people are willing to pay. This sector of the economy has grown very rapidly in recent years. It will remain the area of greatest job growth for the near future.

Over three-fourths of the 15.6 million new jobs that will exist by 2016 will be service oriented. See Figure 2-3 for a list of the 10 occupations that will employ the most people in 2016. All are focused on producing some type of service. The chart shows the numbers of new jobs that will be created during the period, not the millions that already exist. The only U.S. occupations that produce goods are construction, agriculture, forestry, fishing, manufacturing, and mining.

Another focus of today's economy is information. The computer and the Internet are American inventions. These are the tools of the information economy. What we learn with these tools helps us to create new services, improve business methods, and lower costs.

The Commitment to Quality

You will hear the word *quality* spoken in the workplace quite often. To become the very best, businesses of all types

Occupations Offering the Greatest Number of New Jobs, 2006-2016

Occupation	Number of New Jobs (in thousands)	Percent Increase
Registered nurses	587	24
Retail salespersons	557	12
Customer service representatives	545	25
Combined food preparation and service workers, including fast-food	452	18
Office clerks, general	404	13
Personal and home care aides	389	51
Home health aides	384	49
Postsecondary teachers	382	23
Janitors and cleaners, except maids and housekeeping cleaners	345	15
Nursing aides, orderlies, and attendants	264	18

U.S. Department of Labor

2-3
These 10 occupations will see the greatest growth in terms of job openings.

and sizes are constantly seeking ways to improve the quality of their product or service. Quality means different things to different businesses. In a manufacturing business, quality means producing a product with the least possible flaws. In a restaurant, quality means constantly preparing meals that are fresh, appealing, affordable, and served to the customer in a reasonable amount of time.

Quality also includes how well your customers are treated. Quality customer service means making your customers feel that they are welcome and important to you. It means following through in doing what you told the customer you would do. It means being pleasant, friendly, and treating customers fairly.

U.S. companies committed to quality participate in programs such as *Total Quality Management (TQM).* If they do business in other countries, they adhere to globally recognized programs developed by the *International Organization of Standards (ISO).* These programs have procedures and high standards that businesses strive to meet. The programs require management to improve all aspects of quality, including performance and customer satisfaction. Quality is a necessity for doing business in an ever expanding, and more competitive world market.

Resource

Employment Projections by Major Occupational Group, transparency master 2-2, TR. Students review the industry groups to learn which are expected to grow or decline by 2016.

Resource

Workplace Solutions, Activity B, WB. Students examine a case study of an imaginary company, and using concepts from the chapter, recommend ways to make it profitable.

Activity

Group students into three teams to compete in the following two challenges: First, align members according to the range of hair colors present, with black hair first. Next, align members according to birthdays, with January first. When you say "go," teams will work as quickly as possible, shouting "done" when each task is finished. Evaluate results and discuss how teamwork is needed in the workplace.

Reflect

What personal experience do you have working on a team?

As an employee, you will be asked to make suggestions on ways to improve how the business operates. If you have an idea that will improve the quality of a product or service, or can save the company money, you should not hesitate to share the idea with your supervisor. Building quality into a product or service requires constant attention to the way work is done. You will be expected to watch for ways to do your job better and more efficiently.

A Teamwork Approach

Today's workplace uses a team approach as workers jointly seek solutions to problems, 2-4. Employers place high importance on hiring people who work well with others. When interviewing individuals for a job opening, employers look for proof that you have teamwork skills.

The importance of teamwork in your future is so great that one chapter is devoted entirely to the subject. (See Chapter 14, "Being a Team Player.")

Family First

family-friendly programs Work programs that help employees to balance the demand of work and family.

Programs in the workplace that help workers handle the demands of work and family responsibilities are called ***family-friendly programs***. Men as well as women seek the flexibility

2-4
The teamwork approach is used in many workplace settings.

Discuss

What qualities do you appreciate in a teammate? Give examples.

Discuss

Are any family-friendly programs offered where your parents work?

these programs provide. Caring for young children is the main reason for the creation of such programs. Other reasons include caring for elderly parents or sick or disabled family members.

A flexible work arrangement is one type of family-friendly program. ***Flextime*** is a work schedule that permits flexibility in work hours. Companies that offer flextime generally have a daily core period when all employees must be at the work site. This usually consists of four or five hours in the middle of the day. Employees then can schedule their other work hours before or after the core period, depending on their preference.

flextime
A work schedule that permits flexibility in work hours.

Reflect
How does your family handle the challenges of parents working and providing care for children during work hours?

Activity
Ask your parent or another adult who works outside the home this question: How much pay would you willingly sacrifice to work for an employer who offers all-day child care for employees? Share the answer with the class.

Other family-friendly programs that companies may sponsor include the following:

- on-site child care
- vouchers or financial assistance for adult day care or vacation programs for children
- adoption assistance
- on-site shoe repair services, dry cleaners, or employer-sponsored food stores with ready-to-serve food to take home

Employers are also changing their current policies to make existing programs more family-friendly. For example, many companies no longer require workers to take full weeks of vacation time instead of single days. These companies know that many workers with young families prefer taking Mondays or Fridays off. This gives them long weekends for spending time with the family. See 2-5.

Besides voluntary programs in the workplace, a law requires time off for certain employees under certain circumstances. The details of the Family and Medical Leave Act will be covered in the next chapter.

Activity
Have students interview their parents to determine if their grandmothers and great grandmothers worked outside the home. Chart class results.

Example
Cite the similarities between caring for a young child and a live-in elderly relative. (Both the young child and adult often need help getting dressed, eating, and handling everyday tasks.)

Factors Affecting the Labor Market

Forces beyond any individual's control are constantly at work influencing workers. These forces shape the composition of the workforce and the types of jobs available.

2-5
More flexibility in work schedules lets employees plan work around caregiving needs.

Discuss
Cite some examples of change in this society. Does each societal change ultimately affect jobs in some way? Give examples.

Activity
Choose the career that most interests you. Develop a timeline that covers the last 10 years and describes how changes in society have affected it.

Social Change

self-sufficient
Individuals who can take care of themselves; who can earn a salary that will support their needs and wants as well as those of their future families.

Society once discouraged mothers from joining the workforce instead of caring for children at home. In fact, women were generally discouraged from full-time work. That social barrier is long gone. Young women today are encouraged to prepare themselves to be self-sufficient. ***Self-sufficient*** individuals are those who can take care of themselves. This means earning a salary that will support your needs and wants as well as those of your future family.

Except for wartime, most U.S. workers have always been men. That will continue, but the number of new women entering the workforce will almost equal the number of men. From 2006 to 2016, 6.3 million women will join compared to 6.5 million men.

Population Shifts

demographics
The characteristics or makeup of a population.

The characteristics or makeup of a population are called ***demographics***. Key changes within the population demographics affect the workplace. One significant change underway is the increase in minorities in the U.S. population. Employees of Hispanic, Asian, African-American, or Native American heritage will account for a larger share of the workforce in the future. Other minority groups will likewise increase in size, too. Virtually every nation of the world is represented in the U.S. population, making it the most diverse on earth. Diversity is a term commonly used to describe the benefits of working with people different from you. ***Diversity*** is the positive result of people of different racial, ethnic, and cultural backgrounds working together. Business leaders view our diverse workforce as a major resource in addressing the global market.

The greatest population shift occurring now and continuing to 2016 is the age of workers in the labor force. See 2-6. The number of 55-and-older workers will grow by 46.7 percent, while the number of workers between the ages of 16 and 24 will decline by 6.9 percent. The number of all other workers—those between the ages of 25 and 54 will increase by 2.4 percent.

diversity
The positive result of people of different racial, ethnic, and cultural backgrounds working together.

Vocabulary
How do you define *diversity*? Use the word in a sentence to demonstrate understanding.

Discuss
What are some benefits of people from different cultural backgrounds working together? In what ways does your school celebrate diversity?

Activity
Referring to Figure 2-6, divide the class into two teams to list reasons for the percent of change in the labor force by age. (Encourage students to list reasons beyond those covered in the text.)

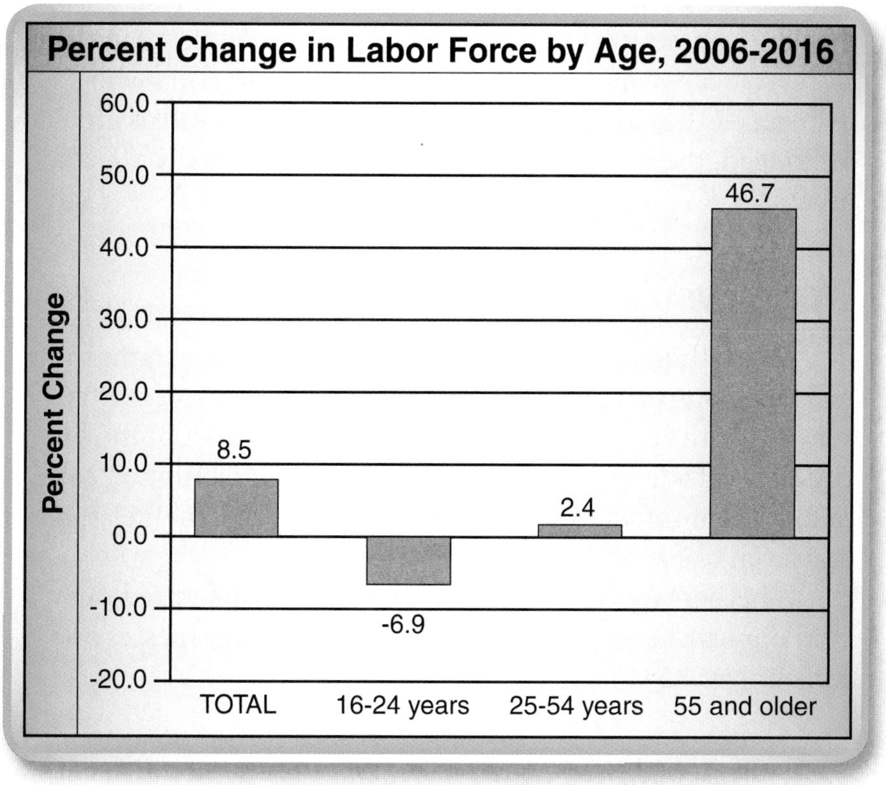

Percent Change in Labor Force by Age, 2006-2016

Age	Percent Change
TOTAL	8.5
16-24 years	-6.9
25-54 years	2.4
55 and older	46.7

U.S. Department of Labor

2-6
This chart shows the projected change in the labor force by age.

Reflect

Do your parents ever talk about the economy? Are you aware of times when the economy is good or bad? Do you ever watch news reports on the state of the economy?

Discuss

Based on what you've heard from news broadcasts or adults conversing, what is the current state of the U.S. economy?

An overall slowdown in growth of the labor force is expected because of the aging and retiring of so many people by 2016. The overall growth rate of the labor force is expected to increase 8.5 percent from 2006 to 2016. This is much less than the 13.1 percent increase of the previous decade.

The Economy

When the economy is strong, demand is high for goods and services. To meet this demand, employers keep their businesses fully staffed, sometimes working their employees overtime. Workers spend their earnings freely when the fear of unemployment is low. They do not worry about losing their jobs.

A weak economy, on the other hand, can cause unemployment for many employees. During periods of economic uncertainty, the fear of losing jobs causes consumers to cut back purchases. Less money is spent on items that aren't really needed, such as movie tickets, CDs, and eating out. Consumers even postpone buying necessary items.

A widespread slowdown in purchasing will cause employee cutbacks in an industry. For example, if clothing sales decrease, there is less need to put new fashions on display. Consequently, there is less need for salesclerks in the stores, truckers moving inventory, and other workers who help get clothes to market. When economic downturns are prolonged, the weak business in one industry usually affects others.

World Events

An earthquake that destroys roads in Taiwan can mean increased business for road-building experts in this country. See 2-7. At the same time, the earthquake can disrupt the country's production of computer chips. That disruption can reduce the number of new computers in the U.S. market and may even cause prices to rise.

Whether world events are natural or manufactured, they hold opportunities and consequences for U.S. businesses and consumers.

2-7
Installing power lines, water systems, and new roads are services in which U.S. companies excel.

Community Connections

Invite a speaker from the nearest office of your state's public employment service. Ask the guest to talk to the class about how the economy affects unemployment rates. Also, discuss the services offered by the employment office and the ways in which it helps people locate jobs.

Government Actions

If you own a busy gas station in town and a new expressway interchange is planned five miles away, your station will probably lose business. Government action can, and often does, affect companies. Actions that affect some companies in a positive way may negatively affect others.

It is important to know that rules, regulations, and other government decisions are generally not made suddenly. Issues are considered for many months or years before a plan is announced. Time is always allowed for affected members of the public to comment before a final decision on the plan is made. The smart citizen stays alert to government plans that may affect his or her livelihood.

Note

Using Figure 2-7, emphasize all the skills needed to install a water system, power line, or new roads.

The Forces of Competition on Staff Size

Success in the global market means developing and delivering products and services quickly. Often this requires hiring more employees. Deciding how many full-time workers

Vocabulary
Define *outsourcing* and give examples. In a sentence, tell why outsourcing is a trend that will continue.

to have is a challenge, especially for smaller companies eager to grow. Employers cannot afford to have employees on the payroll with nothing to do.

Companies often turn to independent consultants before making big changes. Such experts can help companies decide how to best handle a new challenge. If more workers are needed, temporary or part-time help may be considered first. Only when an increased workload is sure to be long-lasting, will companies hire more full-time employees.

outsourcing
The practice of one company contracting with another to handle work more efficiently and keep costs in line.

The reverse is also true. When a company foresees less demand for its products on a long-term basis, it will reduce its workforce.

Sometimes companies turn to other companies for help instead of creating new departments and hiring workers. The practice of one company contracting with another to handle work more efficiently and keep costs in line is called ***outsourcing.*** By outsourcing work, companies can get products quickly and often less expensively. Usually one of the terms of the contract is delivery of the products exactly when and where needed.

What factors shape the composition of the workforce and the types of jobs available?

Companies also contract with service providers for outside help. Outside experts are often used to do payroll tasks, garbage pick-up, and general cleaning. See 2-8. If a company grows unsatisfied with the service provider, it can make changes when the contract expires. Service contracts usually last for one year.

Discuss
Identify some technologies created since your parents were your age. Is it possible to live without some of these? Would life be easier or harder? Which technologies have been great time-savers?

Activity
Contact a local company to interview the manager and learn what tasks are outsourced, if any. Also, ask whether occasional part-time help is used. Report your findings to the class.

technology
The application of scientific principles.

The Technology Revolution

Change is ongoing in the workplace, and technology is the cause of most of that change. ***Technology*** is the application of scientific principles.

New Replaces Old

Look around your school and the businesses in your area. You see computers, fax machines, cellular phones, and other signs of modern technology. This society has moved far beyond the steam engine, electricity, and other discoveries that shaped earlier eras. Today's technology affects how you live and work in more dramatic ways than ever.

2-8
Using an independent service for a specific task, such as cleanup, can result in a high-quality job at a lower cost to the company.

Community Connections

Investigate what types of businesses have existed locally for more than 50 years. Check historical documents about the community in the public library. Summarize your findings in a written report that also answers this question: Which local companies appear to make the best use of new technologies?

Reflect

How might technology change your lifestyle in the next 10 to 15 years? Is there a technology that you would like to see invented to make your life easier?

Resource

Workforce Changes, Activity C, WB. Students list ways in which current changes in the workplace may affect them and their career decisions.

Technology has a snowballing effect, leading to ever more discoveries. More changes in technology have occurred in the last 25 years than in all the preceding years combined. However, what is new today will be old tomorrow. Technology quickens the pace of change.

At one time, an office with a telephone and a typewriter was considered "high-tech." Today, that office would be considered outdated and inefficient. In the office of today, laptop and handheld computers, scanners, wireless networks, fax machines, multitasking copy machines, e-mail, Web-based programs, personal organizers, and cell phones are all considered commonplace.

Some argue that technology causes job losses. Consider the typewriter again and the fact that jobs involving this outdated product are no longer needed. The proper way to judge technology's effect on employment is to compare the number of jobs lost to those created by new technology. In this case, you would compare the total typewriter-related jobs lost to the total computer-related jobs gained. By making a fair

computer revolution
The total change in the way people live and work caused by computers.

Service Learning

If your school has laptops, how might you use them to help needy people or organizations in the community? Think of a plan. Perhaps you could teach someone in a shelter how to create a budget or low-cost menu using Internet resources. Maybe you could acquaint the elderly with the Internet and how it can enhance their lives and keep them in touch with family and friends.

telecommuting
Working at home through an electronic linkup with the central office.

Internet
The global computer linkup of individuals, groups, and organizations in government, business, and education.

comparison, you can see that more jobs result from advances in technology.

Changing Technology in the Workplace

Many of the items you use in your daily activities didn't even exist 20 years ago. For example, CDs, DVDs, and digital cameras were unheard of 20 years ago. Much of the technology in the workplace of today began with U.S. space exploration. The space program created a simple electronic calculator that led to the computer revolution. The ***computer revolution*** is the total change in the way people live and work caused by computers. Technology developed by the space program and defense programs affect the way we work, live, travel, and play.

Defense and manufacturing industries expanded the use of the electronic calculator to help with designing new products. This led to computer systems that link the production, manufacturing, and control functions of a company. The result is shortened cycles for new product introductions and the ability to bring more goods to market quicker than ever.

The introduction of the *PC*, or personal computer, brought enormous computing power, resulting in automating the office and combining systems that formerly were kept separate. Now the work of storing, processing, and communicating information has merged into a single system. This allows several computer users to communicate with each other.

Laptop computers can tap into this system while freeing people from their desks. Laptops are small, notebook-size computers that contain the work of one or more people. Workers can take them to the factory, a meeting room, or a project area, and back to their desks. This also allows more work to be done at home, 2-9. All that is needed to send information back and forth is an electronic linkup with the central office. This is known as ***telecommuting***.

Information can also be sent and received via the ***Internet***—the computer linkup of individuals, groups, and organizations. The Internet has revolutionized the business world. With the right equipment and connections, workers in different locations can share voice or voice/picture communications anytime and anywhere.

2-9
Laptop computers are especially useful for those who work outside a central location and must access a central data source.

Discuss
What are signs of a technologically advanced school? Do you think technology is replacing too many jobs? Explain.

Resource
Can You Make These Computer Connections? reproducible master 2-3, TR. Students write the correct terms for the chapter definitions described and illustrated.

The personal computer also changed the way products are sold and purchased. The selling and buying of goods and services over the Internet has offered many new opportunities in ***e-tailing*** (electronic retailing) or ***e-commerce*** (electronic commerce). Both terms are often used to refer to business conducted over the Internet. Both large and small businesses conduct business over the Web. E-commerce has become a multibillion-dollar industry. Web sites such as *Amazon.com* and *eBay.com* are e-commerce sites. The two major forms of e-commerce are Business-to-Consumer (B2C) and Business-to-Business (B2B). While companies such as Amazon.com cater mostly to consumers, other companies provide goods and services exclusively to businesses.

e-tailing
Electronic retailing.

e-commerce
Electronic commerce.

Discuss
How has computer technology changed since you started school? When did you first use a computer? Has it been easy to keep up with the changes in the computer field?

Fiber-optics has replaced the way data is transmitted. Fiber-optic lines are strands of optically pure glass as thin as a human hair. Fiber-optic lines transmit digital information over long distances. They are also used in medical imaging, mechanical engineering inspection, and for cable television.

The development of the *global positioning system (GPS)*, once used only by the military, is now common in vehicles, hand-held

Reflect

Describe your personal experience with technology. What do you wish technological tools could do that can't be done now?

Resource

Technology Impacts the Job Market, color transparency CT-2, TR. Use the transparency to discuss how various forms of technology affect jobs in the workplace.

devices, and cell phones. GPS uses a series of satellites to identify the user's location. GPS is funded and controlled by the U. S. Department of Defense and is currently used extensively in the shipping and transportation industries, 2-10.

It has been suggested that advances in technology will multiply dramatically in the coming years. As a future worker, you will have to adapt to an ever-changing workplace.

The New World of Work

The workplace has changed as a result of using the tools of technology. Consequently, employers have different expectations of themselves and their employees.

Instant communications, for example, has quickened the overall pace of the business world. Speed is all-important, but so is accuracy. There is no place for slow or wrong responses in today's high-tech environment.

Knowing how to keystroke and operate a computer are skills expected of new employees. You should know how computers are used in the career field you select. You should also know how to access information important in that field.

Today the addition of personal organizers, wireless connections, and portable data devices allow companies and workers to have flexibility in their working environment.

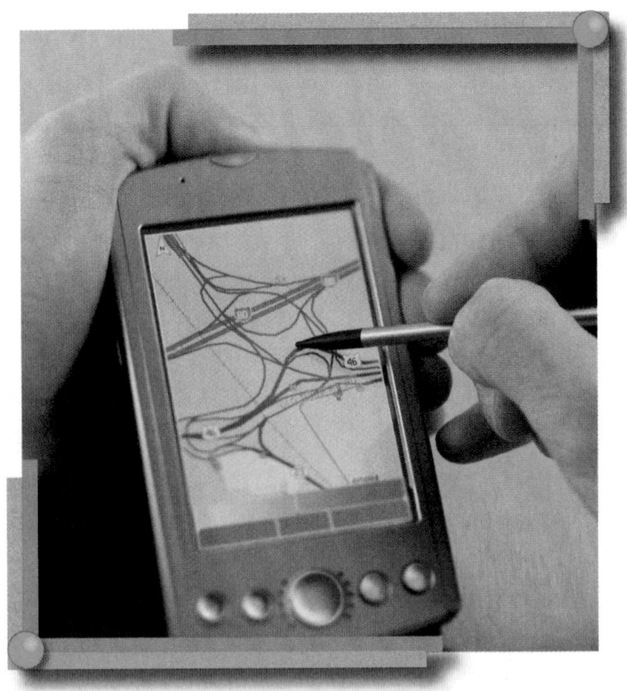

2-10
GPS systems are useful in helping salespeople locate their customers more easily.

The availability of technology has increased expectations that workers will work off-site, often beyond normal work hours.

Only a small percentage of workers will actually work on high-technology assignments. Everyone else will feel the effects of technology in the new tools and processes they use to do their jobs well. Keeping up with advances in technology will require lifelong learning. ***Lifelong learning*** is continually updating your knowledge and skills. It is a term that means your need for learning will never end.

The discussion of technology brings us back to the subject of teamwork. Many firms find that installing the biggest and best equipment does not always guarantee top results. In fact, companies with less-advanced equipment but total employee involvement do a better job. This demonstrates that how employees use equipment is what counts most. This also underscores the importance of your future role as part of a work team. You will be expected to help find solutions to work challenges rather than merely follow orders.

lifelong learning
Continually updating your knowledge and skills.

How does technology affect the workplace?

Resource

The Computer Revolution, Activity D, WB. Students describe how various forms of technology have affected the way people work.

Activity

Give an example of someone who exemplifies the value of lifelong learning. Recall former students and their experiences in lifelong learning.

Resource

What Are the Changes Around Me? reproducible master 2-4, TR. Use the adapted worksheet to reinforce chapter concepts in students who are low functioning.

Summary

Several trends indicate new directions for the workplace in a global economy. Product and service quality is continually examined to make sure it meets customer expectations. Teamwork is the primary way that work is accomplished. Family-friendly programs are helping to lessen the challenge of balancing family and work responsibilities.

Many factors work together to shape the labor market. Social changes, population shifts, the age of workers economic conditions, government action, world events, and forces of competition affect jobs.

Many high-tech tools are reshaping work. To be successful in the workplace, employees must know how to use the computer quickly and accurately. They must update their knowledge and skills continually.

Reviewing Key Concepts

1. What is another name for the free enterprise system?
2. The decline of the U.S. manufacturing sector has paved the way for a new economy based on what sectors of the economy?
3. Name three factors that are inspiring new ideas about the world of work.
4. Companies are *not* likely to outsource ______.
   A. custodial services
   B. landscaping
   C. management functions
   D. payroll services
5. Name four factors that affect the labor market.
6. In your own words, define *technology* and *computer revolution.*
7. Technology will *not* ______.
   A. change the way work is done
   B. process information faster
   C. slow the pace of work
   D. link companies and customers around the world
8. True or false. Changes in technology will cause unemployment to increase.
9. True or false. Technology will require workers to constantly keep learning throughout life.
10. Which of the following is generally *not* a desired quality in today's workers?
    A. computer ability
    B willingness to learn
    C. teamwork skills
    D. an ability to command

Answers to *Reviewing Key Concepts*

1. market economic system
2. service and information
3. (Name three:) a global perspective, the shift to a service and information economy, commitment to quality, a teamwork approach, family-friendly programs
4. C
5. (List four:) social change, population shifts, the economy, laws and regulations, world events, forces of competition
6. (Student response.)
7. C
8. false
9. true
10. D

Building Academic Skills

1. **Social Studies.** Prepare a Venn diagram, comparing employment opportunities of the free enterprise system with the economic systems of the international job market (traditional, command, and market). What are the basic principles of each system regarding the production, consumption, and distribution of goods and services? How do these principles impact the types of jobs people hold?
2. **History.** Investigate historical events that have created growth for business. Write a report that answers the following questions: What types of businesses have existed for more than 100 years? In the last 10 years, what businesses have appeared? have disappeared?
3. **Social Studies.** Write a report explaining aspects of one example of societal change and how the change has affected your chosen career field by giving examples of jobs that were created, altered, or eliminated because of the change.

Building Career Knowledge and Skills

1. Research information about the future of service jobs in our economy and make a brief presentation to the class.
2. Identify one new technology or piece of equipment. Explain in a written report how you think it will influence the workplace.
3. Write a letter inviting a representative from an area business or organization to speak to the class about the technology skills desired in new employees today.
4. Discuss how you think changes in technology might change the workplace in the next 10, 20, and 50 years.
5. Interview current workers regarding the teamwork experiences where they work.
6. Interview past and present workers regarding family-friendly programs that did/do exist at their places of employment. Write a report summarizing your interviews.
7. Find media examples of how technology is changing the workforce and workplace.

Building Technology Skills

1. Conduct an online search using the words *teamwork activities*. Propose two classroom activities and identify the Internet sites where they were found.
2. Conduct online research on FMLA. When did the law become effective? Is the employee paid while on a leave? How does an employee become eligible?
3. Access the Internet to search adult day care for elderly family members. Summarize the services discussed and identify any such facilities in the community.
4. Compose and send an e-mail to a classmate, summarizing the main points covered in class. Relate this to a workplace situation.

Building Workplace Skills

Join a team of three or four classmates to analyze technology changes in the telephone and their effect on the workplace. As a team, determine the five changes you believe were most significant and explain why in a 10-minute presentation to the class. Conclude your presentation with one prediction about future phone capabilities and cite the source of the prediction. Explain how the predicted capability may change the workplace further and enhance globalization.

What laws protect me in the workplace?

Chapter 3
The Law in the Workplace

Key Terms

discrimination
Equal Employment Opportunity Act
EOE
Equal Pay Act
piecework
Americans with Disabilities Act
Age Discrimination Act
sexual harassment
Family and Medical Leave Act

Chapter Objectives

After studying this chapter, you will be able to

- **define** discrimination and list several workplace examples.
- **identify** the laws that make workplace discrimination illegal in the areas of employment opportunity, pay, physical disability, and age.
- **describe** two general forms of sexual harassment.
- **propose** the steps to take to stop any sexual harassment or discrimination at work directed toward you.
- **list** the four conditions addressed by the Family and Medical Leave Act.

Key Concepts

- Knowing your rights can help you to avoid discrimination.
- Sexual harassment is illegal and there are actions to take to deal with it.
- The Family Medical Leave Act helps employees balance family and workplace demands.

What Is Discrimination?

This chapter discusses the laws regarding behavior in the workplace. (Laws concerning health and safety are discussed in Chapter 15, "Keeping Safety First.")

Several laws exist to assure everyone a fair and equal opportunity for employment. These laws protect job seekers and workers from discrimination. ***Discrimination*** means treating a person or group of people differently from the others. This unequal treatment in the workplace is illegal. See 3-1.

discrimination
Unfairly treating a person or group of people differently.

Equal Opportunity

The ***Equal Employment Opportunity Act*** makes discrimination in the workplace illegal when it is based on race, color, religion, sex, or national origin. More recent laws make it illegal to discriminate against people for other reasons. These reasons include physical disability, age, and marital status.

Equal Employment Opportunity Act
A law that makes it illegal for an employer to discriminate because of race, color, religion, sex, or national origin. More recent laws make it illegal to discriminate against people for other reasons, such as disabilities, age, and marital status.

3-1
The law forbids illegal discrimination in all workplace policies and procedures, beginning with a firm's hiring practices.

Resource

Reinforcing Vocabulary, Activity A, WB. Students identify examples of discrimination and determine the law that applies to each.

Example

Employers can set "skill" qualifications for job candidates, such as the following: "Requirements for the position of office assistant include accurately keyboarding 60 words per minute." It is legal for employers to turn away any job candidate who does not possess this minimum qualification.

Employers are prohibited from treating workers unfairly in all work practices. These include hiring, training, promoting, and firing employees. For example, an employer cannot reserve certain jobs for men and prevent women from applying or being considered. That is discrimination.

Some employers include the initials *EOE* in their ads and recruitment materials. ***EOE*** means *equal opportunity employer.* Of course, all employers must abide by the law and treat all job candidates equally. By including *EOE* in ads, an employer is emphasizing a commitment to equal opportunity.

EOE
Equal Opportunity Employer.

Discuss
Why do employers use the letters *EOE* in their job ads? What does EOE mean?

Adapting the Lesson
Have students who are low functioning make a poster showing the benefits of the Equal Employment Opportunity Act. Advise them to use magazine pictures to add visuals to the poster and to display a job ad that refers to *EOE*.

Employers look for workers with just the right skills and qualifications to do the job well. Employers are not guilty of illegal discrimination when they pass over unqualified job seekers. For example, an employer can require job applicants for a data processing position to keystroke 60 words per minute. An auto repair shop can require that technicians be certified to do repair work. Employers can legally turn away applicants who do not meet minimum job requirements.

Equal Work, Equal Pay

As a worker, you can count on being paid the same as others for doing the same job. The ***Equal Pay Act*** was a significant step in achieving equal pay protection.

Equal Pay Act
Law that prohibits unequal pay for men and women who are doing essentially the same work for the same employer.

The law was designed to help women get equal pay for equal work. It applies to all workers regardless of sex or other differences, 3-2. Basically, the law does the following:

- It prohibits unequal pay for men and woman doing basically the same work for the same employer.
- The law prevents employers from lowering the wages of either sex to comply with the law. (For example, suppose men are paid more than women for the same work. An employer cannot reduce the men's pay to match the women's level. Instead, the women's pay must be raised to match the men's.)
- The law also prevents labor organizations from forcing an employer to violate the law. In other words, unions cannot force companies to pay union members a higher wage than nonmembers receive.

Resource
Equal Work, Equal Pay, transparency master 3-1, TR. Students discuss the Equal Pay Act and legal reasons for pay differences in the workplace.

Activity
Divide the class into five groups. To help visualize the concepts in this chapter, assign each group to make a poster about one of the laws described.

Because of the Equal Pay Act, everyone can be assured of getting the same wage from an employer for doing the same job.

3-2
The Equal Pay Act requires employers to make pay levels uniform regardless of the race, color, religion, sex, or national origin of the jobholder.

Adapting the Lesson

Have students who are high functioning interview a male and female having the same job title and working for the same employer. Ask them to prepare a list of questions to ask each, including their job duties, hours worked, total experience with the employer, current pay level, and so forth. Ask them to compare the results and determine if the Equal Pay Act is being obeyed.

Reflect

Do you feel it is fair to get higher pay if you have been with a company longer? How do you feel if you get less pay because of less experience in the job?

Pay Differences

In some cases, certain factors can be considered that result in different pay levels. The following legal factors can result in higher pay for some people doing the same job:

- length of time with the company
- experience in the job
- advanced training
- productivity, or greater work output

Productivity is most easily measured when a job involves ***piecework***. This term refers to a job in which something is produced by an individual that can easily be counted. People who do piecework usually have control over how much they can accomplish. An example of piecework is sewing buttons and buttonholes onto men's shirts. One completed shirt equals one piece.

piecework
A job in which something is produced by an individual that can easily be counted.

By considering these four legal factors, employers can reward workers who are faster, better trained, and more experienced. An employer cannot use any practice, however, that unfairly sets pay differences.

A Barrier-Free Workplace

One of a country's greatest resources is its people. Many people with physical disabilities can contribute greatly to

Resource

Barriers to Work Are Coming Down, color transparency CT-3, TR. Students discuss the provisions of the Americans with Disabilities Act.

Resource

A Case of Discrimination, Activity B, WB. Students decide if discrimination has occurred in two case studies.

an employer's business. Workers who are disabled are just as much a part of the team as all other workers. They can contribute a great deal in the workplace. Enabling a person who is disabled to work, however, may require certain changes to the workplace. Employers must attempt to accommodate an applicant with a disability.

Americans with Disabilities Act
Law that prohibits employers from discriminating against people with physical disabilities.

The ***Americans with Disabilities Act*** prohibits employers from discriminating against people with a physical disability. A wheelchair ramp that allows more people to enter and exit the building is one of the most common changes made. Perhaps a piece of machinery may need to be lowered. Employers must make reasonable changes to provide employment free of physical barriers, 3-3.

Reflect

Think about the adaptations that would be needed if a person in a wheelchair came to live with you. What could you do to help the person adapt to the new surroundings?

Medical and physical requirements of workers must be related to business needs. For example, a homebuilder can require a bricklayer to climb scaffolds and read blueprints. The builder cannot, however, require the worker to have

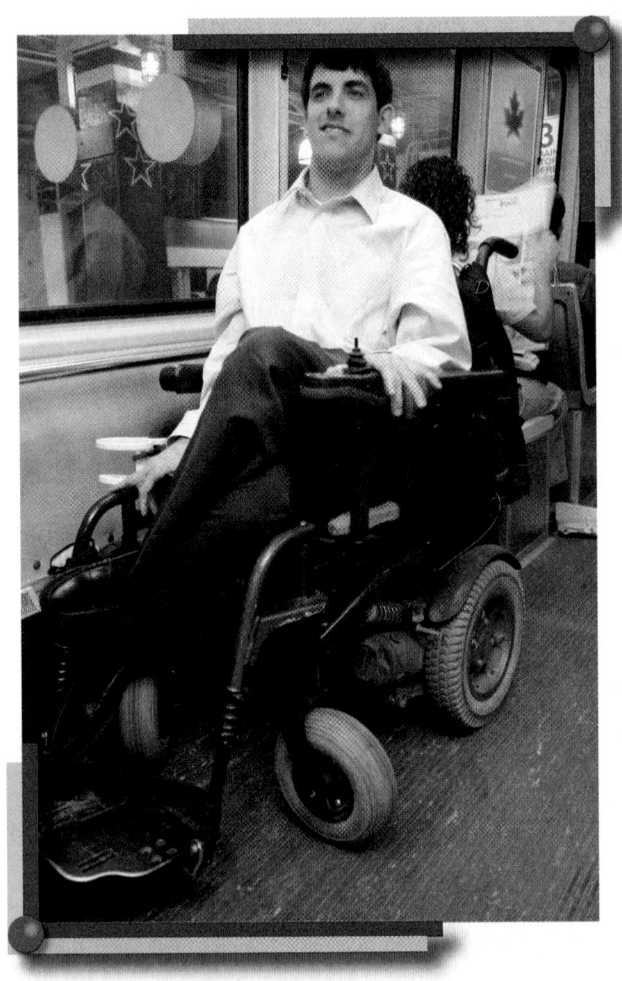

3-3
Offices and mass transit systems must not restrict workers who need a special chair to move around.

Community Connections

Investigate whether workplaces are free of barriers for people with physical disabilities. Students can learn which local companies and organizations have added wheelchair ramps or have made other necessary modifications. Report your findings to the class.

perfect hearing since that is not needed for the job. Any physical exam required by an employer must reflect the duties of the job. Consequently, the builder cannot require the physical exam to cover hearing ability.

An employer cannot ask an applicant about a disability. An employer can, however, ask questions about the person's ability to do the job. Employers need not lower their standards or work quality to satisfy the law's requirement. They can make performance a *condition of employment*. This means keeping the job depends on doing what the job requires.

Making a Difference

Investigate items that you can make for people with disabilities. (The local United Way is a good contact.) Nursing home residents could use bags that carry their personal items and attach to wheelchairs and walkers. Such bags can be created from scrap material. Find out what other items are needed and involve members of your class in deciding ways to make them.

Age Discrimination

This form of discrimination applies most often to people over 40 years old. The ***Age Discrimination Act*** prohibits employers from not hiring older people simply because of their age. It also forbids employers from denying any person a promotion, benefit, or favorable job assignment because of age. The law applies to all employers with 20 or more employees. See 3-4.

Several decades ago, people in their 40s were often considered too old for sales positions. No legitimate reason existed for closing these jobs to people over 40. Instead, it was an industry practice based on discrimination.

3-4
Older workers have the same right to employment as everyone else.

Age Discrimination Act
Law that prohibits employers from not hiring people simply because they are older.

Discuss

Use Figure 3-4 as the basis for a discussion on age and job performance. What qualities do you think this man would bring to an architect's job compared to an employee 30 years younger?

Reflect

What are your attitudes about salespeople of different ages—for example, one 25 years old and one 55—selling you a DVD player, winter coat, or car? Do you think age makes a difference?

Age discrimination continues to draw attention today. The issue usually involves experienced older workers who are left jobless after a company reorganizes. Often, workers retire from one job and seek employment in another job to supplement their retirement income. These older workers have a vast amount of knowledge and experience upon which to draw in making a contribution in the workplace. Age discrimination also affects women returning to the workforce after raising their children.

Setting age preferences or limitations as a job requirement is generally unlawful. In certain cases, however, it is legal. For example, if state or federal laws set age requirements, these must be followed. When legal age restrictions are set, they must be applied to everyone in the same manner.

Consider the job of a forklift operator. If state or federal law requires a person to be 18 years of age to operate a forklift, a 16-year-old cannot be hired to operate a forklift no matter how well he or she can do the job. Other restrictions could also be set. For example, it is legal for the job to also require several years of driving experience with a clean driving record.

What Is Sexual Harassment?

sexual harassment
Unwelcome sexual advances, requests for sexual favors, and other verbal or physical conduct of a sexual nature when it is made a condition of employment or of a person's work performance or environment.

All forms of sexual harassment in the workplace are against the law. ***Sexual harassment*** is unwelcome sexual advances. It can be a request for sexual favors. It can also be verbal or physical conduct of a sexual nature. It is illegal in the workplace under the Civil Rights Act and many state human rights laws. The harasser and the victim can be either sex.

Advances from Authority Figures

There are two basic kinds of sexual harassment. The first type is described as *something given to get something in return*. The legal name is *quid pro quo harassment*. A supervisor or someone in authority usually initiates this kind of sexual harassment. It almost always involves a threat or the promise of a reward.

Resource

The Law and Sexual Harassment, reproducible master 3-2, TR. Students learn more details about the evolution of legal protection from sexual harassment.

A group leader may threaten to fire or block a promotion if the victim rejects his or her advances. A supervisor might promise to promote or give a pay raise to the victim. Often sexual harassment involves the use of power to control a new employee or one with less importance or rank in the organization.

A Hostile Environment

The second kind of sexual harassment deals more with the workplace. In this case, a person makes an environment unpleasant enough to interfere with the other worker's performance. Aspects of the workplace that are considered hostile include sexual pictures, signs, objects, and music. A hostile environment also includes offensive language, jokes, gestures, and comments.

Recognizing Sexual Harassment

Threats and rewards for sexual actions are clear and easy to identify. This behavior is always wrong and illegal! Identifying a hostile environment, however, is not as easy. It can even be confusing. The signs of sexual harassment can be physical, verbal, or nonverbal.

- *Physical harassment* is touching, holding, grabbing, and all other unwanted physical contact.
- *Verbal harassment* is telling offensive jokes, using offensive language, and making suggestions of a sexual nature.
- *Nonverbal harassment* involves offensive gestures and actions, such as staring at a person's body or circulating letters, e-mails, cartoons, or other material of a sexually oriented nature.

Discouraging Sexual Harassment

As an employee, you can discourage cases of sexual harassment by following these guidelines.

- Dress appropriately for the job. See 3-5.
- Become familiar with your right to a workplace free from sex discrimination.
- Know your company's policy and procedures for reporting harassment.
- Conduct yourself in a businesslike manner at all times.

Community Connections

Ask your school principal about the sexual harassment policy at your school. Discuss situations that students may not realize could get them into trouble. Review how you should handle suspected cases and discourage sexual harassment at school.

Note

The harasser and the victim can be either sex. List student examples of sexual harassment on the board for clarification.

Activity

Role-play scenes that involve sexual harassment from previously written scripts. Have students point out aspects of each scene that make the conduct illegal.

Resource

Identifying Sexual Harassment, transparency master 3-3, TR. Students review a list of questions to determine what constitutes sexual harassment.

3-5
If your job does not require a uniform, you will be expected to wear clothing that is appropriate for that workplace.

Your Reading

How can you recognize and discourage sexual harassment?

You should receive a copy of the company's sexual harassment policy during your first week as a new employee. If not, ask what the procedure is so you are informed.

Resource

Is This Sexual Harassment? Activity C, WB. Students determine if various cases involve sexual harassment.

Reflect

Do you feel that the way a person dresses can contribute to sexual harassment? Do you agree that the ways listed in the text would discourage sexual harassment?

Discuss

Use Figure 3-6 as a basis for discussion about sexual harassment. In what ways is this person avoiding sexual harassment and conducting herself in a businesslike manner?

Facing Discrimination or Sexual Harassment

Reputable employers want to provide a workplace free of harassment for their employees. It is in their best interest to provide a productive environment. A workplace with constant tension is not productive. Large and midsize companies have at least one person who handles equal rights matters. The human resources office is usually where they work.

Your greatest weapon against discrimination and harassment at work is to know your rights. When you do, you can confidently proceed.

Action to Take

If you are faced with discrimination or sexual harassment at work, you should follow these steps:

- **Remain professional.** Avoid being too emotional. See 3-6.
- **Speak to the offender.** Let that person know what he or she is doing is illegal and you want it stopped. If the harassment continues, report the person's actions to your immediate supervisor. Most employers have a form that employees can complete to register complaints. Make sure you get a copy of any forms you complete.
- **Record the facts.** Write down all the important details of any continuing event as soon after it occurs as possible. Explain the who, what, when, where, and how of the incident. Be prepared to provide names of witnesses or others who can support your claims.

Resource

Stop Sexual Harassment Before It Starts, transparency master 3-4, TR. Students discuss being assertive and avoiding clothing and behavior that may send the wrong message.

Activity

Have students close their texts and form pairs to take turns explaining what to do if faced with discrimination or sexual harassment. As one student speaks, have the other student carefully write down what they hear.

Resource

Taking Action, Activity D, WB. Students review a case study relating to sexual harassment and decide the action to take.

3-6
It is important to always act businesslike with coworkers in all settings.

Your Reading

What actions can you take if you face sexual harassment?

Activity

In your notebook, write the four conditions that the Family and Medical Leave Act addresses. Ask students if they know anyone who has taken more than six weeks off work to stay home with a new baby or adopted child.

Example

Name specific people or businesses in your community that provide day care or special help to new parents. Name community options for helping care for a sick family member.

Discuss

Do employees get paid during this time? How long can they take off? What happens to their pay level and company benefits during this time?

Family and Medical Leave Act
A law that allows 12 weeks off without pay per year in certain cases to handle special family matters.

- **Report the offense if it does not stop.** Report it to your supervisor, unless he or she is the source of the offense. Then go to someone higher in the company. Contact the person designated by your company to handle such complaints. If you are a union member, you can also go to your union representative. Outside the company, you can contact the Equal Employment Opportunity Commission (EEOC) or your state's Department of Human Rights. Going outside the company is a step to take only after contacting the appropriate source within the company.

As a last resort, the Civil Rights Act gives you the right to take your case to court. If you win the case, you can receive money that you lost because of the discrimination. Loss of money may be due to dismissal, demotion, lost benefits, or other reasons. Employers cannot retaliate against employees who file a complaint or testify as witnesses.

The Family and the Workplace

Workplace demands sometimes clash with family demands. How to care for young or sick children while at work is one of the biggest issues facing employees. Child care issues especially affect single-parent households and those with both parents working outside the home. Caring for sick family members and aging parents are additional concerns. See 3-7.

Juggling family and workplace demands can cause workers to arrive late or go home early. Employees with special family demands often find it difficult to keep their minds on their work. Often workers use up their sick days caring for other family members.

The ***Family and Medical Leave Act*** allows some flexibility in the normal work routine to handle special family matters. The law addresses the following four conditions:

- having or caring for a new baby
- adopting a child or adding a foster child to the family
- being unable to work because of serious illness
- caring for a sick child, spouse, or parent

3-7
Too many employees use up all their sick days caring for other sick family members.

Resource

What Are the Laws That Help You? reproducible master 3-5, TR. Use the adapted worksheet to reinforce chapter concepts in students who are low functioning.

Your Reading

What law helps employees balance the demands of family and the workplace?

The law applies to employers of 50 or more employees. It generally covers those working at the same company for at least 12 months. Under this law, employees can take a total of 12 weeks off without pay. Also, they can keep their health insurance during the time off and return to their jobs or similar jobs with no loss of benefits or pay.

Summary

Employers cannot discriminate against anyone in their hiring, training, promoting, or firing practices. Laws prohibit using race, color, religion, sex, national origin, age, a disability, or marital status as a requirement for employment. Discrimination occurs when there is different treatment of one person or group of people.

Discrimination sometimes affects a person's pay. All workers must receive equal pay for equal work with the same employer. Sometimes pay can be higher for some when certain legal factors are considered.

Sexual harassment in the workplace is illegal. It involves unwelcome advances of a physical, verbal, or nonverbal nature. Sexual harassment can affect the way people do their jobs and feel about themselves. When faced with discrimination or harassment, it is important for employees to know their rights under the law and exercise them.

The law also allows greater flexibility in work schedules for some workers with special family demands.

Reviewing Key Concepts

1. True or false. It is *not* discrimination if a bank hires only applicants who have a driver's license.
2. True or false. It is *not* discrimination if an employer requires all employees to complete special training programs to be promoted.
3. Productivity is most easily measured when a job involves _____.
4. Under the Americans with Disabilities Act, employers must make reasonable changes to provide employment free of physical _____.
5. True or false. Sexual harassment only occurs between a man and a woman.
6. List three steps an employee can take to discourage sexual harassment in the workplace.
7. What is the greatest weapon against discrimination and sexual harassment at work?
8. What are the four steps to take if you are the target of discrimination or harassment at work?
9. What government agency is responsible for enforcing the fair treatment of people in the workplace?
10. Under the Family and Medical Leave Act, an employee of a company with at least 50 employees can take a total of _____ weeks off without pay to handle special family matters.

Answers to
Reviewing Key Concepts

1. false
2. true
3. piecework
4. barriers
5. false
6. Behave in a businesslike manner at all times. Dress appropriately for the job. Become familiar with employee rights to a work environment free from discrimination based on sex.
7. knowing your rights
8. Remain professional. Speak clearly and directly with the offender. Record the facts. Report the offense if it continues.
9. Equal Employment Opportunity Commission (EEOC)
10. 12

Building Academic Skills

1. **Social Studies.** Research the issue of gender equality and sexual harassment in the workplace. Find out the number of males versus females in various occupational areas and write a report on your findings. Are the number of sexual harassment cases higher in some occupational areas than others?
2. **Social Studies.** Investigate which president was in office when the Family and Medical Leave Act was signed into law. Do other countries allow more or less time away from work to handle special family matters? Research at least three other industrial nations.

Building Technology Skills

1. Videotape an interview with the principal or district superintendent of your school to discuss how your school complies with the Equal Pay Act, Americans with Disabilities Act, and Age Discrimination Act. View the tape in class and discuss what you learned.
2. Conduct an online search to learn more about the Equal Employment Opportunity Commission (EEOC). Find the answers to these questions: What powers does the Commission have? What happens when the EEOC determines that an employer is guilty of discrimination or sexual harassment?

Building Career Knowledge and Skills

1. Research the psychological effects of discrimination on people. What are the three most important facts you learned? Share them with the class.
2. Write a paper explaining how to distinguish between innocent flirting and sexual harassment involving people your age.
3. Invite a lawyer to class to discuss how he or she prepares for a sexual harassment case. What kind of information is needed to substantiate a sexual harassment claim?

Building Workplace Skills

Contact a large employer in your community. Find out who in the organization is responsible for making sure equal employment laws are followed. Schedule a telephone or in-person interview to get answers to the following questions: How does the company make sure the rules regarding sexual harassment and discrimination in the workplace are followed? What training programs are offered to company employees, and who is required to attend? What handouts are given to employees on the subject? Prepare a presentation for your class describing your findings. Use any materials gathered in your contacts.

Part Two

Exploring Career Options

4 Learning About Careers
5 Types of Careers
6 A Business of Your Own

Where can I learn about careers?

Chapter 4 Learning About Careers

Key Terms

traits
education
training
skills
entry-level jobs
advanced training
internship
promotion
fringe benefits
cost of living
job shadowing
cooperative education

Chapter Objectives

After studying this chapter, you will be able to

- **list** factors to consider when choosing a career.
- **describe** sources for obtaining career information.

Key Concepts

- Choosing the right career will affect your future.
- Various sources of information can help you explore careers.

Basic Job Factors

What do you want to do when you grow up? This is a question you probably began hearing very early in life. It may have inspired you to picture yourself at work in various jobs. Maybe you have already made a mental list of jobs that sound interesting and others that do not.

Choosing the right career is important to your future happiness and success. Making the right choice involves considering several factors. See 4-1.

Job Duties and Responsibilities

The first factor to consider about a job is its duties and responsibilities. These will determine how you will spend your workday. Job duties are often described by the tasks that must be done. Does the job require you to file reports, take photos, or drive a truck? Maybe you would be required to mix chemicals, use power tools, or conduct research.

The duties of common jobs, such as truck drivers and cashiers, are easily described by their tasks. Getting these jobs may depend on previous experience with similar tasks.

Job duties and responsibilities are sometimes described by worker traits. ***Traits*** are noteworthy characteristics. They are often seen in want ads. The following traits are examples of some common job responsibilities:

- ability to plan and organize
- memory for details
- desire to help people
- ability to persuade

Resource

Reinforcing Vocabulary, Activity A, WB. Students review key chapter terms and use the terms in sentences.

Discuss

When you were younger, how did you answer this question: What do you want to do when you grow up? Has your answer changed?

Resource

Choosing A Career? What You Need to Check Out, color transparency CT-4, TR. Students review the factors to consider when choosing a career.

Vocabulary

What are traits? Give examples.

Resource

Investigating Job Factors, Activity B, WB. Students examine the job factors relevant to their desired career.

traits
Noteworthy characteristics.

Basic Job Factors
• Job duties and responsibilities
• Job prospects
• Education, training, and skills
• Salary and fringe benefits
• Advancement opportunities
• Work location and environment

4-1
For any career you explore, review these basic job factors.

Reflect

Has anyone said that you would be good at a particular career? Have you started collecting information about careers?

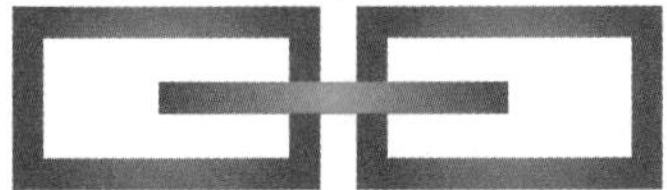

Community Connections

Collect classified sections of the newspaper to answer the following questions: What career areas advertise the most job ads? How many job prospects are there for part-time jobs? What kind of training is required for the most numerous job openings? Share your findings in class.

education
Gaining knowledge to live and work in today's society.

training
Applying knowledge through practice.

skills
Abilities that result from education and training.

entry-level jobs
Jobs that require no previous training.

New or service-oriented jobs are usually described in terms of the traits required. For example, the job responsibilities of a director of customer satisfaction might be described by all four of the traits just listed. Jobs that stress jobholder traits generally do not require previous experience in a similar job. However, you would need to demonstrate that you possess the required traits.

Job Prospects

After you identify a career choice, determine your chances of finding a job in that field. By examining job prospects, you learn about long-term opportunities predicted for the field. What is the outlook for jobs in the next 10 to 20 years for the career you have selected? Will there be openings for job seekers in that field by the time you are ready to enter it? Will this career area grow so you can advance? Only so many teachers, salesclerks, and mechanics are needed at any given time. Many Web sites have information on careers and job opportunities locally, in your state, or even nationally and internationally.

You would not want to prepare for a career field in which jobs are quickly disappearing. The Department of Labor continually examines the outlook for all types of U.S. jobs. It reports that manufacturing jobs are declining, which you learned in Chapter 1. Consequently, you might not want to plan on a life-long future in factory work.

Education, Training, and Skills

You will need to prepare yourself to be ready to handle whatever job you choose. This requires knowing what education, training, and skills are required for the career you seek.

Education is gaining knowledge to live and work in today's society. ***Training*** is applying that knowledge through practice. ***Skills*** are the abilities that result from education and training. Education and training requirements for jobs are generally divided into the following three levels.

Entry-Level Jobs

Entry-level jobs require no previous training. These are jobs that are easily learned, 4-2. Training for these jobs may

4-2
Working as a check-out clerk is an example of an entry-level job.

Activity

List job duties that you would, and would not, enjoy doing. Save the lists so you can compare them to career options that you investigate later.

Vocabulary

What is an entry-level job? If a job requires advanced training, what does it mean? What is a bachelor's degree?

Activity

Use the classified section of the newspaper and list the entry-level jobs in your area. Also, list the jobs for which you would qualify.

Activity

Have students write the name of a career that interests them on a half-sheet of paper in big letters. Collect all papers and, as a class, sort the careers into one of the following piles: *entry-level*, *advanced training*, and *college degree*.

be provided on the job. A high school diploma is usually required. These jobs usually pay low wages and can be phased out as an employer's workforce requirements change.

Jobs Requiring Advanced Training

Jobs requiring ***advanced training*** mean that some job skills are needed. These skills may be obtained in high school through a career or technical program. Skills may also be obtained after high school by attending a community college, public technical school, or private trade school. Some companies operate their own training schools where employees are sent for training. An apprenticeship program is another way to acquire skills.

advanced training
Special skills and training required for a specific job.

Jobs Requiring a College Degree

Jobs requiring a *college degree* mean that a student completes a college or university program of study. College degrees are available for two-year programs, four-year

Resource

The "Math" That Leads to Job Success, transparency master 4-1, TR. Students are introduced to the two factors that lead to successful development of workplace skills.

Discuss

What are the job prospects for careers in your community? In the country overall, what job categories have shortages?

internship
An occupational training program during which a person works at a job, learning from a more experienced person. It can be paid or unpaid, lasting for several weeks, months, or for a year.

Reflect

Would you rather be an hourly or salaried employee? Do you think workers should be paid extra for overtime work in all cases?

programs, and more advanced studies. Usually when a college degree is a requirement for a job, a four-year degree is assumed. (The types of degrees available are discussed in further detail in Chapter 9, "Options for Education and Training.")

Other Educational Requirements

Some jobs require you to have a license or the appropriate certification. The local, state, or federal government issues licenses. Certification is obtained through the association that represents the profession. To obtain a license or certification, you generally must meet specific educational requirements. Sometimes you must also meet specific experience requirements, too.

Some occupations require you to serve an internship as part of training. An ***internship*** is an occupational training program during which a person works at a job, learning from a more experienced person. An internship can be paid or unpaid. It can be for several weeks, months, or for a year. Medical doctors or teachers are examples of people with occupations requiring internships.

Getting the right education, training, and skills is a big part of career preparation. Because it requires time and effort, it is usually accomplished in steps. For example, a dental hygienist must get a state license in order to work. To get the license, he or she must pass a test that measures knowledge and skills. That person must also be a graduate of a recognized dental hygiene school. However, being accepted by a dental hygiene school requires one or two years of college first. See 4-3.

Some careers require more education and training steps than others. You will need to know what your career choice requires in order to prepare yourself for the job.

Salary and Fringe Benefits

The starting salary for a job depends on the job specifications and the experience of the applicant. Entry-level jobs usually pay minimum wage, which is set by law. This is the lowest hourly wage that employers are permitted to pay. Your state employment office will be able to tell you what the minimum wage is at the present time. Most unskilled jobs pay minimum wage.

Education and Training Requirements for Dental Hygienists

You must have a license from the state in which you will practice, which requires:

- a passing grade on a national written and clinical examination, which requires:
- proof of graduation from an accredited dental hygiene college program, which requires:
- one or two years of study at the college level before being accepted by a school of dentistry

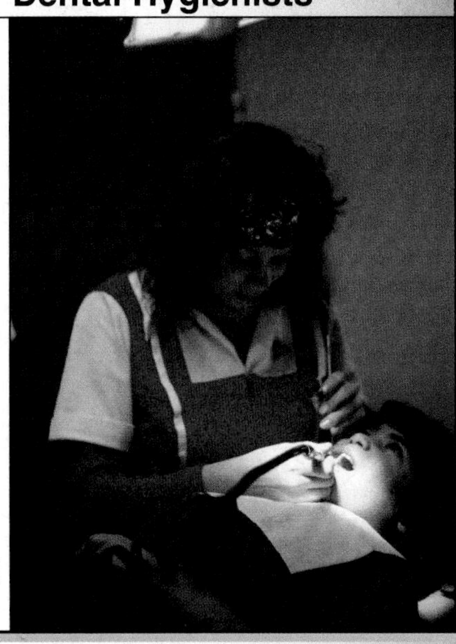

4-3 To understand the education and training required for a specific job, outline the steps needed to fill the requirements. These steps are needed to become a dentist's assistant.

Community Connections

Invite speakers to class to represent unions. Ask the speakers to describe how they operate. Ask them to explain the benefits of belonging to a union. Prepare a list of questions ahead of time.

Union wages are set by contract between the employer and the union. If you take a job covered by a union contract, you will receive the pay scale established for that job. The same union jobs in the company will have the same hourly wage scale. Raises are uniform for everyone in the same job category. The size and timing of raises are covered by the union contract.

In most jobs, you will receive an annual review. Your annual review should allow for a raise for satisfactory performance. Check to see how the organization has handled worker reviews in the past. Read the company handbook and talk to employees to learn more.

The best way to make more than the minimum wage is to get a promotion. A ***promotion*** is a move up to a higher position that has increased job responsibilities and requires increased skills and knowledge. Promotions generally result in higher pay. The more promotions you receive, the better your paycheck will look at the end of the week.

promotion
A move up to a higher position that has increased job responsibilities and requires increased skills and knowledge.

A regular hourly wage is normally paid for the first 40 hours of work. Overtime pay usually applies to time worked beyond 40 hours. There also may be a pay difference for evening hours and shift work. Working overtime is usually

Discuss

Talk about the special training requirements to become a dental hygienist. What other types of careers require certification and/ or a special license?

paid at a time-and-a-half rate, which is 50 percent more. Therefore, a job that pays $8.50 per hour would pay $12.75 per overtime hour. ($8.50 + $4.25 = $12.75)

As you conduct your research, check the organization's policy regarding overtime. Depending on the job, you may be exempt from overtime pay. Check to see if you can receive future time off for working extra hours in a week. Receiving future time off is called *compensatory time* or *comp time.*

Salaried workers are paid an annual salary. They normally work a 40-hour week. However, they may work evenings and weekends with no overtime pay. The extra hours are figured into their annual salary. Salaried workers may receive bonuses and raises based on their performance and the company's earnings. See 4-4.

Fringe benefits are financial extras received in addition to salary or wages. Fringe benefits include such benefits as paid vacation and sick time, health and life insurance, and pension contributions. When you begin working, company-paid pensions and health benefits may not seem important to you. You will probably be more concerned with your paycheck. As you get older, fringe benefits become as important as your paychecks, if not more so.

Activity

Find out what the minimum wage is. If you work 40 hours a week at the minimum wage, what is the total of a weekly paycheck before taxes are deducted?

Discuss

How many hours do you think some salaried people work per week? What are the pros and cons of an hourly wage versus a salary?

fringe benefits
Extra rewards given to workers in addition to salary or wages, such as insurance coverage and paid vacation time.

Vocabulary

What are fringe benefits? Give examples.

4-4
Project managers are examples of salaried workers. If they need to arrive early or stay late, they do so without receiving overtime pay.

Advancement Opportunities

Advancement opportunities play a major role in selecting a job. Very few people start at the top of the pay scale. Your goal should be to move upward at a steady and reasonable pace. The best way to do that is to get promotions for doing an outstanding job. When you research your job choices, ask yourself the following questions:

- Is there opportunity for advancement inside the company, or is it limited?
- Does the company fill openings by promoting its employees, or by hiring outsiders?
- Is there opportunity for advancement outside the firm due to rapid growth in the field?

Look at the opportunities for advancement inside and outside the company. As you master each job function, you become a more valuable worker because of your additional skills and experience.

Reflect

What are the advancement opportunities within your desired career field? Do you want the highest job available in your career? How would you feel about having the same job all your life?

Discuss

If you could work in any city in the United States, decide where and explain why? Would you want to walk, drive or take public transportation to work? Would you take a job that required frequent travel away from home?

Vocabulary

What does *cost of living* mean? Name a U.S. city that you believe has a very high cost of living.

Reflect

How much time are you willing to spend traveling back and forth to work each day?

Activity

Find out how much time the national average is for traveling to and from work each day.

Work Location and Environment

Another major factor to consider when exploring a career is location and environment. How far must you travel to get to your work location? How much time will it take and what will it cost? Will your salary enable you to live comfortably after paying for travel to the job?

When considering jobs in different areas, compare the differences in the cost of living. The ***cost of living*** includes rent, food, travel, and other everyday expenses. Living costs may be much higher in a large metropolitan area than in a small town or rural area. Another very important consideration is the quality of recreational facilities and educational opportunities that are available.

cost of living
Amount of money needed for rent, food, travel, and other everyday expenses.

Even if you like a job itself, you may still choose not to pursue it if you dislike the day-to-day work environment. The sights, smells, sounds, physical demands, and working conditions of the workplace make up the work environment.

Sights may range from a windowless office to sunlight and outdoor views. Smells could involve food cooking, wet paint, or hospital disinfectant. Sounds may include the roar of jet engines or the quiet of a computer keyboard. Physical

Your Reading

Why should you consider basic job factors as you choose a career?

demands could involve carrying a few lightweight files to lifting heavy bags or boxes. Working conditions may involve a comfortable office or the extremes of outdoor weather.

You can't always know in advance if you will like the location and the work environment. You can, however, ask yourself some questions that can lead to a better decision. See 4-5.

Obtaining Career Information

Your next step in exploring careers is to look for facts about the jobs that interest you. Begin your search by checking the most complete, up-to-date information from the Department of Labor. Then talk with your school counselor. Also, search for more information on the Internet.

Department of Labor References

Perhaps the best material on careers is provided by the Department of Labor. Some of the following references exist as publications. Helpful references are available online, too.

4-5

Finding answers to these questions will help you determine if the career you are considering is right for you.

Activity

Complete these unfinished sentences about your dream job: My career is located (*where?*). The sights I see at work are (*what?*). The physical demands of the job are (*what?*).

Enrich

Contact an employer for whom you would like to work and find out if tours are available at that workplace. If you can schedule a tour, record what you see, hear, and feel.

Concerns About Work Location and Environment

- Will I enjoy this type of work?
- Where will I be employed? Is it close to where I live? Can I easily relocate?
- How will I get to work? Can I afford the transportation costs and travel time?
- What is the daily routine of people working in this career?
- Am I compatible with the culture of the company?
- Do I like the working conditions? If not, do I like the job enough to tolerate the conditions?
- Does the work require much travel? Are many evenings and weekends spent away from home?
- Will the work responsibilities match my family/caregiving responsibilities?
- Will the pay support the lifestyle I choose to live?
- Is the work stressful or do stressful conditions exist only with certain employers?
- Is there frequent turnover with personnel?

- The *Occupational Outlook Handbook*, updated every two years, is designed to help with decisions about your future work. The *Handbook* describes what workers do on the job, the working conditions, and the training and education required. It also includes earnings information and expected job prospects. The publication's Web site is **bls.gov/oco**.
- The *Guide for Occupational Exploration* is designed to help people understand what traits are required for certain occupations. The *Guide* categorizes occupations into 12 interest areas that are further divided into work groups. Each work group describes jobs that require the same worker traits. The *Guide* makes it possible to determine how suited you are for a job, based on how well your abilities and interests match job requirements.
- The Occupational Information Network, called the O*NET, is an excellent online resource from the Department of Labor. O*NET can be used to explore careers, related job skills, and trends. It also provides tools for assessing a person's abilities and interests. O*NET's job-classification system links to other labor market information. Consequently, it is the most complete occupational resource available. Access O*NET at **http://online.onetcenter.org/**. (O*NET replaces the *Dictionary of Occupational Titles.*)

The Department of Labor offers career information for youth and adults through its Education and Training Administration. The site also links with other helpful sources of career information. Access the Web site at **doleta.gov**.

School Counselors

Guidance and career counselors are professionally trained to assist you in researching careers. They can save you a great deal of research time by directing your efforts to areas that provide useful facts. Your counselor can help you explore the following areas:

- careers and their educational requirements
- colleges and trade or technical schools offering specific programs

Adapting the Lesson

Have students who are high functioning search the Internet for an online career-interest survey, take the survey, and report its findings. Ask students to swap Web addresses, find one other such survey, and take it. Ask students what they learned from the exercise.

Resource

Obtaining Career Information, Activity C, WB. Students provide missing letters to key terms and complete statements that contain them.

Reflect

Are you interested in the careers recommended to you by others?

Activity

Ask several people what type of career they foresee you holding. Check with a friend, parent, and teacher. Ask them for the reasons behind their suggestions?

Enrich

Invite a guidance counselor to class to administer a career interest survey. Explain how the results can be used to help narrow career choices.

Reflect

What will help you choose a future career? Have you ever talked with a guidance counselor about career options?

Activity

Have students do an Internet search to determine which newspapers serving the community have their classified sections online. Also, have students search for their state's listing of employment opportunities. Ask students to describe what they learned through this exercise.

Enrich

Conduct an online search to see what new career Web sites are available. Compile a list and share your results with the class.

Discuss

Do you know anyone who has used the Internet to search for job information? Did they find it helpful? Were they able to locate a job from online sources?

- government service and recruiting information
- local opportunities to observe jobs in your career field, 4-6

In addition, your school counselor can provide career counseling on a one-to-one basis. Try to schedule a conference early in the school term to speak to the counselor about your career interests.

The Internet and Your Career

The Internet is one of the most valuable sources of career information. Many computers connected to the Internet have all-in-one career sites built into their Web browser. By clicking on the careers block, dozens of online career sites are available. Some of the most popular career Web sites follow:

- Job Bank USA (**jobbankusa.com**)
- America's Job Bank (**ajb.dni.us**)
- *Career* Magazine (**careermag.com**)
- Career Resource Center (**careers.org**)

You can also search the Internet for job information provided by many sources. These include unions, professional associations, employment agencies, and companies. Other sources include colleges, universities, government agencies, and hundreds of newspapers and periodicals.

4-6
Observing the work of others is a good way to learn about job tasks and responsibilities.

Enrich

Conduct an online search to find addresses of electronic message boards that would allow you to chat about careers and post information about career options. Share the results with the class.

A popular method for getting career and job information from the Internet is through newsgroups and electronic message boards. Newsgroups are special interest groups composed of people with similar interests. Using newsgroups to search for career information helps you limit your Internet search.

Online Internet chat groups and electronic message boards are also useful in gathering career information. Through them, you can talk with others who share your interests.

Your Reading

What methods can you use to obtain career information?

Additional Ways to Investigate Careers

There are many other ways to learn more about careers. These include researching other sources, talking with people, volunteering, working in career-related jobs, and attending career events.

Resource

Getting to Know Career Information Sources, Activity D, WB. Students examine several sources of career information and report what each source provides.

Research

Researching careers means gathering information about your career choices before you commit to a specific career. It means weighing the pros and cons of the career. You can use many combinations of the following sources to gather information:

Libraries

Your school and local libraries carry a wide selection of books, CDs, and videotapes on careers. Classified ads in newspapers, trade magazines, and professional journals provide additional information. Most libraries offer Internet access, too.

Trade Unions and Professional Associations

These organizations offer a great deal of information on jobs in their specific career fields. If you seek a highly specialized career, this is one of the best information sources.

Public Employment Services

These employment service centers exist to help people find employment. You can locate the nearest site by looking in the state government listing of a telephone directory under *Job Service*.

Community Connections

Visit both your school library and community library. Ask librarians at each library about career resources they offer. Ask them to highlight the trade and professional magazines that each library has. Learn how to access career-related references at both libraries.

Interviewing Workers

Resource

Interviewing for Career Information, reproducible master 4-2, TR. Students interview a person who has a satisfying career and report the worker's answers to their questions.

Activity

Have students create a spreadsheet to record answers on their job shadowing experience. Use Figure 4-7 to form the categories. Have students share their results with other students in similar career areas.

After narrowing your list of career considerations to two or three, contact people who work in these fields. Ask them questions about their careers. A good starting point is your family, teachers, and friends. Do any of them work in a career field that interests you? Ask them to introduce you to anyone they know who works in an area you are investigating.

Generally, people are very eager to talk about their jobs and give advice to interested listeners. Be prepared to ask career-related questions whenever you have an opportunity to discuss a person's job. This opportunity may arise when talking with individuals or when taking part in a career study tour. See 4-7.

Job Shadowing

job shadowing
Accompanying a person to his or her job to learn about that person's job.

One of the best ways to investigate a career choice is to accompany workers on the job. This is called ***job shadowing***. Job shadowing usually lasts for a short time, only a few days to a week or two. This period is long enough to experience the work environment firsthand and get your career questions answered. You also witness the type of duties commonly performed.

Your school counselor might be able to schedule a job-shadowing experience for you. You would stay with a worker at his or her job site during normal work hours. The experience would help you know if a career in the field is worth exploring.

Activity

Set up a job shadowing experience in a career that interests you. Prepare questions ahead of time about that career. Write a report on what you learned.

4-7
Some of the most helpful career information you can get is from workers themselves.

Career Questions to Ask Workers

- Do you enjoy your work?
- What skills and abilities are needed?
- How would you describe a typical day?
- Is there room for advancement in this career?
- What working conditions would you like to change?
- Do you recommend this career to others?

Reflect

How would you respond to people who say they do not enjoy their work? Do you think a person's career should be fun?

Community/Service Learning

If your dream career involves working with community or service organizations, gaining firsthand experience will be easy. These groups always have work for willing volunteers.

Your school can arrange learning experiences with cooperating agencies in the community. These often include hospitals, senior centers, YMCA/YWCA centers, food pantries, and nursing homes. Through community/service learning, you have an opportunity to use classroom knowledge while performing a service for others. The following activities are just some of the many available to explore:

- Community service agencies need help with their office work.
- Hospitals and health care agencies need helpers to run errands and deliver food to patients.
- Peer tutoring uses students to help other students with their studies. See 4-8.

Activity

Name some ways in which a person your age can help teach skills to others who are less capable?

Example

Share information about openings for part-time jobs in the community and the average pay. What types of skills are needed for the jobs?

Resource

What Can I Do Well? reproducible master 4-3, TR. Use the adapted worksheet to reinforce chapter concepts in students who are low functioning.

4-8
Helping other students with their studies develops interpersonal and information skills that you can later use in your career.

Enrich

Set up a career morning by inviting representatives from various local employers to school. Ask speakers to give 20-minute presentations in three consecutive sessions, so students can sign up to hear three different presenters. Have students organize the event, assign separate classrooms to each speaker, and prepare an attractive agenda. Advise students to allow enough time for questions after each speaker and movement between sessions. (Consider advance student sign-up to determine which speakers need the larger rooms.)

Making a Difference

Create (or update) a list of service agencies in the community that need volunteers. Contact the agencies and find out what types of volunteers are needed, for what tasks, and during what hours. Consider filling a position and to report back to class on the experience.

cooperative education
A program between schools and places of employment that allows students to receive on-the-job training through part-time work.

- Assistants are needed in parks and recreational facilities to serve as referees, camp counselors, and craft instructors.
- The Habitat for Humanity organization builds homes for those who cannot afford shelter. Youth volunteers are needed to help carry supplies, food, and water to the workers, and litter to trash bins.

Part-Time Jobs

It is not always possible to obtain an entry-level job in the career area you desire. If jobs exist, age or educational restrictions may exclude you. For some career fields, however, entry-level jobs do not exist for teenagers.

You can gain valuable work experience of a general nature by holding a part-time job. You can obtain part-time employment after school, on weekends, or during the summer. You will learn to follow company policies and interact with fellow workers. You will understand more about job performance and expectations. All of these valuable learning experiences will help you find a full-time job when you are ready.

Your school may have a cooperative education or co-op program. ***Cooperative education*** is a program between schools and places of employment that allows students to receive on-the-job training through part-time work. You work under the supervision of your employer and your co-op teacher. (Cooperative education will be described in greater detail in Chapter 9.)

Career Events and Job Fairs

Take advantage of career days, job fairs, employment workshops, and tours offered by your school or community. These are excellent ways to investigate specific jobs and employers while learning about different career fields.

Most speakers at career events answer audience questions. They will give you helpful hints on how to learn more about your particular interests. Many presenters bring materials to help you better understand what they do.

Tours to career sites are especially helpful. They let you see firsthand what workers actually do on their jobs. You can also experience the sounds and sights of the work environment.

Your Reading

List four ways you can investigate careers.

Summary

Knowing as much as possible about a given occupation will help you make intelligent career choices. Research as much as you can about job duties and job prospects for the careers you are considering. Identify the education, training, and skills necessary. Salary and fringe benefits are very important. Also, consider advancement opportunities, work location, and the work environment.

Begin your career exploration by checking Department of Labor information. Then talk to your school counselor to focus your search.

Check many sources to find out as much as possible. Talk with workers in the career you are considering. Enroll in a job-shadowing program to get a firsthand look at the work environment. To obtain valuable work skills, volunteer for community activities and hold a part-time job. Attend career events to ask questions of the presenters.

Reviewing Key Concepts

1. List five factors to explore when investigating basic information about a career.
2. In what two ways are job duties and responsibilities described?
3. Name the three basic levels of education and training.
4. List four fringe benefits.
5. Name the five main qualities of the work environment.
6. List three career references from the Department of Labor.
7. Which Department of Labor publication provides career information in terms of worker traits?
8. Why is it a good idea to talk with your school counselor about your career considerations?
9. True or false. Most workers do *not* like to talk about their jobs.
10. Identify six sources of community/service projects to explore.

Answers to *Reviewing Key Concepts*

1. (List five:) job duties and responsibilities; job prospects; education, training, and skills; salary and fringe benefits; advancement opportunities; work location and environment
2. by the tasks that must be accomplished, by the traits needed in workers to do the job well
3. entry-level, advanced training, college degree
4. (List four:) paid sick time, paid vacation time, health insurance, life insurance, pension contributions
5. sights, smells, sounds, physical demands, working conditions
6. *Occupational Outlook Handbook*, *Guide for Occupational Exploration*, O*NET
7. *Guide for Occupational Exploration*
8. because he or she can direct your career search and help you find useful and current facts quicker
9. false
10. (List six: Student response.)

Building Academic Skills

1. **Research, writing.** Search the U.S. Department of Labor Web site (**dol.gov**) to find out what other career information and assistance is available. Summarize your findings in an easy-to-read, one-page handout.
2. **Writing, Math, and Science.** Select four or five common entry-level jobs. Make a chart showing the job duties plus the school subjects that most directly relate to each job. Write a paragraph about what math, writing, or science skills are needed in each job.

Building Technology Skills

1. Use a spreadsheet program to create a chart with the job factors listed in 4-1. Save this spreadsheet and add information as you investigate careers.
2. Research the starting pay for three occupations in your preferred career field. Search the Web site of the Occupational Outlook Handbook (**bls.gov/oco**) for average monthly incomes. What is it for beginners? for experienced workers? Summarize your findings in a table prepared with a word processing program.
3. Check out two of the popular career Web sites listed to search for a job in your career area of choice. Report the number of jobs and write a reaction to the information you find.
4. If attending a career day at your school is not possible, go into the community to videotape interviews with various local employers. Show the video to the class.

Building Career Knowledge and Skills

1. Using the O*NET, research four job titles that interest you. For each, record the Standard Occupational Classification (SOC) code and write a short job description.
2. Give a two-minute presentation to the class on your top career choice. Describe it in terms of the basic job factors.
3. Listen carefully to your classmates' career presentations (described in the previous item). List the pros and cons about their career choices as they apply to you.
4. Organize a community/learning project involving your school and community.
5. Visit an online source for employment information. Record how many openings were listed for your top five job titles.
6. Interview a person about his or her job responsibilities and the education and training that was needed to qualify for the job.

Building Workplace Skills

Using online and print resources, research your top career choice. Find out what group or organization represents the profession, and phone or write for the name of three people to contact. Indicate that you would like to interview people with practical experience in the career field. Phone the recommended contact people to schedule a phone interview with each. Prepare a list of questions in advance that will provide information you can't get any other way. Summarize your experience in a report to the class. Are you more or less interested in the career as a result of the interviews? Keep your interview findings for future career reference.

How can career clusters help me?

Chapter 5
Types of Careers

Chapter Objectives

After studying this chapter, you will be able to

- **identify** 16 career clusters.
- **describe** a wide range of pathways and career options within each career cluster.
- **determine** the requirements for and opportunities in one or more careers that interest you.

Key Concepts

- Knowing the growth potential of various industries and occupations can help you choose a career that will be in demand.
- Each career cluster has a range of pathways and career options to consider.

Key Terms

paraprofessional
logistics
e-marketing

paraprofessional
A trained aid with one to three years of advanced training who assists professionals.

logistics
The process of managing, controlling, and moving goods, energy, information, services, or people from a point of origin to a destination in the most timely and cost-efficient manner possible.

e-marketing
Computer technologies combined with marketing and sales of goods and services.

Resource

Reinforcing Vocabulary, Activity A, WB. Students match the chapter terms with their definitions.

Resource

Where Will Your Career Take You? transparency master CT-5A and CT-5B, TR. Students discuss the 16 career clusters and the various jobs they contain.

Activity

Make an occupational family tree. List the jobs that your parents, grandparents, aunts, uncles, cousins and older siblings have had. Which career clusters appear most often?

Resource

Classifying Occupations, reproducible master 5-1, TR. Students identify the 16 career clusters and, for each cluster, eliminate job titles that do not belong in a list of representative careers.

Resource

Occupational Research, Activity B, WB. Students research a chosen occupation and determine if they are suited for such work and how to become qualified.

Note

The Web sites for the *Occupational Outlook Handbook* and the O*NET are **bls.gov/oco** and **online.onetcenter.org**.

Resource

Exploring Career Clusters, Activity C, WB. Students examine career clusters and occupations that interest them.

Exploring Careers

In this chapter, you will read about the 16 career clusters identified by the U.S. Department of Education. The careers in each cluster are based on common interests and skills. If one career interests you, it is likely that other careers in the same cluster will also interest you.

A variety of jobs requiring different levels of education and training exist within each cluster. You may notice that some jobs belong in more than one cluster. For example, *food scientist* belongs in the Agriculture, Food, and Natural Resources cluster and the Science, Technology, Engineering, and Mathematics cluster.

When you find a career that appeals to you, you will want to find out more about it. You may want to research several career paths. Keep your interests in mind. This will help you choose a career that you will enjoy.

You learned in Chapter 1 that transferable skills can be used successfully in many different careers. For example, foodservice workers, office assistants, and salespeople are just a few of the workers who must know how to schedule activities. Customer service representatives, waiters, and nurses must have good listening skills. If you begin a career and your interests change, many skills used in one career can be used in another.

Using the techniques you learned in Chapter 4, begin exploring the career clusters. The *Occupational Outlook Handbook* and the O*NET contain extensive information to help guide you in choosing a career.

Job Growth

In general, employment between 2006 and 2016 is expected to increase by 15.6 million jobs. This growth will be seen in some industries and occupations much more than others. The chart in 5-1 shows the occupational areas that will experience the greatest growth of salaried and paid positions across the nation. (Your teachers may have similar information that pertains specifically to your state.)

Top 10 Areas of Largest Employment Growth, 2006–2016		
Occupational Areas	**Percent Job Increase**	**Total Jobs in 2016**
Management, scientific, and technical consulting services	77.9	1,639,000
Home health care services	55.4	1,348,000
Computer systems design and related services	38.3	1,768,000
Offices of physicians	24.8	2,687,000
Employment services	18.9	4,348,000
Colleges, universities, and professional schools, public and private	14.5	3,933,000
General medical and surgical hospitals, public and private	13.9	5,679,000
Limited-service eating places	13.2	4,548,000
Local government, excluding education and hospitals	10.9	6,206,000
Elementary and secondary schools, public and private	7.6	8,983,000
Note: Covers all wage/salary positions		

U.S. Department of Labor

5-1 The top 10 fast-growing occupational areas all involve positions in the services sector.

Activity

Create a PowerPoint presentation to show the variety of careers in each career cluster.

Adapting the Lesson

Have students who are low functioning create a poster showing pictures of people or objects cut from magazines that relate to the occupational areas in 5-1.

Resource

Learn More About Jobs, reproducible master 5-2, TR. Use the adapted worksheet to reinforce chapter concepts in students who are low functioning.

An overall picture of the sectors that make up the U.S. job market shows that the agriculture sector will offer little job growth, while the goods-producing sector will offer somewhat more. The services sector, however, currently employs the vast majority of U.S. workers and will continue to outpace the job growth of all other sectors combined.

As you examine the career clusters in this chapter, consider their potential for job growth. When an occupational area is expanding, many new workers are needed. These areas often present the greatest employment opportunities for individuals.

How can knowing about career clusters guide your career decisions?

Agriculture, Food & Natural Resources

Careers in this cluster involve working with plants, animals, and food processing. Power, structural, and technical systems as well as natural resources, the environment, and agribusiness are also included in this cluster.

Farmers grow crops, and ranchers tend livestock. Food scientists and technologists discover new food sources, analyze food content, and develop ways to process, preserve, package, and store food. Foresters plan and supervise the growing and using of trees. Conservationists and environmentalists work on problems regarding the responsible use of air, land, and water. They also preserve marine life and wildlife. Animal scientists study genetics, nutrition, and reproduction.

Entry-level jobs are available in this career cluster. Many technical jobs require two or more years of advanced training. Engineers, scientists, and top managers need to complete at least four years of college.

An expanding population, globalization, and an increasing public focus on diet will result in more job opportunities in this career cluster. Many specialists work for the Environmental Protection Agency, the National Park Service, and the Fish and Wildlife Service. The federal government is one of the biggest employers in this career area. Other possible employers include landscape nurseries, golf courses, mining and logging operations, and oil exploration companies.

Agriculture, Food, and Natural Resources

Pathways and Career Options

Pathway	Career Options
Food Products and Processing Systems	Agricultural Communications Specialist • Business-Educator • Food Scientist • Meat Processor • Toxicologist • Biochemist • Nutritionist • Dietician • Food Broker • Food Inspector • Meat Cutter-Grader • Food Meal Supervisor • Cheese Maker • Microbiologist • Produce Buyer • Bacteriologist • Food & Drug Inspector • Bioengineer • Biochemist • Food & Fiber Engineer
Plant Systems	Bioinformatics Specialist • Plant Breeder & Geneticist • Biotechnology Lab Technician • Soil & Water Specialist • Crop Farm Manager • Agricultural Educator • Plant Pathologist • Aquaculturalist • Sales Representative • Greenhouse Manager • Grower • Farmer • Rancher • Botanist • Tree Surgeon • Education & Extension Specialist • Agricultural Journalist
Animal Systems	Agricultural Educator • Livestock Producer • Aquaculturalist • Animal Caretaker • Poultry Manager • Equine Manager • Veterinarian • Veterinary Assistant • Feedlot Specialist • Animal Scientist • Embryo Technologist • Pet Shop Operator • USDA Inspector • Livestock Buyer • Feed Sales Representative • Vivarian Technician • Wildlife Biologist • Livestock Geneticist • Animal Nutritionist
Power, Structural, and Technical Systems	Machine Operator • Electronics Systems Technician • Agricultural Engineer • Heavy Equipment Maintenance Technician • Recycling Technician • Waste Water Treatment Plant Operator • Parts Manager • Welder • Machinist • Communication Technician • Agricultural Applications Software Developer • Programmer • Database Administrator • Information Lab Specialist • Engineering Specialist
Natural Resource Systems	Cartographer • Wildlife Manager • Range Technician • Ecologist • Park Manager • Environmental Interpreter • Fish & Game Officer • Fishing Vessel Operator • Logger • Forest Technician • Log Grader • Pulp & Paper Manager • Soil Geology Technician • Geologist • Mining Engineer
Environmental Service Systems	Pollution Prevention & Control Manager • Pollution Prevention & Control Technician • Environmental Sampling & Analysis Scientist • Health & Safety Sanitarian • Environmental Compliance Assurance Manager • Hazardous Materials Handler • Hazardous Materials Technician • Manager • Water Environment Manager • Water Quality Manager
Agribusiness Systems	Field Representative for Bank, Insurance Company, or Government Program • Farm Investment Manager • Agricultural Commodity Broker • Agricultural Economist • Farmer • Rancher • Feedlot Operator • Farm Manager • Livestock Rancher • Breeder • Dairy Herd Supervisor • Agricultural Products Buyer • Animal Health Products Distributor

People in this career cluster design and build roads, bridges, and buildings. They construct homes, offices, shopping centers, hospitals, and factories. Engineers make sure all structures are sound. Employees in maintenance/operations inspect and move new equipment into position. They determine the correct placement of machines in a plant, repair structures and machinery, and perform preventive maintenance. Most careers involving planning, designing, and engineering require college degrees or completion of certificate programs.

Many other workers with special training actually build, restore, repair, and maintain the structures. These workers include roofers, bricklayers, cement masons, ironworkers, welders, glaziers, and painters. They work on-site wherever structures are built. Much of their work occurs outdoors and in potentially dangerous conditions.

Most construction workers learn their skills in technical schools or apprenticeship programs. Industry plays a major training role by supporting apprenticeships, craft training, joint industry/training programs leading to certification, and college training.

Many opportunities exist within this high-skilled field. Employment opportunities vary by specialty and level of responsibility

Architecture and Construction

Pathways and Career Options

Design and Pre-Construction	Architect • Drafter • Regional & Urban Planner • Designer • Industrial Engineer • Materials Engineer • Environmental Designer • Civil Engineer • Programmer • Mechanical Engineer • Electrical Engineer • Preservationist • Environmental Engineer • Surveyor • Fire Prevention & Protection Engineer • Cost Estimator • Electrical & Electronic Engineering Technician
Construction	General Contractor & Builder • Construction Foreman • Estimator • Project Inspector • Sales & Marketing Manager • Education & Training Director • Safety Director • Construction Inspector • Subcontractor • Field Supervisor • Mason • Iron & Metalworker • Carpenter • Electrician • Boilermaker • Electronic Systems Technician • Sheetmetal Worker • Painter
Maintenance and Operations	General Maintenance Contractor • Construction Engineer • Construction Manager • Estimator • Facilities Engineer • Environmental Engineer • Demolition Engineer • Project Inspector • Manufacturer's Representative • Equipment & Material Manager • Maintenance Estimator • Security Controls Manager • Preservationist • Remodeler • Safety Director • Construction Inspector

People with careers in the arts, audio/video technology, and communications include photographers, printers, painters, sculptors, singers, and dancers. Others are agents, cartoonists, stage managers, and lighting directors.

You notice the results of work done in the communications field every day. You see newspapers, magazines, books, photographs, and movies. You hear music, radio, and movie sound effects. People in these careers work for publishers, radio and television stations, movie studios, and telephone companies.

Many careers in this cluster are rewarding, creative, and challenging. They are constantly changing, too, because of technological advances. Satellites and computers have led the way for these advances. The creative aspects of this cluster are rapidly merging with the technological aspects.

Careers in this area require the ability to communicate effectively in both oral and written form. The training and education needed are as varied as the careers themselves. Some people have special talents and become instant successes. However, most people spend years training to gain the skills and knowledge needed.

Arts, Audio/Video Technology, & Communications

Pathways and Career Options

Pathway	Career Options
Audio and Video Technology and Film	Video Systems Technician • Video Graphics, Special Effects, & Animation Designer • Audio-Video Designer & Engineer • Technical Computer Support Technician • Audio-Video System Service Technician • Audio Systems Technician
Printing Technology	Graphics & Printing Equipment Operator • Lithographer & Platemaker • Computer Typography & Composition Equipment Operator • Desktop Publishing Specialist • Web Page Designer
Visual Arts	Commercial Photographer • Commercial Interior Designer • Residential & Home Furnishings Coordinator • Graphic Designer • Computer-Aided Design Technician • Fashion Illustrator • Textile Designer • Commercial Artist • Illustrator • Artist • Curator • Gallery Manager • Fashion Designer
Performing Arts	Production Manager (Digital, Video, or Stage) • Cinematographer • Video Editor • Dancer • Playwright • Screen Writer • Screen Editor • Script Writer • Director & Coach • Performer • Actors • Musician • Make-Up Artist • Costume Designer • Stagecraft Designer & Lighter • Set Designer & Painter • Stagecraft Sound Effects & Acoustics Coordinator • Composer • Conductor • Music Instructor
Journalism and Broadcasting	Audio & Video Operations • Control Room Technician • Station Manager • Radio & TV Announcer • Editor • Journalist • Reporter • Broadcast Technician
Telecommunications	Telecommunication Technician • Telecommunication Equipment, Cable, or Line Repairer • Installer • Telecommunication Computer Programmer & Systems Analyst

Business, Management & Administration

Careers in this cluster involve clerical, computer, accounting, management, and administrative work. An office setting is the most common job site for people working in these careers.

Most entry-level jobs require basic data entry, bookkeeping, and filing skills. Technological advances are forcing workers to upgrade their computer skills. Knowledge of commonly used software programs is especially important. The educational background required to work in this career cluster depends on the level of job responsibilities.

Administrative assistants, clerks, word processors, and receptionists are needed in all kinds of offices. Some workers input data, organize documents, prepare work schedules, and assemble reports. Managers and administrators solve problems, analyze data, and make decisions.

Because of technological innovations, changes in government regulations, and growing environmental concerns, employers will need well-trained, well-informed business, management, and administrative professionals. Career opportunities are available in every sector of the economy and require specific skills in organization, time management, customer service, and communication. Jobs in this career cluster occur everywhere there is office work. Business and administration functions exist throughout government, education, and business.

Business, Management, and Administration

Pathways and Career Options

Pathway	Career Options
Management	Entrepreneur • Chief Executive • General Manager • Accounting Manager • Accounts Payable Manager • Assistant Credit Manager • Billing Manager • Business & Development Manager • Compensation & Benefits Manager • Credit & Collections Manager • Payroll Manager • Risk Manager • Operations Manager • Public Relations Manager • Human Resources Manager
Business Financial Management and Accounting	Accountant • Accounting Clerk • Accounting Supervisor • Adjuster • Adjustment Clerk • Assistant Treasurer • Auditor • Bookkeeper • Budget Analyst • Budget Manager • Billing Supervisor • Cash Manager • Controller • Merger & Acquisitions Manager • Price Analyst • Top Collections Executive • Top Investment Executive • Treasurer • Chief Financial Officer • Finance Director
Human Resources	Human Resources Manager • Human Resources Coordinator • Industrial Relations Director • Compensation & Benefits Manager • Employee Assistance Plan Manager • Training & Development Manager • Corporate Trainer • Arbitrator • Employer Relations Representative • Affirmative Action Coordinator • Equal Employment Opportunity Specialist • Pay Equity Officer
Business Analysis	Systems Analyst • E-commerce Analyst • Requirements Specialist • Marketing Analyst • Operations Research Analyst • Business Consultant • Business Analyst • Budget Analyst • Product Manager • Price Analyst
Marketing	Marketing Manager • Sales Manager • Assistant Store Manager • Department Manager • Salesperson • Customer Service Supervisor • Customer Service Clerk • Research & Development Manager • Small Business Owner & Entrepreneur • E-commerce Manager & Entrepreneur • Wholesale & Retail Buyer • International Distribution Manager • Warehouse Manager • Logistics Manager
Administration and Information Support	Administrative Assistant • Executive Assistant • Office Manager • Medical Front Office Assistant • Information Assistant • Desktop Publisher • Customer Service Assistant • Data Entry Specialist • Receptionist • Communications Equipment Operator • Computer Operator • Court Reporter • Stenographer • Dispatcher • Shipping & Receiving Worker • Records Processor • Library Assistant

People who enjoy working with and helping people will find this career cluster very rewarding. People with careers in education and training include teacher's aides, parent educators, counselors, and librarians. They work with individuals on a one-to-one basis as well as groups of students. Often the job site is a school. However, other sites include offices, gyms, health clubs, private homes, and business settings. Related occupations include occupational trainers, administrators, and human resource specialists.

People in this field need a solid background in academic, technical, and presentation skills. Teachers and trainers must have the ability to communicate, inspire trust and confidence, and motivate learners as well as understand their educational needs. They must be able to recognize and respond to individual differences in diverse learners and employ different teaching and training methods that will result in learner achievement. Most of these occupations require licensing or certification. Practically all occupations in this career cluster, even for entry-level positions, require training beyond high school. Most occupations require an advanced college degree.

A growing emphasis on improving education will increase the demand for workers in this cluster. Training programs will be needed in response to the increasing complexity of many jobs and technological advances across all industries.

Education and Training

Pathways and Career Options

Administration and Administrative Support	Superintendent • Principal • Administrator • Supervisor & Instructional Coordinator • Education Researcher • Test Measurement Specialist • College President • Dean • Curriculum Developer • Instructional Media Designer
Professional Support Services	Psychologist (Clinical, Developmental, or Social) • Social Worker • Parent Educator • Counselor • Speech & Language Pathologist • Audiologist
Teaching and Training	Preschool Teacher • Kindergarten Teacher • Elementary Teacher • Secondary Teacher • Special Education Teacher • Teacher Aid • College & University Lecturer • Professor • Human Resource Trainer • Physical Trainer • Coach • Child Care Director • Child Care Worker • Child Life Specialist • Nanny • Early Childhood Teacher & Assistant • Group Worker & Assistant

People holding jobs in this career cluster generally handle tasks that involve money. Some professionals work for individual clients, while others work for various firms and organizations.

Professionals who work with clients may sell banking services or other financial products. They may give investing advice or arrange a mortgage. They may give credit counseling or process an insurance claim. Whatever their job, they explain the pros and cons of various financial decisions so people can choose what's best for their particular situation.

Every organization, whether profit-making or nonprofit, has one or more financial specialists to prepare the required financial reports. They may also manage the accounting and purchasing departments and credit card operations. If the firm buys or sells beyond U.S. borders, these specialists must know the financial systems of other countries.

People in this cluster need a solid background in math, organization, time management, customer service, and communication. Although people in positions such as bank tellers and other clerks usually need only a high school education, most occupations in this cluster require advanced training or a college degree. Professional organizations offer certification programs that are recognized levels of competency in the profession. Examples are Certified Financial Analyst, Certified Financial Planner, and Certified Public Accountant. Securities and commodities sales agents must meet state licensing requirements, which usually include passing an examination.

Career opportunities are available in every sector of the economy. Jobs will increase due to greater levels of global investments in securities and commodities along with the growing need for investment advice. Advances in technology and trends toward direct marketing provide challenging opportunities for careers across all areas of the cluster.

Finance

Pathways and Career Options

Pathway	Career Options
Financial and Investment Planning	Personal Financial Advisor • Tax Preparation Professional • Securities & Commodities Sales Agent • Investment Advisor • Brokerage Clerk • Brokerage Assistant • Development Officer
Business Financial Management	Accountant • Financial Analyst • Treasurers, Controllers & Chief Revenue Agent • Auditor • Economist • Tax Examiner • Collector • Revenue Agent
Banking and Related Services	Credit Analyst • Loan Officer • Bill & Account Collector • Teller • Loan Processor • Customer Service Representative • Data Processor • Accountant • Internal Auditor • Compliance Officer • Title Researcher & Examiner • Abstractor • Credit Report Provider • Repossession Agent • Network Service & Operations Manager • Debt Counselor
Insurance Services	Claims Agent, Examiner, & Investigator • Claims Clerk • Insurance Appraiser • Underwriter • Actuary • Sales Agent • Customer Service Agent • Processing Clerk • Direct Marketing

Careers in this cluster provide government, legislative, administrative, security, and regulatory services. All of these services are needed at federal, state, and local government levels.

People in this career cluster need a solid background in social studies, political science, foreign language, and history. People involved in revenue and taxation need a strong background in accounting. Many occupations in public service are also called *civil service jobs*. These are government jobs obtained by taking a competitive exam. Many public service positions have residency requirements. A *residency requirement* demands that an applicant live in a certain area. Usually, this is the area served by the branch of government offering the job. For many federal occupations, U.S. citizenship is required.

The qualifications for public service careers vary. All branches of the armed forces require high school graduation or its equivalent for certain enlistment options. Many jobs require education beyond high school. Administrative assistants and secretaries can obtain entry-level jobs, but office training or experience is often expected. Administrators generally need college degrees. Regulators may be required to hold the same licenses, certifications, or registries as practitioners in the industries or activities they regulate.

The factors that influence government employment levels are unique. Elected officials determine the payroll budget of the government. Each administration has different public policy priorities, which increase employment levels in some programs and decrease it in others.

Government and Public Administration

Pathways and Career Options

Pathway	Career Options
Governance	President • Vice President • Governor • Lieutenant Governor • Mayor • Cabinet Level Secretary (Federal or State) • Representative (Federal or State) • Senator (Federal or State) • Assistant, Deputy, & Chief of Staff • Commissioner (County, Parish, or City) • Commissioner (State Agency) • Congressional Aide • Legislative Aide • Legislative Assistant • Specialist • Lobbyist • Policy Advisor
National Security	National Security Advisor • Staff or Field Officer • Electronic Warfare Specialist • Combat Operations Officer • Infantry Field Officer • Artillery Officer • Air Defense Artillery Officer • Special Forces Officer • Nuclear Weapons Officer & Specialist • Missile & Space Systems Officer • Military Intelligence Specialist • Signals Intelligence Officer • Surface Ship Warfare Officer •
Foreign Service	Ambassador Foreign Service Officer • Consular Officer • Administrative Officer • Political Officer • Economic Officer • Diplomatic Courier
Planning	Business Enterprise Official • Chief of Vital Statistics • Commissioner • Director (Various Agencies) • Economic Development Coordinator • Federal Aid Coordinator • Census Clerk • County Director • Census Enumerator • Census Planner • Program Associate • Global Imaging Systems Specialist
Revenue and Taxation	Assessor • Tax Auditor • Internal Revenue Investigator • Revenue Agent & Officer • Tax Examiner Assistant or Clerk • Inspector General • Tax Attorney • Tax Policy Analyst
Regulation	Business Regulation Investigator • Chief of Field Operations • Code Inspector or Officer • Equal Opportunity Officer, Inspector, Investigator, or Examiner • Chief Bank Examiner • Bank Examiner • Aviation Safety Officer • Border Inspector • Cargo Inspector • Election Supervisor • Enforcement Specialist • Immigration Officer
Public Management and Administration	City Manager • City Council Member • City or County Clerk • Court Administrator or Clerk • Executive or Associate Director • Officer • General Service Officer • Management Analysis Officer • Program Administration Officer

The health science career cluster offers many opportunities for employment in careers that promote health, wellness, and diagnosis as well as treat injuries and diseases. Jobs are available in hospitals, clinics, and nursing homes. Other workplaces include laboratories, dentists' offices, and pharmacies.

Workers in this cluster help people recover from illness or injury and stay healthy. Dietitians help people meet their nutritional needs. Dentists and orthodontists focus on keeping teeth healthy. Podiatrists specialize in the care of feet. Optometrists and ophthalmologists are concerned with proper vision and good eye care.

Because the health field is so broad, there are jobs at all levels. Entry-level jobs include those of orderlies and stockroom attendants. ***Paraprofessionals*** are trained aids, with one to three years of advanced training, who assist professionals. Many of their jobs require licensing. Examples of workers at this level are dental hygienists, medical data analysts, physical therapists, practical nurses, paramedics, laboratory assistants, and X-ray technicians. Advanced degrees are usually needed for professions in specialty areas such as pharmacists and registered nurses. Professions, such as physician or dentist, require a doctoral degree.

Health care is the largest and fastest-growing industry in the United States. Based on an aging population and increased use of technology, the demand for health care workers will grow.

Health Science

Pathways and Career Options

Therapeutic Services	Acupuncturist • Anesthesiologist Assistant • Art, Music, or Dance Therapist • Athletic Trainer • Audiologist • Certified Nursing Assistant • Chiropractor • Dentist • Hygienist • Dietician • Emergency Medical Technician • Home Health Aide • Licensed Practical Nurse • Massage Therapist • Medical Assistant • Mortician • Occupational Therapist or Assistant • Optometrist • Paramedic
Diagnostics Services	Cardiovascular Technologist • Clinical Lab Technician • Computer Tomography (CT) Technologist • Cytotechnologist • Diagnostic Medical Sonographer • Electrocardiographic (ECG) Technician • Electronic Diagnostic (EEG) Technologist • Exercise Physiologist • Geneticist • Histotechnician • Histotechnologist • Magnetic Resonance (MR) Technologist
Health Informatics	Admitting Clerk • Applied Researcher • Community Services Specialist • Data Analyst • Epidemiologist • Ethicist • Health Educator • Health Information Coder • Health Information Services • Healthcare Administrator • Medical Assistant • Medical Biller • Patient Financial Services Coordinator • Medical Information Technologist • Medical Librarian & Cybrarian
Support Services	Biomedical Engineer • Clinical Engineer • Biomedical Technician • Clinical Technician • Environmental Services Worker • Facilities Manager • Food Service Worker • Hospital Maintenance Engineer • Industrial Hygienist • Materials Manager • Transport Technician
Biotechnology Research and Development	Biochemist • Bioinformatics Associate • Bioinformatics Scientist • Bioinformatics Specialist • Biomedical Chemist • Biostatistician • Cell Biologist • Clinical Trials Research Associate • Clinical Trials Research Coordinator • Geneticist • Genetics Lab Assistant • Lab Technician • Microbiologist • Molecular Biologist • Pharmaceutical Scientist • Quality Assurance Technician

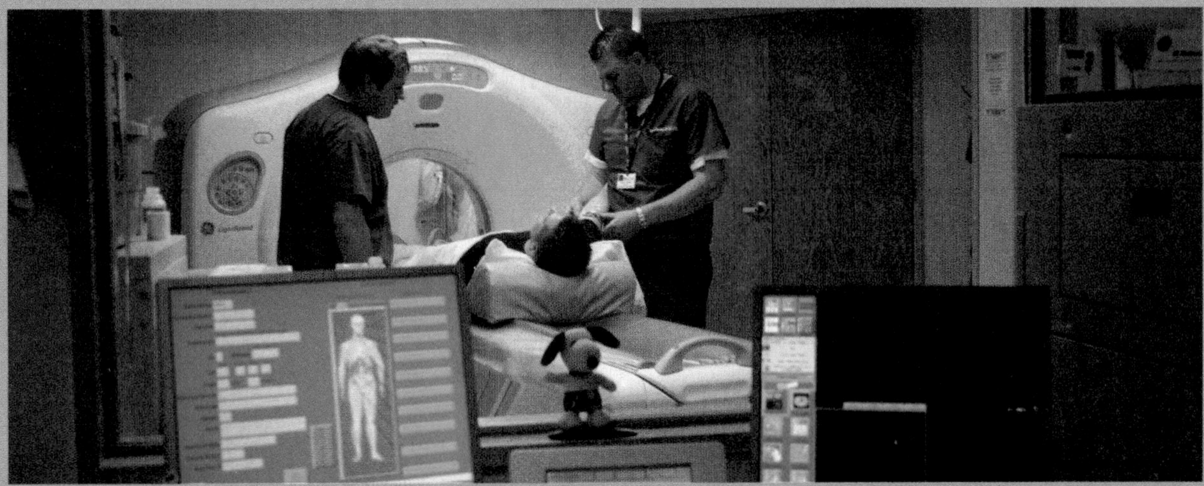

Hunterdon Medical Center, Flemington, New Jersey

This cluster prepares people for careers in the management, marketing, and operations of restaurants, other food services, lodging, attractions, recreational events, and travel-related services. People in this career cluster work in hotels, restaurants, travel agencies, amusement parks, country clubs, tourist attractions, and on cruise ships. In general, their work focuses on making visitors happy. Hospitality and tourism operations are located throughout the world.

Hotel employees, from greeters to managers, try to make visitors comfortable. Food and beverage service workers satisfy customer appetites. Travel agents, tour guides, and ticket takers make sightseeing trips and vacations enjoyable. People learn to ski, play golf, tennis, and other recreational activities with the help of teaching pros on staff.

The level of education required depends on the level of job responsibilities. Knowledge of geography and the psychology of dealing with people and their expectations are very important. Also important are computer and map-reading skills and strong problem-solving skills. Being familiar with foreign languages is a plus. Many careers in hospitality and tourism offer on-the-job training. Experience and/or career/technical training may help workers advance. College degrees are usually needed for top jobs. Many colleges offer degrees related to hospitality and tourism. Some technical schools offer training programs. Many trade associations offer seminars that lead to certifications.

An increase in leisure time and personal income means more business in this career cluster. Also, business-related travel is common. Both trends are likely to keep the number of jobs in the hospitality and tourism industry growing. People who enjoy hard work, variety, and working with people will have many opportunities to advance in this industry.

Hospitality and Tourism

Pathways and Career Options

Restaurants and Food and Beverage Services	General Manager • Food & Beverage Manager • Kitchen Manager • Catering & Banquets Manager • Service Manager • Maitre'd • Restaurant Owner • Baker • Brewer • Caterer • Executive Chef • Cook • Pastry & Specialty Chef • Bartender • Restaurant Server • Banquet Server • Cocktail Server • Banquet Set-Up Employee • Bus Person • Room Service Attendant
Lodging	Front Office Manager • Executive Housekeeper • Director of Sales & Marketing • Director of Human Resources • Director of Security • Controller • Food & Beverage Director • General Manager • Quality Assurance Manager • Owner & Franchisee • Communications Supervisor • Front Desk Supervisor • Reservations Supervisor • Laundry Supervisor • Room Supervisor
Travel and Tourism	Executive Director • Assistant Director • Director of Tourism Development • Director of Communications • Director of Visitor Services • Director of Sales • Director of Marketing & Advertising • Director of Volunteer Services • Events Manager • Sales Manager • Destination Manager • Convention Services Manager • Travel Agent • Event Planner • Meeting Planner
Recreation, Amusements, and Attractions	Club Manager & Assistant Manager • Club Membership Developer • Parks & Gardens Safety & Security • Parks & Garden Ranger • Resort Trainer & Instructor • Gaming & Casino Manager • Gaming & Casino Dealer • Gaming & Casino Security & Safety • Fairs & Festival Facility Manager • Fairs & Festival Promotional Developer • Theme Parks & Amusement Parks Area Ride Operations Manager

Human Services

The many job opportunities available in this career cluster all relate to families, human needs, and improving a person's quality of life. Some jobs assist individuals or families. Others involve entire communities.

People in human services work in homes, schools, child care centers, clinics, and community centers. They work with all age groups. Sometimes they work with people who are underprivileged or have physical or mental disabilities. At times, they serve as consultants to doctors, nurses, and other professionals. They can work as counselors or in consumer services. People in personal care services can work as barbers, spa attendants, or funeral directors.

People in this career cluster need a solid background in communication, science, and technical skills. Some occupations in this career cluster require only on-the-job training. Many require career/technical training. Each state has its own licensing requirements that regulate training for many of the careers in this area. Professionals in this field have college degrees, many of which are advanced.

Based on statistics, human services careers have a good employment outlook, especially those careers that involve working with the elderly. The employment outlook is also growing for people working in consumer services.

Human Services

Pathways and Career Options

Pathway	Career Options
Early Childhood Development and Services	Childcare Facility Director • Childcare Facility Assistant Director • Elementary School Counselor • Preschool Teacher • Educator for Parents • Nanny • Teachers' Assistant • Childcare Assistant or Worker
Counseling and Mental Health Services	Clinical & Counseling Psychologist • Industrial-Organizational Psychologist • Sociologist • School Counselor • School Psychologist • Substance Abuse & Behavioral Disorder Counselor • Mental Health Counselor • Vocational Rehabilitation Counselor • Career Counselor • Employment Counselor • Residential Advisor • Marriage, Child, & Family Counselor
Family and Community Services	Community Service Director • Adult Day Care Coordinator • Volunteer Coordinator • Licensed Professional Counselor • Religious Leader • Religious Activities & Education Program Director • Human Services Worker • Social Services Worker • Vocational Rehabilitation Counselor • Employment Counselor • Career Counselor • Vocational Rehabilitation Service Worker
Personal Care Services	Barber • Cosmetologist, Hairdresser, & Hairstylist • Shampooer • Nail Technician, Manicurist, & Pedicurist • Skin Care Specialist & Esthetician • Electrolysis Technician • Electrologist • Funeral Director • Mortician • Embalmer • Funeral Attendant • Personal & Home Care Aide • Companion • Spa Attendant • Personal Trainer • Massage Therapist
Consumer Services	Consumer Credit Counselor • Consumer Affairs Officer • Consumer Advocate • Certified Financial Planner • Insurance Representative • Banker • Real Estate Services Representative • Financial Advisor • Investment Broker • Employee Benefits Representative • Hospital Patient Accounts Representative • Customer Service Representative • Consumer Research Department Representative

Occupations in this career cluster design, develop, manage, and support hardware and software information systems. Careers in this area are available in every sector of the economy—from financial services to medical services, from business to engineering and environmental services. People with careers in this cluster might be network administrators, technical writers, game programmers, or Web designers.

Many information technology careers are available for people with strong computer, math, and science skills. Workers in this field attend computer workshops, seminars, and classes after earning a college degree. They must constantly upgrade their skills because of ever-changing technology. They continue earning various certifications to verify their advanced knowledge and skill level.

Careers tend to cluster in four areas of concentration. Some workers design and run network systems. Some focus on providing technical support and services. Others focus on programming and software development. Yet others concentrate on interactive media.

This career cluster is perhaps the fastest growing and most rapidly changing of all career areas. People who pursue careers in the information technology field will discover ongoing opportunities to learn about and work with new technologies that are transforming the world.

Information Technology

Pathways and Career Options

Pathway	Career Options
Network Systems	Data Communications Analyst • Information Systems Administrator • Information Systems Operator • Information Technology Engineer • Technical Support Specialist • User Support Specialist • Telecommunications Network Technician • Network Administrator • Network Analyst • Network Engineer • Network Operations Analyst • Network Security Analyst • Network Transport Administrator
Information Support and Services	Data Administrator • Data Analyst • Data Modeler • Database Administration Associate • Database Developer • Knowledge Architect • Systems Administrator • Technical Writer • Desktop Publisher • Instructional Designer • Online Publisher • Technical Support Analyst • Call Center Support Representative • Customer Service Representative • Product Support Engineer
Interactive Media	2D & 3D Artist • Animator • Audio & Video Engineer • Media Specialist • Media Designer • Instructional Designer • Multimedia Author • Multimedia Developer • Multimedia Specialist • Producer • Production Assistant • Programmer • Streaming Media Specialist • Virtual Reality Specialist • Web Designer • Web Administrator • Web Page Developer • Web Site Developer • Webmaster
Programming and Software Development	Applications Analyst • Applications Engineer • Business Analyst • Computer Engineer • Data Modeler • Operating Systems Designer & Engineer • Operating Systems Programmer • Operating Systems Analyst • Program Manager • Programmer • Analyst • Software Applications Specialist • Software Applications Architect • Software Applications Design Engineer

This career cluster involves planning, managing, and providing judicial, legal, and protective services. Employed by state and local levels, emergency service personnel fight fires and prevent crime. Attorneys, dispatchers, bailiffs, security guards, and inspectors are some related positions in this cluster.

At the federal level, public safety work is more specialized. FBI agents work on cases involving terrorism, organized crime, and violations of federal law. Treasury Department agents investigate the suspicious use of credit cards and illegal gun sales.

Criminal matters plus many other issues are handled by the U.S. court system. Other issues include labor disputes, wills, divorces, business contracts, real estate, and bankruptcy. Lawyers advise clients of their legal rights and represent them in court. Law clerks help research the facts of a case.

Many careers in this cluster require, at minimum, technical training and successful completion of preemployment tests. For instance, applicants for firefighting jobs generally must pass a written exam as well as tests of strength, physical stamina, coordination, and agility. Law enforcement officers are often trained in their agency's police academy, which includes classroom instruction in laws and accident investigation along with training in traffic control, use of firearms, first aid, and emergency response. Training requirements in legal services depend on the type of work performed. Some careers require a two-year degree, and many require a master's or doctoral degree.

Renewed national interest in public safety and security has expanded opportunities for employment in this career cluster. Numerous job openings will stem from employment growth in corporate, industrial, and homeland security.

Law, Public Safety, Corrections, and Security

Pathways and Career Options

Pathway	Career Options
Correction Services	Warden • Jail Administrator • Mid-level Manager • Program Coordinator & Counselor • Public Information Officer • Correctional Trainer • Case Manager • Community Corrections Practitioner • Probation & Parole Officer • Corrections Educator • Corrections Officer • Detention Deputy • Youth Services Worker • Facility Maintenance Worker • Transport Officer •
Emergency and Fire Management Services	Emergency Management & Response Coordinator • Emergency Planning Manager • Emergency Medical Technician • Fire Fighter • Fire Fighter Manager & Supervisor • Forest Fire Fighter • Forest Fire Fighter Manager & Supervisor • Forest Fire Inspector & Investigator • Hazardous Materials Responder • Dispatcher • Training Officer • Grant Writer & Coordinator • Rescue Worker
Security and Protective Services	Security Director • Security Systems Designer & Consultant • Information Systems Security Specialist • Computer Forensics Specialist • Private & Corporate Investigator • Loss Prevention & Security Manager • Security Trainer & Educator • Security Sales Representative • Loss Prevention Specialist • Security Systems Technician • Private Investigative Assistant
Law Enforcement Services	Animal Control Officer • Bailiff • Child Support Investigator • Missing Persons Investigator • Unemployment Fraud Investigator • Criminal Investigator & Special Agent • Gaming Investigator • Bomb Technician • Highway Patrol • Immigration & Customs Inspector • Police & Detective Manager & Supervisor • Police Detective & Criminal Investigator • Police, Fire, & Ambulance Dispatcher • Police & Patrol Officers
Legal Services	Attorney • Case Management Specialist • Court Reporter • File & Document Manager • Information Officer • Investigator Judge • Law Clerk • Legal Assistant • Legal Secretary • Magistrate Mediator & Arbitrator • Negotiator • Paralegal

Manufacturing

People in manufacturing careers produce cars, computers, appliances, furniture, toys, and other products. They refine ore and produce steel. They knit and weave textiles. They process chemicals and foods. They work in quality assurance, maintenance, installation, and repair. Health, safety, and environmental assurance are a part of this cluster. This cluster also includes inventory control and logistics. (***Logistics*** is the process of managing, controlling, and moving goods, energy, information, services, or people from a point of origin to a destination in the most timely and cost-efficient manner possible.) Most people in this career cluster work in factories or plants.

People in the manufacturing cluster need a solid background in math, science, and technical skills. Although entry-level jobs exist, the next level, *semiskilled labor*, requires experience and/or technical training. To qualify for most of the *skilled labor* positions, workers must complete a formal training program beyond high school, such as an apprenticeship or community college program. Companies and trade unions also offer training programs.

Skilled labor positions are called *skilled trades*. Examples of workers in skilled trades are machinists, tool and die makers, drafters, and welders. The manufacturing field also employs people in positions such as engineers and scientists, which require a college degree.

Due to manufacturing plants moving toward more automation of their processes, the employment outlook for this career cluster will grow more slowly than other fields. However, people with a broad range of skills or a specific skill that cannot be automated will experience job growth and find their services in demand.

Manufacturing

Pathways and Career Options

Pathway	Career Options
Production	Assembler • Automated Manufacturing Technician • Bookbinder • Calibration Technician • Electrical Installer & Repairer • Extruding & Drawing Machine Setter • Extrusion Machine Operator • Foundry Worker • Grinding, Lapping, & Buffing Machine Operator • Hoist & Winch Operator • Instrument Maker • Large Printing Press Machine Setter • Milling Machine Set-Up Operator
Manufacturing Production Process Development	Design Engineer • Electrical & Electronic Technician & Technologist • Electronics Engineer • Engineering Technician & Technologist • Engineering Technician • Industrial Engineer • Labor Relations Manager • Manufacturing Engineer • Manufacturing Technician • Power Generating & Reactor Plant Operator • Precision Inspector, Tester, & Grader
Maintenance, Installation, and Repair	Biomedical Equipment Technician • Boilermaker • Communication System Installer & Repairer • Computer Installer & Repairer • Computer Maintenance Technician • Electrical Equipment Installer & Repairer • Facility Electrician • Industrial Facilities Manager • Industrial Machinery Repair Technician • Industrial Maintenance Electrician
Quality Assurance	Calibration Technician • Inspector • Lab Technician • Process Control Technician • Quality Control Technician • Quality Engineer • Statistical Process Control (SPC) Coordinator
Logistics and Inventory Control	Communications, Transportation, & Utilities Manager • Dispatcher • Freight, Stock, & Material Mover • Industrial Truck & Tractor Operator • Logistical Engineer • Logistician • Material Associate • Material Handler • Material Mover • Process Improvement Technician • Quality Control Technician • Traffic Manager • Traffic, Shipping, & Receiving Clerk
Health, Safety, and Environmental Assurance	Environmental Engineer • Environmental Specialist • Health & Safety Representative • Safety Coordinator • Safety Engineer • Safety Team Leader • Safety Technician

Careers in this cluster involve the marketing, promoting, buying, selling, and distribution of goods and services. Market researchers look for ways to find new customers. Advertisers try to promote products and services by making them appealing. Buyers and purchasing agents get the supplies, equipment, and products their companies need to conduct business. People in marketing information management and research work to maintain customer databases and use statistics to predict trends and buyer behavior. People in distribution and logistics handle products and materials, manage movement and storage of raw materials and finished products, and coordinate inventory.

Unlike most other career clusters, sales and service offer many opportunities for semiskilled and skilled workers. Warehouse workers and stock clerks are examples of entry-level jobs. An increasing number of positions, however, require familiarity with a computer. Those who provide services such as Web page design need technical training. Real estate agents must be licensed. College degrees are helpful in many jobs and are required for positions in promotion and management. Advancement in this career cluster is accelerated by participation in company training programs, training programs sponsored by various industry and trade associations, and conferences and seminars.

Opportunities in this cluster may change from year to year because sales are affected by changing economic conditions, legislative issues, and consumer preferences. Earnings vary widely by industry, occupation, type and level of responsibilities, and experience. Employment opportunities for retail salespeople are expected to be good. People with a college degree or computer skills will be sought for managerial positions in sales, logistics, management information systems, marketing, and e-marketing. (***E-marketing*** is computer technologies combined with marketing and sales of goods and services.)

Marketing, Sales, and Service

Pathways and Career Options

Pathway	Career Options
Management and Entrepreneurship	Entrepreneur • Owner • Small Business Owner • President • Chief Executive Officer • Principal • Partner • Proprietor • Franchisee • Independent Distributor • Administrative Support Representative
Professional Sales and Marketing	Inbound Call Manager • Channel Sales Manager • Regional Sales Manager • Client Relationship Manager • Business Development Manager • Territory Representative • Key Account Manager • National Account Manager • Account Executive • Sales Engineer • Sales Executive
Buying and Merchandising	Store Manager • Retail Marketing Coordinator • Merchandising Manager • Merchandise Buyer • Operations Manager • Visual Merchandise Manager • Sales Manager • Department Manager • Sales Associate • Stock Clerk • Receiving Clerk
Marketing Communications and Promotion	Advertising Manager • Public Relations Manager • Public Information Director • Sales Promotion Manager • Co-op Manager • Trade Show Manager • Circulation Manager • Promotions Manager • Art & Graphics Director • Creative Director • Account Executive • Account Supervisor • Sales Representative
Marketing Information Management and Research	Database Manager • Research Specialist & Manager • Brand Manager • Marketing Services Manager • Customer Satisfaction Manager • Research Project Manager • Constituent Relationship Management (CRM) Manager • Forecasting Manager • Strategic Planner • Product Planner • Planning Analyst
Distribution and Logistics	Warehouse Manager • Materials Manager • Traffic Manager • Logistics Manager • Transportation Manager • Inventory Manager • Logistics Analyst & Engineer • Distribution Coordinator • Shipping & Receiving Administrator • Shipping & Receiving Clerk
E-Marketing	Fulfillment Manager • E-Merchandising Manager • E-Commerce Director • Web Site Project Manager • Internet Project Director • Brand Manager • Forum Manager • Web Master • Web Designer • Interactive Media Specialist • Internet Sales Engineer • Site Architect • User Interface Designer

Science, Technology, Engineering & Mathematics

People working in this career cluster provide basic research as well as laboratory and testing services. Often their work results in a new discovery with the potential for improving life.

Careers range from engineers to teachers to technologists. Conducting research is often involved in this career area. Researchers generally specialize in one area of the life, physical, earth, and space sciences or technology. Technical writers are needed to interpret scientific and mathematical results.

Engineers generally specialize in distinct branches of their profession. They take scientific principles and apply them in new ways. Engineers focus on designing efficient machinery, products, systems, and processes.

Often scientific work goes in unexpected directions. It is common for researchers and engineers to work closely with experts in other disciplines. Computer-aided tools allow scientists and engineers to quickly modify experiments and run tests.

Advanced degrees are common among scientists, mathematicians, technologists, and engineers. Even entry-level jobs in this cluster, such as lab technicians, often require a four-year college degree. Many people can receive training and experience through the armed forces.

Advancing technology will compel companies to improve and update product designs and processes. The job outlook for this area is good for people with highly developed technical, science, and math skills.

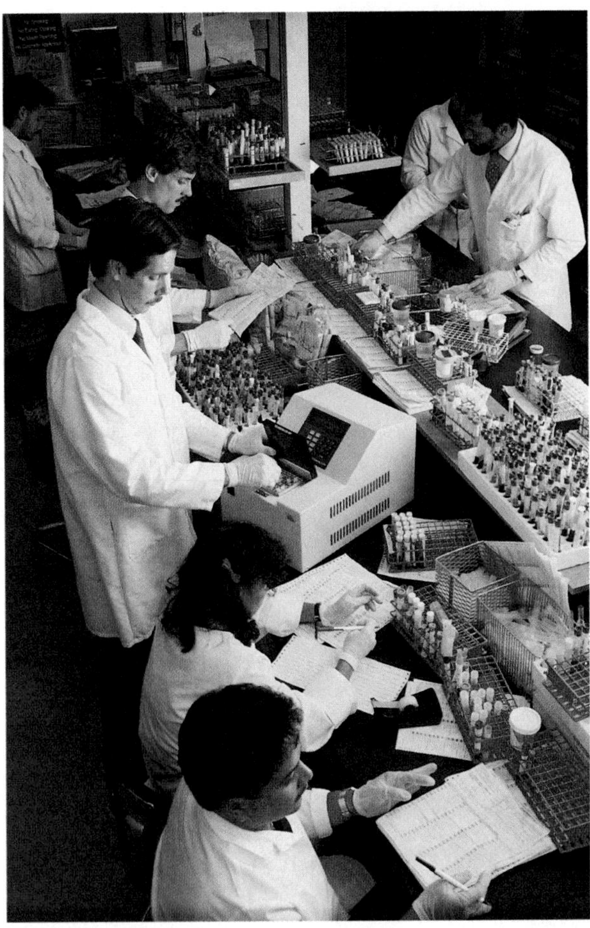

Science, Technology, Engineering, and Mathematics

Pathways and Career Options

Engineering and Technology	Aerospace Engineer • Application Engineer • Automotive Engineer • Biotechnology Engineer • Chemical Engineer • Civil Engineer • Energy Transmission Engineer • Environmental Engineer • Facilities Technician • Geothermal Engineer • Hazardous Waste Technician • Human Factors Engineer • Industrial Engineering Technician
Science and Math	Research Chemist or Technician • Science Teacher • Lab Technician • Scientific Visualization & Graphics Expert • Statistician • Analytical Chemist • Anthropologist • Applied Mathematician • Archeologist • Astronomer • Astrophysicist • Atmospheric Scientist • Biologist • Botanist • Computer-Aided Design (CAD) Operator

Transportation, Distribution & Logistics

Transportation involves moving passengers, cargo, and mail on land, at sea, and in the air. Workers are needed to design, operate, and maintain the vehicles used and the systems that track them. Planning, management, customer service, and regulation of transportation systems and their effects on safety and the environment are also a part of this cluster. Distribution and logistics are behind-the-scenes activities that make the transportation system run well. Workers in this career area make sure shipments arrive in good condition at the correct destinations on time in the most economical manner. They also arrange for adjustments for lost or damaged goods.

Transportation workers on land include school bus drivers, railroad workers, repair technicians, and shipping and receiving clerks. Workers at sea include ship captains and deckhands. Airline and helicopter flight engineers and air traffic controllers are needed for air transportation.

Jobs in the transportation industry rely on computers. Even repair technicians and shipping clerks now use computerized tools to do their jobs. One such important tool is the GPS system. A *global positioning system (GPS)* is a highly accurate satellite-based tracking system. It signals where specific cargo is in the world at any given time.

Most jobs in this career cluster require technical training. Drivers need a commercial driving permit called a *chauffeur's driver's license* or *commercial driver's license (CDL)*. Airline pilots and ship captains must have on-the-job experience and a federal license. Many career/technical schools and community colleges offer training programs in equipment maintenance and repair.

The growth in the nation's economy is expected to require significant increases in the use of air, rail, and ship transportation operations. Companies increasingly depend on technicians and engineers to guard against equipment malfunction. As tourism and business travel expands, growth is expected in this career cluster.

Transportation, Distribution, and Logistics

Pathways and Career Options

Transportation Operations	Air & Space Transportation Manager • Airplane Pilot & Copilot • Flight Attendant • Air Traffic Controller • Aircraft Cargo Handling Supervisor • Rail Dispatcher • Locomotive Engineer • Railroad Brake, Signal, & Switch Operator • Train Crew Member • Yard Worker • Water Transportation Manager • Captain • Sailor & Marine • Ship & Boat Captain • Ship Engineer
Logistics Planning and Management Services	Logistician • Logistics Manager • Logistics Engineer • Logistics Analyst • Logistics Consultant • International Logistics Manager
Warehousing and Distribution Center Operations	Warehouse Manager • Storage & Distribution Manager • Industrial & Packaging Engineer • Traffic, Shipping, & Receiving Clerk • Production, Planning, & Expediting Clerk • First-Line Supervisor & Manager • Laborer & Material Mover • Machine & Vehicle Operator • Laborer & Freight Stock Material Mover • Car, Truck, & Ship Loader • Packer & Packager
Facility and Mobile Equipment Maintenance	Facility Maintenance Manager & Engineer • Industrial Equipment Repair Technician • Industrial Electrician • Electrical & Electronic Technician • Mobile Heavy Equipment Repair Technician • Aerospace Engineering & Operations Technician • Aircraft Repair & Service Technician • Power Plant Technician • Aircraft Engine Specialist • Aircraft Body & Bonded Structure Repairer
Transportation System Infrastructure	Urban & Regional Planner • Civil Engineer • Engineering Technician • Surveying & Mapping Technician • Government Service Executive • Environmental Compliance Inspector • Air Traffic Controller • Aviation Inspector • Traffic Engineer • Traffic Technician • Motor Vehicle Inspector • Freight Inspector • Railroad Inspector • Marine Cargo Inspector • Vessel Traffic Control Specialists
Health, Safety, and Environmental Management	Health & Safety Manager • Industrial Health & Safety Engineer • Environmental Scientist & Specialist • Environmental Science & Protection Technician • Environmental Manager & Engineer • Environmental Compliance Inspector • Safety Analyst
Sales and Service	Marketing Manager • Sales Manager • Sales Representative (Transportation & Logistics Services) • Reservation, Travel & Transportation Agent or Clerk • Cargo & Freight Agent • Customer Service Manager • Customer Service Representative • Customer Order & Billing Clerk • Cashier, Counter, or Rental Clerk

Summary

Learning about different types of careers is interesting. It is also important. The career you eventually choose will be a major factor in your life. You should do all you can to prepare to make a wise choice.

Sixteen career clusters are described in this chapter. Each includes a wide variety of jobs from entry-level to professional positions.

Watch and listen to other people as they work in different careers. Think about how you would feel as a worker in various jobs. The more you do to prepare yourself, the more likely you are to make a satisfying career choice.

Answers to *Reviewing Key Concepts*

1. True
2. (Student response.)
3. 15.6
4. Agriculture
5. Architecture
6. Hospitality
7. True
8. False
9. B
10. civil service

Reviewing Key Concepts

1. True or false. Some jobs can belong in more than one cluster.
2. Give an example of how transferable skills can be used successfully in many different careers.
3. In general, employment between 2006 and 2016 is expected to increase by ______ jobs.
4. Careers in the ______, Food, and Natural Resources cluster involve working with plants, animals, and food processing.
5. People in the ______ and Construction career cluster design and build roads, bridges, and buildings.
6. An increase in leisure time and personal income means more business in the ______ and Tourism career cluster.
7. True or false. Renewed national interest in public safety and security has expanded opportunities in the Law, Public Safety, Corrections, and Security career cluster.
8. True or false. To qualify for a skilled labor position, no training beyond high school is required.
9. Which of the following people would need to pass a written exam as well as tests of strength, physical stamina, coordination, and agility?
   A. Engineer.
   B. Firefighter.
   C. Broker.
   D. Hairstylist.
10. Many public service jobs are also called ______ ______ jobs, which are government jobs obtained by taking a competitive exam.

Building Academic Skills

Writing. Make a career ladder to illustrate your personal career plans, to the extent you currently envision them. (The career ladders should contain information ranging from the current year to 10 years from now.) Write a report identifying the transferable skills that relate to the occupations you have listed.

Building Technology Skills

Use a software program to create a chart of your key interests and aptitudes for use in examining potential career paths. List your interests and aptitudes on the left side of the chart. Across the top, identify five jobs that appeal to you.

Building Career Knowledge and Skills

1. Find a news story about a change in technology. What jobs or career cluster will be affected? Discuss the story in class.
2. Visit your guidance office and obtain three pamphlets describing jobs you think you would like.
3. Interview someone in a career that interests you. Ask questions about the pros and cons of the career. Find out what a typical day at work involves. Prepare an oral report on your findings.

Building Workplace Skills

Work with a team of three or four classmates to create individual posters for six career options within a career cluster. Determine who will do which tasks. Prepare a brief fact sheet for each career that covers the basic job factors discussed in Chapter 4. Use Department of Labor references for your research. Use the computer to conduct your research and create the posters. Determine which facts to display on each poster. Identify the career field and career cluster on each. Present your posters to the class and summarize the key points about each. Attach the appropriate fact sheet to each poster to allow classmates to learn more details later, if they so desire.

Could I succeed with a business of my own?

Chapter 6 A Business of Your Own

Key Terms

entrepreneurship
retail business
franchise
service business
working capital
wholesale
sole proprietorship
partnership
corporation
stockholder

Chapter Objectives

After studying this chapter, you will be able to

- **give examples** of retail and service businesses.
- **decide** whether you are the right type of person to own your own business.
- **summarize** the financial considerations of starting a business.
- **name** and **describe** three types of business organizations.

Key Concepts

- Entrepreneurs own their own retail or service businesses.
- Being an entrepreneur has advantages and disadvantages.
- The first step to entrepreneurship is forming a business plan.
- There are three basic types of business organizations.

Your Own Business

Does the idea of being your own boss appeal to you? Have you ever thought about starting a business of your own? If so, entrepreneurship may be right for you. See 6-1. ***Entrepreneurship*** means starting and owning your own business. A person who starts a business is called an *entrepreneur.* Being an entrepreneur is not easy, but it can be very rewarding. Entrepreneurs need to have good imaginations. They look for business ideas and new and better ways to solve problems. They work to successfully sell their new products and services to others.

Entrepreneurs generally start with small businesses, but their businesses may grow to be quite large. Gas stations, restaurants, and beauty salons are examples of small businesses that are often owned by entrepreneurs. Most small businesses are involved in retail sales or providing services.

All businesses, even those owned by entrepreneurs or Internet entrepreneurs, depend on customers for their success. The customer is the reason may entrepreneurs stay in business or go out of business.

entrepreneurship
The starting and owning of a person's own business.

Resource
Reinforcing Vocabulary, Activity A, WB. Students match chapter terms with their definitions.

Discuss
If you wanted to start your own business, where would you consider getting the money? What skills does it take to start a business?

Example
Bill Gates of Microsoft is probably the best-known person who started his own business.

Discuss
Give examples of people in the community who have started their own businesses.

Retail Businesses

Entrepreneurs who own a ***retail business*** sell products, such as food, clothing, and cars, to consumers. Many retail

retail business
A business that sells products, such as clothing or cars, to consumers.

Sam's Wash 'N Shine Service

Sixteen-year-old Sam is an entrepreneur. He began last summer when a neighbor asked if he would like to make some money by washing and waxing her car. He agreed and spent a full day working on the car. When he finished, the car looked like new.

Sam's neighbor was so pleased that she told a friend. The friend called Sam to see if Sam would wash and wax his car. Sam agreed and did another excellent job. The word got around, and soon Sam had more cars to wash and wax than he had days left in his summer vacation. Sam called a friend and hired her to help with the work.

Sam now has two people working for him. This summer he and his two employees plan to work full-time washing and waxing cars. Sam has enrolled in an auto body repair program that starts at the local career/ technical school next fall. Someday Sam wants to have his own auto body repair shop.

6-1
Some people become entrepreneurs by turning part-time work experiences into full-time businesses.

franchise
The right to sell a company's products in specified areas.

Resource

Retail and Service Businesses, Activity B, WB. Students answer questions about retail and service businesses to check their understanding.

Discuss

Would you ever consider buying a franchise? Name some franchises in the community.

Activity

Find out the financial and other requirements for buying a franchise business.

service business
A business that performs tasks for its customers.

businesses are located in shopping malls and business districts.

Some entrepreneurs own one-of-a-kind shops. Others own franchises. A ***franchise*** is the right to sell a company's products in a specified area. Many of the regionally known chains of stores and restaurants are franchises.

Some entrepreneurs who own retail businesses make the products they sell. Others sell products that are made by others. For example, someone who owns a bakery may make the pastries he or she sells. However, someone who owns a clothing shop probably buys clothes from manufacturers and resells them to the public.

Service Businesses

The service industry makes up a large portion of the businesses in the United States. Entrepreneurs who own ***service businesses*** perform tasks for their customers. Their businesses may involve such services as hair styling, cleaning houses, landscaping, or dry cleaning. See 6-2.

6-2
Hairstylists provide the service of washing, cutting, and styling hair for their customers.

Your Reading

Why do entrepreneurs need to have good imaginations?

Do You Want to Be an Entrepreneur?

Entrepreneurs often start their own businesses to achieve certain goals. You may want to become an entrepreneur some day if you have some of the following goals:

- making more money
- developing a new idea
- being your own boss, setting your own working hours, and making your own decisions
- gaining recognition in the community
- doing a better job than anyone else

Not everyone is the right type of person to start a business. Your answers to the following questions may help you decide if entrepreneurship is for you:

- Do you have unlimited ambition and drive?
- Are you self motivated?
- Do you have a good knowledge of the product or service you want to provide?
- Do you make good decisions quickly?
- Can you manage time, energy, and resources wisely?
- Can you supervise people well?
- Can you motivate people to do their work well?
- Are you comfortable around strangers?
- Do you have strong people skills?

Starting a business can present some disadvantages. Knowing some of these may help you decide whether you want to become an entrepreneur. One disadvantage is the amount of work to do. Small business owners often work many more hours than people who work for others. See 6-3.

Another disadvantage is the financial risk. Opening a business can be very expensive. Business owners must pay rent,

Community Connections

Invite two or three entrepreneurs from the community to class. Prepare questions for the guests about how they started their businesses, what the special challenges are, and why they like owning their own businesses. Ask the speakers for advice for initiating any business ideas you may have.

Resource

Is Entrepreneurship for You? Activity C, WB. Students examine whether they desire a career as an entrepreneur.

Reflect

How would your family react to you being an entrepreneur? Has anyone in your family started a business? Would your friends be supportive if you decided to start your own business?

Activity

Take the "entrepreneurship test" on this page by answering the questions honestly. Based on your answers, do you think starting your own business is a possible career path for you?

6-3
Entrepreneurs often spend weekends and late weekday hours doing paperwork for their business.

Reflect

Do you feel you have the skills it takes to run your own business? How much time do you think it would take to make a business successful?

Resource

Business Advice, Activity D, WB. Students interview an entrepreneur to learn about being an independent businessperson.

Your Reading

Why is opening a business a financial risk?

wages, and taxes. They must buy equipment and supplies, too. If a business fails, the owner risks losing the entire financial investment.

For these and other reasons, entrepreneurs must deal with more stress than average workers feel. This is another disadvantage of entrepreneurship.

Planning a Business

Discuss

Take a class poll by asking, "Who would like the challenge of operating your own business?" What types of businesses would interest you?

Resource

Planning a Business, Activity E, WB. Students plan a business that could be started now.

After evaluating your goals and deciding to become an entrepreneur, your first step to entrepreneurship is forming a business plan. What type of business do you want to start? Will you provide a service or a product? Who will your customers be? How will you service them?

Decide what you are capable of doing. It is not wise to start a business doing something you have never done. Most business experts recommend working in a field for a few years before starting your own business. In that way, you will be better prepared to handle problems that arise. See 6-4.

6-4
Working in an established business for a few years can prepare a person for starting his or her own business.

Activity
Use Figure 6-4 to write a paragraph on a day in the life of an entrepreneur. Share your stories.

Activity
Make a list of service businesses in your community. What are some services for which you must travel to other communities?

People in the Small Business Administration (SBA) office in your area can help you as you make plans to start a business. They can tell you what legal steps must be followed. They can help you register with the proper state and federal agencies. They can provide detailed information on how to plan your firm, advertise, and manage operations. There are also volunteer organizations, such as SCORE (Senior Core of Retired Executives), that provide information and guidance in starting and operating a business.

The SBA can also help you get ***working capital***. This is the money needed to start and maintain a business. Government-funded small-business loans are available to entrepreneurs who qualify.

working capital
Money needed to start and maintain a business.

Community Connections

Invite a speaker from the Small Business Administration to discuss starting a business. Find out what the agency provides. Ask the speaker why so many new businesses fail. Prepare questions that would help you get started in a business of your own.

Financial Considerations

One of the biggest mistakes entrepreneurs make is not planning for business expenses. Some businesses, particularly retail businesses, require a great deal of money to open. To open a clothing shop, for example, you must first buy the clothing.

Service businesses may cost less to start. For instance, you only need yourself and a lawn mower to begin a lawn maintenance service. The following questions and comments can help would-be entrepreneurs realize what business expenses they may have. The answers to these questions will become part of your business plan.

Adapting the Lesson

Have students who are high functioning create a checklist titled "Tips for Owning a Business as a ..." Ask students to focus on their respective career choices as they list helpful tips for their desired occupational area. Have students share their lists with the class.

wholesale
A large quantity of items packaged in bulk with a per-item cost below the retail price.

Activity

Divide the class into "business teams" to discuss how to form their own business. Have them decide a title for their business, the goals, and the products to sell or services to provide. Students will need to decide where to locate their business and how it would operate.

- **Must equipment be purchased?** Equipment may include anything from a computer to many pieces of expensive equipment. See 6-5. Sometimes entrepreneurs can rent equipment instead of buying it. Another alternative might be to lease equipment with the option to buy. This type of lease allows payments to apply toward the purchase price of the item.
- **What kind of supplies are needed?** Paper, pencils, computers, gasoline, and food may be some of the supplies needed for different businesses. Sometimes a business owner can purchase supplies ***wholesale***. This is a large quantity of items packaged in bulk with a per-item cost below the retail price.
- **What kind of advertising should be done?** Many businesses cannot survive without advertising. Through advertising, customers learn about businesses and the goods or services they offer. Many small businesses advertise by using direct mail leaflets, newspapers, radio, and cable television. Advertising can be expensive, so it is important to spend advertising dollars wisely. Business owners must reach the people who are most likely to buy their products or services.

6-5
Many small restaurants are owned and operated by entrepreneurs.

Activity

Have students regroup into "business teams" to develop plans for advertising. What kinds of advertising would be most effective for their business? Where should they advertise?

- **At what price should the goods or services be sold?** Business owners must think about many things when setting prices. The cost of providing the goods or services is a chief consideration. Generally, the lower the business owners' costs are, the lower the selling prices can be. Another factor to consider is the price charged by competitors offering similar goods or services.
- **Are employees needed?** Sometimes one or two people are enough to run a small business, particularly when it is just opening. Later, a few employees may need to be hired to help with the work. Each added employee increases the company's expenses. The value of what a new employee produces must be greater than the extra labor costs.
- **What type of work space is needed?** Some people can run their businesses from an apartment or home. This is usually cheaper than renting office or store space. As a business grows, space can be rented as needed. Sometimes the type of work involved requires a particular type of space.

Your Reading

Why do most business experts recommend working in a field for a few years before starting your own business?

Types of Business Organizations

When you start a business, decide how you will organize it. The following businesses are the three basic types of organization:

- sole proprietorship
- partnership
- corporation

Enrich

Contact a real estate salesperson to determine rental costs for office and warehouse space. Share these costs with the class along with estimated costs for utilities.

Resource

Business Expenses, transparency master 6-1, TR. Students discuss the various types of expenses entrepreneurs have.

Sole Proprietorship

One person owns a ***sole proprietorship***. It is the easiest type of business to start and dissolve because no other owners are involved. The owner makes all business decisions, does most of the work, and earns all the profits.

sole proprietorship
A business owned by one person.

Being a sole proprietor also has disadvantages. Being the owner means you are responsible for all bills and expenses. If the business fails, the owner's personal property may be taken to cover any outstanding debts. Many people are good at

Reflect

Are you the type of person who could handle a business partnership? What is the key to a successful partnership?

partnership
A business owned by two or more people.

making a product or providing a service. However, not all of these people have the skills to successfully run a business.

Partnership

Two or more people own a ***partnership***. The partners combine their money and energy. They often share the work, responsibilities, debts, and profits.

An advantage of a partnership is having one or more partners with whom to share ideas and discuss problems before making decisions, 6-6. If the business fails, the losses are shared with the partners. Partnerships may have problems, too. One of the partners may feel that he or she is being treated unfairly. Partners may disagree on how to run the business. Such feelings can cause partnerships to fail.

Resource

Business Organizations, Activity F, WB. Students examine the advantages and disadvantages of the three basic types of business organizations.

Corporation

A ***corporation*** can legally act as a single person, even though many people may own it. To *incorporate* means to organize a business as a corporation. People buy a part of the company by purchasing stock. The owners of the stock are called ***stockholders***. Selling stock in a company provides a greater amount of money to the business. Stockholders risk the amount of their original stock investment if the business fails.

corporation
A business that can legally act as a single person, but may be owned by many people.

stockholder
A person who owns a share or shares of stock in a corporation.

Although they are the owners, stockholders have little responsibility for business decisions. Those decisions are left to the board of directors. The directors, elected by the stockholders, make most of the decisions for the company.

Corporations can be publicly held or privately held. *Publicly held* corporations are corporations in which the public can buy stock. They are generally very large, having thousands of stockholders. In a *privately held* corporation, the stock is held by a few individuals, usually family members or the people who started the business. These corporations can be a very small company of one or two people who have chosen to incorporate their business. This type of organization offers some different legal and tax advantages than a partnership or sole proprietorship.

Name the three basic types of business organizations.

6-6
Business partners must consult each other about important decisions.

Discuss

What would you consider before inviting a person to become a business partner? What do you think should be done when the partners cannot agree? How many people do you think can successfully operate a business partnership?

Resource

Types of Business Organizations, color transparency CT-6, TR. Students use examples of local businesses to classify the three types of business organizations.

Resource

What Is the World of Business All About? reproducible master 6-2, TR. Use the adapted worksheet to reinforce chapter concepts in students who are low functioning.

Summary

Entrepreneurs are people who own and operate their own businesses. Most entrepreneurs begin by opening small retail or service businesses. The businesses may stay small, or they may grow.

If you are thinking of starting your own business, you should look at both the pros and cons. You should also take a good look at the type of person you are. Most successful entrepreneurs share certain characteristics.

Once you decide to start a business, plan carefully. You may want to contact the nearest Small Business Administration office for help. Entrepreneurs must decide what type of organization is best for their businesses. They may choose to run their businesses as sole proprietorships, partnerships, or corporations.

Reviewing Key Concepts

1. What is the difference between retail businesses and service businesses? Give an example of each.
2. The right to sell a company's products in a specified area is called a ______.
3. List five goals entrepreneurs often have for starting their own business.
4. Name two disadvantages of entrepreneurship.
5. How can the Small Business Administration help entrepreneurs get started?
6. List five financial considerations when planning to open a business.
7. Describe an advantage and a disadvantage of organizing a business as a sole proprietorship.
8. Describe an advantage and a disadvantage of a partnership.
9. True or false. Selling stock in a company provides a greater amount of money for operating a business.
10. True or false. Although stockholders own a corporation, they have little responsibility for business decisions.

Answers to *Reviewing Key Concepts*

1. Retail businesses sell products, such as food, clothing, and cars, to consumers. Service businesses perform tasks or services for their customers. (Examples are student response.)
2. franchise
3. (Student response.)
4. (Name two:) longer work hours, high financial risk, high stress
5. by explaining the legal steps that must be followed, by helping them register with the proper state and federal agencies, by providing detailed information about planning and managing, by helping them get working capital
6. (List five:) purchasing equipment, buying supplies, deciding how to advertise, pricing the goods or services, deciding staffing questions, finding office or store space
7. (Student response.)
8. (Student response.)
9. true
10. true

Building Academic Skills

Math. Conduct research and calculate the percentage of start-up business money that should be allocated to tools, equipment, other supplies, utilities, rent, wages, and so forth. Make a chart of the costs.

Building Technology Skills

1. Conduct an Internet search using *starting a business* as the search words. Find at least three good references to write a report on the helpful hints found. Also, cite your sources.
2. Interview teenagers or young adults who have become entrepreneurs. What businesses have they started? How is technology used in their businesses? What do's and don'ts can they offer about their experience? Share your findings with the class.
3. Research the stock market online. Compile a list of do's and don'ts for stock investors. Report your findings to the class.

Building Career Knowledge and Skills

1. Conduct a brainstorming session. List types of businesses that might have a market in your community.
2. Design a bulletin board that shows various opportunities for entrepreneurs.
3. Research the success of an entrepreneur. Write a report about how the business was started and how it grew.
4. Interview three entrepreneurs in your community. Ask them what they did to get their businesses started. Find out if they think they should have done anything differently. What advice would they give to a young entrepreneur?
5. Contact the nearest Small Business Administration office. Find out what it takes to qualify for a government loan for working capital.

Building Workplace Skills

Imagine yourself as an entrepreneur and determine the type of business that might interest you. What product or service would you offer? Research who your competitors are by checking library and Internet sources. If you prefer a neighborhood business, learn about your competitors through conversations with friends and family members. What are the strong points of your competitors? What would you do to offer a better product or service than your competitors? Which of the three basic ways to organize a business would you choose? Indicate whether you feel well-suited to entrepreneurship. Give a brief oral report to the class, citing the references you used.

Part Three

Making Plans for Career Success

How do I get to know the real me? What do I need to know about myself when choosing a career?

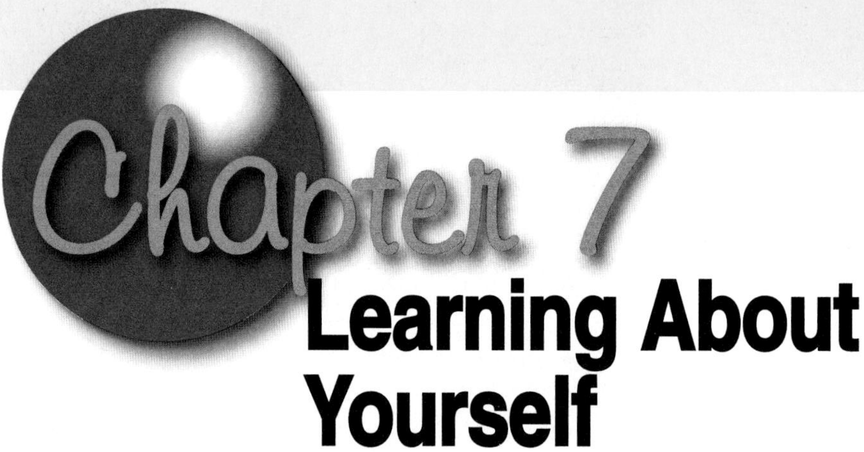

Chapter 7 Learning About Yourself

Key Terms

resource
personality
self-concept
interests
attitude
aptitudes
abilities
values

Chapter Objectives

After studying this chapter, you will be able to

- **determine** how personality, self-concept, interests, attitudes, aptitudes, abilities, and values affect career decisions.
- **analyze** how self-concept can affect job performance.
- **relate** personal values to work values.

Key Concepts

- By knowing yourself, you can choose a career that suits you.
- Your personality, self-concept, interests, attitudes, aptitudes, abilities, and values are important to choosing a career you will like.
- You can evaluate yourself by taking an honest look at yourself.

The Importance of Knowing Yourself

What career path will you follow? In Chapter 4 of this text, you learned how to explore the various career options available to you. The choices you face may seem overwhelming. Choosing a satisfying career requires knowing about careers, but that's only half the search. The other half is knowing yourself.

In this chapter, you will learn how to better understand yourself. Only then will you be able to choose a career that suits you.

Resource

Reinforcing Vocabulary, Activity A, WB. Students match the chapter terms with their definitions and give examples.

Discuss

How can parents and teachers help you become successful? Your friends are a resource; how will they help you? What resources are available in your community?

Vocabulary

What is the definition of personality? Write a description of your personality.

Examining the Real You

Most of us know ourselves better than anyone else does. However, we are not always honest with ourselves. "You are only kidding yourself" is a common saying. Being honest with yourself is important for knowing the real you and choosing a satisfying career path.

Understanding yourself begins by understanding your resources. A ***resource*** is anything a person can use to help reach his or her goals. Money is a resource you can get. Time is a resource everyone has. The desire to do well is a resource within you. (You will learn more about resources in Chapter 10, "Making a Career Plan.")

resource
Anything a person can use to help reach his or her goals.

The resources within you are important to choosing a career you will like. Your resources include your personality, self-concept, interests, attitude, aptitudes, abilities, and values. Each of these can affect the career choice you make. Understanding these characteristics about yourself may be as important to career success as your academic preparation.

Your Reading

How does knowing what your resources are help you to choose a career path?

Your Personality

Everyone has a one-of-a-kind personality. ***Personality*** is the group of traits that makes each person unique. Some of these traits may be intelligence, enthusiasm, and honesty. Others are listed in Chart 7-1.

personality
The group of traits that makes each person unique.

Have you ever described someone as having a good personality? You probably meant the person was friendly,

7-1
Identifying the personality traits that describe you can help you choose a career that will suit your personality.

Resource

Your Ideal Personality, reproducible master 7-1, TR. Students identify their personality traits and consider how they may relate to future career success or failure.

Activity

Use the personality traits listed in Figure 7-1. On a separate piece of paper, write down all of the traits from the chart that describe you. Put a plus sign by traits that are positive and a negative sign by traits that are negative. Could you add any other traits to your list?

Personality Traits		
cooperative	dependent	unreliable
agreeable	talkative	tolerant
stubborn	loyal	critical
self-disciplined	honest	jealous
friendly	dishonest	capable
shy	pleasant	lazy
intelligent	enthusiastic	moody
thoughtful	outgoing	nervous
impulsive	quiet	patient
energetic	confident	kind
ambitious	happy	religious
generous	sad	polite
greedy	funny	respectful
aggressive	witty	sarcastic
assertive	boring	helpful
independent	dependable	selfish

happy, pleasant, and kind. Such a person is usually popular. People react in a positive way to someone with a good personality. Your personality is important to your career in the following two ways:

- First, understanding your personality helps you choose a career you will like. For example, a talkative person might do well in sales. A supportive person might do well in customer service or health occupations. Your chances for happiness and success are best when your career is suited to your personality. See 7-2.
- Secondly, having a pleasant personality helps you get jobs and do them well. Employers and coworkers react positively to pleasant personalities. They enjoy working with such people. Employers avoid hiring people with poor personalities. People with poor personalities are usually a sign of future problems.

Your Reading

Name two ways in which your personality is important to your career choice.

7-2
People with friendly, supportive personalities often become teachers.

Discuss
Does a person's personality affect his or her ability to get a job? Do you think employers try to figure out your personality during a job interview?

Activity
Write a description of your self-concept.

Resource
Your Personality Traits and Self-Concept, Activity B, WB. Students analyze their personality traits and how they affect their self-concept.

Activity
In three paragraphs, summarize the following: your strengths, your weaknesses, and a plan to turn your weaknesses into strengths.

Your Self-Concept

What you know and feel about yourself is your ***self-concept***. Your self-concept affects your personality. When you have a healthy self-concept, you recognize both your strengths and weaknesses. You accept and feel good about your positive qualities. Factors that influence a healthy self-concept include a realistic and complete self-concept and high self-esteem.

self-concept
Recognition of both your strengths and weaknesses. Accepting and feeling good about yourself.

You have high self-esteem when you feel good about yourself. You respect yourself and feel that you are a worthwhile person. You recognize what you like and dislike about yourself. You know what to change about yourself to raise your self-esteem.

You develop a realistic self-concept by seeing yourself as you really are, not as you would like to be. As you think seriously about your self-concept, consider your relationships with others.

Reflect
What factors do you think influence what you feel about yourself? What would help a person develop a more positive self-concept?

Resource
What Are Your Interests? color transparency CT-7, TR. Students discuss the different interests that can be pursued within each career area.

Discuss
Do you think a person's interests affect his or her career choice?

Your self-concept becomes more complete as you learn more about yourself. New experiences and interactions with a variety of people can help you develop a more complete and healthy self-concept.

Your self-concept can affect your chances of getting and keeping a job. Self-confident employees have a positive attitude. They are able to accept new challenge s and responsibilities. People with a healthy self-concept tend to do well in the workplace so employers try to hire them.

Forming and Changing Your Self-Concept

A good self-concept doesn't just happen. What you have learned to believe about yourself forms your self-concept. If you have a good self-concept, you can strengthen it. If you have a poor self-concept, you can change it.

How do you develop a realistic self-concept?

To change your self-concept, you must first be honest with yourself. Often people who brag about what they can do have a poor self-concept. They brag because they want others to think they are able to do more than they really can.

How you feel about yourself also affects how others see you. If you feel good about yourself, others will see you in a positive way. If you know your strengths and your weaknesses, and are honest with yourself, others will respect you. Knowing your strengths does not mean always knowing the answer. It means that when you are unsure of something, you aren't afraid to ask. You aren't afraid to make a mistake. You know that you can succeed only by trying.

Your Interests

interests
The ideas, subjects, or activities a person enjoys.

Everyone has a unique set of interests. ***Interests*** are the ideas, subjects, or activities a person enjoys. Right now, you may be interested in music and singing. Some of your friends may be interested in the computer, while others enjoy sports and hobbies. No person's interests are better or worse than another's. They simply are different.

Resource
Identifying My Interests—People, Data, Objects, Activity C, WB. Students examine their preference for working with one or more interest areas.

Interests play a key role in your career. People who find their work interesting are usually successful and happy. If you like your job, work can be fun and exciting.

Which do you enjoy most? Interacting with people, working with information, or using tools? In other words, do you prefer to work with people, data (ideas), or objects (things)?

Activity

Figure 7-3 shows a career in the service sector. How many other careers can you list that fall into this category? Why is an interest in working with people important for these careers?

Reflect

Do your interests show a desire to work with your hands? Do you like to work with tools and machines? Do you enjoy indoor or outdoor activities?

People

Are you a person who prefers to be around others? Do you like to talk with people? Do you make friends easily? Are you outgoing? See 7-3.

Students who are people-oriented prefer socializing to reading a book or watching TV. These students are usually active in many school functions and clubs. They like to assist others. They volunteer to help with community functions. They like to solve conflicts between others.

Data

Are you an information seeker? Do you enjoy gathering information from books, magazines, newspapers, TV, or the Internet? Do you know all the football scores and statistics? Do you like to read and research information?

7-3
Jobs in the service sector need workers who enjoy helping people.

Activity

Match your interests to possible career opportunities.

Activity

On a blank sheet of paper, draw three columns titled *Past Interests*, *Current Interests*, and *Future Interests*. In the appropriate columns, list the ideas, subjects, or activities that you have enjoyed in the past, are presently involved in, or wish to pursue in the future. Classify each interest as people-, data-, or object-related. Where are your interests concentrated?

Enrich

Select an adult role model and describe that person's attitude. Do the same for several other successful adults in other career areas. What similarities exist in their attitudes? Do their qualities match yours?

Your Reading

How do your interests play a key role in your career choice?

People interested in data like to discover facts. Some enjoy working with figures. They are comfortable spending time alone and often prefer that to socializing with others.

Objects

Do you like to repair broken objects or assemble things? Do you enjoy working on a car, sewing a new outfit, or cooking a special meal?

People who like to work with tools and instruments enjoy making items with their hands, 7-4. They like to take objects apart and put them back together.

Sometimes they enjoy working with others on a hands-on project, but often they enjoy working alone.

Few jobs focus exclusively on people, data (ideas), or objects (things). Most jobs involve more than one interest area. Many careers, like those of a *carpenter, teacher,* and *reporter,* have primary and secondary interests. Knowing your particular interests will help you focus on a good career match.

7-4
Carpenters and other craftspeople have jobs that focus on tools and the objects that result from using them.

Resource

Aptitudes, Abilities, and Values, Activity D, WB. Students provide definitions and examples.

Discuss

What effect should a person's aptitude have on choosing a career? Should people consider pursuing a career that does not make use of their aptitudes?

The Three A's

Attitude, aptitude, and ability are the three A's. You can improve your attitude and abilities, but you have no control over your aptitude.

Your Attitude—Positive or Negative?

Your attitude is very important. ***Attitude*** is how you react to a situation. Your reaction shapes how other people view you. Is your attitude positive or negative, happy or angry?

You probably know people who are friendly, pleasant, and kind. These are signs of a positive attitude. People with this attitude are very popular. Employers tend to hire these people, and employees like to work with them.

People with a negative attitude are just the opposite. They often complain and are rarely satisfied. They think their ideas are the best and are unwilling to compromise. These people become very difficult coworkers. Employers try to avoid hiring individuals with a negative attitude.

Your Aptitudes and Abilities

Many people have natural talents and can learn to do new things quickly and easily. Natural talents and the potential to learn easily and quickly are ***aptitudes***. For instance, some people can play a song on a musical instrument after hearing it only a few times. They have an aptitude for music.

If you have an interest and an aptitude for something, you would probably be very successful in a related career. If you enjoy writing and do it well, you would probably be a good author or journalist.

Some people discover their aptitudes on their own. They may discover their aptitudes when learning something new. Sometimes others can see your aptitudes when you can't. Your friends, family, teachers, and employers can all help you discover your aptitudes. You can also discover new interests and aptitudes by doing volunteer work, having an after-school job, or by exploring a hobby.

Making a Difference

List your aptitudes and abilities. Prepare a list of volunteer jobs that could utilize your talents. Choose a job from your list and perform a volunteer service. Reflect on how this experience made you feel about yourself.

attitude
How you react to a situation.

aptitudes
The natural talents a person has or the potential to learn certain skills easily and quickly.

Community Connections

Interview at least two factory workers to find out what skills are needed for their jobs. Make a list of the abilities needed for the work. Share results of the interviews with the class.

abilities
The skills a person has developed.

Your Reading

What are the three A's and how do they determine the direction of your career?

Activity

Title a blank sheet of paper *Abilities.* Draw three columns titled *I do well, I'm working on,* and *I want to learn.* List abilities in the appropriate columns. Which column is longest?

A school counselor can give you an aptitude test. Such a test does not have right or wrong answers. It just helps you learn about your aptitudes.

Skills you must develop are your ***abilities***. Sometimes abilities are aptitudes that you have developed and improved. For instance, an aptitude for quick, coordinated movements could be developed into the ability to type quickly and accurately or play the piano well. Different jobs require different abilities, 7-5.

Sometimes people choose careers for which they have no aptitudes or abilities. This puts them at a disadvantage next to workers who have the natural ability to perform well. For example, an individual may want to be a professional singer. Without an aptitude for music or the ability to sing, that person does not have the personal resources for a successful singing career. It is very important to recognize your aptitudes and abilities when considering a career.

The average person has many aptitudes and abilities, but not all lead to a career. For example, one of your favorite pastimes may be repairing cars. This does not mean you should become a full-time automotive technician. You may simply enjoy fixing cars as a hobby. If so, your other interests would determine the direction of your career.

7-5
This assembly line task requires skillful finger manipulation. Such coordination is an aptitude, but with practice, a less coordinated person could develop the ability.

Resource

Abilities and Values Influence Careers, reproducible master 7-2, TR. Students examine several careers, identify the abilities needed for success in several jobs, and list the values such jobholders would likely possess.

Your Values

Values are all the beliefs, ideas, and objects that are important to you. People have different values. Your family, friends, and community influence your values. Your life experiences and religious beliefs also influence them. See 7-6.

Each individual has a unique set of values. Consider yours and be honest with yourself. Try to decide what is most important to you. Then try to act according to your values. If education is important to you, put your best efforts into your schoolwork. If you appreciate good health, take time to exercise and learn about nutrition.

Besides personal values, you also have *work values.* These are related to work that is important to you. Some common work values are listed in 7-7. Take time to think about what you want from your work. Some of your values may be the same personally and professionally. People who value honesty with family members and friends also believe it is important with coworkers.

Being able to identify what is important to you will help you make career choices. If you believe time with your family is important, you would not be happy traveling for long periods. If you seek creative outlets, you would not enjoy working on a factory assembly line. If you value high status in the community, you might want to become a doctor or police officer. Consider your personal values and work values when you choose a career.

values
All the beliefs, ideas, and objects that are important to an individual.

Community Connections

Interview someone you admire, based on your values. (Your values may include honesty, health, family, friends, religion, and education, among other topics.) Write a paragraph that explains why you admire the interviewed person.

Reflect

List five values that are very important to you. How did you learn or acquire them?

Values	
Honesty	Are you always sincere and truthful? Do you expect the same in return?
Health	Do you enjoy practicing good health habits? Do you eat right, exercise, and get enough rest?
Family, Friends	Do you like to be surrounded by the people you love, or do you prefer to see them only at certain times?
Religion	Do you have certain beliefs or rituals that must be maintained?
Education	Do you enjoy gaining knowledge? Do you want to earn an advanced degree?

7-6
Beliefs, ideas, or objects that are important to you are your values.

Your Reading

How do your values affect career choices?

7-7
Answering these questions honestly will help you identify some of your work values.

Resource

What Is Important to You? reproducible master 7-3, TR. Use the adapted worksheet to reinforce chapter concepts in students who are low functioning.

Community Connections

Ask three adults who know you well the following questions: What are my greatest skills? What future career can you see me pursuing? What is one thing I need to work on to be successful in that career? Write a summary of the responses.

Your Reading

What is the best way to evaluate yourself?

Work Values	
Ethics	Do you believe in being honest and fair in all business situations?
Independence	Do you like to work as part of a team or on your own?
Variety	Should your workdays be very similar or very different?
Creativity	Do you want a job that involves following directions, or would you prefer a job where no directions exist so you could figure them out for yourself?
Competition	Do you enjoy leading or following your coworkers?
Recognition	How important is it to you that others know what you do?

How to Evaluate Yourself

There are many ways to evaluate all the characteristics that make *you*. Your school may evaluate you to help you make choices and identify classes. Employers will evaluate you, too. They often use written tests to evaluate your personality, aptitudes, and abilities. They may also use interviews and supervisor reports to assist their evaluation.

You, too, can evaluate yourself. You can recognize your attitude and change it. Simple activities, such as listing your positive and negative attitudes, can be the first step. Deciding which attitude to change and how to do so are the next steps.

Abilities can be changed in the same way. Your ability to play a musical instrument can change with more practice.

Taking an honest look at yourself periodically is the best way to evaluate yourself. Asking your family, teachers, and school counselor what they see in you will also help. When weak points are discovered in you, work to correct them. Then, map your progress.

Summary

Being aware of the resources within you can help you choose a satisfying career. Begin with positive personality traits and a healthy self-concept. Employers and coworkers enjoy working with people who possess these resources.

Your interests, attitude, aptitudes, and abilities are other resources you can use to choose a satisfying career. You are likely to be happy and successful if you are interested in your work and able to do it well.

Think about what you want from your personal life and your work. Knowing what is important to you will guide you to satisfying career choices. Work toward knowing yourself better. Change any weaknesses in you that could negatively affect your career choice.

Reviewing Key Concepts

1. What are resources?
2. What resources do you have that can help you choose a satisfying career?
3. Name a career and five personality traits that would help a person succeed in it.
4. Describe how you can develop a complete and healthy self-concept.
5. Why should you think about your interests when searching for a career?
6. What are the three basic areas of career interests?
7. How can your attitude affect your career?
8. List three ways people discover their aptitudes.
9. What is the difference between aptitudes and abilities?
10. Which of the following statements is *not* true?
    A. Family, friends, community, life experiences, and religious beliefs influence values.
    B. Each individual has a unique set of values.
    C. An individual's work values tend to be very different from his or her personal values.
    D. Both personal and work values may affect career choices.

Answers to
Reviewing Key Concepts

1. Resources are all the things or qualities you have or can use to help you get what you want.
2. personality, self-concept, interests, attitudes, aptitudes, abilities, values
3. (List five. Student response.)
4. New experiences and interactions with a variety of people can help you develop a more complete and healthy self-concept.
5. People who find their work interesting are usually successful and happy.
6. people, data (ideas), objects (things)
7. Employers and workers enjoy working with people with positive attitudes and avoid those with negative attitudes.
8. (List three. Student response.) on their own; when learning something new; by having friends, family, teachers, or employers point them out; by doing volunteer work; having an after-school job; by exploring a hobby; by taking aptitude tests
9. Aptitudes are natural talents and the potential to learn easily and quickly. Abilities are skills that have been developed.
10. C

Building Academic Skills

1. **Technology Education.** Invite the technology teacher to class to discuss the skills needed to produce various products. Ask questions about specific items that interest you. You may bring actual items to class or pictures from magazines.
2. **Math.** Create a bar graph that indicates your attitudes about various topics. Vertically on the left, alphabetically list your courses, extracurricular activities, hobbies, and other favorite pursuits and interests. Across the bottom, label a scale from *1* to *10*. (A rating of *10* indicates the highest enjoyment.)

Building Technology Skills

1. Take an online personality test using one of the following Web sites: **2h.com/personality-tests.html** and **queendom.com/tests/personality**. Write a summary paragraph that describes what these tests revealed about your personality.
2. Use PowerPoint software and a digital camera to create a presentation that reflects your personality. You can show your skills and talents through pictures of yourself in sports, intramurals, community activities, hobbies, and family activities.
3. Use a word processing program to list everything you enjoy doing. Color-code the items as follows: red = *solitary pursuits;* blue = *pursuits involving one or more people;* green = *costs money;* and yellow = *involves sports.* (Note: Items may have two or three colors.)
4. Use a spreadsheet program to keep track of what you have learned about yourself. Document your abilities, skills, personality, personal priorities, attitudes, and interests.

Building Career Knowledge and Skills

1. Working in a small group, identify and list personality traits you would want your coworkers to have. Compare lists. Which personality traits did everyone in the group list?
2. Research the background of a successful person. Write a one-page report on how the person's interests, aptitudes, and abilities helped him or her succeed.
3. Consider a famous book or popular television show. List the personal and work values displayed by the main character. How do they affect the character's life and career?
4. Design a bulletin board that shows how different interests can lead to careers.
5. List your positive and negative attitudes. Identify those that you would like to change or improve. Develop a plan that will enable you to change. (Keep this activity private or, if you desire, share it with your teacher.)

Building Workplace Skills

Interview local employers to find out how they try to determine if job candidates have the personality traits, attitudes, and work values they desire in employees. Working with two or three classmates, decide how to divide the following tasks. Interview at least two local employers to obtain the information. Summarize your findings in a one-page report, and create an interesting cover page that focuses on one of the key points you learned. Use a computer to develop both the report and cover page. Present your cover page to the class, briefly describing what inspired your team to create it.

Decisions, decisions! How do I decide?

Chapter 8 Making Decisions

Chapter Objectives

After studying this chapter, you will be able to

- **distinguish** between different types of decisions.
- **list** the seven steps of the decision-making process.
- **apply** the decision-making process to real-life situations.
- **explain** the role trade-offs play in making decisions.
- **explain** the importance of personal, career, and work decisions.

Key Terms

decision
routine decision
impulse decision
decision-making process
alternatives
implement
trade-off

Key Concepts

- You make different types of decisions every day.
- The decision-making process helps you to arrive at a well thought-out decision.
- The decisions you make involve trade-offs.
- You can use the decision-making process to make personal, career, and work decisions.

Decision Making—A Daily Task

decision
A choice or a judgment.

Vocabulary
Define the word *decision*. What decisions are easy for you to make? Give an example of decisions that are hard to make.

Resource
Reinforcing Vocabulary, Activity A, WB. Students complete a crossword puzzle with the chapter's key terms.

Activity
Divide a blank piece of paper into three columns and title them: *Children's Decisions, Teenager Decisions*, and *Adult Decisions*. List all the decisions you can. Which list is longest? Which group has the hardest decisions to make?

Vocabulary
Give examples of routine decisions and impulse decisions to demonstrate understanding.

When you make a ***decision***, you make a specific choice or judgment. You arrive at a conclusion. You make up your mind. You make many decisions every day. Most of them are fairly simple. You make them quickly, without much thought. Some of your recent decisions may have involved the following choices:

- walking to work or riding
- seeing a movie or going to a dance
- studying or watching television
- eating a hamburger or tacos

Other decisions are more difficult to make. You must think about them and plan for them. The following decisions are examples of those requiring thoughtful planning:

- when to get a job
- what courses to take in school
- what to do after graduation
- what career path to follow

As you read this chapter, you will learn more about making both the easy and the difficult decisions. You will also learn ways to make the difficult decisions easier to handle.

Routine Decisions

routine decision
A decision made often.

Resource
Use the Decision-Making Process, color transparency CT-8, TR. Students discuss the steps they must follow to make good decisions.

Routine decisions are decisions you make often. Choosing what time to get up in the morning, what clothes to wear, and what to eat for breakfast are all routine decisions. You make these decisions automatically. At one time, each of these decisions took some thought and planning. By now, they are part of your daily routine. Less and less planning is needed as decisions become automatic or routine. See 8-1.

Impulse Decisions

impulse decision
A decision made quickly, without much thought.

Impulse decisions are snap decisions. They don't require much thought or planning. Instead, these decisions are made quickly. They are based on feelings or reactions to certain situations. You may grab an umbrella as you leave for school

8-1
Wearing a raincoat on a rainy day is a routine decision.

Resource

The Decision-Making Process, Activity B, WB. Students examine a thought process involved in making a decision and link each thought to a step in the decision-making process.

Note

The decision-making process can be used by anyone of any age. Point out that adults use the decision-making process when making major purchases, career decisions, and so forth.

if dark clouds are in sight. You may decide to walk home from school instead of riding if the sun is brightly shining.

At times, impulse decisions can be fun and exciting. However, important decisions in life should not be made on impulse.

Your Reading

What decisions do you make every day? Are they routine or impulse decisions?

Thoughtful Decisions and the Decision-Making Process

Many of the decisions you will face in life will be difficult decisions. They will be too unfamiliar to treat as impulse or routine decisions. They will be too important to treat as impulse decisions. You will need to take time to think about these important decisions.

The ***decision-making process*** will help you sort through your thoughts. It is a seven-step guide for making decisions based on careful thinking and planning. See 8-2.

decision-making process
A seven-step guide for making decisions based on careful thought and planning.

8-2
The decision-making process is a tool you will need to use throughout life to make good decisions.

Making a Difference

Interview someone involved in local government to find out what issues and concerns are currently being discussed regarding the community. Also, ask if there are any projects with which students in the class could help. Report your findings to class and assess the project suggestions. As a group, use the decision-making process to decide what project(s) you will choose.

alternatives
Options a person has when making a decision.

Resource
Learning from Decisions, reproducible master 8-1, TR. Students review recent decisions and the steps they used to make them.

The Decision-Making Process

1. Define the issue.
2. Make a self-inventory.
3. List all possible alternatives.
4. Forecast the outcome of each alternative.
5. Choose the best alternative.
6. Make a plan of action.
7. Evaluate the results.

1. Define the Issue

To make a thoughtful decision, you must first define the question or issue. Identify just what it is that you need to choose, judge, or conclude. Sometimes the decision can be stated as a problem that needs to be solved. You must understand a situation before you can make a good decision about it.

2. Make a Self-Inventory

When facing a question or problem, it is best to review your strengths and weaknesses. What can you do to help solve this problem? Which of your talents and abilities can you use? Knowing what you can do well helps to identify possible alternatives.

3. List Possible Alternatives

Many people fail to think through the many alternatives they have. ***Alternatives*** are choices or options. As a result, people often never consider the best possible decision. Make a list of all the alternatives you have before you make a decision.

You may not even know what all of your choices are. In that case, do some research. Read books, magazines, check out the Internet, and talk to people. Get all the information you need. Do not limit yourself. The longer your list of alternatives is, the better your chances are of making a good decision.

4. Forecast Possible Outcomes

Think through each of your alternatives. Try to predict what would happen as a result of each choice. As you play the "what if?" game, consider both the pros and cons of each choice. Think about short-term and long-term results. Consider how each choice might affect other people as well as yourself.

Enrich

Create a chart showing all the steps of the decision-making process. Use the chart to solve problems together as a class.

Activity

Steps 4-6 in the decision-making process are listed here. Talk about each step and give examples.

Note

Forecasting possible outcomes is not easy. It requires a very open-minded approach to questions and a persistent effort to try to identify all probable "what ifs."

5. Make a Decision

After carefully considering each alternative, one will probably stand out as the best choice. This is the time to make your decision. If you have followed the first five steps carefully, you will probably be happy with your decision. See 8-3.

6. Make an Action Plan

After making a decision, you need to put it into action, or ***implement*** it. When you implement a decision, you are carrying out a plan.

implement
To put a plan into action.

8-3
The color, style, and fit of each alternative should be considered when deciding what to buy.

Your Reading

With what types of decisions would you use the decision-making process?

Resource

Trade-Offs, Activity C, WB. Students recommend trade-offs to consider in order to reach specific goals.

Adapting the Lesson

Have students who are low-functioning cut apart the steps in the decision-making process and practice putting them in the correct order. Then, give students a problem that was solved using the steps. Have them cut the sentences apart and put them in order.

Activity

Have students write a list of decisions that fellow classmates must make each year. Collect the lists. Divide the class into pairs and give each group two problems to solve. Have the pairs trade papers to read how the problems have been solved.

If you aren't sure how to act on your decision, ask the *who, what, when, where, why,* and *how* questions: Who should take action? What should happen? When do you want it to happen? Where should it happen? Why should it happen? How should it happen? The answers to these basic questions will help you implement your plan.

7. Evaluate Results

Finally, look at the results of your decision. This last step is an important one. Take time to judge the outcome of your decision. Good or bad, you must accept responsibility for it. If the outcome turns out as expected and you are pleased, you made a good decision. If not, make an effort to learn from your experience. Determine why you are not pleased. Think again about your alternatives. You may need to alter your decision or make a different decision to get the results you want.

Trade-Offs

Every time you make a decision, you are making a choice. By choosing one alternative, you give up the others. When you choose to get married, you give up being single. When you choose to take a job in a big city, you limit your chances to enjoy the peacefulness of the countryside. There is a ***trade-off*** or exchange for every decision you make. One thing must be given up in return for another. See 8-4.

trade-off
The giving up of one thing for another.

You may decide to purchase an expensive sweater for the dance next month. To do this, you will need some money. Therefore, you must set up a savings plan. To reach your goal, you must consider all possible trade-offs. Getting more money to buy a new sweater may mean working more hours at a part-time job. If you don't have a job, buying a new sweater may mean not doing some of the following:

- going to a movie
- buying a new CD or DVD
- stopping for pizza after a game

Do not make important decisions too quickly. The trade-off principle is always at work. Keep this in mind when you make decisions.

Your Reading

How do trade-offs influence the decisions you make?

Bergen County Technical School

8-4

Not joining the tennis team this year may be a necessary trade-off for choosing to join the archery team and learning a new sport.

Community Connections

Attend a meeting of local government leaders to observe decision making in action. (You may be able to view the meeting on television if your community has a cable show devoted to local events.) For each of the issues discussed at the meeting, identify how closely the formal decision-making process was followed. What trade-offs were involved in the decisions? What did you learn from the experience?

Personal Decisions

Personal decisions are choices that affect you personally. They are influenced by your likes and dislikes. Your personal decisions will determine such areas as the following:

- your hairstyle
- the clothes you wear
- your friends
- the lifestyle you lead

Your personal decisions may affect your career decisions. If you choose to wear casual clothes to work in a very conservative bank, you may not fit into the conservative work culture of the bank. If you choose friends that have questionable character or a bad reputation, you may have trouble getting a good job. Personal and career decisions are often interwoven.

Your Reading

How can personal and career decisions be interwoven?

Career Decisions

Many people spend more time planning their vacations than they do planning their careers. Explore many career

Who can help you in making career decisions?

Resource

Preparing for Career Decisions, Activity D, WB. Students are asked questions to get them thinking about a future career.

Reflect

When you make decisions, do you consider how it will affect your family? your future?

paths to find one or more that you might like to pursue. Then match your traits with the requirements of the career paths you are considering. See 8-5.

Gather as much information as you can to assist you in making a wise career choice. Discuss your career plans with your teachers and guidance counselors. Talk to friends, family members, and neighbors. They can help you explore career paths. Do additional research in libraries, if necessary. Do not limit yourself.

Analyze your career alternatives so you can choose a career path that suits you. Once you decide on a career, draw up a plan of action that will help you reach your career goal. As you make career decisions, consider the following factors:

- What courses and programs will you take in high school?
- How much effort will you put into your studies?
- What skills will you develop?
- What schooling and training beyond high school are you willing to pursue?

8-5
If you can think clearly and speak persuasively, you have some of the important traits needed for becoming a lawyer.

Adapting the Lesson

Pair students who are low functioning with students who are high functioning. Direct the students to take turns interviewing each other about their career plans and goals. Have students write scripts of the interviews for a nightly news show. Let the students keep the scripts about their career plans and goals.

- What careers will you explore?
- In what extra-curricular activities will you participate to explore career options, personal skills, and talents?

Your Reading

How would you follow the steps of the decision-making process when making a work decision?

Work Decisions

In the workplace, you will face many decisions. These decisions may affect your job. They may also affect other people. See 8-6. Remember, decisions are choices. As a worker, you will make decisions every day. The following decisions are some that you might face:

- Should I complete this order or go on break?
- Should I work overtime?
- Should I tell my boss about a faulty product?
- Should I take this promotion or wait for another?

Resource

Making Decisions at Work, Activity E, WB. Students use the decision-making process by examining workplace case studies.

8-6 A customer service agent frequently must decide how to deal with impatient customers.

Activity

Talk to your parents to find out what decisions they must make at work. What is the hardest decision they have had to make at work? What advice do they have to share with you about making decisions at work?

Activity

Prepare an oral or written plan describing the specific factors considered in the decision-making process used to solve a simulated career problem.

Resource

What Will Help Me Make Decisions? reproducible master 8-2, TR. Use the adapted worksheet to reinforce chapter concepts in students who are low functioning.

Discuss

Have students talk to three people in the community who are known to "get things done" to gather firsthand advice on good decision making.

Often the answers are obvious, but sometimes they are not. In some cases, you may face two or more choices that seem good. Simply follow the seven steps of the decision-making process. See 8-7.

Remember, *making no decision* is actually a decision. It is choosing to take no action. It is deciding to accept whatever happens or whatever other people choose for you. It is giving up a chance to manage your own life.

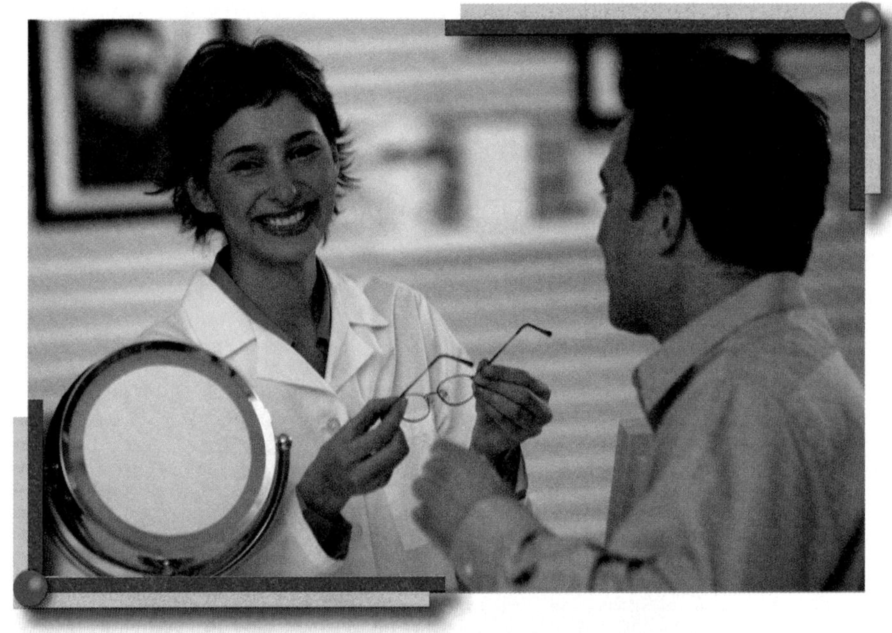

8-7
In some work situations, you will help others to make decisions.

Summary

You make many decisions every day. You make most of them quickly and easily, without much thought. Important decisions that will affect your future deserve careful consideration. The decision-making process is a seven-step guide based on careful thinking and planning. It can be applied to any situation.

All decisions involve trade-offs. Be sure to consider the trade-offs involved in your decisions. The results of personal decisions sometimes affect more than just your personal life. They may influence your career and family life.

Career questions and work issues are often difficult. Use the decision-making process to help sort through your thoughts. If you follow each step, you are likely to make good decisions and get the results you want.

Reviewing Key Concepts

1. Give five examples of routine decisions.
2. On what are impulse decisions based?
3. List and explain the seven steps of the decision-making process.
4. What should you consider when forecasting the possible outcome of each alternative to a decision?
5. When people implement plans, what are they doing?
6. Why is the last step of the decision-making process an important one?
7. What is the relationship between decisions and trade-offs?
8. Which of the following is an example of the results of personal decisions?
   A. classes offered by your school
   B. the friends you have
   C. your football team's opponents
   D. businesses that offer entry-level jobs
9. True or false. Personal decisions are not related to career decisions.
10. What happens when you do *not* make a decision?

Answers to *Reviewing Key Concepts*

1. choosing what time to get up in the morning, what to wear, what to have for breakfast, what time to leave for school, whether to walk or ride to school (Students may justify other examples.)
2. feelings or reactions to certain situations
3. Define the issue. Make a self-inventory. List possible alternatives. Forecast possible outcomes of each alternative. Decide which alternative best meets your needs. Develop a plan of action. Evaluate the results. (Explanation is student response.)
4. Consider both the pros and cons of each alternative. Think about short-term and long-term results. Consider how each choice might affect other people as well as yourself.
5. putting decision into action
6. It is important to evaluate the results of a decision because, good or bad, you must accept responsibility for it. You can also learn from it.
7. There is a trade-off or exchange for every decision you make since something must be given up in return for another.
8. B
9. false
10. You choose to take no action and thereby decide to accept whatever happens or whatever others choose for you. You give up a chance to manage your own life.

Building Academic Skills

Science. Compare the steps in the decision-making process to the scientific methods of problem solving. Examine how they are similar as well as how they are different.

Building Technology Skills

1. Search the Internet, using the key word *decision making*. Research the resources available, making a list of the most helpful Web sites. Share them with the class.
2. Videotape the decision-making process in action. Working in a group, bring in several items of clothing and pretend you are shopping. In the production, use the decision-making steps to decide which outfit to buy.

Building Career Knowledge and Skills

1. Write a short story in which the main character makes both routine and impulse decisions.
2. In class, discuss ways in which personal decisions may influence career decisions. Also discuss ways in which career decisions may influence personal decisions.
3. As a class, make a list of common work-related matters that require decision making.

Building Workplace Skills

Apply the seven steps of the decision-making process to a real or imaginary career-related example. Work with two or three classmates and determine as a team who will do which tasks. Use the example to explain the decision-making process in a class presentation. Include posters and/or handouts designed with the help of a computer.

What education and training are a part of my future?

Chapter 9

Options for Education and Training

Chapter Objectives

After studying this chapter, you will be able to

- **explain** the importance of basic skills in any career choice.
- **determine** the impact of technology on the job market.
- **list** the opportunities that are available for job training and higher education.

Key Concepts

- Training, education, and basic skills are needed no matter what your career choice is.
- Preparing for a career involves checking out training and education requirements.
- Further training and education often involves financial decisions.

Key Terms

career/technical program
apprenticeship
associate degree
bachelor's degree
graduate degree
master's degree
doctoral degree
intern

Discuss

How many of your parents have had to learn more about technology for their jobs? In what types of training or classes have you seen or heard adults participating?

Resource

Reinforcing Vocabulary, Activity A, WB. Students match terms with their definitions.

Vocabulary

Define foundation skills. What are some examples of basic skills? of thinking skills?

Enrich

Use a graphing software program to make a list of your foundation skills. Rate how well-developed your skills are by using a scale of 1 to 5, with 5 indicating the highest level of development. (A rating of 1 indicates *does not possess the skill.*) Color-code your results.

The Need for Further Training and Education

Jobs are changing quickly, primarily because of technology. Before the computer revolution, a high school diploma often was adequate preparation for the workplace—but no longer. High school graduates without special training are rarely considered for good-paying jobs today. The higher-paying jobs go to workers with more education, training, and experience.

Further training and education are very likely to be a part of your future. Prepare yourself for that step by perfecting your foundation skills *now.*

The Importance of Foundation Skills

Any career you choose will require you to have good *foundation skills.* These involve the following basic skills and thinking skills:

- *Basic skills* include reading, writing, math, speaking, and listening abilities.
- *Thinking skills* include thinking creatively, making decisions, solving problems, visualizing ideas, knowing how to learn, and reasoning.

Suppose you plan to apply for work as a cashier. You must be able to read and write in order to fill out the job application form. As a cashier, good math skills are crucial, 9-1. You would also need good reasoning skills to be able to handle customer questions and unexpected events.

The best way to perfect your foundation skills is to work on them now while in school. Study as much as possible to get ahead. Take advantage of your schooling and gain as much knowledge and experience as possible. Perfecting these skills now will pay off in the future. Employers appreciate a job applicant who has performed well in school. Employers realize that a good student is likely to be a good employee.

9-1
People who work with money must have good math skills.

Discuss
Make a list of the careers that need math skills. Where are math skills needed in daily life?

Resource
Basic Skills for the Workplace, Activity B, WB. Students identify the tasks involved and the basic skills needed for two careers that interest them.

Reflect
Do your favorite subjects have anything to do with how good you are in the subject? If you are good in math, is it one of your favorite subjects?

Resource
Types of Training, reproducible master 9-1, TR. Students discuss the types of training available to prepare for their future career.

Discuss
What is a career/technical program? Do you have these programs in your school district? What is a cooperative education program?

Preparing for a Career

As you learn about different types of jobs, check the education and training needs. What is required by the career you seek? Is prior work experience necessary? Once you know all the requirements of a career field, you can begin preparing for it.

For some careers, you can enter training programs while in high school. A career/technical school is one example.

Most of the advanced training and education programs, however, are available after high school. Some of the options are private trade schools, business schools, colleges, and universities. Most higher education programs are at least one year in length. Often, day and evening classes are available.

Career/Technical Training

Many schools throughout the country offer a ***career/technical program***. In these programs, you learn and develop the skills necessary for entry-level employment. You also learn the technical information required for earning a living. These programs are offered in the areas of health, business, agriculture, skilled trades, and marketing.

career/technical program
A program that teaches students skills necessary for entry-level employment.

Some career/technical programs are offered to students who are still in high school. See 9-2. These programs are

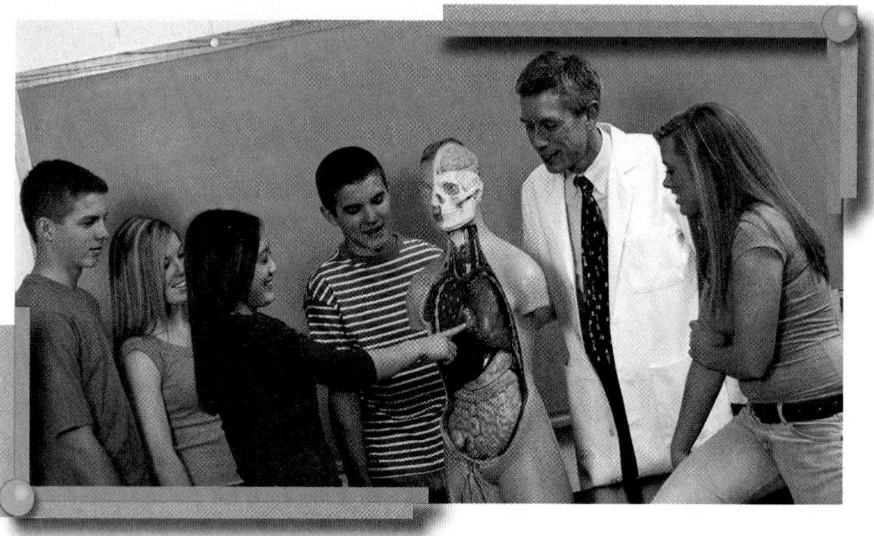

9-2
Career/technical schools teach high school students entry-level skills in areas such as health-related fields.

Making a Difference

Contact the local training schools and community colleges that offer career/technical programs to determine if they need help collating program brochures or mailings. Ask them to put your group on a list to help with future projects.

Resource

Cooperative Educations, color transparency CT-9, TR. Students discuss how the cooperative education program relates to school and the workplace.

Discuss

What is an apprenticeship? Give examples of occupations that have an apprenticeship program. What are the advantages and disadvantages of apprenticeship programs? Do you feel more career areas should offer this type of additional training?

often called *Tech-Prep programs.* Tech-Prep programs begin in the junior year and usually involve two years of additional schooling after high school. They allow students to receive college credit for work done in high school.

For information about technical or career programs in your area, talk with your teacher or guidance counselor.

Cooperative Education

Many schools offer cooperative education programs, also called co-op programs. Cooperative education is an arrangement between schools and places of employment. The program allows students to receive on-the-job training through part-time work. At the same time, students attend classes part-time.

In co-op programs, students earn money for their work. They also earn credits toward graduation. Their grades are based on their performance at work and on class assignments. Often their class assignments relate to their jobs. For instance, students may be asked to do the following projects:

- Research a career ladder for their occupation.
- Write reports about the occupations in the companies for which they worked.
- Research their career fields
- Write about their cooperative education job experiences.

Apprenticeships

Another kind of training for an occupation is an ***apprenticeship***. An apprenticeship consists of two parts. One part is on-the-job training under the direction of a skilled worker. The other part is related classroom instruction and theory.

apprenticeship
Occupational training involving learning a trade by working under the direction and guidance of a skilled worker and receiving related classroom instruction and theory.

Apprenticeship is a formal employment relationship designed to promote skill training and learning on the job. An apprenticeship usually requires three to five years of training. Training is a combination of practical and related instruction. Related instruction is usually conducted in a classroom setting, often at a community college or technical school. The related classroom instruction, or theory portion, is taught by a person knowledgeable in the technical aspects of the occupation. Related instruction may include mathematics, technical writing, and problem solving.

Apprenticeships can lead to over 900 different careers. The following are some examples:

- automotive technician
- carpenter
- chef
- jeweler
- photographer
- tailor
- upholsterer

Most apprenticeships are for adults who have already graduated from high school. However, anyone who is at least 16 years old can apply for an apprentice program. While working and learning, the apprentice is paid entry-level wages for a beginner in that field. Those who complete a registered apprenticeship receive a certificate of completion. Certificates of completion are nationally- and internationally-recognized by employers of skilled workers.

Note
Increasing numbers of women are entering jobs traditionally dominated by men, such as automobile mechanics, carpenters, heavy equipment mechanics, telephone installers, and repair workers. Women should be encouraged to follow the apprenticeship route for skilled trade occupations.

Reflect
How would you feel about having an apprenticeship program available for the career you desire? Do you feel you would be better prepared for that career by having this kind of training?

Resource
Plans for Career Training, Activity C, WB. Students examine the varied career goals they can consider, depending on the type of career training they pursue.

Company Training Programs

Some large companies offer their own training programs. These programs are designed to prepare employees to do specialized jobs. The programs may train employees to operate certain types of equipment or teach them specific skills.

Resource
Educational Choices, reproducible master 9-2, TR. Students review case studies and decide what education choices seem best for each person discussed.

Note
Emphasize that not everyone needs a bachelor's degree to get a good job.

The length and quality of training programs vary. A short-term program may involve up to one month of on-the-job training. Long-term training involves more than one year of on-the-job training or a combination of training and classroom instruction. Most people who take part in company training programs consider them very helpful, 9-3.

Community and Junior Colleges

associate degree
The award granted after completing a two-year college program.

Community colleges and junior colleges usually offer programs that are two years in length. When you complete a two-year program, you usually receive an ***associate degree***. After completing an associate degree, it is very common to transfer to a four-year college for additional studies.

Many high schools link their course offerings to community or junior college programs in the area.

Colleges and Universities

bachelor's degree
The award granted after completing a four-year college or university program.

When you complete a four-year program at a college or university, you receive a ***bachelor's degree***. Hundreds of majors are offered at thousands of colleges around the world.

9-3
Company training programs focus on teaching information or skills needed by employees to do their jobs better.

Discuss
Give an example of a career that uses an associate degree. Give an example of a career for which an employee must have a bachelor's degree. Give examples of people you know who have bachelor's degrees.

Discuss
What training methods do you see in Figure 9-3? What are some reasons for company training sessions?

A *major* is an area of study in which you specialize while in school.

Information about programs of higher education is available in many places. Start with the guidance department at your school. Guidance counselors have books that list programs and give information about schools. These books can also be found in libraries.

Write to or e-mail the schools you might want to attend and schedule appointments to visit the campuses. During your visits, talk to administrators and teachers as well as students. Doing so will help you determine if a particular school is right for you.

Jobs requiring an advanced degree require schooling beyond a bachelor's degree. An advanced degree is also called a ***graduate degree***. Basically, there are two levels of graduate degrees.

- A ***master's degree*** involves one to two years of study beyond a bachelor's degree.
- A ***doctoral degree***, the most advanced degree, often requires three years of study beyond a bachelor's degree. This degree is also called a *doctorate.*

Try not to make quick decisions when choosing a program or school. Higher education is quite expensive and time-consuming. A poor decision may result in wasted time and tuition on courses that may not be accepted by another school. Many colleges and universities have information on their Web sites about the programs they offer and their admissions requirements. Some colleges and universities offer virtual tours of the campus as well. You can use the on-line links to contact college or university representatives to ask questions. Some colleges and universities offer on-line classes to allow you to earn a degree.

Internships

An internship is another type of occupational training program. An internship may be a paid or unpaid period when a high school or college student or college graduate gains practical experience under supervision. Internships may be part-time or full-time. Typically, they are part-time during the school year. Some may be full-time in the summer. The usual internship lasts 6 to12 weeks, but can be shorter or longer.

Community Connections

Investigate the community colleges and career training schools in the area so you are aware of the educational and training options that exist locally. Check the schools' Web sites to find answers to the following questions: What degree programs are offered? What types of financial assistance are available? What percentage of each school's graduates find careers in their chosen area?

graduate degree
An advanced degree requiring education beyond a bachelor's degree.

master's degree
An advanced degree involving one to two years of study beyond a bachelor's degree.

doctoral degree
The most advanced degree, often requiring three years of study beyond a bachelor's degree; also called a doctorate.

intern
A student, seeking skills for a career, who works in a temporary position with an emphasis on on-the-job training rather than employment.

Community Connections

Look for people in the area who have completed an internship program and invite them to speak to the class about their experiences. Prepare questions in advance, including: What did they learn? What were the program requirements? What are the advantages and disadvantages of completing this type of program?

Enrich

Investigate military training programs. Find out what transferable skills can be developed through these programs.

Resource

Figuring Education and Training Costs, Activity D, WB. Students determine the costs linked to pursuing a specific educational or training program.

An ***intern*** is a student, seeking skills for a career, who works in a temporary position with an emphasis on on-the-job training rather than employment. Student internships may provide opportunities for students to gain experience in an area of their interest. They may also help students determine if they have an interest in a particular career, assist them in creating a network of contacts, or gain school credit.

Teachers, doctors, nurses, dentists, dietitians, broadcasters, and others must successfully complete an internship before they can work in their career fields. A classroom, hospital, and television newsroom are just some of the sites of an internship.

Types of Internships

Various types of internships are available in different industries or settings, depending upon the purpose of the internship. These include the following:

- *Work experience internship*: The placement can be for varying periods of time during the school year. During this period, the student is supposed to use the knowledge and skills learned in school and put it in practice. This way, the student gains work experience in his or her field of study.
- *Research internship*: In this type of internship, a student does research for or about a particular company. The student may choose a topic within the company to study. The results of the research study are compiled into a report and often are presented.
- *Diversity internship program*: This type of program provides internships for minorities. These programs are most often sponsored by community and special groups organized to offer minorities training opportunities.

Military Training

Another way to gain experience is through military training. Many military duties are the same as those done by civilian workers. The military offers a variety of jobs that are similar to those in nonmilitary communities. Many workers start their career training while serving in the military. Military service is also a way to pay for higher education. The military provides scholarship and grant programs for people who complete an active duty enlistment.

The branches of the U.S. military are the Army, Navy, Air Force, Marines, and Coast Guard. After basic training and a series of aptitude tests, a person is usually sent for further training. In the military, you can begin to prepare for such careers as *automotive technician*, *chef*, or *electronics technician*. See 9-4. All branches of the service also offer apprenticeships and college degree programs.

Your Reading

Why should you know the training and education requirements of a career as you prepare for it?

Financing Further Training

Many young people have career goals that require education beyond high school. If you choose this path, consider how to pay for the training.

Higher education can be costly. Suppose you decide to enroll in a one-year program at a trade school. If the school is far from home, you will have daily living expenses to pay in addition to tuition. You will need money to cover items such as room and board, school supplies, clothing, and health care. You should know how much money you have available for education and how much your education will cost.

The costs of attending school may be high, but you may be able to lower these costs. Perhaps you could obtain financial aid to help pay tuition. Student financial aid is intended to

Activity

List and explain all the educational and/or training alternatives that are available after high school.

Discuss

What are the resources available to help meet the cost of education beyond high school?

9-4 Military training can prepare people for careers in many technical fields.

Activity

Select a career area that interests you. Chart all the education and training options discussed in the chapter that can provide the skills needed for that career. Compare the costs of each program.

Resource

What Training Programs Are Available, reproducible master 9-3, TR. Use the adapted worksheet to reinforce chapter concepts in students who are low functioning.

Activity

Develop a chart classifying employment opportunities based on educational and training requirements of careers in your interest area.

What financial considerations are involved in planning for training and education?

help students pay educational expenses. Those expenses include tuition, fees, room and board, books, and supplies. You may be able to get financial help in the form of loans, grants, or scholarships.

Financial aid may be classified into two types—merit-based or need-based. *Merit-based financial aid* includes scholarships and grants awarded by colleges, universities, trade schools, or organizations. Merit-based scholarships and grants are typically awarded for outstanding academic achievements. Some merit scholarships can also be awarded for special talents, leadership potential, or other personal characteristics. Scholarships may also be given because of group affiliation, such as student or community organizations. Athletic scholarships are a form of merit aid that takes athletic talent into account. *Need-based financial aid* is awarded on the basis of the financial need of the student. The government offers a variety of loans and grants.

You may want to investigate tax-advantaged savings plans designed to encourage saving for future college costs. These plans include prepaid tuition plans and college savings plans. They are sponsored through states, state agencies, or educational institutions. The school you will attend probably offers various forms of financial assistance, too. Private sources provide a variety of loans and scholarships. Your guidance counselor or a financial planner will be able to tell you more about the options available to you. See 9-5 for more tips on financing further training.

Another way to save money may be living with a relative in a nearby town. Perhaps you could work part-time while going to school or attend a school nearby.

Tips for Financing Further Training

- Know how much money you have to spend and how much your education will cost. Then plan for ways to make up the difference.
- Plan ahead. Save the money you earn from part-time and summer jobs. Apply that money toward your education.
- Work while in school to help cover your costs. You may want to work part-time or participate in a work-study program. You may prefer to work full-time and be a part-time student.
- Choose an education option you can afford. Local community colleges are a fairly low-cost option. State colleges and universities are less costly than private colleges and universities. Tuition is often less if you attend school in your state than if you attend school in another state.
- Live at home or with a relative while attending school.
- Apply for government funded loans, grants, and scholarships. This is done by filling out forms describing your family's financial status. Aid is given to those who show financial need.
- Apply for any other scholarships for which you might qualify. These might be based on need, athletics, or academics. They are available from many sources.
- Consider borrowing money from a person or a financial institution.
- Join the military and arrange to have all or part of your education costs paid through military funding.
- Talk with your guidance counselor and do library research to learn more about financing further training.

9-5
Many resources are available to help meet the high costs of career training.

Reflect

How many ideas in Figure 9-5 are options for you to consider?

Summary

Education plays a key role in a person's career and future lifestyle. The basic skills of reading, writing, math, speaking, and listening, together with the thinking skills, are needed for success in any job. Further education is often necessary due to technological change. The more education a person has, the better his or her chances are of moving up the career ladder and the greater his or her job satisfaction.

Training is available in different forms to prepare people for various careers. Options include career/technical training, cooperative education programs, and apprenticeships. Other options are company training programs, colleges, universities, internships, and military training.

Financing higher education can be costly. Students can lower this cost by planning ahead and seeking financial assistance from other sources.

Answers to *Reviewing Key Concepts*

1. all jobs
2. Employers realize that a good student will probably be a good employee.
3. (Name three:) private trade schools, business schools, colleges, universities
4. (List three:) health, business, agriculture, skilled trades, marketing
5. work performance and class assignments
6. apprenticeship
7. An associate's degree usually involves completion of a two-year program; a bachelor's degree, completion of a four-year program.
8. (List three:) doctor, nurse, dentist, dietitian, teacher
9. A poor decision may result in wasted time and tuition on credits that may not transfer to other schools.
10. (List two:) automotive technician, chef, electronics technician

Reviewing Key Concepts

1. For which jobs are foundation skills needed?
2. Why do employers appreciate a job applicant who performs well in school?
3. Name three advanced training and education programs that are available after high school.
4. Name three subject areas in which career/technical programs are offered.
5. What is the basis for grades in cooperative education programs?
6. What kind of training involves learning a trade by working under the direction and guidance of a skilled worker?
7. What is the difference between an associate degree and a bachelor's degree?
8. Name three jobs that require internships.
9. Why should you think carefully before choosing a program or school of higher education?
10. Name two nonmilitary careers for which military training can help you prepare.

Building Academic Skills

Writing. Write a letter to the university of your choice, seeking information on programs in your area of interest. Check the letter for correct format and appropriate grammar and style.

Building Technology Skills

1. Conduct an online search with the words *wages* and *education.* Document what you learn regarding the link between a worker's level of education and income, especially in occupations that interest you. Summarize what you learn in a written report.
2. Investigate a local company that offers a training program to learn answers to these questions: What types of skills are taught to employees? How long is the training? What training methods are used—classroom instruction, on-site demonstrations, an Internet program, or some other method? Are skills taught that employees should have learned in high school?

Building Career Knowledge and Skills

1. Explore the Web site of a college or technical school. Make a list of the admission requirements. List the courses offered that relate to your career path. Calculate the cost of tuition, room and board, and any fees that may be required.
2. Interview someone in a career field that interests you. Find out what education and training he or she would recommend for a person entering that field today.
3. Visit the Web site of the U.S. Department of Labor, Bureau of Apprenticeship and Training. Locate a list of occupations in which a person can become an apprentice.
4. Examine the help wanted section of the newspaper for job openings. Sort the ads into the following categories: Jobs out of high school, jobs requiring a two-year college degree, jobs requiring a four-year college degree, and jobs for which there is an apprenticeship program.

Building Workplace Skills

Research a career field that interests you. Identify the education and training required and the associated time and costs involved. Talk with your guidance counselor to learn which schools offer this training. Then write to two schools for information about program specifics and costs. Obtain as much information as possible through the Internet. If your schooling would force you to live away from home, find out costs for room, board, and travel. Summarize your findings in a written report. Indicate the career researched, the education and training needed, and the schools selected. Also report all related costs, itemized per school year, and your ideas about how to pay for them. Based on what you have learned, which school would you choose? Share your decision and the facts that led to your decision in a brief written report.

How can a career plan help me reach my goals?

Chapter 10 Making a Career Plan

Key Terms

human resources
nonhuman resources
goals
career plan

Chapter Objectives

After studying this chapter, you will be able to

- **explain** the importance of setting goals.
- **identify** your resources.
- **list** your personal and professional goals.
- **develop** a career plan.

Key Concepts

- The planning and decisions you make today lay the groundwork for your future career.
- Identifying and using your resources can help you to achieve your career goals.
- Your career interests and setting personal and professional goals can help you determine which career is right for you.
- A career plan helps you to focus on your career goal and how you plan to achieve it.

The Importance of Planning

What do you want to achieve by planning your career? You might answer, "to get a job." However, would you really accept any job? If you are honest with yourself, you can name some jobs that you would not accept under any condition.

Like everyone else, you want a job that you will enjoy. A satisfying job doesn't just happen. You must plan for it. Without plans, you're likely to have no direction in life. See 10-1. People without direction often end up with whatever jobs are left, or no job at all.

The actions you take and decisions you make today lay the groundwork for your future career. This may sound overwhelming at first, but it really isn't. Choosing a career involves several steps. Planning helps you take those steps in an orderly way. Planning keeps you organized and on track.

Check Your Reading

How is planning the key to finding a satisfying career?

Reflect

How often do you plan first before taking action? What personal benefits do you get from having a plan?

Exploring Your Resources

One of the first steps of the career planning process is to identify your resources. A resource is anything a person can use to reach his or her goals. Chapter 7 discussed the resources within you, such as your interests and aptitudes. The resources within you are ***human resources.***

Some other human resources available to you are your teachers, counselors, and family members. They know you almost as well as you know yourself. Talk with them to help sort through your interests and explore career questions.

human resources
The resources that people have within themselves.

Resource

Reinforcing Vocabulary, Activity A, WB. Students complete statements with the correct chapter terms and give examples where requested.

Why Plan?	
Alice:	*"Would you please tell me which way I ought to go from here?"*
Cheshire Cat:	*"Well, that depends a good deal on where you want to go."*
Alice:	*"I don't much care where."*
Cheshire Cat:	*"Then it doesn't much matter which way you go."*

Lewis Carroll: *Alice's Adventures in Wonderland,* 1865

10-1
Without a plan, you will lose your way and wander, just as Alice in Wonderland did.

Resource

With a Career Plan, You Know the Way, transparency master 10-1, TR. Students are introduced to the importance of a career plan.

nonhuman resources
Time and all the material resources around you.

Activity
Make lists of all your human and nonhuman resources. Which resources will help you with your daily life? with career plans?

Reflect
Why is it hard for some students to choose a career? Why do you think some classmates have already made up their mind and know what career they want?

Discuss
Do you think students with more resources have more career choices?

Other resources that can help you reach your goals are nonhuman resources. ***Nonhuman resources*** include time—24 hours every day—and the material resources around you. Time to study as well as participate in a sport and rest is an example of the nonhuman resource of time. A car to travel to school and money for career training are examples of nonhuman material resources.

Other material resources that will help you prepare for your career are your school and community. Within these material resources are people—human resources—who can help you. See 10-2. Explore all that your school and community have to offer.

Your School

The library contains reference material relating to jobs and careers for you to explore. The Internet, often available through your school library or computer lab, has resources for current job openings and is also a source of job market trends.

10-2
Your teacher is a human resource, but your school is an example of a nonhuman resource.

Adapting the Lesson
Give students who are low functioning a form that lists human and nonhuman resources so they can circle those available for their career planning. Include *Teachers, Counselors, Parents, Relatives, Friends,* and *Personality Traits* as well as *Time, Money, School, Community, Books, Computer, Volunteer Work,* and *Part-Time Job.*

More importantly, your guidance counselor has a wealth of information on careers, their educational requirements, and schools for further training.

A guidance counselor will also help you choose classes related to your career interests. If college is required, he or she will help you select the courses needed for college acceptance. Extracurricular activities can provide opportunities for developing your special skills as well as learning teamwork skills.

Making a Difference

Volunteer to help work behind the scenes at a career fair. Assist the presenters with setting up materials before the presentation and with distributing information afterward.

Your Community

A wide variety of volunteer activities are available to help you experience job duties firsthand. You can learn about employers in the area and possibly tour their facilities. You can make contacts with various people who can give you inside tips about their careers. They can provide job leads for you when you search for part-time or full-time work. Also, when you need job references, community contacts are usually very willing to serve that role.

Your Reading

How can your resources help you to achieve your career goals?

Reflect

Do you have a clear idea of your likes and dislikes? Do you know if you want to work in an office or outdoors? What will help you create a list of career "likes" and "dislikes"?

Resource

Job Likes and Dislikes, Activity B, WB. Students review various work situations and identify which they like, which they don't like, and what other types of situations they want in a career.

Examining Career Interests

When you imagine yourself in a career, you try to picture what you would like about the job. Your likes and dislikes help you sort through potential careers to one that will satisfy you. Often, your likes are identical to your interests. By making a list of your likes and dislikes, you will see a pattern develop. From that pattern, you can conclude which career areas might interest you and which will not.

For example, the person whose interests are listed in Figure 10-3 might enjoy the following careers:

- child care worker
- teacher
- exercise instructor

Figure 10-3 also lists that person's dislikes. Based on those dislikes, he or she probably would not enjoy the following careers:

- data processor
- landscaper
- wallpaper hanger

10-3
A simple list of your likes and dislikes will help you discover your career interests.

Exploring Interests
Dislikes
Traveling and driving for long distances
Reading technical material
Painting or working from a ladder
Cutting grass and doing yard work
Likes
Talking and being with people
Working out and exercising
Leading a group or teaching
Planning activities for children

Resource
Career Interests and Abilities Inventory, Activity C, WB. Students list their interests and abilities and identify possible jobs for each.

Your Reading
What role do your interests play in career planning?

Your list of likes and dislikes will be much longer than the example shown here. If you have difficulty with creating a list, talk with your guidance counselor. He or she will help you determine your interests.

Sometimes interests are determined through aptitude tests. These tests are fun to take because there are no right or wrong answers. The tests match your interests with jobs that involve tasks you enjoy. Your answers to these tests paint a clearer picture of which career areas are best for you.

Discuss
Give some examples of long-term and short-term goals. What kinds of goals can you set related to this class?

Setting Career-Related Goals

Have you ever seen people at work and imagined yourself in their shoes? Have you read about someone's interesting life and thought about yourself in a similar role? Without knowing it, you were considering those careers as goals for yourself. ***Goals*** are aims or targets a person tries to reach or achieve.

goals
The aims a person tries to achieve.

Successful people plan for their success. They set goals for themselves and then work to reach them. To succeed in life, you cannot just wait for things to happen to you. You must make them happen. The best way to make things happen is to set goals.

Resource
Goals Are the Target, color transparency CT-10, TR. Students review key definitions and give examples.

Your goals may be grouped into two categories—long-term or short-term. Generally, *long-term goals* are those that will take more than six months to accomplish. *Short-term goals* can usually be accomplished within several days or weeks. See 10-4.

The goals you want to achieve for yourself are your personal goals. As a student, many of your personal goals may be tied to your education. Some will also be related to your career. Wanting to achieve good grades and to graduate on time are two examples. Other examples of personal goals include the following:

- to talk to a guidance counselor about taking an aptitude test next week (short-term)
- to practice your math skills during the summer break (short-term)
- to join the debate club next season (long-term)

As you think about a career, you should also consider your professional goals. Any target you want to reach in your career is a professional goal. The following are some examples:

- to begin a college program in accounting next month (short-term)
- to obtain an entry-level accounting job in a large company after graduating from college (long-term)
- to have a management position within three years of working for the company (long-term)

Resource

Setting and Reaching Goals, Activity D, WB. Students list various goals they want to set and develop plans for reaching them.

Reflect

How confident do you feel about your career choice? What do you think would happen if you had to make adjustments to your career plan in the next few years?

Adapting the Lesson

Have students who are low functioning make a list of goals for this course and circle the goals on which they are currently working. Be sure they break the list down into manageable steps. Share this list with their resource or support teachers.

10-4
Catching a fish is a short-term goal. Becoming a fish and game warden is a long-term goal.

Your Reading

How is setting goals related to career success?

Often, personal goals are closely related to professional goals. For example, the personal goal of living in a big city may be due to your professional goal of working downtown. Writing your goals down and reviewing them often is a good way to keep them foremost in your mind.

Activity

Determine how to state a goal and list the steps to reach it by referring to Figure 10-5. Write a similar example for a short-term goal.

Discuss

What are the questions you must consider when setting career-related goals? Will your career goals change? Will the steps taken to achieve those goals change?

Activity

Make a list of 10 questions you have about your future career and answer them completely to the best of your ability.

Taking Steps to Achieve Career Goals

After setting your goals, you must decide how you will achieve them. Be specific about what steps you will need to take to reach each goal. Writing the steps down on paper will help you think clearly. An example is shown in 10-5.

Sometimes people set goals without knowing how to achieve them. If you don't know what to do, ask your friends, family members, and teachers. Perhaps they can share experiences with you that will help you plan for your future.

When you complete a step toward reaching your goal, cross that step off your list. It will make you feel a great sense of accomplishment. When you finally reach your goal, you will have reason to celebrate.

Questions to Consider

Sometimes you may find that one of your goals is unrealistic or can't be achieved in the time period set. If this happens, you may need to change your goal or time frame. Don't be afraid to adjust your goals so you can reach them.

10-5
Writing down the steps needed to reach a goal can help you see what actions are needed.

How to Reach a Goal

The goal: to get a part-time job in a department store within the next two months *(short-term)*

Steps to reach the goal:

1. Look for a job in the classified section of the newspaper.
2. Stop at local department stores and fill out applications in their human resources departments.
3. Set up interview times.
4. Prepare for the interviews.

Note

Stress to the students that career goals give direction to their lives and help them make other decisions.

You may be better able to work toward a goal if you modify it. There are three questions to consider when setting career-related goals.

What Do You Want to Achieve?

This may be the most difficult question of all to answer. Rarely do people know their exact career goal at an early age. Even after reaching the career of their dreams, some people go on to explore other careers.

You should try to narrow your search to one career area that most interests you. However, staying alert to other interesting career areas is important in today's fast-changing workplace.

Activity

Identify the high school courses related to your specific career choices.

Activity

Think of a goal your younger brother, sister, or neighbor might have. Write down the goal and a list of the steps needed to reach the goal. Share this advice with them and report their reaction back to the class.

What Can You Realistically Achieve?

As you investigate the job that interests you, learn what is required to get the job. For example, some employers in the trades require their employees to have their own tools, 10-6. If you cannot afford to buy tools immediately, you may need to look at an alternative job until you can afford them.

Sometimes special training or education is required for a job. If your career goal is to be an engineer, you will need a bachelor's degree. You may not have the grades necessary to get into college, requiring you to take classes to prepare for higher-level study.

While the goal of *engineer* is a good one, you may have to start at a different level. For example, you might start as a draftsperson or a clerk in an engineering office. You may also look at other related careers, such as an engineering technician or a land surveyor. It may take a little longer to reach your goal, but the additional work experience will greatly benefit you.

Community Connections

Talk with some tradespeople in the community to determine if they must buy their own tools and bring them to work each day. Find out how much the required tools cost. Would this aspect of a career persuade them to decide on another type of career?

What Is a Realistic Period to Accomplish What You Want?

Your level of motivation will help to determine what you can accomplish in a given period. If you are willing to give up other activities and concentrate on reaching your goal, you may reach it in a relatively short period. The less time you spend working toward your goal, the longer it will take to achieve it.

Reflect

Is it getting easier to make decisions about a future career? Do you see how important it is to plan? What questions do you still have?

10-6
Often automotive technicians and other trades people must provide their own tools.

Your Reading

What should you do if a goal is unrealistic or can't be achieved in the time period set?

Activity
List the elements of a career plan. What are some items to include in a career plan for becoming a teacher?

career plan
A list of steps a person takes to reach his or her career goals.

Resource
Chart Your Career Plan, transparency/reproducible master 10-2, TR. Show students the career-planning form and how to fill it out. Then, students use the form to create their own career plans.

Activity
Access career information using print and online resources to complete an educational and/or training plan for a career pathway.

Developing a Career Plan

Knowing your resources and understanding what you want to do in life prepares you for the next step—creating a career plan. A ***career plan*** is a list of steps you need to take to reach your career goal. It should include the following:

- extracurricular and volunteer activities that help prepare you
- entry-level jobs that provide experience
- education and training requirements

A career plan is simply a guide. It helps to focus your attention on your career target and how you plan to achieve it. A career plan can be developed for any career. If your goals should change, your plan can be changed to reflect them.

One possible career plan is shown in 10-7. It shows the steps that one person might take to achieve the dream of becoming a landscape architect. Landscape architects design public outdoor areas so they are beautiful and useful. Notice the career plan

Career Plan for a Landscape Architect	
Junior High School	Mow neighborhood lawns for the experience and extra money. Grow ornamental plants for state fair competition. Volunteer to help at cleanup events for neighborhood parks and highways.
High School	Join the local horticulture club. Start a neighborhood lawn care service. Work at a garden and nursery center part-time. Take classes in drawing and a college preparatory program emphasizing art, botany, and mathematics.
College	Earn a bachelor's degree in landscape architecture. Work during summers at a golf course to help maintain the greens. Intern in the senior year with a respected landscape firm.
After College	Work for two or three years in the occupation. (Some states may require a license to work in this area.) Consider obtaining a master's degree.

10-7
As you accomplish each step of a career plan, your activities move you closer to your goal.

Resource
How Do I Make a Career Plan? reproducible master 10-3, TR. Use the adapted worksheet to reinforce chapter concepts in students who are low functioning.

Activity
Using Figure 10-7 as an example, write out your own career plan. Then, explain your career plan to a classmate and ask for additional ideas or suggestions. Share your career plan with your parents.

Activity
Using Figure 10-7 as an example, identify extracurricular activities, service-learning activities, and other experiences during high school that would lead to your desired career.

focuses on successive stages in life. It also lists the activities—ranging from easy to advanced—that can be handled in each.

In developing your career plan, it is important that you are true to yourself. You may know people that entered a career path because their friends were planning to do so. Sometimes people follow a certain path because they want to fulfill their parents' wishes. If you feel pressured by a similar situation, it is important that you talk about how you picture your future. Explain that you appreciate their concern for your well-being. Let them know that you hope they will support you and your career choice.

It may take several conversations before they understand your view. However, they may never agree with your decision. Still, you must address the issue with them so they know that you have thought carefully about your future.

What is the purpose of a career plan?

Summary

Choosing a career is an important step in your life. If you have a plan, you will stay focused on your goals and reach them sooner than you would without a plan.

Use the resources that are available to you. In addition to those within you, teachers, counselors, family members, your school, and your community are other resources to use. Resources help you achieve goals.

Setting goals for yourself is a way to make things happen. Goals help you achieve success. You may have both long-term and short-term goals. Some of your goals may be personal, and some may be professional.

Once you have set your career goals, decide how to achieve them in a career plan. Then work toward your goals, making changes to the plan if and when they are necessary. There is more than one way to arrive at your goal. Consider all possibilities and create a plan that best suits you.

Reviewing Key Concepts

1. Why is career planning important?
2. What two basic types of resources are available to you?
3. Why should you examine your likes and dislikes?
4. How do long-term goals differ from short-term goals?
5. Are personal goals related to professional goals?
6. What three questions should you consider when setting goals?
7. Name two reasons why a person might need to enter a career later than planned.
8. What is a career plan?
9. When should a person first write a career plan?
10. What three types of activities are included in a career plan?

Answers to *Reviewing Key Concepts*

1. (Student response.)
2. human, nonhuman
3. Examining your likes and dislikes helps you sort through potential careers to identify one that will satisfy you.
4. Long-term goals are those that will take more than six months to accomplish. Short-term goals can be accomplished within a few days or weeks.
5. yes
6. What do you want to achieve? What can you realistically achieve? What is a realistic period to accomplish what you want?
7. (Name two. Student response.)
8. a list of steps to take to reach a career goal
9. now, in the teen years
10. extracurricular and volunteer activities, entry-level jobs that provide experience, education and training requirements

Building Academic Skills

1. **History.** Review the career and early years of a famous historical figure. Document the steps that person took to acquire the career for which he or she is famous. Give an oral report on what you learned.
2. **Speaking.** Use graphic organizers to visualize your career plans. Prepare a speech in which you identify your unique career goal and list the steps necessary for achieving it. Also address the skills and knowledge you still need to learn. Form pairs to review each other's graphic organizers and provide helpful comments for improvement.

Building Technology Skills

1. Conduct an Internet search using the words *career planning*. How many sites can be found for helping you to plan careers? What types of information do the sites contain? Which of the sites provide the best help for career planning? Become acquainted with five career-planning sites and share their Web addresses and features with the class.
2. Produce a short video of resources in the school and around the community that help with career planning. Share the video with other classes or play it on your school media programs.
3. Research *aptitude test* online. Determine if the test you found can help you refine your list of career likes and dislikes. What did you learn from the online test? Can you find any other free aptitude tests online?

Building Career Knowledge and Skills

1. Research a career that interests you. Include in your report the educational requirements for this career and any special training that may be needed.
2. List all your likes and dislikes in separate columns. Using your list, identify careers that match the items in your "likes" column.
3. Make a list of personal and career goals. Share the list with at least three people. Ask them for advice in reaching the goals. Summarize their suggestions.

Building Workplace Skills

Map the steps of a career plan for the career that interests you most. Make your career plan cover at least the next 10 years. Be sure to list community and school activities plus volunteer or paid positions that will be helpful. Also identify any special training or education that is required. Give separate copies of your career plan to your teacher and guidance counselor for their review. Consider their recommendations and incorporate them in your plan if you desire. File your plan in a safe place for reference and update it when necessary.

Part Four

Acquiring Workplace Skills

How should I hunt for a job?

Chapter 11 Job Search Skills

Key Terms

want ads
open ad
closed ad
networking
private employment agency
public employment service
electronic bulletin boards
résumé
references
portfolio
job application form

Chapter Objectives

After studying this chapter, you will be able to

- **use** want ads, the Internet, and other job search tools.
- **prepare** a personalized résumé, list of references, and portfolio.
- **develop** a list of potential employers.
- **complete** a job application form.

Key Concepts

- Knowing where and how to find a job is a valuable skill.
- Résumés and portfolios tell potential employers about you.
- A job application form helps employers compare your job qualifications to those of other job candidates.

Sources of Information About Jobs

want ad
A source of information about available jobs, found in the classified section of the newspaper.

open ad
A classified ad providing specific information about a job.

closed ad
A classified ad giving general information about a job.

The job search is one of the most important steps in your career. Knowing how and where to find a job is a valuable skill. As a new worker, you should be careful in your choice of employment. The job you choose may last for many years.

Think carefully before making a career choice. Study the companies in your area. Ask questions about the kinds of jobs they offer. Think about your hobbies and other interests. These can help you select a job you might enjoy. When looking for a job, use as many sources of information as you can.

Want Ads

Want ads appear in the classified section of the newspaper. See 11-1. Want ads are also called *classified ads*. They are a common source of information about available jobs. Some want ads are easy to read and understand. Other ads are more difficult to read because they include many abbreviations. Common abbreviations are listed and explained in 11-2.

Classified ads may be either open or closed. An ***open ad*** gives you specific information about the job, pay range, and company. A ***closed ad*** gives general information about the job. The company's name and a salary figure are rarely given. Instead, you are directed to send your résumé to a post office box, a fax number, or an e-mail address.

Resource
The Job Search, color transparency CT-11, TR. Students are introduced to the various aspects of a job search.

Resource
Reinforcing Vocabulary, Activity A, WB. Students match the correct terms to various descriptions.

Enrich
Invite a school counselor to talk to the class about resources available to students trying to decide on career choices. Report sources of information to help in the decision-making process.

Networking

One of the best ways to find job openings is by ***networking***. This involves checking with family, friends, and other people you know. Ask if their employers are hiring. Perhaps they know someone who works for a company that is looking for help. Generally, people will be eager to help you in your job search.

Internet

networking
Checking with family, friends, and other people you know to find out about job openings.

Searching the Internet is a good way to find information and leads for a job. The Internet provides information on

11-1
Check the want ads in the classified section of your local newspaper for leads to jobs.

Community Connections

Invite representatives from local employers who are involved with placing want ads for their companies. Prepare questions in advance, such as the following: How much work goes into developing a job ad? Do the companies place open or closed ads? Where are the ads placed?

Discuss

Identify which ads in Figure 11-1 are open ads and which are closed ads. To which type of ad are you more likely to respond?

Activity

Count the total number of ads in a Sunday newspaper's classified ad section. Then, count how many include EOE. What percentage of ads do so?

Classified Section		
Employment Opportunities		
Help Wanted	**Help Wanted**	**Help Wanted**
ADMINISTRATIVE ASSISTANT Expd. administrative assistant for expanding law firm. Must be organized, detail-oriented, and able to work in fast-paced environment. Previous law office exp. a plus. Résumés to: Human Resources, 135 S. LaSalle, Cleveland, OH 45204	DRIVER West side electrical contractor has opening for driver. Will train. Some overnight travel required. EOE. Send résumé to MHX 288, Journal 45211	MARKETING SPECIALIST Immediate opening for marketing specialist. Assist in the coordination, implementation of current marketing and new business initiatives. Identify business objectives for new and existing programs that drive the data selection and targeting processes. Send résumé to D. Beckman, Center Bank, 8743 Manor Drive, Cleveland, OH 45216. No calls/e-mails/faxes. EOE
CABINET MAKER Position open for expd. furniture maker. Good opportunity for advancement. Call Mike 555-2376	EDITOR Editor needed to review manuscripts for textbooks. Strong writing skills req. Teaching exp. a plus. Send résumé, recent writing samples, and salary requirements to: Box MHX 592, Journal 45211	
CHEF Seeking executive chef for new retirement community. Call 555-8605 bet. 1 & 3 p.m.	MACHINIST Expd. machinist needed to repair and rebuild all plant equipment. First shift. Good salary and benefits. Apply at ACE MFG. CO. 5716 W. Roosevelt Rd. EOE	TECH SUPPORT MANAGER Computer/Info system company has opening for IT manager. Maintain network/software/phones/website. Provide direction in using IT to improve performance/service to public. Municipal exp. desirable. E-mail résumé to jwatson@homewood.oh.us. EOE

Abbreviations in Want Ads	
a/p—accounts payable	mfg.—manufacturing
a/r—accounts receivable	mgr.—manager
asst.—assistant	mgt.—management
BA—Bachelor of Arts degree	min.—minimum
bet.—between	nat'l—national
bkkg.—bookkeeping	nec.—necessary
BS—Bachelor of Science degree	neg.—negotiable
bus.—business	oppty.—opportunity
co.—company	o/t—overtime
comm.—commission	p/t—part time
dept.—department	refs—references
EOE—equal opportunity employer	req—required
eves.—evenings	sal.—salary
exc.—excellent	secy.—secretary
exp.—experience	steno—stenography
f/t—full time	temp.—temporary
g/l—general ledger	trans.—transportation
hrs.—hours	wk.—week or work
immed.—immediate	wpm—words per minute
lic.—license	yrs.—years

11-2
Knowing these abbreviations will help you understand the want ads.

jobs in your area and across the country. Sometimes the information resembles newspaper want ads. When you use such search words as *job opportunities* or *careers*, hundreds of sources of information appear.

You can use the Internet as a job search tool in two ways. First, you can search the Internet for specific jobs. Also, you can post your résumé on job-search bulletin boards. These electronic bulletin boards are sites that many employers review to find employees. When you post a résumé on the Internet, many employers know you are available for work.

A résumé posted on the Internet becomes public information. It is wise to take precautions to safeguard your privacy. Omit your home address and the address of your current employer. You can provide that information later at an interview.

Reflect
Would you feel more comfortable replying to an ad posted on the Internet or one printed in a local paper?

Resource
Want Ad Abbreviations, Activity B, WB. Students rewrite ads without abbreviations.

Activity
Divide the class into four teams. Have one person from each team go to the board and write the want ad abbreviation for each word you call out.

Resource
Using Want Ads, Activity C, WB. Students find a job ad in their career area of interest and analyze it.

Activity
Survey the class to find the career areas of interest. Write each on the top of a piece of poster board. Have students use the Internet to find a job posting that fits his or her area of interest. Print out the job postings and paste them under the appropriate headings. Have students sign the poster next to their respective job posting.

Adapting the Lesson

Have groups of two or three students who are high functioning make a video of an interview with a counselor from a public or private employment agency. Students are to learn about the agency's services and the help it provides jobseekers. Have students share the video with the class.

The Internet is becoming one of the primary sources of job leads. To access these leads, take some time and plan. You should first organize your search materials to prevent becoming overwhelmed with responses. If you do not organize your search, you could receive information on countless jobs that do not interest you. See 11-3.

When you use the Internet to search for a job, you will need an electronic résumé. This will be discussed in more detail later in the chapter. Electronic bulletin boards are also discussed later in this chapter.

Employment Agencies

private employment agency
A business that helps people find jobs for a fee.

Employment agencies fall into two categories, private and public. ***Private employment agencies*** are businesses that help people find jobs. This type of employment agency receives a fee from either the employer or the applicant. Find out the exact cost and who is responsible for paying it before using the service.

Activity

Use an online directory to list names of both public and private employment agencies found in your community.

The fees charged by private employment agencies vary. Some are only as much as the applicant earns in one week on the new job. Others are thousands of dollars.

public employment service
A government-supported group that helps people find jobs for free.

The government supports ***public employment services***. They receive no fees. They help people find jobs in government, industry, and other areas. Most large cities have

11-3
The Internet puts information about thousands of jobs at your fingertips. Focus on those that match your interests.

Note

Some private agencies specialize in certain fields and can be very helpful to job hunters wanting work in that field. However, always find out their fees before accepting any employment service.

public employment services. To find the office nearest you, look in the "State government" telephone listings under *Job Service* or *Employment*.

Community Connections

Examine the want ads posted on bulletin boards throughout the community. Also, answer the following questions: How many job openings were posted at each site and how many job-wanted ads were also posted? What types of jobs were posted there?

The Yellow Pages

The Yellow Pages give information about businesses in your community. It is another source to check when looking for a job. The Yellow Pages can help you select employers based on your areas of interest. To use the Yellow Pages, look up a topic of interest, perhaps *computers*. Then look below that heading to find companies you would like to contact.

Community Bulletin Boards

People often place ads on community bulletin boards. These can be found in places like supermarkets, bus stations, and drugstores.

You may wish to place your own ad on a bulletin board. It might read as follows:

Wanted—Lawn care position

Have experience and my own car

Call 555-7272.

electronic bulletin boards
These allow you to post and read messages on the computer, acting as a media for the exchange of information among large groups of people, combining the features of electronic mail with private computer conferencing.

Electronic Bulletin Boards

Electronic bulletin boards allow you to post and read messages on the computer. Electronic bulletin boards act as a media for the exchange of information among large groups of people. They combine the features of electronic mail with private computer conferencing. They have a much larger audience than a community bulletin board, so there is more of an opportunity to interact and get a job.

Your Reading

Which sources of information would you find most useful in finding job opportunities?

résumé
A formal written summary of a person's education, work experience, and other qualifications for a job.

Resource
Finding Job Leads, reproducible master 11-1, TR. Students hunt for potential employers for jobseekers in various occupations.

Resource
Résumé Guide, transparency master 11-2, TR. Students review the various facts to include in résumés.

Example
Share with students the types of records and paperwork needed to begin working on a résumé and suggest they begin keeping these files.

Resource
Sample Résumé, transparency master 11-3, TR. Students examine a sample résumé and identify ways to improve it.

Résumés

Suppose you decide what kind of work you want and where to apply for a job. The next step is to get your paperwork in order. Many employers will ask for a copy of your résumé. A ***résumé*** describes your education, work experience, and other qualifications for work.

Preparing Your Résumé

The employer's first impression of you may come from your résumé. It is important that the information be correct and neatly organized. Your full résumé should include the following information:

- name
- address
- telephone number
- cell phone number
- e-mail address
- career or employment objective
- current employer and date of employment
- past employers and dates of employment
- schools attended, dates of attendance, and general course of study
- school and community activities and honors
- special skills
- the availability of references

Each section of the résumé is important. You should keep your résumé current, updating it as changes take place. See the example in 11-4.

A good résumé contains facts about you that are important to the job you seek. Employers will want to know about your experience and education. Facts about activities and honors are important, too.

People with little or no work experience will want to report extracurricular activities that demonstrate the qualities employers seek. These qualities include dedication, a willingness to cooperate, and originality.

JOYCE Q. HENRY
123 South River Street
Trenton, NJ 07864
609-555-1141
jqhenry@serviceprovider.com

JOB OBJECTIVE
Administrative Assistant

EMPLOYMENT

- J.B. Van Buran, Inc.
  13 West End Avenue
  Trenton, NJ 07864

  Retail Sales Person: Assisted customers with selections; straightened merchandise displays; processed returns; closed sales.
  2/20XX to present

- Speedy Serve
  Route #31
  Trenton, NJ 07864

  Counter help: Filled customer orders; cleared tables; cashier.
  11/20XX to 2/20XX

EDUCATION

- Trenton High School
  Chambers Street
  Trenton, NJ 07864
  Graduated June, 20XX

  Major: Office Occupations Program, including classes in Microsoft Office, WordPerfect, Microsoft Word, Excel, and PowerPoint

- Junior High School No. 2
  Olden Avenue
  Trenton, NJ 07864
  Graduated June 20XX

  Major: General Studies

ACTIVITIES AND HONORS

- President, Business Professionals of America local chapter—20XX
- Vice President, Student Council—20XX
- Member, Ski Club
- Member, Mercer County 4-H Club

SPECIAL SKILLS

- Keyboarding, word processing, microcomputer applications, and business mathematics
- Fluent in Spanish

REFERENCES

- Available on request

11-4
A good résumé is neat and accurate.

Discuss
The résumé in Figure 11-4 is a beginning résumé. What information did this individual include? Was the information complete? Was the résumé neat and easy to read?

Enrich
Invite a career counselor to share helpful hints on writing a résumé and cover letter. If he or she provides services to the community, ask for a report of these.

Resource
Résumé Worksheet, Activity D, WB. Students fill in the worksheet with the information they would include in a résumé.

People with special skills may list them in a separate category. This helps to highlight a person's specialty area.

Personal information, on the other hand, should never be included. Examples of such information involve your age, height, or marital status. Including this information may

Enrich

Interview your parents to find out if they ever wrote a résumé for their job search. Find out what information they included on the résumé and what advice they have for you in writing one.

Note

Résumés that are e-mailed or posted to an Internet database must not contain special formatting codes.

Example

Save a copy of your existing résumé document as *text* (or an ASCII file). Some computers have built-in applications to do this, such as Notepad for Windows or TextEdit for Macintosh.

convince some employers that you have no further job-related facts to provide.

Many students are finding they need two basic forms of résumé. The traditional form, which is a printed résumé, is used to take to interviews and to respond to newspaper ads. An electronic form is used for job searches on the Internet.

Carefully proofread your résumé. Also, have someone review your résumé before you send it to potential employers.

Electronic Résumés Sent to Potential Employers

Your job search on the Internet requires a different style of a résumé. A résumé used on the Internet is often referred to as an *electronic résumé*. Electronic résumés use simplified formats because they must be readable to many different types of computers. The simplified format is often called *plain text* or *text only*. The example in 11-5 is a plain text résumé.

Create an electronic version by opening your existing résumé document and saving a copy as a text file. (Be sure to preserve the original formatted document.) Saving a copy as a text file eliminates formatting codes. Electronic résumés do not contain columns, indents, bullets, or bold or italic type.

Although electronic résumés eliminate normal formatting, some attention-getting devices can be used. Notice the use of capitalization and asterisks in the example. See 11-5. When you develop your electronic résumé, follow certain rules.

- Use an 11-point, standard-width typeface, not a condensed style.
- Make sure no line exceeds 65 characters. Hit the *enter* key to force additional words to another line.
- Include every keyword that applies to you. For example, do not simply write *word processing*. Instead, list all the specific computer programs you use.
- Never e-mail an attachment. Send your cover letter and résumé as text in a single message.
- Close your e-mail message stating that a fully formatted hard copy is available.
- Before e-mailing your résumé to an employer, send it to yourself and a friend. Check whether the document appears as planned upon arrival. If not, adjust the format before using it.

Sample Electronic Résumé

JOYCE Q. HENRY
123 South River Street
Trenton, NJ 07864
609-555-1141
jqhenry@serviceprovider.com

JOB OBJECTIVE
Administrative Assistant

EMPLOYMENT
*Retail Sales Person: Assisted customers with selections; straightened merchandise displays; processed returns; closed sales. 2/20XX—present
J.B. Van Buran, Inc.
13 West End Avenue, Trenton, NJ 07864

*Counter Help: Filled customer orders; cleared tables; cashier. 11/20XX to 2/20XX
Speedy Serve
Route #31, Trenton, NJ 07864

EDUCATION
*Trenton High School, graduated June, 20XX
Chambers Street, Trenton, NJ 07864
*Major: Office Occupations Program, including classes in Microsoft Office, WordPerfect, Microsoft Word, Excel, and PowerPoint

*Junior High School No.2, graduated June, 20XX
Olden Avenue, Trenton, NJ 07864
Major: General Studies

ACTIVITIES AND HONORS
President, Business Professionals of America local chapter—20XX
Vice President, Student Council—20XX
Member, Ski Club
Member, Mercer County 4-H Club

SPECIAL SKILLS
*Keyboarding, word processing, microcomputer applications, and business mathematics
*Fluent in Spanish

REFERENCES
Available on request

11-5
An electronic résumé that you would send to potential employers is simple and plain so that it is readable on different types of computers.

Use this electronic résumé when responding to a specific want ad or employer. If posting a résumé to a site that anyone can view, you will want to remove your private information, as discussed next.

Discuss
What are the advantages of posting your résumé on a job search Web site? Why do you think a specific format is used to submit résumés?

Reflect
How do you feel about the facts you have for a résumé? Do you think you have enough activities and volunteer work to add to your résumé?

Enrich
Invite an employer that gets electronic résumés to come to class. Have them talk about the types of résumés they receive. Ask about the information they seek in résumés.

Enrich

Some employers use computer software to search résumés posted on the Internet. Adding keywords related to your career field will increase the chances that your résumé is noticed. Find three want ads for similar jobs in your area of interest. Circle the words and phrases that an employer might use in a keyword search. How could you add these words to your résumé?

Electronic Résumés for Internet Posting

The type of résumé shown in 11-6 should be used in general Internet job searches. It follows the same format as the electronic résumé to be sent to potential employers with one important difference. All personal information is deleted. Internet postings of personal information are sources for identity theft and Internet stalking.

Your posted résumé should only report your specific qualifications and work experience. This form may be posted on Internet job boards or Internet employment sources.

11-6
An electronic résumé for Internet posting should never include personal information, such as your name and address.

Sample Electronic Résumé for Internet Posting

JOB OBJECTIVE
Administrative Assistant

EMPLOYMENT
*Retail Sales Person: Assisted customers with selections; straightened merchandise displays; processed returns; closed sales. 2/20XX—present

*Counter Help: Filled customer orders; cleared tables; cashier. 11/20XX to 2/20XX

EDUCATION
*High School Graduate

*Major: Office Occupations Program, including classes in Microsoft Office, WordPerfect, Microsoft Word, Excel, and PowerPoint

ACTIVITIES AND HONORS
President, Business Professionals of America local chapter—20XX
Vice President, Student Council—20XX
Member, Ski Club
Member, Mercer County 4-H Club

SPECIAL SKILLS
*Keyboarding, word processing, microcomputer applications, and business mathematics

*Fluent in Spanish

REFERENCES
Available on request

REPLY TO: jqhenry@serviceprovider.com

Making a Difference

Check the local sections of the paper or any special newspaper sections that list volunteers needed. Check for any listings that might be from a community agency with which you could obtain work experience. You should include this work experience on your résumé.

References

References are people who know you. They can comment on your character and skills.

When choosing references, choose people who will be respected by an employer. Such individuals include coaches, teachers, school counselors, and former employers. Choose three or four people who know you well enough to answer an employer's questions.

Do not choose a friend, parent, or relative as a reference. Employers will probably not trust the accuracy of any reports they give about you.

Always ask for permission to use a reference's name. Get permission before you give that person's name to an employer.

In your résumé, say that references are available on request. When an employer asks for your references, provide a separate page that lists them. Do not guess about names, job titles, addresses, or phone numbers. Be sure everything is accurate.

references
People who can speak about a person's character and skills.

Your Reading

What is the difference between a traditional résumé and an electronic résumé for Internet posting?

Portfolios

A ***portfolio*** is a selection of materials that you can use to document your accomplishments over a period of time. To compile a portfolio, select your best work samples to showcase your achievements. These items might provide evidence of career skills as well as academic skills. Some of the items you might include in your portfolio are

- career summary and goals
- work samples (including photographs and videos) that show mastery of specific skills
- writing samples that show communication skills
- a résumé
- letters of recommendation that document specific career-related skills
- certificates of completion
- awards and recognition
- memberships in student organizations and participation in conferences and workshops

portfolio
A selection of materials that you can use to document your accomplishments over a period of time.

Activity

List types of people who are regarded as good references. Write down what you would say to ask an individual to be a reference for you. Make a list of people whom you would like to use right now as references.

Note

A professional three-ring binder can be used to compile a portfolio. Use tabs and dividers to separate material and include a table of contents.

Your Reading

What should your portfolio reflect about you?

- transcripts, licenses, and certifications
- volunteer work/community service
- reference list

Portfolios encourage self-reflection and self-assessment. The portfolio is assembled to reflect your skills and talents. It can be a useful tool in interviews with potential employers. Once you have developed your portfolio, keep it current and up-to-date. In addition to the traditional portfolio, you might consider developing an online Web-based portfolio.

Job Application Forms

job application form
A form completed by a job applicant to provide an employer with information about the applicant's background.

Many companies will ask you to complete their ***job application form***. This form asks for information about you and your background. It helps employers compare your job qualifications to those of other job candidates.

Whenever you apply for a job, be prepared to complete a job application form. If you have your résumé and a pen, you will be ready. You will have the information you need.

Read through the entire application before starting it. If you do not understand a question on the application, ask someone to explain it to you.

It is important that you complete the application neatly and correctly. Look at the two applications in 11-7. If you were the employer, which person would you hire?

First, read the directions carefully. Take your time and print the information requested. Always use a pen, never a pencil.

Respond to all questions. If a question does not apply to you, draw a short line in the space. If you leave a space empty, the employer may think you overlooked it or forgot to answer it. Sign your full name. Do not use a nickname.

If you can take the unanswered application form home with you, do so. This allows you to be very careful as you complete it. Remember to return the application promptly. Usually, though, you will be asked to complete the application form in the company's office either online or on paper.

Remember, the employer forms an opinion of you from your application. If the form is sloppy, incomplete, or inaccurate, you may never get a chance to be interviewed.

Activity
Have students write career summaries and goals to include in their portfolios. Refer students to Chapter 10 if they need help writing career goals.

Resource
Applying for Employment, Activity E, WB. Students complete a job application form.

Activity
Have students write five questions addressing what information is asked on job application forms and how to complete them. Read the questions and have the class answer them as a review.

Incorrect

APPLICATION FOR EMPLOYMENT

PERSONAL INFORMATION Date 6-18-XX Social Security Number 634-12-8308

Name Davis Charlie G.
Last First Middle

Present Address 318 W Lincoln Chicago IL
Street City State

Permanent Address 318 W Lincoln Chicago IL
Street City State

Phone No. (312) 555-8830

If related to anyone in our employ, state name and department Fred Davis Referred by

EMPLOYMENT DESIRED

Position Any Date you can start Anytime Salary $8.00/hr

Are you employed now? If so, may we inquire of your present employer?

Ever applied to this company before? Where When

EDUCATION Name and Location of School Years Completed Subjects Studied

Grammar School Robert Frost 6

Crestwood Jr. High 2

High School Central High 3

College

Trade, Business or Correspondence School

Subject of special study or rese...

Correct

APPLICATION FOR EMPLOYMENT

PERSONAL INFORMATION Date 6-15-XX Social Security Number 239-46-8956

Name CARVER CHARMAYNE MARIE
Last First Middle

Present Address 2636 N. CLYBORNE ST. CHICAGO IL
Street City State

Permanent Address 2636 N. CLYBORNE ST. CHICAGO IL
Street City State

Phone No. (312) 555-2653

If related to anyone in our employ, state name and department — Referred by GELISIA BROWN

EMPLOYMENT DESIRED

Position CHECKOUT CLERK Date you can start 6-20-XX Salary $8.30/HOUR

Are you employed now? NO If so, may we inquire of your present employer?

Ever applied to this company before? NO Where When

EDUCATION Name and Location of School Years Completed Subjects Studied

Grammar School WHITTIER ELEMENTARY 8 GENERAL
WEST OAKTON, OR

High School P.S. 387 2 TYPING, MATH,
CHICAGO, IL BUSINESS

College

Trade, Business or Correspondence School

Subject of special study or research work ACCOUNTING, OFFICE MACHINES

11-7
Compare these two job applications. Always complete job application forms neatly and correctly.

Discuss

What impression does the top application form pictured in Figure 11-7 convey? Do you think this individual would do the job well? What impressions do you have from reading the second application?

Note

Emphasize that the neatness and completeness of the job application form affects your chances of getting a job interview.

Resource

Learning About Job Ads, reproducible master 11-4, TR. Use the adapted worksheet to reinforce chapter concepts in students who are low functioning.

Gaps in Employment

Don't be overly concerned or worried about applications that ask for information about gaps in employment or your reason for leaving your last job. Be clear, but do not go into too much detail. Some reasons for leaving a job or gaps in employment include the following:

- laid off
- health issue
- family issues

Your Reading

Why is it important that you complete the job application form neatly and correctly?

- travel issues—shorter commute
- promotional offer
- educational pursuits
- financial opportunity

Explaining the gap in your employment is only a small part of getting a new job, 11-8. It is important to stress that you are a strong candidate for the job. Stress your strong points, interest in the job, and skills. Also, point out any volunteerism and community involvement as well as education and training.

11-8
Stress that you are a strong candidate for a job by pointing out your skills and training.

Summary

During a job search, use as many sources of information as you can. Talk to friends and others. Read the want ads. Check the Internet. Visit employment agencies. Use the Yellow Pages. Read ads and place your own ad on community and electronic bulletin boards. The more you learn about job openings, the more likely you are to get a job.

Prepare a résumé that will help you make a good impression. Present your qualifications in an honest, positive way. Be sure to include all the information that employers need.

Be ready to complete job application forms during your job search. Use a pen to fill them out neatly and correctly. Respond to all questions.

Reviewing Key Concepts

1. Where should you look to find want ads?
2. Which kind of want ad gives you more information?
3. Who pays a fee to a private employment agency?
4. How can you use the Yellow Pages in your job search?
5. What information should a full résumé include?
6. What information should *not* be included in a résumé?
7. Why should you *not* choose a friend, parent, or relative as a reference?
8. True or false. You should ask your references for permission to use their names before giving them to an employer.
9. Why should you have your résumé handy when you complete a job application form?
10. If a question on a job application form does *not* apply to you, what should you do?

Answers to *Reviewing Key Concepts*

1. Want ads can be found in the classified section of a newspaper and on the Internet.
2. open
3. either the employer or the applicant
4. Look up a topic of interest. Then, look below that heading to find companies to contact.
5. applicant's name; address; telephone number; cell phone number, e-mail address, career or employment objective, current employer and date of employment; past employers and dates of employment; schools attended, dates of attendance, and general course of study; school and community activities and honors; special skills; and the availability of references
6. personal information such as age, height, and marital status
7. because employers feel these people may not give accurate reports about the applicant
8. true
9. to provide most of the information needed to complete a job application form
10. Draw a short line in the space.

Building Academic Skills

Writing. Evaluate a résumé pulled from an Internet site for important criteria such as grammar, spelling, punctuation, and vocabulary. What recommendations would you make for improving the résumé?

Building Technology Skills

1. Create a database of job categories and online job search sites. Work together in teams according to career areas of interest. Each team should share their results with the class.
2. Use the Internet to check jobs posted online and find five that interest you. Conduct your search using the following Web sites: **monster.com**, **worktree.com**, **employment911.com**, **jobonline.com**, and **careerbuilder.com**.
3. Create a file of résumé examples from the Internet to bring to class. Discuss the information included on the résumés and discuss the formats used to create them.
4. Go to the **jobbankusa.com** Web site and use the "résumé builder" feature. You will be prompted to fill in basic information. Create your résumé on this site for practice and compare your finished résumé to the samples given in the text. What are the similarities and differences between them?
5. Write and send an e-mail message to a friend that was absent from class today. Share with the friend five facts about completing a job application form. Also, inform the friend about the importance of starting a file to document activities and accomplishments that will be useful in future résumés.

Building Career Knowledge and Skills

1. Find a want ad with many abbreviations. Rewrite the ad without abbreviations. Discuss your ad in class.
2. Contact the nearest public employment service. Request pamphlets that explain the services offered.
3. Look in the Yellow Pages for places where you would like to work. List your top five employers.
4. Following the guidelines presented in this chapter, prepare three résumés for your preferred career area and a list of references.
5. Obtain a job application form from a local company. Complete it neatly and correctly.

Building Workplace Skills

Search three sites on the Internet for a job that interests you. One site to explore is **http://www.ajb.org**. (The U.S. Department of Labor provides the information on this site.) Search two other sites for the same job title and note which sites you searched. Print copies of all three. Compare and contrast the information you obtained and report your findings to the class.

How do I get hired?

Chapter 12
Interviewing Skills

Chapter Objectives

After studying this chapter, you will be able to

- **prepare** for an interview.
- **describe** what to do and what not to do during an interview.
- **write** a follow-up letter.
- **evaluate** a job offer.

Key Terms

interview
interviewer
interviewee
telephone interview
personal interview
job description
follow-up letter

Key Concepts

- Since the interview is the most important step in getting a job, preparation is important.
- Knowing what to do and what not to do can help you during an interview.
- After an interview, take time to review what happened and write a follow-up letter.

The Most Important Step

interview
A talk between an employer and a job applicant.

interviewer
An employer who talks with a job applicant.

interviewee
A job applicant who receives an interview.

The interview is the most important step in a job search. It can be a good experience if you are prepared and know just what to expect.

An ***interview*** is a talk between an employer and a job applicant. It may also be described as a talk between an interviewer and an interviewee. An ***interviewer*** is an employer. In large companies, an interviewer may be a company representative who has the task of talking with job applicants. An ***interviewee*** is a person who is looking for a job. This person is also called a *job applicant*.

In large companies, the personnel department or the human resources department often conducts interviews. The function of these departments (or departments with similar names) is to find the right people to fill available positions.

An interview is usually your first chance to meet with an employer. Remember that first impressions are lasting impressions. Your interview is your chance to make a good first impression. See 12-1.

Your Reading

Why are first impressions important?

Preparing for Interviews

Do a little homework to learn about the company. You should know what the company does. Does it make a product

12-1
An interview gives a job applicant and an employer a chance to find out how well they might work together.

Note
Emphasize to students that the interview will be a critical test of their ability to "sell" their skills and present themselves as valuable employees.

Resource
Reinforcing Vocabulary, Activity A, WB. Students match chapter terms with their definitions.

or provide a service? Does the company participate in civic and community projects? Have you ever used the company's product or service? Were you satisfied? Be prepared to say something positive about the company. For example, if you have used its product and are pleased with it, say so. Above all else, be truthful in whatever you say. Never tell a lie to get a job.

Be prepared to tell the interviewer about the skills you have that fit the job. If you are applying for a clerical job, for instance, be prepared to talk about your clerical skills. Think about the questions that the interviewer might ask and be ready to answer them. You may be asked, "Do you have keyboarding skills?" Your answer may be, "Yes, I prepare all my school reports and papers on the computer. I also prepare a monthly newsletter for a student organization."

Think of ways to let the interviewer know you are dependable. Be prepared to talk about anything you have done in the past that would help you do the company's job well. Assemble a portfolio of examples that show the quality of your work. Also, prepare a list of questions that you can ask the potential employer to make sure that this is a good job fit for you.

In what ways can you prepare for an interview?

Resource

Landing a Job Begins with a Successful Interview, color transparency CT-12, TR. Students are introduced to successful interviewing techniques.

Resource

Company Research, Activity B, WB. Students research a company and answer questions about it.

Telephone Interviews

A want ad may list only a telephone number. To answer the ad, a job applicant must have a ***telephone interview***. This is a telephone conversation between a company representative and a job applicant. It often includes a variety of interview questions. Usually, if a telephone interview goes well, the job applicant is invited for a personal interview.

telephone interview
A telephone conversation between a company representative and a job applicant.

Before you call for a telephone interview, take paper and pen and go to a quiet room to make the call. Introduce yourself and state your purpose. For instance, say, "My name is John Wright, and I'm calling about your ad in Sunday's paper for a stock clerk. I'm a senior at Franklin High School. I can work in the afternoons and on weekends. I am very interested in working as a stock clerk and coming in for an interview."

When you make the call, be ready to accept a specific day and time for a personal interview. Try to fit your schedule around the interviewer's time schedule. If you can't meet when the interviewer suggests, explain why and offer another

Discuss

Explain what happens in a telephone interview. What should you be prepared to discuss during a telephone interview?

Activity

Role-play telephone interviews. Bring in two telephones for props. Interviews can involve a teacher and a student or two students. Critique the conversations.

time and date. Whenever possible, change your schedule to be available for the interview.

Your Reading

How can you prepare for a telephone interview?

Personal Interviews

A ***personal interview*** is a face-to-face meeting between an employer and a job applicant. It usually determines whether or not the applicant will be hired.

personal interview
A face-to-face meeting between an employer and a job applicant.

Plan what you will wear to the personal interview. Clothes should be clean and pressed. You must look clean, neat, and dressed for the type of job you seek. You should wear businesslike attire for an office or sales position, 12-2. You may wear casual clothes when applying for a construction job. Observe how the employees holding the job you seek are dressed and arrive looking as good or better.

Your shoes should be spotless and polished. Your hair should be styled in a businesslike fashion and neatly combed. Male job applicants should be clean-shaven or have a neatly

12-2
A business suit or something similar is appropriate attire when interviewing for an office position.

Discuss
What can you do to make a good impression during an interview? What do you take along to an interview?

trimmed beard. Female applicants should have a proper style and size handbag, if they carry one at all. Also, they should not wear heavy makeup or lots of jewelry.

Be Well Groomed

Proper grooming tells people you care about yourself. A major part of the interview is convincing the interviewer that you're the best person for the job. Take a bath or shower, and brush your teeth before going to an interview. Use a deodorant. Your hair, hands, and fingernails must be clean. Be aware that many employers do not appreciate tattoos or body piercings. Don't let poor grooming spoil your chances for getting a job.

Be on Time

Get a good night's sleep. You want to be at your best for the interview. If you are tired, it will show. Go to bed early if you have an early morning interview.

Too many times a job is lost because an applicant is late for the interview. Arriving late gives the interviewer the impression that you believe tardiness is okay. If you must depend on public transportation, make sure you know the schedule and the time needed for the full trip. If you are not sure how to get to the interview, practice the drive or commute. Plan to be at least 15 minutes early.

You should know the exact time and place of your interview. If you aren't sure of the time or place, telephone the company. Identify yourself and say, "I am checking about my interview. Where should I arrive and at what time?" See 12-3.

Plan to Go Alone

The interview is an important step in getting a job. It is something you must do by yourself. Do not bring a friend to the interview. An interviewer expects you to speak for yourself. If your friend wants a job in the same place, it would be better to let your friend set up a separate appointment. An applicant who rushes through the interview for a waiting friend is not likely to get the job.

Community Connections

Invite workers who conduct interviews as one of their job responsibilities with area employers. Have the guests discuss how they expect the interviewee to dress. What questions do they often ask during an interview? What are helpful hints in preparing for an interview? Prepare questions in advance.

Reflect

Are you well groomed? How do you think an employer would evaluate your grooming skills?

Example

Help students recognize what to wear on an interview by preparing index cards with the following pictures of males and/or females in: a suit, sports shirts and dress pants, a skirt and blouse, a dress, and dress pants with a shirt and tie. For an interview as a cashier, business manager, construction worker, or teacher, show the student the appropriate card of what to wear.

Discuss

When should you take a friend along to a job interview? (*never*)

12-3
Always arrive at the interviewer's office at least five minutes before your appointment.

Your Reading

Why should you be well-groomed and on time for an interview?

Interviewing Tips

The interview is a chance for the company to meet you. It is also a chance for you to learn more about the company. The interviewer is looking for a person who can do the job and work well with other people.

It is natural to be nervous during an interview. However, remember that the interviewer is interested in you. Try to relax and answer all questions honestly. You know your good points, and an experienced interviewer will learn them through your answers. Be yourself!

Reflect

How would you handle nervousness during an interview? What can you do that would make you feel more comfortable during an interview? What do you feel your interview strengths are?

Reflect

How will you feel sitting in a chair waiting for your first interview? Will you feel confident? Will you feel nervous? How will you prepare for that first interview?

Enrich

Create a poster titled "Interview Do's and Don'ts." Use pictures from magazines to help illustrate your tips. Display the posters in school.

What to Do

Knowing what to do will make the interview easier. By knowing how to behave, you will also appear confident. For each interview, prepare to do the following:

- Introduce yourself when you meet the interviewer and smile. Use the interviewer's name. For example, say, "Good morning, Mr. Brown. I'm Josephine Smith."
- Shake hands firmly if the interviewer extends a hand.
- Remain standing until you are offered a seat. Be relaxed, but sit straight in your chair. If you slouch in your chair, you probably won't get the job.

- Look at the interviewer. Don't stare at the wall, ceiling, or your lap. Making eye contact with the interviewer says you are interested in the job and the company.
- Keep a pleasant smile. Speak clearly and loud enough to be heard. Let the interviewer lead the discussion.
- Talk freely. Give more than just yes and no answers. The interviewer needs information to make a hiring decision.
- "Sell" yourself. Tell the interviewer why you are interested in the company and the job. Talk about your skills and why you're the best person for the job.
- Be prepared to discuss how you can be a quality team member.
- Be polite and have a positive attitude.
- Thank the interviewer for the opportunity to be interviewed.

What Not to Do

Serious job applicants display their best behavior during an interview. Consequently, they avoid the following behaviors:

- being late
- chewing gum or smoking
- laying things on the interviewer's desk
- acting like a know-it-all
- saying, "I'll take anything," instead of describing the kind of work you want to do
- trying to run the interview by talking too much
- discussing personal problems
- trying to read the material on the interviewer's desk
- answering questions with lies
- tapping pen, playing with a ring on your finger, etc.
- arguing or displaying a negative attitude. See 12-4.

Adapting the Lesson

Have students who are low functioning list types of jobs on index cards that they might have during or right after high school. Have each student draw a card. His or her job is to prepare for the interview by finding magazine pictures of someone dressed appropriately for that job.

Discuss

What do facial expressions say about an interviewee? Why do you think it is important to smile during an interview? What facial expressions would indicate the person is nervous? What facial expressions indicate the person isn't interested in the job?

Example

Take each of the items listed in the section "what not to do" and give possible consequences if the advice is not followed. For example, what is the possible result of being late for an interview? (*not getting the job because the company may think the applicant would come to work late, too*)

Discuss

What type of papers do you think the interviewer will have on the desk during your interview? Should you try to read the papers? (*no*)

Interview Pluses	Interview Minuses
Some people are hired because they	Some people are not hired because they
• show interest in the company and the job	• show no interest in the company or the job
• know about the company's products or services	• know nothing about the company
• have clearly defined career goals	• have no career goals
• are qualified for the job	• do not have the knowledge and skills needed for the job
• express themselves clearly	• communicate poorly
• have a record of past accomplishments	• appear lazy
• are mature	• are immature
• get along well with others	• do not get along with others
• have a positive attitude toward life and work	• have a bad attitude
• are well groomed	• are poorly groomed
• have good manners	• have poor manners

12-4 Showing positive characteristics can help you get a job. Showing negative characteristics will encourage the interviewer to end the interview early.

Discuss

As you refer to Figure 12-4, discuss the possible reasons that some people are not hired. Talk about ways to overcome some of these points and improve the chances of getting a job.

Activity

Role-play appropriate interviewing techniques for an employment opportunity in your interest area.

Resource

Interview Questions, Activity C, WB. Students answer questions they might be asked by an interviewer.

Resource

Interview Practices, Activity D, WB. Students assess whether interviews were handled well or poorly, and then identify what should have happened in the poorly handled cases.

Resource

Interview Success Factors, reproducible master 12-1, TR. Students assess various factors to determine which would increase or decrease chances for interview success.

Questions to Answer

An interviewer gets to know you by asking questions. You will be rated on your answers throughout the interview. Simple *yes* and *no* answers are not enough. Answer the questions completely. How you answer the questions will help to determine whether or not you get the job. Be ready to answer questions such as the following:

- What are your goals for the future?
- What were your favorite and least favorite subjects in school?
- In what school activities have you participated?
- What teaming skills do you have?
- How well can you follow instructions?
- How dependable are you?

- What is your major weakness?
- What salary do you expect?
- Why do you think you might like this particular job?
- What kind of work do you eventually hope to do?

Before you are asked any questions, the interviewer may say, "Tell me about yourself." This is your opportunity to summarize your best points and emphasize their benefits to the job. Be ready with a brief reply, just in case.

Activity

Put each of the "questions to answer" on individual large sheets of paper, measuring approximately 24 by 36 inches. Divide the class into teams of four or five people. Give each team two questions and have them write a group response to answer the question. When time is called, have the teams switch papers and critique the answers, listing advice below the answer. Return papers to original teams.

Questions to Ask

The interviewer is not the only one who can ask questions. You can and should ask questions. Your questions should show the interviewer that you are interested in the job.

At some point during the interview, you should learn more about the job than the brief description provided in the want ad. You will have an opportunity to read (or hear the interviewer read) the job description. A ***job description*** details the tasks you are to perform. Make sure you completely understand what the job involves.

job description
An explanation of tasks to be performed by an employee in a specified position.

Don't ask questions unrelated to the job. Do not ask questions just to have something to say. Above all, do not ask questions that the interviewer has already answered in earlier remarks. Some common questions asked by job applicants follow:

- What are the work hours?
- Is much overtime work involved?
- Is there room for promotion?
- What are the job duties?
- Is travel expected?
- What fringe benefits are available?
- Is there flexibility to meet family needs?
- What skills does an employee need to succeed in this job?
- What training does the company provide for employees?

Activity

Select an "open ad" from the classified section of the newspaper. Predict what types of questions you might be asked in the interview. Make a list of these questions. Think about the skills the employer will probably question.

Enrich

Have students select a local company at which they would like to work. Have them prepare a list of five questions to ask during an interview.

Your Reading

How can you appear confident during a job interview?

Adapting the Lesson

Have students who are low functioning practice giving answers to common interview questions with parent volunteers or learning support aides. Tape-record their answers, then play them back individually with the respective student present as you critique the answers.

Your questions tell the interviewer that you are interested in the job. Your questions and the interviewer's answers also help you decide if you would like to have the job. See 12-5.

After the Interview

Soon after the interview, find a quiet place and go over the interview in your mind. Write down any questions that gave you trouble. This will help you develop answers if you are asked back for a second interview. It will also help you in future interviews with other companies.

Evaluate the Job and the Company

You should be ready to accept or reject a job if it is offered to you. In order to make your decision, honestly evaluate the job and the company. The time to do this is right after the interview while the experience is still fresh in your mind.

Bristol-Myers Squibb Co.

12-5
By asking relevant questions, you show the interviewer that you are interested in the job.

Note

Figure 12-5 indicates the use of good eye contact during an interview. Point out that everyone is nervous, but if you avoid looking at the interviewer, he or she may think you lack self-confidence or are not trustworthy.

Reflect

What will help you decide if the job for which you had an interview is right for you? What qualities are you looking for in the job and the company?

How can you tell if a job is right for you? Make a list of what is important to you. Consider your needs, career goals, and the type of work you want to do. Compare your list with the opportunities and working conditions offered by the employer. Do you like the results?

Your list of positive and negative feelings will help you make a final decision about the job. The following sample questions provide a starting point in making your own list:

- Does the job seem right for you?
- Are the working conditions comfortable?
- Did the other employees seem to like their work?
- Does the company offer training and opportunities for promotions?
- Is the salary right?
- Are fringe benefits available?
- Would this job help you in your long-range career goals?
- Do you have enough information to make a decision?

Making a Difference

Publish a brochure on what you have learned about searching for a job, filling out a job application, and interviewing. (Ask your teacher to verify its accuracy.) Then give your brochures to a school counselor, local shelter, welfare-to-work program, or some other group of local job seekers.

Write a Follow-Up Letter

Shortly after the interview, write a follow-up letter to the interviewer. A ***follow-up letter*** is a brief letter written in business form to thank the interviewer for the interview, 12-6. Your letter should include the following points:

- a short thank-you for the interview
- a statement about your interest in the job
- additional points that are important but were not discussed, such as job qualifications you possess and failed to mention
- a request to hear from the interviewer about the company's decision

follow-up letter
A brief letter written in business form to thank an interviewer for an interview.

If your evaluation has made you realize that you would be interested in the job, state this in your letter. Likewise, if your evaluation has shown that you would not be interested, you should politely indicate this. A follow-up telephone call can be made within a week if you have not heard from the interviewer.

Your Reading

What steps should you take following an interview?

12-6
Sending a follow-up letter shows an interviewer that you are a serious job candidate.

32 Ashland Avenue
Mountain View, CA 94043
August 10, 20XX

Ms. Judith Samson
Goodright Company
117 Main Street
Oceanport, CA 94702

Dear Ms. Samson:

Thank you for taking the time yesterday to talk with me about the maintenance job with the Goodright Company. The information you provided was very helpful.

During my interview, we discussed my experience as a carpenter's assistant with the Build-It Construction Company last summer. However, I didn't have an opportunity to mention the plumbing and electrical systems classes I've taken at the Mountain County Area Career/Technical School. I believe the skills I've learned in these classes have prepared me for many of the maintenance tasks I would perform if employed by your company.

I am excited about the possibility of joining your company, and, if offered the job, I will do my best to be a good employee. I look forward to hearing from you soon.

Sincerely,

Michael King
Michael King

Activity

On the board, write good salary, comfortable working conditions, convenient location, chance for promotions, pleasant supervisor, and good company benefits. Have students prioritize their own list and summarize what is most important to them in a few sentences.

Discuss

What impression does the letter in Figure 12-6 create for the person receiving it? What information about yourself can you include in the letter?

Discuss

What are reasons for writing a follow-up letter? How should the letter look and what do you say in the letter?

Resource

Sample Follow-Up Letter, transparency master 12-2, TR. Students review a well-written follow-up letter.

Resource

Follow-Up in Writing, Activity E, WB. Students critique a poorly written follow-up letter and write an improved version.

Adapting the Lesson

Have students who are low functioning copy a sample follow-up letter you prepared. Leave blanks for them to insert personal information.

Receiving a Job Offer

You may be offered a job at the end of an interview. However, do not be upset if the interviewer does not offer you a job on the spot. The interviewer may want to check your references or interview others. You should be told when to expect an answer. If you have not been told, ask if you can call back in a few days.

When a job offer is extended to you, you may wish to ask for a day to think about it. The interviewer will usually say yes, but you might be asked to decide right away. The job may need to be filled quickly, and more interviews may be necessary.

If you still want the job, tell the interviewer you are pleased to accept. Be sure to ask *where*, *when*, and *to whom* you should report for work. Some companies offer specific orientations for new employees. Find out if you will need to bring anything with you to the work site. If you will need a uniform, ask where and when you should get it.

Find out everything you need to know to feel ready for your first day at work. If the interviewer doesn't know the answers to your questions, he or she will refer you to your supervisor. Your supervisor will be able to tell you anything else about the job you may need to know.

If you decide not to accept a job offer, thank the interviewer. Be polite. The interviewer will appreciate your honesty. Remember, the company wants employees who want to work there. They know that every job does not appeal to everyone, and they are looking for the right person for the job.

Resource

Get Ready for the Job Interview, reproducible master 12-3, TR. Use the adapted worksheet to reinforce chapter concepts in students who are low functioning.

Adapting the Lesson

Have students who are low functioning imagine being interviewed, but not getting the job. Have them make a list of steps to follow in this situation, such as: *Learn from each interview. Think about what happened. Practice interview questions. Find out if my skills need improvement. Talk to a teacher for more help. Do not give up.*

Steps to Follow if You Do Not Get the Job

It is rare to get a job after only one interview. You may have many interviews before you get a job. This is true for most people throughout their careers.

You should learn from each interview, especially if you do not get the job. Think about what happened during the interview. Did you have a specific job in mind when you applied? Did you know about the company's business? Were you able to give good answers to all the interview questions? Would you have hired yourself for the job?

If the answer to any of these questions is no, then perhaps you already know why you did not get the job. Sometimes the reasons are not so simple. You could politely ask the interviewer to tell you why you did not get the job. This information might help you on your next interview.

Another question you might ask yourself is, "Do my skills need improvement?" If so, you may want to talk to your career counselor or teacher. Most importantly, do not get discouraged. Recognize the importance of being a good match for the existing work environment. The job needs to be a good match for you as well as for the company. There is a job out there for you. You just need more time to find it.

Summary

The interview is the most important step in getting a job. Prepare for it carefully. Find out about the company's products or services. Be ready to discuss your skills and other job qualifications.

Pay attention to your clothes and grooming when you get ready for an interview. Plan to go alone and arrive on time. Be positive, pleasant, polite, and truthful. Be prepared not only to answer questions, but also to ask them.

After the interview, take time to review what happened. Be sure to write a follow-up letter. If you are offered a job, evaluate the offer carefully. Think about your needs and career goals before you make a decision. If you are not offered a job, do not be discouraged. Learn from the experience and try again.

Answers to *Reviewing Key Concepts*

1. The job applicant is invited for a personal interview.
2. true
3. Being late gives the interviewer the impression that you think tardiness is okay. You would probably not be hired.
4. false
5. (Student response.)
6. (Student response.)
7. (Student response.)
8. where, when, and to whom you should report for work; if you will need to bring anything with you to the work site; anything else you need to know to be ready for your first day at work
9. a short thank-you for the interview, statement about your interest in the job, additional important qualifications you possess that were not discussed, a request to hear from the interviewer about the company's decision
10. (Student response.)

Reviewing Key Concepts

1. What usually happens if a telephone interview goes well?
2. True or false. A personal interview usually determines whether or not the job applicant will be hired.
3. Why is it important to be on time for an interview?
4. True or false. If both you and your friend are applying for jobs at the same place, you should go to your interviews together.
5. List five behaviors you should demonstrate during an interview.
6. List five behaviors you should *not* demonstrate during an interview.
7. List five questions to ask an interviewer during an interview.
8. If you accept a job offer, what should you be sure to ask?
9. What four points should be included in a follow-up letter?
10. List five questions you would ask yourself when evaluating a job offer.

Building Academic Skills

1. **Speaking.** Practice public speaking and telephone skills. Invite an English teacher from your school to play the role of an employer. Pretend to place a phone call to this teacher to inquire about a part-time job advertised in the newspaper. When you finish the telephone inquiry, ask the English teacher to critique the phone call.
2. **Speaking.** Prepare for a successful job interview by practicing answers to interview questions, such as "tell me about yourself" and "what do you have to offer my company?" Present a one-to-two minute presentation on selected interview questions.

Building Technology Skills

1. Search the Internet for a company at which you would consider working. One Web site to check is hoovers.com. Document the information you learned about the company. Based on your findings, what new questions might you ask at an interview?
2. Select three "interview pluses," as indicated in 12-4. Illustrate them with a drawing or a piece of clipart from a software program. Use the artwork to create one-page flyers that tell why the "interview pluses" are important and how to accomplish them.
3. Conduct an online search for examples of follow-up letters from the cover-letter library of this Web site: careerlab.com. Also, check careercity.com and monster.com. Ask students to document some ideas proposed by these Web sites for writing follow-up letters.

Building Career Knowledge and Skills

1. Write an article for your school newspaper about what you should and should *not* do during interviews.
2. Discuss how you would prepare for interviews for the following jobs: gas station manager, file clerk, and salesperson in a fashion shop. (Remember that dressing appropriately is part of the preparation process.)
3. Work with a partner to practice telephone interviews.
4. Prepare a list of questions that an interviewer might ask you in an interview.
5. Write a sample follow-up letter to an interviewer.

Building Workplace Skills

Practice your job interview skills with two classmates. Plan to have each person of the team interviewed jointly by the other two in separate sessions. Together, schedule appointment times for the three interviews. Also, determine what type of position you seek as "interviewee" and let the interviewers know. (This will allow the two interviewers enough time to develop questions related to the position you seek.) Carefully record the job positions your teammates plan to seek so you can develop appropriate questions when you interview them. Interviewers should take notes during the interviews and, after each interview, discuss the strengths and weaknesses observed. As a team, share your reactions to the interview process with the class.

How can I excel as an employee?

Chapter 13
Good Employee Skills

Key Terms

work ethic
penalty
reprimand
termination
punctual
dependable
privilege
mentor

Chapter Objectives

After studying this chapter, you will be able to

- **determine** what you may gain as an employee if you succeed in winning at work.
- **identify** expectations of employers.
- **describe** how you can do your best as an employee.

Key Concepts

- Having a good work ethic will help you win your employer's approval.
- Doing your best as an employee involves meeting your employer's expectations, having a good attitude, and accepting responsibility for your work.

Winning at Work

"Winning at work" means that you gain something from your job. You may feel you have won just by getting a job. That is an accomplishment. As you work, however, you will have many more chances to win. You will be able to win respect if your work pleases your employer. You also win self-esteem when your work meets your personal standards.

In order for you to win at work, it is not necessary for someone else to lose. When you win, you will be a contented employee. This will allow your company to win through your contributions of effort and ideas. See 13-1.

Community Connections

Select a local employer and ask if it has an employee awards program. If the employer has such a program, find out answers to the following questions: Of what does it consist? In what special way are award-winners treated? Why does the company sponsor the program? Share your findings with the class.

Consider Your Employer's Expectations

To give an honest day's work for an honest day's pay is a common work ethic. A ***work ethic*** is a standard of conduct and values for job performance. Having a good work ethic will help you win your employer's approval.

work ethic
A standard of conduct and values for job performance.

When you win with your employer, you may be rewarded with job security, raises, and promotions. The best way to win with your employer is to meet his or her expectations.

Imagine yourself as an employer. What traits would you want your employees to have? How would you expect them to behave? What kind of employees would you reward with raises and promotions? Your answers to these questions should help you understand how employers think and act. Your answers are probably similar to the list of employer expectations in 13-2.

Employee of the Month Award given to

Bill Martinez

In recognition of outstanding performance during the month of April

Cardinal Engineering Services

13-1
Employees gain self-esteem when they excel, and companies gain profits.

Vocabulary

Use *work ethic* in a sentence to demonstrate understanding.

Resource

Reinforcing Vocabulary, Activity A, WB. Students complete a crossword puzzle with the chapter's key terms.

The Work Ethic

Employers expect employees to:

- come to work every day on time
- work hard
- follow company rules and policies
- get along with coworkers
- lend a helping hand whenever asked
- appreciate privileges without abusing them
- have a good attitude
- be honest
- show loyalty
- do the work correctly, completely, and on time
- take pride in their work
- make an effort to improve
- accept responsibility for their work
- show initiative

13-2 Considering your employer's expectations will help you become a winning employee.

Adapting the Lesson

Have students who are low functioning use the chart in Figure 13-2 to make a poster on what employers expect. Have students use magazine pictures to illustrate the ideas and explain them aloud to demonstrate understanding. Display the posters.

Making a Difference

Form teams of four to develop a plan to make chocolate chip cookies faster and better than anyone else. Write out your strategy. You will be judged on how well your plan reflects teamwork. On the following day, put your chocolate chip cookie company strategy to work, making the cookies and donating them to a kitchen that feeds the needy in your community. Evaluate how well the strategies of the teams worked.

Employers want what you want. They want to be treated fairly and with respect. They want employees who can get along with others and make the company a success.

Getting Along with Others

You will be expected to get along with your employer. Getting promoted is not likely if you can't get along with your employer. You might even be fired in such a case.

All employers are different so their personalities differ. Their styles of supervision also vary. The best way to get along with your employer is to do your job well.

As a new employee, don't try to tell your employer how to change the operation. You should get to know your employer and the operation before making suggestions for change. If you don't know how to handle a task, ask questions and be willing to learn. Let your employer know that you want to do a good job.

Your employer will expect you to get along with your coworkers. If you are unable to cooperate with others, you will reduce the productivity of your department. Employers cannot afford to keep employees who interfere with the company's ability to get a job done.

Your employer will also expect you to get along with customers and business contacts, 13-3. You need to deal with people outside the company in a helpful, friendly, professional way. If you fail to treat these people with respect, they are likely to get a bad impression of your company. They may even stop doing business with your company. If your attitude or actions hurt your company's business, they will hurt your chances of keeping your job.

Activity
In your notebook, write a description of a teacher who has a good work ethic. List positive qualities this teacher displays.

Discuss
Use Figure 13-3 to talk about the expectations employers have regarding employees. How many of these are the same as the expectations of the classroom teacher? In what ways does the teacher prepare you to work with employers?

Compliance

Complying with company rules and policies is another employer expectation. As a new employee, you may be told these rules and policies, or you may receive a written copy. It is your responsibility to learn the rules and policies and follow them. Ask your employer to explain any company rule or policy that you do not understand.

Breaking company rules and policies usually results in a penalty. A ***penalty*** is a loss or hardship due to some action. The specific penalties that apply to different cases are detailed

penalty
A loss or hardship due to some action, such as breaking company rules or policies.

13-3
Smiling and being courteous to customers are requirements for service-oriented jobs.

Reflect
Have you ever encountered a grumpy salesperson? How did you feel afterward? What do you think happens to people with that attitude?

in a company's rules and policies manual. For instance, a construction company may require you to wear a hard hat at all times when on the job. If you failed to comply with this company policy, you could be penalized in the following way:

reprimand
A severe expression of disapproval.

- First offense is a verbal reprimand. A ***reprimand*** is a severe expression of disapproval.
- Second offense is a written reprimand and a fine. The written reprimand goes into your personnel file. It affects future decisions about your pay level and job opportunities.

termination
The end of employment or the loss of a job.

- Third offense is termination. ***Termination*** is the end of employment or the loss of a job.

Punctuality

punctual
On time.

One company policy is likely to involve your working hours. Employers expect their employees to put in a full day's work. To do so, you must be ***punctual***. This means being on time. You should try to be at your workstation at least five to ten minutes early. You should not leave before the official quitting time.

Discuss
Ask employed students to volunteer to talk about their company's rules. What happens if these rules are not followed? Explain how you learned about the company rules. Why does an employer need rules?

Employers have many ways of checking on the starting and quitting times of employees. Some companies use time clocks. You punch your time card when arriving and when leaving work, as well as when taking your breaks. See 13-4. Many offices use sign in/sign out sheets. Employees are required to sign a logbook when entering or leaving the building.

13-4
Some employers record employees' punctuality by using time cards punched by a time clock.

Resource
If You Were an Employer, Activity B, WB. Students identify the expectations they would have for employees if they had the role of employer.

No matter what system is used at your place of employment, you should get into the habit of being early. Then, you will not need to worry about being late.

Dependability

Employers, coworkers, family, and friends expect you to be dependable. Being ***dependable*** means being reliable. This means workers expect you to be a person of your word. Not only must you be punctual, you must also stay busy at doing your assignments. Being dependable means not taking time off for nonessential purposes.

dependable
Being reliable.

Many people depend on you to do the job you were hired to do. This means accomplishing the tasks you were expected to complete, as outlined in your job description. It also means doing tasks according to your supervisor's directions.

Resource

Winners or Losers? Activity C, WB. Students identify positive and negative work traits in case studies.

Activity

Make a list of behaviors that show you are dependable. Divide the list into two categories: dependable at school and dependable at home.

Employers and coworkers appreciate dependable people. Dependable workers are usually the first to be considered for job advancements and raises.

Do Not Abuse Privileges

Some company policies may concern certain privileges for employees. A ***privilege*** is a right that is given as a benefit or favor. Most employees have several privileges at work. Two examples are breaks and the use of office equipment. Do not abuse or take advantage of such privileges.

privilege
A right that is given as a benefit or favor.

Breaks from work allow employees to relax and return to work refreshed. If you are given a 15-minute break, do not stretch it into a 20-minute break. Your supervisor depends on you to return to work promptly.

Reflect

What do you think your parents would say about your dependability? Are there any tasks you could do to be more dependable at home?

Discuss

What are some types of company privileges? Have you ever received classroom privileges and then had them taken away? Why did this happen? Do you think the same thing could happen in the workplace?

Your company may allow you to use the telephone to make some important local telephone calls. Don't abuse this privilege. Keep your personal calls to a minimum. Use this privilege to call home when you'll be late or to take care of an urgent personal matter. Don't chat with family members and friends, and don't allow them to call you at work just to chat.

Likewise, do not send personal faxes or e-mails on company equipment. To prevent this from occurring, many companies have strict rules regarding the use of office equipment. Abusing these privileges robs your employer of your work time. It also creates unfair expenses for your employer. More importantly, your activities may tie up communication

Community Connections

Interview a company supervisor or manager. Ask him or her for answers to these questions: How are employee evaluations handled? What happens if an employee is not honest? What happens if an employee does not get along with others? What is done to an employee who is caught stealing? Share your findings with the class.

Discuss

Imagine that you work for a major retailer and observe a fellow employee taking office supplies home. What effect do you think this has on the company? Would you tell your boss? Would you talk to that employee?

Your Reading

How can you win at work and meet your employer's expectations?

channels and prevent customers from easily reaching the company. This could result in lost sales and customers.

Honesty

Your employer expects you to be an honest employee. One type of dishonesty that is a problem in some workplaces is stealing. Stealing does not always involve taking money from your employer. Stealing also includes taking company supplies, tools, or equipment for personal use.

Stealing *any* amount of your employer's property is dishonest. Even taking something as minor as a package of pencils is considered stealing. This is just like taking money from the cash register. Your employer must replace the stolen pencils at a cost to the company.

Another form of dishonesty is taking too much time for breaks. Doing so cheats the employer out of time that workers should be devoting to work. It also cheats the employer out of wages that are not earned. Most companies have a definite starting and quitting time. Don't arrive at work late, and don't quit work early. Coming in late or sneaking out early is unfair to the company. Also, it will cause discontent among coworkers and could be grounds for dismissal.

You should be honest in all your dealings with your employer. An employer is likely to go to great lengths to keep an employee who is honest. See 13-5.

Loyalty

Would you remain friends with a person who always tells others about your faults and secrets? Would you continue to like a person who always "puts you down"? You probably wouldn't. You want friends who are loyal. You want friends who talk about your strengths, not your weaknesses.

Employers are very much like you. Employers expect their employees to be loyal. They want employees who speak highly of the company and their employers. They want employees who will not give away company secrets or grumble about decisions the employer makes.

Being loyal to your employer, however, means keeping company business within the company. It does not mean you must ignore those things that should be improved. Instead, loyalty means always working to make the company better. As a loyal employee, you earn the respect of your employer.

13-5
Honest employees do not stretch their breaks beyond the specified time allowed.

Do Your Best as an Employee

To win at work, you must do your very best as an employee. This means doing your job to the best of your ability. It means looking for ways to improve and being willing to learn new skills. Doing your best as an employee involves accepting responsibility for your work and having a good attitude. If you make a true effort at this, you will win. You'll win self-esteem by knowing you're doing the best job you can do.

Use All Your Abilities

Your first challenge is getting a job. Your next challenge is keeping the job. Many people spend a lot of time working to get a job. Once they have the job, they relax. Don't let this happen to you. You should put your best foot forward at all times. "Do an honest day's work for an honest day's pay" is an old saying that still applies. Your employers and your coworkers expect you to do the job you were hired to do. Doing your job to the

Vocabulary

In your own words, define loyalty. Give examples of behaviors demonstrated by students who are loyal to their school.

Adapting the Lesson

Have students who are high functioning research loyalty in the workplace. Have students find answers to these questions: Has employee loyalty to employers increased or decreased in recent years? What are the causes for the change? What can employers do to increase employee loyalty? Have students share their findings with the class.

Reflect

Do you think it is important for an employer to recognize employees, such as giving employee-of-the-month awards? How do you feel about getting a reward when you "go the extra mile"?

Example

Recall an individual that you feel excelled in the role of "student." Share how this student demonstrated this quality.

Resource

Actions to Avoid, reproducible master 13-1, TR. Students examine poor employee actions or attitudes and identify what each reflects about the individual.

Reflect

What do you think are the most important qualities in keeping a job? Why do people you know lose their jobs?

Resource

Winning Work Habits, Activity D, WB. Students evaluate their work habits and identify which need improvement.

Activity

Use Figure 13-6 to list possible behaviors that would demonstrate this employee takes pride in his work. How could he "go above and beyond"?

best of your ability has another benefit, too. It allows you to feel good about yourself and build your self-esteem.

Some employees do only what they are told to do and no more. Employees who work to the best of their abilities, however, notice other tasks that need to be done. These employees do extra tasks without being asked. For instance, your assigned task may be to dust the shelves. While dusting, you may find items like rubber bands and paper clips lying on the shelves. If these items do not belong there, remove them. To simply dust around these items is not doing the job to the best of your ability.

Don't simply ignore other tasks that need to be done while doing an assigned task. On the other hand, if the extra tasks require considerably more time or expertise, first check with your employer. Always make sure you are using your time on the job in the way your employer wants.

Take pride in what you do. If you are sweeping floors, sweep them as clean as you can. If you are baking pastries, try to make them perfect in shape, texture, and taste. If you are writing a report, try to write it without a single error. Treat each task like the most important task the company could give you. See 13-6.

There is truth in the old saying "practice makes perfect." Visualize each step of your job. Work at perfecting whatever you do. Go over each detail until the steps become automatic. Be patient. Developing skill takes determination and practice.

13-6
Take pride in your work to do the best job you can do.

Discuss

Compare the responses in the discussion activity above to a student performing his or her job. What are some signs that a student takes pride in his or her work, works to maximum ability, and performs above and beyond expectations?

Watch for Ways to Improve

Your first obligation to your employer is to do the job you were hired to do. When your end result does not meet your employer's standards, seek your employer's help. Try to improve your skills. A positive attitude, training, and practice will help you improve.

After you master your job, look for new skills to develop. This will help you become more valuable to your employer. Watch the more experienced workers do their jobs. Ask them to show you how to do some advanced tasks. Don't be afraid to try new assignments.

Let your employer know that you want to handle additional responsibilities. Volunteer for extra training and other job assignments. Take self-improvement courses that help you advance on the job. The more you learn and do on the job, the more valuable you become to your employer.

Reflect

How do you feel when you master a new skill? Does all the hard work seem worthwhile then?

Adapting the Lesson

Have students who are high functioning make a video showing employees who use all their abilities. Ask students to create scenes showing employees taking pride in their work and giving "an honest day's work for an honest day's pay." Also, have students include contrasting scenarios of employees.

Discuss

Why do companies need to keep workers up-to-date? Why does an employee need to be willing to learn new skills? How does the boss react when an employee is eager to learn new skills for the job?

Be Willing to Learn

You must be willing to learn your company's way of operating. Every company operates somewhat differently. For instance, the style of typing a letter for one company may differ from the style used by another company.

Your willingness to learn and keep your skills updated is important to your company. Your company will provide you with on-the-job training. It might even send you to seminars or school to improve your skills. Skilled workers help the company earn higher profits. Higher profits help pay for more jobs and higher wages. See 13-7.

Mentors

Perhaps you will be fortunate to have a mentor. A ***mentor*** is a more experienced person who provides his or her expertise in order to help less-experienced workers advance in their careers, enhance their education, and build networks. A mentor can be a friend, counselor, or teacher. Some companies often pair new employees with a mentor who can guide the new employee through advice and example as the new employee advances in the company.

mentor
A more experienced person who provides his or her expertise in order to help less-experienced workers advance in their careers, enhance their education, and build networks.

13-7
Be willing to learn the skills needed to keep up with your company's changing needs.

Resource

What Type of Worker Are You? reproducible master 13-2, TR. Use the adapted worksheet to reinforce chapter concepts in students who are low functioning.

Reflect

How do you feel when you make a mistake? If a mistake occurs on the job, what do you do?

Discuss

How does it feel to work in a group in which students have a positive attitude? How do you handle a person in your group who does not have a positive attitude?

Resource

Winning at Work, color transparency CT-13, TR. Students discuss what employees can do to be successful at work and reach their career goals.

Accept Responsibility for Your Work

There will be times when you make mistakes on the job. Don't be afraid to admit your mistakes. Everyone makes mistakes at one time or another. Learn from your mistakes. Try not to make the same mistake twice. Whatever you do, don't blame others for your errors. Rather, accept responsibility for them. You will get more respect from your employer and your coworkers when you do.

Your Reading

What are ways you can do your best as an employee?

Have a Good Attitude

A positive attitude will help you accomplish your tasks to the best of your ability. Try to develop a "can do" attitude. This attitude shows you are willing to try any task. It also shows your belief in your own ability to succeed.

Having a good attitude ranks high with most employers. Many prefer workers with positive attitudes to workers with perfect skills. Employers can teach workers the skills they need. The workers themselves, on the other hand, must develop a positive attitude. See 13-8.

Signs of a Good Attitude

- Listen to the suggestions of others.
- Avoid making excuses for mistakes or blaming others for them.
- Live up to the expectations of supervisors and coworkers.
- Try to see things from the other person's point of view.
- Respect the opinions of others.
- Give a day's work for a day's pay willingly.

13-8
An employee with a good attitude will win an employer's respect.

Making a Difference

Contact a local hospital, nursing home, or Meals on Wheels group. Ask the group to recommend noteworthy volunteers who have shown loyalty and a positive attitude. Ask if individuals would be willing to discuss their volunteer experiences with you or the class.

Summary

Winning at work means benefiting from your job. You do this by meeting your employer's expectations and doing your best as an employee. It means having a good work ethic.

Employers seek employees who will comply with company rules and policies. They also seek employees who will be honest, dependable, and loyal. Employers know that employees who meet these expectations will help the company be successful.

You should always excel in your role as an employee. Living up to your personal standards will allow you to develop pride in your work. Your self-esteem and self-confidence will grow. You will be a winner at work!

Reviewing Key Concepts

1. List 10 expectations employers have regarding their employees.
2. Why is it important to comply with company rules and policies?
3. Why must an employee be punctual?
4. Give two examples of abusing company privileges.
5. Describe honesty on the job.
6. Explain how an employee can show loyalty at work.
7. Explain why it is important to do your job to the best of your ability.
8. Describe two ways you can improve on the job.
9. What should you do when you make a mistake on the job?
10. List five characteristics of a person with a good attitude.

Answers to
Reviewing Key Concepts

1. (List 10. See Figure 13-2.)
2. There are usually penalties for breaking them.
3. to put in a full day's work
4. (List two:) taking long breaks, using the phone to chat with friends, using office equipment to send personal faxes or e-mails
5. Honesty means not stealing company property or wasting time at work.
6. (Student response.)
7. (Student response.)
8. (Describe two:) asking experienced workers to show you how to do advanced tasks, volunteering for extra training and other job assignments, taking self-improvement courses
9. Admit it, accept responsibility for it, and learn from it.
10. (List five. See Figure 13-8.)

Building Academic Skills

Writing, speaking. Write a speech on the importance of honesty in the workplace and the effect it has on the work environment. Present your speech to the class.

Building Technology Skills

1. Use the computer to create a flowchart. Imagine yourself as an employer as you tackle the following tasks: Write down the name of your company and the services it provides or the products it produces. List job titles in your company, and below them, the qualities that employees holding them should have.
2. Search the Internet for *positive attitude.* (You might be surprised at the number of Web sites that appear.) Use several sites to create a PowerPoint presentation or a Web page on what happens to people with positive attitudes.
3. Use the computer to develop a list of common employee work rules that would be applied to a chocolate chip cookie manufacturer. You may use the Internet to research *work rules.* Also, list the consequences of breaking any rules.

Building Career Knowledge and Skills

1. Interview three workers from different companies. Ask them about the workplace importance of dependability, honesty, and getting along with others. Summarize your findings in a brief report.
2. Interview an employer to learn his or her idea of a good employee. Report your findings to the class.
3. Obtain a company's rules and policies manual. Make a list of all actions that lead to penalties. Beside each action, describe its penalty. Put a check mark beside actions that can lead to termination.

Building Workplace Skills

Working with three or four classmates, develop two short skits depicting "good" and "bad" employer/employee interactions over an employer expectation discussed in this chapter. (Two examples are honesty and compliance.) Develop a two-minute script for each skit. Decide as a team what the performers should say and do to deliver a memorable message. Together determine who should do which tasks. Present the skits to the class live or videotape the skits and play them back during class. Summarize the point of the message at the end of the skits.

How can I be a team member at work?

Chapter 14
Being a Team Player

Key Terms

teamwork
brainstorming
constructive criticism
ridicule
sarcasm
conflict
compromise
argumentative
rumor
grapevine
gossip
harassment

Chapter Objectives

After studying this chapter, you will be able to

- **explain** the importance of being a team player at work.
- **list** several tips for new workers.
- **describe** how to accept constructive criticism positively.
- **distinguish** between a good sense of humor and the poor use of humor.
- **state** the importance of avoiding arguments, rumors, harassment, and comparisons to coworkers.

Key Concepts

- To achieve success at work, you must work well as a member of a team.
- It is important to gain the acceptance of your fellow employees.
- Accepting instruction and constructive criticism positively show you are a team player.
- A positive attitude and a good sense of humor can get you through difficult situations at work.
- Being a team player means avoiding arguments, rumors, harassment, and comparisons to coworkers.

Teamwork Leads to Success

Being hired by a business as an employee is only the first step. You need to work well as a member of the team in order to achieve success.

Consider how a high school drill team functions. It can function only if every member cooperates. It is important for all members to be team players. When one member fails to cooperate, the entire team looks bad.

Companies depend on teamwork in the same way. ***Teamwork*** is two or more people working toward a common goal. If one employee fails to cooperate, the entire company can look bad. Without cooperation, the company cannot produce products as quickly or provide services of the highest quality. If customers feel they are not getting the best a company can offer for the price, they shop elsewhere. A company that disappoints its customers will lose business as a result.

Resource

Reinforcing Vocabulary, Activity A, WB. Students fill in the blanks of partial definitions with correct terms from the chapter.

Reflect

How would you describe your teamwork skills? Do you feel you get along with everyone in the group?

Resource

Be a Team Player, color transparency CT-14, TR. Students suggest ways they can be team players at school and work.

teamwork
Two or more people working toward a common goal.

Becoming an Effective Team Member

No single employee, no matter how good he or she is, can make a company successful. Employees must work as a team to achieve that goal. As a new employee, make it your business to be a team player at your company. Don't focus on what great work *you* can do. Focus on what great work *your company* can do because you are part of the team.

Employers are looking for people who can work together harmoniously. They are looking for people who can share ideas and solve problems. Strong interpersonal skills are workplace skills workers need to be effective.

No single characteristic or trait makes a team member effective. It requires a combination of interpersonal skills. This chapter discusses several interpersonal skills important in the workplace and ways to develop them.

Community Connections

Interview a coach from your school. Ask him or her how skills learned from being on a school team relate to being on a workplace team. Write a report and share it with the class.

Developing an Effective Team

A capable team can accomplish more than one person left to do a job alone. Forming such a team is not easy. It requires the skills, talents, trust, and cooperation of all members.

Teams must learn to work together before they can be successful. Consider a successful sports team, chorale group,

Resource

The Goose Story, reproducible master 14-1, TR. Students analyze a story for its teamwork significance.

Discuss

Why is it important to keep an open mind when working on a team? What happens to the team if a few members take over and prevent ideas and contributions from others on the team?

brainstorming
A way to come up with many ideas in a short time by listing everyone's ideas, no matter how ridiculous the ideas may seem, and then discussing and evaluating them.

or planning committee. Members must get to know each other's strengths and weaknesses. They must develop a plan and an organized way to accomplish it. Most importantly, they must learn to trust each other and function as a team. The following behaviors are signs of an effective team.

Sharing Ideas

Every member of an effective team is encouraged to participate. No one feels that his or her input is not valued. All ideas are considered important. One way of sharing ideas is through brainstorming. ***Brainstorming*** is a way to come up with many ideas in a short time by listing everyone's ideas, no matter how ridiculous the ideas may seem, and then discussing and evaluating them.

Being Open to New Ideas

Keeping an open mind is most important to team planning. Predetermining that an idea won't work without first discussing it often discourages members from making suggestions. Not allowing all members to get involved can doom the team to failure. See 14-1.

14-1
Companies want employees to recommend new ideas that could improve the company.

Activity

Divide the class into teams. Provide each team with a bag of marshmallows and a box of toothpicks. Give students 10 minutes to build the tallest free-standing structure. When time is up, evaluate the results as well as the entire process.

Sharing Leadership

The leader's function is to facilitate the group's efforts. That person has the responsibility to encourage everyone to participate. However, no single person is likely to have strengths in all the areas needed. For that reason, the leader of an effective team welcomes seeing others contribute to the group's effort.

Making a Difference

Contact the United Way. Inquire about the ways this organization uses teamwork. Find out how volunteers are used in the agencies that are part of the United Way. Inquire about projects in which you could become involved to develop teamwork skills.

Creating an Action Plan

After much thought and discussion, the members decide a course of action. Goals, objectives, and timetables are developed.

Working Toward a Common Goal

All members of an effective team have a clear understanding of the task at hand. Each individual knows what he or she must do to accomplish the group's goal. The plan of action is followed carefully, but modified if the team considers it necessary.

Showing Trust

Every member shows support for his or her fellow team members. Each speaks freely, without fear of being criticized or ridiculed for their input. Everyone tries to do his or her assigned tasks as well as possible and on time.

Reflect

Are you the type of person who could be a good leader? What qualities do you have that can put you in a leadership role?

Staying Focused

The hardest part of teamwork is keeping everyone focused on the task at hand. It is easy to get sidetracked and lose focus, especially if the task takes a long time. Periodically, the members of an effective team remind each other of the importance of their mission.

Teams become effective after going through several stages. Experts who study group behavior identified the four stages of team development. Recognizing and understanding these stages will help you succeed as a team player. These stages are summarized in 14-2.

Your Reading

Why is teamwork important to a company?

14-2
Before a team becomes effective, members must know, accept, and trust one another.

Stages of Team Development
1. Forming Team members share personal information as they try to get to know and accept one another. It is an exciting new adventure, but not everyone is comfortable.
2. Storming Team members usually compete for status and often question why the team was formed. Tensions arise as members jockey for control. Leadership from members may not be evident.
3. Norming The team begins to work as a unit. A leader emerges and members begin to listen to one another. Trust forms.
4. Performing This is the highest level of team performance. The team accomplishes complex challenges. Tasks are handled efficiently.

Making a Difference

Form groups to work on a volunteer project for a local agency. Plan your project and then carry it out. Upon completion of the project evaluate the results. (Project ideas include baking bread for a local food bank, making drawstring bags for the American Red Cross or Salvation Army, or making small stuffed animals for the emergency room of a hospital.)

Tips for New Employees

On your first day of work, your main concern should be learning to do the job. However, even at this early date, devoting some of your attention to your coworkers is important. Your early dealings with them may have long-term effects. You are the new person on the job. You need to be accepted by your supervisors and coworkers. Being a friendly, respectful, likable person will help you gain the acceptance of your fellow employees.

Be Friendly

When you start a new job, introduce yourself to other employees with a smile and a firm handshake. Get to know your coworkers by name. Greet them when you arrive, and say good-bye to them when you leave.

Don't overdo it. Trying too hard to be friends with your new boss can be a mistake. You might be labeled an "apple polisher."

In short, be friendly and pleasant. However, do not expect everyone at work to be your friend. Attaining the friendship of your coworkers is nice, but receiving their respect and cooperation is your main goal.

Discuss

Use Figure 14-2 to talk about the stages that effective teams go through. How do you think these stages help you succeed as a team player?

Respect Your Coworkers

As you meet your coworkers, remember they deserve your respect as workers and as people. As workers, respect your coworkers for their knowledge and skills. They would not be working for the company if they did not have useful talents to offer

Respect your coworkers for their positive qualities. Like all people, your coworkers have good and bad traits. Don't focus on their bad traits. Instead, look for their good traits.

Resource

Tips for Getting Along, Activity B, WB. Students interview three workers for their tips on getting along with coworkers.

Adapting the Lesson

Have students who are low functioning circle the positive actions to take on the first day of a job from a list that you provide. Have them explain why they should avoid the actions that were not circled.

Present Yourself as a Likable Person

Your new coworkers will start to form impressions of you from your very first meeting. Consequently, you want to present yourself as a likable person who gets along with everyone.

Avoid appearing self-centered. Your coworkers will quickly tire of hearing you talk about yourself endlessly. You will bore them by always talking about your own problems and interests. Listen to what they have to say. Talk about your common interests.

Also avoid acting like a know-it-all. Don't assume a superior attitude and pretend to know all the answers. Listen to instructions and follow them. Ask questions when necessary. See 14-3.

As a new employee, do not tell your boss or experienced workers how to do their jobs. There will be plenty of time to offer suggestions after you get to know the job and your coworkers better.

Your Reading

In what ways can you gain the acceptance of your fellow employees?

14-3
Successful companies rely on employees who have good interpersonal skills with coworkers and customers.

Enrich

Invite a guest speaker to share with the class how important teamwork is at his or her workplace. Have the guest discuss the results of no leadership or lack of teamwork in the workplace.

Accept Constructive Criticism Positively

constructive criticism
The process of offering judgmental remarks about you or your work.

When you start a new job, you should be prepared to accept instructions and some constructive criticism. ***Constructive criticism*** is the process of offering judgmental remarks about you or your work. As you work, your supervisor may show you a better way to do a job. A coworker or your boss may tell you when you have done something wrong. See 14-4.

No one likes to be criticized. Being told that you have done something wrong is not fun. However, when employees make mistakes, their supervisors must tell them what they did wrong. This helps the employees learn. If employees were not told what they did wrong, they would continue to make the same mistakes. Your supervisor understands that new employees may make some mistakes. You must understand that mistakes can cause a company to lose business and money.

The way you react to constructive criticism shows how willing you are to be a team player. You can react to constructive criticism in two ways: negatively or positively. Being defensive is a negative response to criticism. You defend yourself by blaming others or making excuses. Another negative response is getting angry with yourself. Staying upset about constructive criticism for a long time is also negative.

Activity
Role-play a situation in which an employee accepts constructive criticism about his or her job. Also role-play an employee who does not accept the criticism, makes excuses, and blames others. Have the class evaluate what they observed.

Adapting the Lesson
Have students who are low functioning write how they would handle each of these constructive criticisms from a boss: Your handwritten phone orders are hard for others to read. Some customers complain that you talk too softly on the phone. You are too slow in checking out customers.

14-4
Your supervisor may use constructive criticism to help you improve your work. Learn to accept it positively.

Discuss
Figure 14-4 shows a boss explaining something to an employee. What do you think is happening in the picture? How do you think the employee is feeling, based on the look on her face?

None of these responses will help you or your coworkers achieve the team goal of getting a job done.

To respond in a positive way, try to keep a good attitude. Listen to what is said. Accept it as a suggestion for a better way to do your job. Think of it as a learning experience. Do not overreact and assume that you are a failure. Remind yourself that you are a valued employee. Tell yourself that you can and will do better next time. Then apologize and express your desire to improve. Recognize that no one is perfect and there is always room for improvement. Most job performance reviews will suggest ways to become a better worker. Do not take offense by this, but rather view it as a natural part of performance reviews.

A positive reaction to constructive criticism will help you be a better team player. You will save yourself from being too upset. Your supervisors and coworkers will be impressed with your willingness to improve. If you improve enough, you may be promoted!

Why should you view constructive criticism as a learning experience?

Have a Positive Attitude

People like to be with coworkers who have a *positive attitude.* Those with a positive attitude see the optimistic side of everything. They are upbeat, cheerful, and eager to find solutions to problems. On the other hand, people with a *negative attitude* only see the problems. They look at the gloomy side of everything. They are grumpy and full of complaints.

Negative attitudes do not help team members achieve goals at work. Positive attitudes do, 14-5. Try to develop behaviors that reflect a positive attitude. Try to be a worker who does the following:

- smiles often
- shows enthusiasm
- seldom complains
- makes changes willingly
- tries to understand the views of others
- seldom criticizes others
- volunteers help

Resource

Studying Work Attitudes, Activity C, WB. Students analyze a case study and identify how they would respond to various situations.

Activity

Write a short description of people who have a positive attitude. What qualities do they have? Why would you like to work with them?

Activity

Design a poster to encourage students to have a positive attitude. Include the qualities listed on this page. Display the posters around the school. Generously use color and pictures from magazines to illustrate your points.

14-5
Working cooperatively is a sign of the positive attitude needed to achieve goals at work.

Activity
Write a paragraph about a time when a good sense of humor helped get you or your team through a difficult situation. Point out what you learned in that experience.

Your Reading
Why is it important to have a positive attitude at work?

Discuss
Name situations in school and in the workplace when "goofing off" is inappropriate.

Discuss
Talk about times when jokes are not appropriate. How should you handle someone who tells crude or hurtful jokes? When a worker has a poor sense of humor, how do you think the boss will react?

- avoids making excuses
- accepts responsibility for mistakes
- always tries to perform at a high level

A positive attitude can be reflected in what you say. Saying something positive about someone is just as easy as saying something negative. Your coworkers are more likely to accept you as a team player if you speak kindly of them.

Keep a Good Sense of Humor

A good sense of humor can help your team get through difficult situations at work. Having a sense of humor is being able to laugh at yourself when you do something foolish or silly. When this happens, try not to get angry at yourself or at others. Try to laugh it off and avoid repeating the mistake. No one likes a person who acts too seriously. Don't take yourself so seriously that you forget how to laugh.

Avoid the Poor Use of Humor

Knowing how to use your sense of humor in the workplace is important. However, you must not get carried away.

Most people like to hear and tell jokes. Jokes make people laugh. Jokes are fine to tell as long as they do not deliberately offend anyone. Crude jokes should be avoided. Crude jokes are vulgar and in bad taste. They are offensive to most people. A person who tells crude jokes is seldom held in high regard by coworkers.

Having a sense of humor does not mean spending a lot of time at work telling jokes or acting silly. You may get a laugh or two, but your coworkers might begin to see you as a clown. Your supervisor may consider you a *slacker.* That is a person who avoids work or responsibility. You might put your job or your chances for promotion in danger.

You should not cause laughter at the expense of someone else's feelings. Ridiculing another person is never funny. To ***ridicule*** a person is to make fun of him or her. A person who ridicules another person is cruel and insensitive. You should always try to respect the feelings of others.

Like ridicule, sarcasm is not funny, nor does it contribute to the team effort. ***Sarcasm*** is the use of cutting remarks. The intention is to put another person down. Words can often hurt as much as, if not more than, physical force.

Vocabulary
Use the terms *ridicule* and *sarcasm* in a sentence to demonstrate understanding.

ridicule
To tease or belittle.

sarcasm
The use of cutting remarks.

Your Reading
What is the difference between a good sense of humor and a poor use of humor?

Do Not Cause Conflict

Being a team player means cooperating with your coworkers to do the best job your company can do. Most of your adult life will be spent working. A good portion of your time will be spent with coworkers. If you don't get along with them, you may not be able to advance in your job, 14-6. In fact, you stand a good chance of losing your job altogether.

People have to work together to get most jobs done. Friction on the job creates unpleasant working conditions. Starting arguments, spreading rumors, and gossiping are three ways to cause conflict. ***Conflict*** is a hostile situation resulting from opposing views. It can become a destructive force if not resolved. You cannot work at peak performance when you, or those around you, cause conflict. In some

Reflect
How do people feel if they are ridiculed or are targeted for sarcastic remarks?

Adapting the Lesson
Have students who are low functioning make lists of ways to handle disagreements. Compile a master list. Give copies to the students and have them circle the five most-constructive ways to handle coworker disagreements.

conflict
Hostile situation resulting from opposing views.

14-6
This case study illustrates how your ability to work well with coworkers can affect your chances of getting a promotion.

You Must Be a Team Player Before You Can Be a Coach

Tom had recently been transferred into Sally's department. Sally was asked to help Tom in his new assignment. Tom made a minor error and Sally became upset. A great deal of friction developed between them. Sally told everyone of Tom's mistake. As the weeks went by, she continued to be highly critical of Tom. The entire department began to feel sorry for Tom because of the treatment he received from Sally.

When an opening for the position of department supervisor became available, Sally applied for it. She knew her skills were excellent. She felt that she was qualified to do the job. However, Sally did not get the promotion.

Sally observed her new supervisor, Kathy, to figure out why Kathy got the job. Like Sally, Kathy had very good skills. She also got along well with other employees. Kathy did her work and helped others when needed.

Sally realized that her attitude toward others had caused her to lose the promotion. She realized that she must learn to get along better with her coworkers. She made up her mind to make an effort to do so.

Discuss

Read the case study in Figure 14-6. How would you describe Sally's attitude? Will people with excellent skills always get the promotion? Why do you think a positive attitude is so important on the job?

Discuss

List ways to handle a disagreement constructively. What happens to workers who are very defensive? What happens to productivity when workers avoid coworkers who are argumentative?

conflict situations, compromise is necessary. ***Compromise*** means giving something up to resolve a conflict.

compromise
Giving something up to resolve a conflict.

Do Not Cause Arguments

Being a team player at work means avoiding arguments. There are two sides to most situations. Try to see the other person's side.

Some people seem to look for arguments. They disagree with just about everything. If you say it's nice outside, they'll say it isn't. These people are described as being ***argumentative***. Don't become this type of person. Most people tend to stay away from people who are argumentative.

argumentative
Easily creating arguments.

If you have frequent and major disagreements with your coworkers, they will shun you. You may lose not only their friendship and cooperation, but also your job or a promotion.

Another situation to avoid is taking sides in other people's arguments. Often the arguing parties eventually make up and you become the outsider. It is best not to get involved in the first place. See 14-7.

Discuss

What are some situations that could start arguments in the workplace?

Discuss

What coworker qualities make the workplace a pleasant experience for all? What would you recommend if a person cannot get along with a coworker?

14-7
Being able to avoid arguments with your coworkers will help you become a more valuable team player at work.

Vocabulary
Define *rumors, grapevine,* and *gossip* as they relate to the workplace. How can these negatively impact the workplace?

Reflect
How do you feel if you hear a rumor about a friend? In what ways can you stop the gossip?

Resource
Strengthening Work Attitudes, reproducible master 14-2, TR. Students write about three strengths that will help them at work and three weaknesses to improve.

Do Not Spread Rumors

Rumors can interfere with your ability to work with your coworkers as a team. ***Rumors*** are bits of information that pass from one person to another without proof of accuracy. At work, rumors pass swiftly along the ***grapevine***, an informal and unofficial flow of information.

rumor
Information passed from one person to another without proof of accuracy.

grapevine
An informal and unofficial flow of information.

gossip
To tell personal information about someone.

Rumors are usually only half-truths. Perhaps someone hears part of a conversation. This person then tells another person what was heard. The person who starts the rumor usually does not have all the facts. The person either invents or adds facts to make sense of the message. As the rumor passes through the grapevine, others add or delete information.

Gossip is part of the rumor mill or grapevine. When you ***gossip***, you tell personal information about another person. Sometimes this information is true. Often it is not true. Gossip, like rumors, is usually information that should not be told to others.

Do not gossip or spread rumors. Your employer and coworkers consider people who gossip and spread rumors as people who can't be trusted. You will lose everyone's respect if you talk about others.

Also avoid letting others spread gossip to you. Some people may try to use gossip to influence your impressions about your fellow workers. Form your own opinions without listening to gossip. Rumors and gossip can deeply hurt your coworkers.

Your Reading

How can conflict affect work performance?

harassment
Doing or saying things that make people feel different or uncomfortable.

Avoid Harassment

Harassment is doing or saying things that make people feel different or uncomfortable. Harassment is unacceptable behavior. Never harass others. Do not tell jokes or make remarks about any of the following:

- age
- birthplace or ethnicity
- color of skin or race
- disability
- family
- gender
- looks
- sexual preference
- political or religious beliefs

Everyone has a right to expect their employer and coworkers to treat them with respect and dignity. Everyone has a right to a safe work environment. If that right is violated, a person should tell a trusted friend or someone in authority about it. There are federal and state laws that protect workers against harassment. (These laws were discussed in Chapter 3.)

Your Reading

Why should harassment be avoided?

Resource

Good Work Habits in Action, Activity D, WB. Students explain how to put various work habits into action.

Avoid Comparisons

As a new worker, you may see some of your coworkers enjoying benefits that are greater than yours. Do not compare your work or benefits with theirs. Although you are players on the same team, senior employees are often entitled to more benefits. They may have worked for the company for many years. Perhaps they have positions that require more responsibility.

Avoid comparing workloads, salaries, and the treatment of coworkers. Senior employees will not appreciate questions about their benefits. See 14-8.

14-8
Employers expect workers to stay focused and not waste time by comparing their assignments to those of their coworkers.

Don't Compare Workloads

Your first obligation to your employer and your coworkers is to do the work described in your job description. It is your responsibility to perform those tasks to the best of your ability.

Always ask your supervisor for more responsibilities when you have completed your assigned duties. You should also be willing to give your coworkers a helping hand when you have extra time. However, do not show off by trying to take on more than you can handle. You do not want your coworkers to think you are trying to put them down.

Never compare your workload to a coworker's workload. Another employee may appear to have a light workload. However, you may not realize how complex his or her tasks are. Let your employer judge the work you do.

Don't Compare Salaries

Employers set different salary levels for different jobs. Employees with more experience usually earn more than workers with little or no experience. Employees with special knowledge may also receive higher wages. As you gain experience and knowledge, your salary will increase.

Activity

Write a job description of a person in the role of student.

Activity

Ask your parents to share their job descriptions with you. See how many tasks they must do that require special training.

Adapting the Lesson

Divide students who are low functioning into small teams to create a poster titled "Teamwork." Encourage students to make their poster colorful and include tips for working together. Display posters in the school.

Resource

Teamwork Equals Success, reproducible master 14-3, TR. Use the adapted worksheet to reinforce chapter concepts in low functioning students.

Don't Compare the Treatment of Coworkers

Senior employees usually receive more benefits than beginning workers. Extra benefits are earned by having more years of experience with the company, 14-9. They may also be earned by holding jobs in the company that involve greater responsibilities. The employees are rewarded with benefits such as the following:

- preferred parking spaces
- longer vacations
- first choice on vacation schedules
- preferred working schedules
- bigger bonuses
- stock options

If these benefits appeal to you, don't just envy those who have them. Work as hard as they did to earn them.

Your Reading

Why should you avoid comparing your benefits to those of other employees?

14-9
Employees often receive special recognition for many years of service to a company.

Activity

Use Figure 14-9 to write a small paragraph on what happened to this employee. What types of recognition do you think employees should receive for many years of service to a company?

Summary

Being a team player at work is necessary if you want to get along with your coworkers and succeed at your job. If you are not a team player, friction with your coworkers will cause unpleasant working conditions. Neither you nor your coworkers will be able to perform to the best of your abilities. The company could suffer losses. You could lose a chance for a promotion. You might even lose your job.

When you are a team player, everyone wins. The work site becomes a pleasant place. All jobs are done well and on time. The employees and the company enjoy success.

You can develop skills and behaviors that will help you become a team player. No one characteristic or trait makes you a team member. It is a combination of effective interpersonal skills. Put forth your best efforts right away, from the very first day at a new job. Be friendly and respect your coworkers. Accept constructive criticism positively and have a positive attitude. Keep a good sense of humor, but avoid the poor use of humor. Do not cause arguments or spread rumors. Finally, avoid comparing your work situation with your coworkers' work situations. Your efforts to be a team player will be rewarded.

Reviewing Key Concepts

1. Why should you, as a new employee, make it your business to be a team player at your company?
2. Which of the following statements are true?
   A. You should always be a team player.
   B. You should *not* expect everyone at work to be your friend.
   C. As a new employee, you should tell experienced workers how they could do their jobs better.
   D. It is easier to be accepted by others if you speak kindly of them.
   E. When coworkers have a dispute, you should get involved right away and help them settle it.
3. Describe a positive way to respond to constructive criticism.
4. List five behaviors that reflect an employee's positive work attitude.
5. How does having a good sense of humor help you when you do something foolish or silly at work?
6. Name three types of humor that should be avoided.
7. Describe an argumentative person.
8. Why should you avoid spreading gossip and rumors?
9. Why should you avoid comparing your workload to that of a coworker?
10. Why do senior employees usually receive more benefits than beginning workers?

Answers to *Reviewing Key Concepts*

1. No single employee can make a company successful. Success results from good teamwork.
2. A, B, D
3. Keep a good attitude, listen to what is said, and accept the comments as a learning experience. Do not overreact and assume you are a failure. Apologize and express your desire to improve.
4. (List five. Student response.)
5. You can laugh it off without getting angry at yourself or others.
6. ridicule, crude jokes, sarcasm
7. one who disagrees with almost everything
8. It causes conflict.
9. You may not realize how complex a coworker's tasks are.
10. because of more years of experience with the company or a job involving greater responsibilities

Building Academic Skills

1. **Research, speaking.** Investigate debate strategies and suggest a topic related to the workplace to debate. Find out how to argue constructively. Plan and prepare a topic to debate.
2. **Research, writing.** Research conflict in the workplace to find out how employers handle it. What effect does conflict have on employee output and the number of sick days taken. Is workplace conflict a major cause of stress? Does stress relate to a company's accident record? Summarize your findings in a written report.

Building Technology Skills

1. Work in small groups. Using video or digital cameras, record role-plays of effective team members in action. Reverse the role-play to show what happens when team members do not work together. Share the pictures or video with the class.
2. Use a computer software program to design a citation to give to a classmate who demonstrates outstanding teamwork skills. Determine the criteria for this award. Vote by secret paper ballot. Ask your teacher to announce the winner and hold a small award ceremony.
3. Search the Internet for sites that address positive attitude. Write a report from your sources on how a positive attitude affects your life and health.
4. Use the Internet to investigate job descriptions for careers of interest to you. Print copies of the descriptions and add them to your personal career information file. Review your future job description to see if you are ready to learn all the tasks you will be asked to perform on that job.

Building Career Knowledge and Skills

1. Write a two-page fictional story about an employee's interactions with coworkers. Then exchange stories with a classmate. What behavior improvements would you recommend for the employee in your classmate's story?
2. Watch a television show in which the main characters are at work together. Make a list of the scenes in which they cooperate.
3. Give a one-minute oral report on why the workplace needs team players.
4. Invite an employer to class to talk about the importance of teamwork. Be prepared to ask questions.
5. Make a list of team player skills you would like to see in your coworkers. Circle the skills you already possess. Pick at least three team player skills you would like to develop and create a plan of action to do so.
6. Interview workers regarding team skills that are expected in the work world. Summarize your findings in a statement.

Building Workplace Skills

With two classmates, visit a local store, library, or government office to observe how coworkers interact with supervisors, customers, and each other. (First talk with the manager and ask permission to observe examples of teamwork and take notes, otherwise people will wonder what you are doing.) Note and record what is said and done when employees work together. Decide with your classmates how to divide the following tasks. Make an oral report to the class summarizing the best example of teamwork skills you saw as well as the worst example. Identify how the second situation should have been handled.

How do I stay safe at work?

Chapter 15 Keeping Safety First

Chapter Objectives

After studying this chapter, you will be able to

- **identify** proper workplace safety procedures.
- **explain** proper safety procedures when working with machinery and tools.
- **describe** safety procedures related to lifting, upkeep, organization, and using ladders.
- **apply** fire safety procedures.
- **list** five lifesaving steps in first aid.
- **describe** responsibilities of employers and employees under OSHA.

Key Terms

dismissal
grounded
flammable liquid
fire triangle
evacuate
first aid
OSHA
FLSA
workers' compensation
disability

Key Concepts

- You must follow safety rules to prevent accidents.
- Follow proper safety procedures when working with machinery, tools, and ladders and those related to lifting, upkeep, and organization.
- Preventing fires and knowing what to do if one occurs can save lives and property.
- You must be alert and healthy to do a job well and safely.
- There are federal laws designed to promote safe and healthy working conditions.

Resource

Reinforcing Vocabulary, Activity A, WB. Students match terms to their definition.

Activity

Read the general safety rules in Figure 15-1. Write a small paragraph on why it is important to keep a work area clean and what that has to do with safety.

Discuss

Explain why "don't goof off" is listed in the safety rules.

Reflect

How can you help keep your school safe?

Thinking and Acting Safely

Accidents on the job cost companies money. Medical bills must be paid. Production goes down. New or part-time workers may need to be hired to take the place of injured workers. Fines and lawsuits are also possible.

Preventing accidents is everyone's business. It is important to always think and act safely. You must know the safety rules, but simply knowing them will not stop accidents. More importantly, you must follow safety rules to prevent accidents.

The first rule of safety is to learn the right way to do your job. That will always be the safe way. Never operate equipment or use tools unless you have been shown the proper and safe method. If you are not sure about any part of your job, ask your supervisor for further instruction. Don't guess! A mistake could cost your life or someone else's.

Ten general safety rules are listed in 15-1. Following them will help keep you safe on the job.

Unsafe Acts

Do you always act safely? At least 95 percent of all accidents are caused by unsafe acts or unsafe conditions. Most of these accidents could be avoided by using common sense.

People cause unsafe acts. No one really wants an accident to happen, but sometimes people act before thinking. For

15-1
Following these general safety rules will help you avoid accidents and injuries on the job.

Ten General Safety Rules
1. Comply with all company safety rules and signs.
2. Follow all instructions. Do not take chances. If you don't know the rule or procedure, ask!
3. Correct or report all unsafe conditions.
4. Use the correct protective equipment. Wear properly fitted clothes.
5. Report all accidents. Get first aid promptly.
6. Use, adjust, and repair equipment only when authorized. Report safety hazards immediately.
7. Use the right tool for the job. Use it correctly and safely.
8. When lifting, bend your knees. Get help for lifting heavy loads.
9. Don't goof off.
10. Keep your work area clean.

instance, some people feel that wearing safety glasses around moving machinery is unnecessary. However, a chip of wood or a tool hitting a person in the eyes could cause injury or blindness. Knowing that, is taking off your safety glasses worth the risk? Beware of the following unsafe acts:

- wiping or cleaning moving machinery
- failing to wear proper protective clothing
- wearing jewelry or loose clothing around equipment
- failing to pull back long hair
- smoking in a nonsmoking area
- failing to follow safety rules and signs
- goofing off
- lifting a load that is too heavy
- removing or not using machine guards
- taking chances

You have to act safely to protect yourself. You must also act safely to protect others. Being careless can hurt not only you, but others as well.

Resource

Preventing Accidents, Activity B, WB. Students analyze possible accidents for various occupations and preventive measures.

Discuss

Most accidents could be avoided by using what? (*common sense*) What unsafe acts have you seen in science or food labs?

Activity

Brainstorm a list of all the things that affect your safety every day. Include ideas from your home, school, and community.

Unsafe Conditions

Unsafe conditions cause accidents. Whenever possible, correct unsafe conditions even if you didn't cause them. For example, clean up spills so no one will slip and fall. Pick up objects left on steps so no one will trip or fall. Do not be responsible for some other person's accident.

You cannot correct all unsafe conditions. Those that can't be corrected should be reported. Your supervisor will thank you for it. Be on the lookout for the following unsafe conditions:

- poor upkeep and organization
- dim lighting
- blocked fire exits
- high stacks of boxes
- overused electrical extension cords
- opened drawers left unattended

Resource

Classroom Safety Check, reproducible master 15-1, TR. Students check the classroom for potential safety concerns.

Activity

Write a list, organized by separate rooms, of safety rules that should be followed at home. Include the basement, garage, and outdoors, if your home has any of these areas. Share the lists you develop with the head of your household to see that all the important areas of concern for your home have been covered.

- dangerous objects overhead
- tools left lying around
- oily rags in paper boxes

Can you think of other unsafe conditions that might occur at work? If so, how would you correct them? See 15-2.

Proper Safety Attitude

Your actions speak louder than words. The way you act on the job reflects your safety attitude. In order to practice safety, you must think about safety. Thinking about and practicing safety requires a proper safety attitude.

Certain attitudes can lead to accidents. Try to avoid these and develop safety-conscious attitudes.

15-2
Correcting unsafe conditions, such as poor lighting, can help prevent accidents in the workplace.

Reflect

If you were the employer, how concerned would you need to be about safety? Have you ever gotten hurt at school or at home? Were those injuries safety-related and preventable?

Forgetfulness

Forgetting safety details can cause you and others serious injury. Make it a habit to follow all the safety steps associated with your job.

Noncompliance

Noncompliance with company safety rules and signs can be the first step toward an accident. Follow instructions. Do not violate orders.

Carelessness

Your job requires your full attention. Daydreaming on the job can result in a mistake that causes someone pain and injury. Keep your mind on what you are doing.

Lack of Anger Management

You are a prime target for an accident if you are not in full control of your emotions. Hotheads react without thinking. It's too late to be sorry after an accident has occurred. Learn to control your anger and think clearly.

Uncertainty

If you are not sure how to perform a task, ask for instructions or a demonstration. A wrong decision can lead to an injury.

Fatigue

You cannot operate at your best when you are tired. Alert people have fewer accidents. Get plenty of rest and pay attention to what you do on the job.

Laziness

People who don't want to make the effort to follow good safety practices are asking for an accident to happen. Ignoring safety rules is a serious matter that could cause your ***dismissal***. That is another term for being fired.

Showing Off

A show-off is a danger to everyone. That person is more interested in gaining attention than in promoting safety. A show-off usually takes unnecessary chances, 15-3.

Note

All the potential accidents discussed on this page could possibly originate from having a poor safety attitude.

Example

Share ways students have demonstrated safety in laboratory settings. Also, give examples of how some students have demonstrated the unsafe attitudes listed on this page.

Community Connections

Interview at least three workers in various occupations to learn more about workplace safety. Find answers to the following questions: What are the special dangers or safety concerns of your job? What training do you receive to prevent workplace accidents? What is the procedure for handling accidents at your job?

dismissal
Another term for being fired.

Discuss

How can the safety attitudes listed on this page affect your role as a student?

15-3
Racing machines or showing off in other ways can cause extensive property damage and serious injury to you and your coworkers.

Your Reading

Why is the first rule of safety to learn the right way to do your job?

Vocabulary
What does grounded mean in reference to an electrical outlet?

Discuss
Check your classroom. Are any electrical outlets grounded? Why is it a good idea to have this type of outlet?

Activity
Make a list of some of the most dangerous careers to have. Identify if they are dangerous because of people, machines, locations, or other factors.

Workplace Safety

Many workers, such as office workers, do not consider their work areas unsafe. Because they feel safe, they often forget to follow simple safety precautions. Accidents, however, do occur in office settings and similar workplaces.

Most workplace accidents are caused by a combination of an unsafe act and an unsafe condition. Workers in office settings and other workplaces need to recognize safety hazards and correct them. Workers should adhere to the following safety practices:

- Close all desks and file drawers when they are unattended or not in use. Make sure drawers do not open into aisles or walkways where people could bump into or trip over them.
- Be careful when using manual paper-cutting machines. Pay attention to what you and those around you are doing. Use extreme caution with blades of any type.
- Turn off all office machines before cleaning, adjusting, or adding fluid or cartridges. Office machines can be as harmful to people as factory machines.
- Make sure all electrical machines and electrical cords are kept in good repair and grounded. A plug that is ***grounded*** has an electrical connection with the earth. It

grounded
Connected to the earth to avoid electrical shock.

prevents shock by causing electricity to flow to the ground rather than into your body.

- Do not touch electrical machines or connections with wet hands. Water is a good conductor of electricity. An electrical shock could cause serious injury or even death.
- Don't lean too far back in a chair or sit on the edge of the seat. It could slip from beneath you. See 15-4.
- Replace worn electrical cords or plugs. Frayed cords and bad connectors can create sparks and cause fires.
- Unplug electrical connections by pulling the plug, not by pulling the cord. Pulling the cord could damage the protective covering and cause a shock or start a fire.
- Do not overload electrical circuits with too many machines or appliances. Overloading can cause wires to heat and start a fire.
- Use the handrails on stairs to prevent falls.

Reflect

Do you think an office is an unsafe place? Do you know anyone who works in an office? What do you think they would say about office safety?

Activity

Look at the list of office safety practices. Pick out the top five that you think cause the most accidents. What can be done to prevent them?

Discuss

Simple things such as chairs can cause accidents. How many students have you seen have an accident in a chair? What caused the accident? Could the accident have been prevented?

15-4
Sitting properly in a chair can help to prevent workplace accidents.

Your Reading

How are most workplace accidents caused?

- Keep the floors clean and dry to prevent slips and falls. Keep telephone wires and extension cords away from places where people could trip on them.
- Never stand on movable office furniture to reach high bookshelves or to replace lightbulbs. Use sturdy ladders or step stools with nonslip treads.
- Read and follow all directions on storing and using chemicals for office machines.
- Be extremely careful of dangling hair, jewelry, scarves, and neckties when working with office machines. Anything that could be caught in machinery should be held back or removed before working with the equipment.

Safely Using Machinery, Tools, and Workplace Items

Factory and construction workers need to be especially aware of safety hazards. Many of the machines and tools used by these workers can be dangerous if not handled properly. See 15-5. A few general guidelines should be followed when working with machinery and tools.

- Work at a safe speed. Rushing and taking shortcuts could cause accidents. Never take a chance. Trying to save a minute or two could cost you a finger or even your life.
- Wear the right clothes. Clothes should fit snugly. Loose clothing can get caught in moving machinery. Keep your outer clothes buttoned. Don't take a chance on getting pulled into moving machinery. Avoid wearing dangling jewelry.
- Protect your feet. Do not wear sneakers, flip-flops, or sandals on industrial or construction work sites. You should wear hard-toed safety shoes. They protect your feet from falling tools and equipment. Safety shoes can save you from pain and serious injury.

Enrich

Invite a fast-food manager to class to discuss potential safety concerns that must be addressed at his or her workplace. Find out about the safety rules and the training each employee receives.

Activity

Consult the Yellow Pages to find companies that deal with making workplaces safer or provide training on safety. Compile a list of resources and share them with others in the class.

Working with Power Tools and Equipment

The first rule of personal safety is *always think first.* This rule applies to all operations. The second rule is *never operate*

15-5
People who work with machinery and tools must take extra precautions to stay safe at work.

Reflect
What types of equipment do you think are the most dangerous? How do you feel about working with dangerous tools?

Discuss
Use Figure 15-5 to discuss potential dangers. Point out safety precautions you see in the picture. What potential dangers exist at this worksite?

Discuss
Whose job is it to ensure safety on the job? What are ways accidents can be prevented in the workplace? In what ways can accidents be prevented in the classroom? Should there be fines for violations of safety rules?

Resource
Understanding Safety Practices, Activity C, WB. Students answer questions about safety.

any power tools or equipment without first receiving proper operating instructions. Power tools should be used correctly and safely. Adhere to the following safety rules with electrical tools and equipment:

- Never operate unfamiliar equipment until you receive specific instructions on its operation.
- Make sure your hands are dry before using an electrical cord. To unplug a cord, grip the plug itself. Do not pull on the cord.
- Keep the starting switch in the off position when plugging in equipment.
- Examine the equipment before turning it on. If an electrical cord is cut or has exposed strands of wire, do not use it.
- Never operate defective equipment.
- Wear the proper protective clothing. Also remember to wear safety goggles to protect your eyes from dust and flying objects, 15-6.

15-6
Workers in many areas need to wear safety goggles or other types of eye protection.

Discuss
What could result from operating defective equipment? Have you ever witnessed an impatient person trying to force a broken tool to operate before having it repaired?

Enrich
Develop a poster to explain the safety features of a piece of laboratory equipment. Use the ideas presented on this page as a reference.

Discuss
What safety precautions are needed in school labs? What other classes require safety precautions with equipment?

- Report defective tools and equipment to your supervisor.
- Keep all safety guards and shields in place.
- Do not oil, clean, or adjust equipment when the power is on.
- Disconnect electrical equipment when not in use.

Proper Use and Care of Hand Tools

Many accidents are caused by improper use and maintenance of hand tools. You should learn to use each tool the correct way. Choosing and using the right tool for the job gets it done faster and more safely.

Tools should be kept clean and in good condition. Dull tools should be sharpened. Broken handles should be replaced.

Each tool should be stored in its own place when not in use. It will be easier to find when needed. Also, properly stored tools will not fall on you or cause you to trip.

Carry sharp or pointed tools in kits or tool belts. Never carry them in your pockets. Always cover points or sharp edges with shields.

Discuss

What are mechanical aids? List some mechanical aids that can help you to save time and muscle power.

Activity

Prepare a brief newsletter article on some aspect of safety. Submit the article to the school newsletter.

Reflect

Do you know anyone who has had back problems? Were the problems related to lifting? How would you feel if you had to lift boxes all day on your job?

Lifting

Improper lifting is a common cause of accidents on the job and at home. Thousands of people injure themselves each year because of improper lifting. Lifting too much at one time or lifting objects incorrectly can cause hernias or back injuries.

A smart worker learns to lift properly. This includes knowing how much, how often, how far, and how high you can lift. You should also know how much help you need and what mechanical aids are available to help you.

The first step is learning how to lift. Always remember that your legs are much stronger than your back. The key to lifting, then, is to use your leg muscles. When lifting an object from the floor, keep your arms and back straight. Bend your knees and lift with the powerful muscles in your legs.

Know your limitations. Know how much you can safely lift. Seek help with loads in excess of your limit. Play it safe. Do not handle more than you can lift.

Use mechanical aids to save time and energy. Learn the proper procedures for using cranes, hoists, elevators, conveyors, and hand trucks. Failure to learn the safe operating procedures of mechanical aids can be more dangerous than manual lifting. Keep the following safety guidelines in mind when lifting:

- Lift with your leg and arm muscles.
- Keep your back as straight as possible.
- Always carry the load close to your body.
- Be sure you have good footing.
- Be sure you can see where you are going.
- Ask for help when necessary.
- Use mechanical aids to save your energy.
- Keep your work area free from tripping hazards.
- Work smarter, not harder. See 15-7.

15-7
Following proper lifting procedures can help prevent strains and back injuries.

National Institute for Occupational Safety and Health

Activity
Have several students demonstrate the proper lifting technique with a large empty box. Class members can critique the demonstration.

Reflect
How would you rate your home for safety awareness? Are the floors clear of clutter to avoid falls and accidents? Does everyone put away tools and materials when finished with them?

Discuss
What types of upkeep and organization practices will reduce hazards? What are the three upkeep and organization rules that you think everyone should follow?

Activity
Ask your custodial staff if they would demonstrate the proper use of their ladders around the school. Demonstrate how to inspect a ladder for safety.

Discuss
Describe how people at your home or in your neighborhood use ladders. Do they always practice safety?

Upkeep and Organization

Good upkeep and organization reduce hazards. A clean work area is a safe work area. Cluttered and messy areas can lead to accidents such as tripping, slipping, or being struck by falling objects.

Keep your work area clean. Always put your tools away after use. A tool on a ledge or overhang could slip and hit someone walking or working beneath.

Clean the floors regularly to remove any hazards that might cause slipping. Pick up scraps and wipe up spilled liquids. When mopping floors, always use safety cones or caution signs to warn of slippery conditions. Place the signs so they can be seen from all directions of approach.

Using Ladders Safely

Many jobs require the use of ladders. Ladders are useful aids, but they must be used with care. See 15-8. Choosing the right ladder for the job is important. Metal ladders should not be used near electrical equipment or high-voltage wires. Metal conducts electricity. Someone standing on or touching a metal ladder could be seriously injured or killed if electrical contact is made with the ladder.

15-8
To safely access high places, use a sturdy, securely positioned ladder and work within an arm's reach.

Reflect

Think of situations when you had to reach things at home that were too high. Did you get a chair or ladder? Did you get adult help? Did you take a risk and try to climb higher yourself?

Activity

List common flammable liquids people often store in their homes or garages. (*gasoline, paint thinner, cleaning solvents*)

Your Reading

Why should factory and construction workers be especially aware of safety hazards?

Always check a ladder before using it. Check to see that all the rungs are in place. Make sure the ladder is steady and strong enough to support you. Never use crates, boxes, or machinery as makeshift ladders. The chances of slipping and falling are too great.

Many people fall off ladders because they overreach. You should never stretch on a ladder. Instead, safely move the ladder within an arm's length of your work. Some other safety guidelines for using ladders are listed in the chart in 15-9.

Fire Protection

Fire is a threat to life and property. You must be on guard at all times to prevent fires. A fire at your workplace could put you out of a job. Even worse, someone could get seriously injured.

Each year, careless smoking and faulty electrical wiring and appliances account for nearly half of all fires. Other major causes include the following:

Enrich

Bring in a newspaper article about a fire that happened in your community. What was the cause? Could the fire have been prevented? Were smoke detectors present?

15-9
Ignoring any of these guidelines could result in a serious injury.

Safety Guidelines for Using Ladders
• Be sure the ladder is in good condition.
• Make sure the ladder has firm footing and is correctly placed.
• Open a ladder to its fullest width and lock it in position before you climb.
• Do not work from a ladder placed in front of a door that could be opened. Lock or block the door first.
• Always face the ladder when climbing up or down.
• Always take one step at a time and use both hands.
• Do not lean off-balance to reach the work. Instead, move the ladder.
• Never stand on the top two steps of a ladder.
• Do not use objects to create a makeshift ladder.
• When working outdoors on a home, make sure an extension ladder extends three feet above the roofline.

Discuss
Of the safety guidelines listed in Figure 15-9, which guideline do you think is ignored most often?

Example
Explain the school's emergency action plan for reporting a fire.

flammable liquid
A liquid that can easily ignite and burn rapidly.

Community Connections

Invite a firefighter to class to explain the use of fire extinguishers and the procedures to follow in the event of a fire. Include how to use the classroom fire extinguisher in the demonstration. Prepare questions in advance.

fire triangle
A symbol representing the three elements that provide the necessary condition for a fire: oxygen, fuel, and heat.

- faulty heating equipment
- grease buildup in kitchen ventilation hoods
- unattended open flames in kitchens and labs
- careless use of flammable liquids

A ***flammable liquid*** is one that can easily ignite and burn rapidly. Gasoline and solvents are flammable liquids.

Fire takes place when three elements are present—oxygen, fuel, and heat. If you remove any one of these three factors, you will extinguish the fire. Figure 15-10 illustrates the classic ***fire triangle***. The triangle symbol represents the three elements required to provide the necessary condition for a fire.

By removing a factor, the triangle opens and you extinguish the fire. If you keep any one factor from joining the other two, you prevent a fire from starting. In the event of a fire, you need to know the following:

- the location of all fire alarms, fire extinguishers, and exits
- how to use a fire alarm pull-box
- how to use the telephone to report a fire—Many regions of the country use *911* for emergency police and fire calls.

15-10
Fire cannot result unless all three sides of the fire triangle—oxygen, fuel, and heat—are present.

Discuss
Explain the fire triangle in Figure 15-10. Using the illustration, explain why a fire grows when people try to extinguish the flame by "beating" it with a towel or magazine.

Reflect
Have you ever administered first aid of any kind?

Enrich
Invite the school nurse as a guest speaker to share with students some basic first-aid steps. Encourage students to remember these when babysitting.

Familiarize yourself with how to contact that outside line from a workplace phone. In the case of a fire, you would give your name and say, "I want to report a fire at XZY Company." Give the building's address and the exact location of the fire or smoke within the building.

- how to evacuate the building—To ***evacuate*** means to empty or vacate a place in an organized manner for protection. Fire drills are a must at work and at home.
- how to use a fire extinguisher on a small fire—The purpose of a fire extinguisher is to put out a small fire or keep a fire from spreading. For the most part, firefighting should be left to trained firefighters.

Additional fire prevention tips are listed in 15-11.

evacuate
To empty or vacate a place in an organized manner for protection.

Your Reading
What could happen if there was a fire at your workplace?

Health and First Aid

Your health affects your performance at work. The food you eat and the amount of sleep you get could affect your work. Fatigue on the job often leads to carelessness and accidents. The same holds true for lack of proper food. A simple rule to follow is *get plenty of rest and proper nourishment.*

15-11
The best way to assure fire safety is to prevent one from ever starting.

Fire Prevention Tips
• Make sure smokers smoke only in designated areas.
• Keep your work area clean.
• Don't overload electrical wires. They can short-circuit and cause a fire.
• Never store oily rags and paper in open containers. They can build up heat and ignite.
• Keep containers of flammable liquids tightly closed and stored in cool areas.
• Always obey all safety rules. When in doubt, ask!

Making a Difference

Work with other classmates to design a newsletter for elementary school children about first aid and general safety. Obtain permission to distribute them in conjunction with giving a short presentation highlighting safety awareness.

first aid
Immediate, temporary treatment given in the event of an accident or illness before proper medical help arrives.

Observe simple hygiene rules. Always wash your hands after working with chemicals or before eating. Workers have transmitted harmful substances into their bodies because they failed to wash their hands before eating or smoking.

Where you eat on the job is important. Observe no-eating and no-smoking signs. Never eat where germs can infect your food and drink. Washrooms are not sanitary eating places, nor are most work areas.

It is best to stop working if you become ill on the job. You will not be working at top performance. Further, your illness may cause you to be careless and injure yourself or someone else. When ill, report to your supervisor. Your supervisor will make sure that you get proper medical assistance.

All injuries should be reported immediately. Get help fast. Report immediately for first aid, regardless of how slight the injury. If a coworker is injured, call for help. Remain calm and wait for proper medical assistance to arrive.

First aid is immediate, temporary treatment given in the event of an accident or illness before proper medical help arrives. Everyone should receive some formal first aid training. Essential lifesaving steps are listed in 15-12.

Your Reading

How does your health affect your performance at work?

OSHA

The Occupational Safety and Health Act is a federal law that calls for safe and healthy working conditions. The law

First Aid

When someone is injured, follow these basic first aid steps until proper medical help arrives.

1. Make sure the injured person has nothing in his or her mouth or throat. Food or gum could prevent the injured person from breathing.
2. Stop any bleeding. Apply pressure over the wound. A tourniquet should be used only as a last resort.
3. Prevent shock. Keep the injured person flat on his or her back with the head low. Keep the person warm.
4. Call for medical help. Stay with the injured person until help arrives.
5. Remain calm. Move the injured person only when there is an immediate threat of further injury if he or she is not moved.

15-12
Knowing how to give basic first aid could help save a person's life.

Resource
First Aid: Be Prepared, reproducible master 15-2, TR. Students research proper first-aid procedures to use in emergencies.

and the government agency that enforces it are both called ***OSHA***. The Occupational Safety and Health Administration is the name of the enforcement agency.

As an employee, you should know what OSHA requires of employers and employees. The law was passed to reduce hazards in the workplace. Both employers and employees have obligations under the law.

OSHA
A government agency and a federal law that calls for safe and healthy working conditions. The Occupational Safety and Health Administration is the agency, while the Occupational Safety and Health Act is the law.

Community Connections

Interview a worker who is responsible for his or her company's compliance with OSHA regulations to learn: What special equipment, procedures, and protective clothing are required of the company? What happens if a company does not follow OSHA requirements? What types of enforcement action does the agency take?

Employers' Responsibilities

OSHA requires employers to provide workplaces free from safety and health hazards. It also requires them to know and follow the standards set forth in the law. Employers' responsibilities include the following:

- providing a safe place to work
- examining conditions in the workplace to make sure they meet safety and health standards
- making sure employees use safe tools and equipment
- requiring employees to use personal protective gear
- using color codes, posters, labels, or signs to warn employees of potential hazards
- keeping OSHA records of work-related injuries and illnesses

Reflect

Do you feel safer knowing a federal agency oversees workplace safety? How do you feel about the rules OSHA has set for employees?

Resource

Personal Protection Equipment, color transparency CT-15, TR. Students discuss various items of protection equipment and the various jobs that require them.

- placing the OSHA poster in the workplace so employees know their rights and responsibilities
- allowing employee representatives to participate in safety inspections

Employees' Responsibilities

OSHA regulations also require employees to follow all rules, regulations, and orders issued under the law. Employees' responsibilities include the following:

- reading the OSHA poster at your job site
- knowing and following OSHA standards that apply to your work
- adhering to all of your employer's safety and health standards and rules
- reporting hazardous conditions to your supervisor
- reporting any job-related injuries or illnesses to your employer and seeking treatment quickly
- cooperating with OSHA compliance officers when they inspect conditions at your job site
- using your rights under the OSHA law responsibly
- wearing and/or using prescribed protective equipment. See 15-13.

What is OSHA and how does it affect you as an employee?

FLSA

FLSA
The Fair Labor Standards Act is designed to protect the educational opportunities of youth and prohibits their employment in jobs that could endanger their health and safety.

The ***FLSA*** (Fair Labor Standards Act) is designed to protect the educational opportunities of youth, and it prohibits their employment in jobs that could endanger their health and safety. The Department of Labor is the federal agency that monitors child labor and enforces child labor laws.

FLSA prohibits minors under age 18 years old from working in any occupation that it defines as hazardous. Among those occupations are excavation, manufacturing explosives, mining, and operating many types of power-driven equipment such as saws and slicers.

Child labor laws vary from state to state. Regulations provide specific information on those occupations. Consult

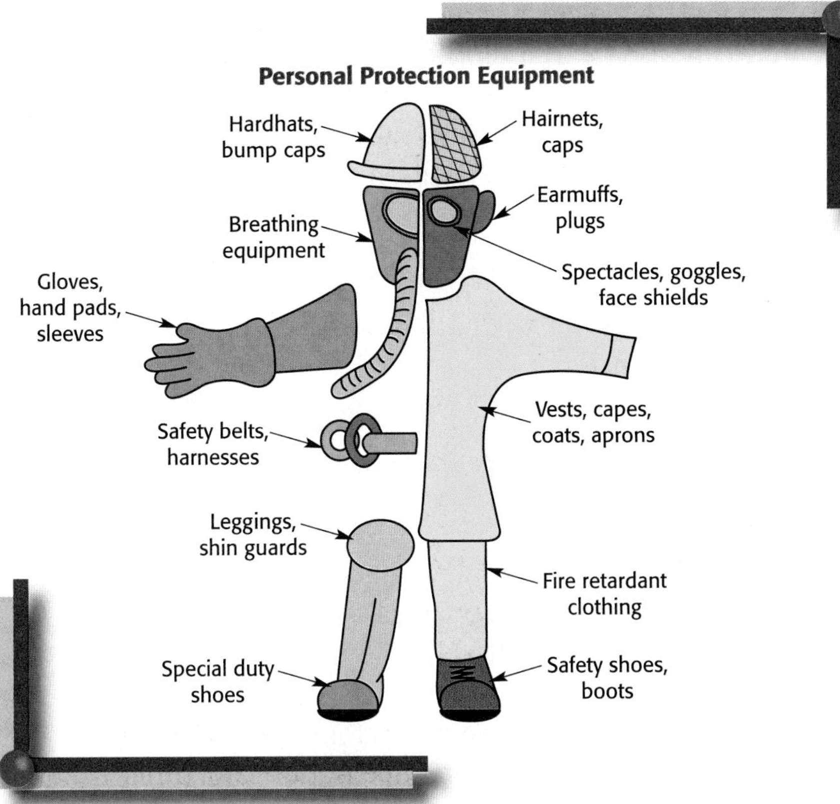

15-13
OSHA requires workers to wear specific kinds of protective equipment based on the potential hazards of their jobs.

Discuss

Use Figure 15-13 to discuss protective equipment on employees. Do you think the protective equipment makes it harder to do the job?

both the U.S. Department of Labor and state department of labor for more information. If a state law differs from the federal law, the stricter of the two laws applies to the employment of minor workers.

Your Reading

What is FLSA and how does it affect you as an employee?

Workers' Compensation

As a worker, a workers' compensation law probably covers you. ***Workers' compensation*** is insurance against work-related accidents. Most American workers are covered by workers' compensation.

workers' compensation
An insurance against loss of income from work-related accidents.

All 50 states have workers' compensation laws. These laws fall into two categories: compulsory and elective. Employers in the *compulsory* category must participate in the plan. Employers in the *elective* category may decide for themselves whether to participate. In the states where participation is elective, most employers provide coverage to limit their risk of negligence suits.

Resource

Do You Know How to Practice Safety? reproducible master 15-3, TR. Use the adapted worksheet to reinforce chapter concepts in students who are low functioning.

Unlike other forms of worker insurance, workers' compensation does not cost you any money through payroll deductions. Employers pay the premiums for workers' compensation. If you are injured on the job, your workers' compensation will cover the following:

- cost of unlimited medical treatment, including doctors, hospital fees, and rehabilitation services
- payment of lost wages (in the form of a percentage of your regular wage)
- death benefits to your family (in the form of a fixed amount of income)
- insurance against occupational diseases caused by working conditions, such as lung diseases
- income benefits for disability

What is the purpose of workers' compensation?

disability
A temporary or permanent physical or mental condition that prevents an employee from working.

A ***disability*** is a temporary or permanent physical or mental condition that prevents an employee from working. Sometimes a temporary disability is called *short-term*, and a permanent disability is called *long-term*. If permanently disabled, you will receive payments for the rest of your life.

The specifics of workers' compensation laws differ from state to state. You can find out about your state's law by contacting your state labor department.

Discuss
How much does workers' compensation cost an employee? (*nothing*) Who pays the premiums? (*the employer*)

Activity
Investigate the worker's compensation laws in your state and find out what is required of employers.

Disability Insurance

If you suffer a long-term disability, social security will pay you monthly benefits. See 15-14. Disability benefits from social security begin after a six-month waiting period. They are payable at any time before age 65, if you've worked long enough. To qualify for disability benefits, you must have worked at least 20 of the last 40 quarters.

Young workers who are disabled can also collect. Young workers may not have worked the entire 20 quarters, but they are still eligible in the event of long-term disability. Young workers' benefits are figured using a different scale. Young workers are eligible for disability benefits 18 months after they begin working.

If you become disabled and can't work, you should contact your local social security office. It will assist you with the needed information and forms.

What is the purpose of disability insurance?

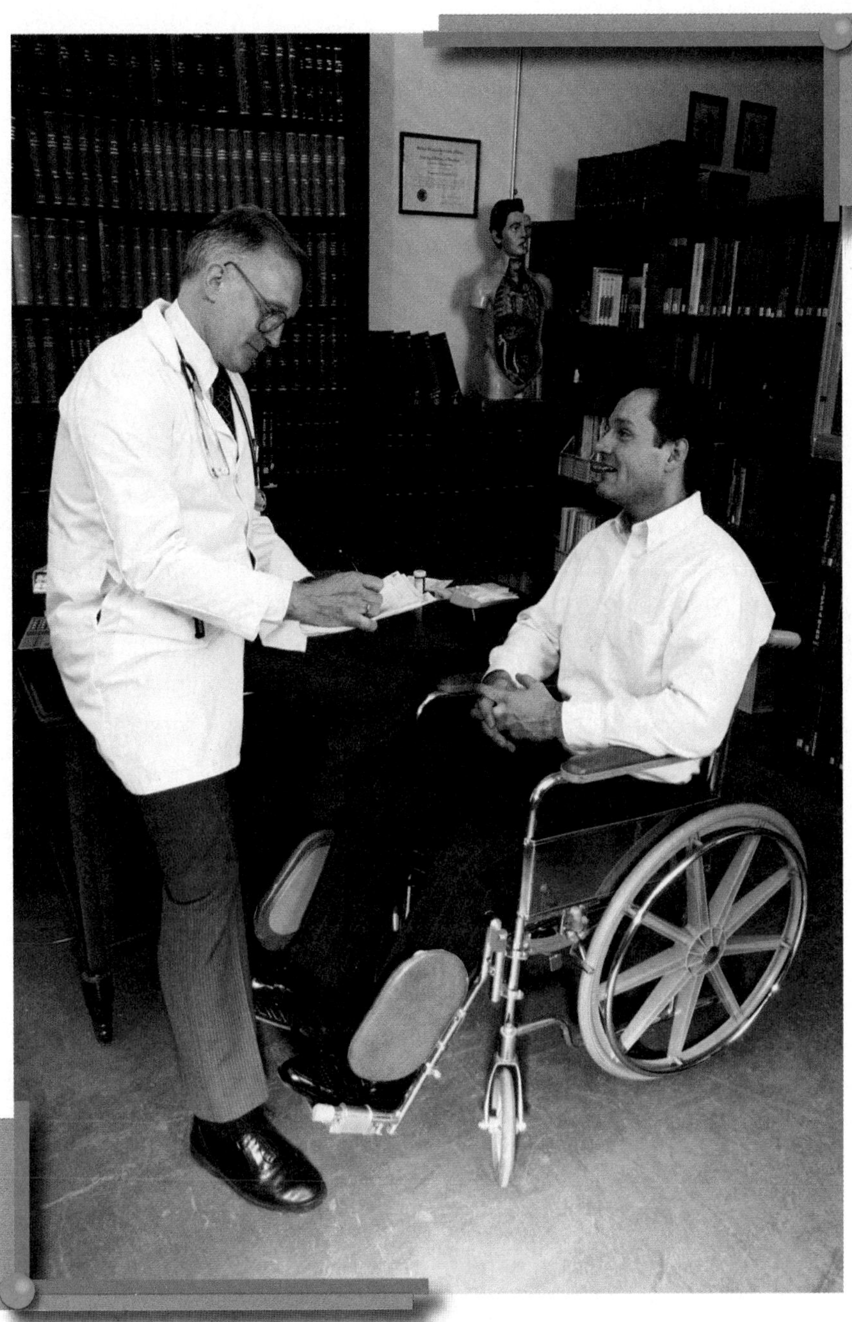

15-14
Disability benefits are paid to workers who cannot work for long periods of time due to job-related injuries.

Reflect

Do you know anyone who has had to adapt his or her life because of a disability?

Enrich

Investigate disability insurance by contacting an insurance agent to learn more about the coverage provided. Be prepared to give an oral report on your findings and demonstrate how to submit insurance claims.

Summary

Safety is everyone's concern. You must avoid unsafe acts and correct unsafe conditions. You also must develop a proper safety attitude. Whether you work in an office or a factory, you must always practice safety when working with tools and equipment. Job safety also includes proper lifting, upkeep, organization, and correct use of ladders.

Fire is a threat to life and property. Do all you can to prevent fires. If a fire does occur, be prepared. You should know what to do and how to report the fire by phone.

You must be alert and healthy to do a job well and safely. Follow good health and hygiene practices. Immediately report any injury you suffer. If you have a chance to take first aid training, do so.

OSHA is a federal law and a federal agency. Both promote safe and healthy working conditions. OSHA places responsibilities on both employers and employees. The FLSA is designed to protect youth in the workforce. Insurance against workplace injuries is covered by workers' compensation. Workers can also be protected with disability insurance.

Reviewing Key Concepts

1. Describe five unsafe acts and five unsafe conditions that lead to accidents.
2. List five safety practices that should be followed by people who work in workplaces such as offices.
3. Describe five proper safety procedures to follow when working with machinery and tools.
4. Name five safety hints to keep in mind when lifting.
5. Give five safety rules to follow when using ladders.
6. Name the three sides of a fire triangle and explain the principle illustrated by it.
7. Explain how you would use the telephone to report a fire in your classroom.
8. List five steps in first aid.
9. Name five employer responsibilities and five employee responsibilities as a result of OSHA.
10. Of what importance is workers' compensation to employees?

Answers to *Reviewing Key Concepts*

1. (Describe five of each. Student response.)
2. (List five. Student response.)
3. (Describe five. Student response.)
4. (Name five. Student response.)
5. (Give five. Student response.)
6. A fire triangle consists of oxygen, fuel, and heat. If you remove any one of these three factors, you extinguish the fire. If you keep any one factor from joining the other two, you prevent a fire from starting.
7. Dial the fire station or *911.* Give your name and say, "I would like to report a fire at (your school)." Give the school's address and the exact location of your classroom within the building.
8. (List the five steps. See Figure 15-12.)
9. (Name five of each. Student response.)
10. It provides insurance against work-related accidents.

Building Academic Skills

1. **Science.** Write the safety rules to follow in a science lab. Compare that list to the rules you must follow in a foods lab. In what ways are the lists similar?
2. **Health Education.** Review the first aid guidelines you have learned (or will learn) in health education or related classes. Make a list of everything you would do if a classmate next to you suddenly showed signs of a serious nosebleed.
3. **Science.** Demonstrate how mechanical devices are used to make the job of lifting easier. Show examples of how levers, pulleys, and other tools can be used to lift and control the movement of heavy objects.
4. **Science.** Talk with your science teacher to obtain a list of flammable liquids and learn if any are common household chemicals. Describe the proper storage for these chemicals and check your own home to see if they are being stored properly. Report any improperly stored chemicals and their fire potential to the head of your household.

Building Technology Skills

1. Use an Internet search engine, such as **google.com** or **hotbot.com**, to research safety attitudes. Select an article, read it, write a summary, and be prepared to share it with the class.
2. Conduct an Internet search on *workplace injuries*. Write a summary of the most frequently reported injuries as well as ways to avoid them. Also, investigate lighting and ventilation to determine if there are any special concerns in these areas.
3. Select a power tool or small electrical appliance that is used in your home and review the operating manual and/or use-and-care guide written for it. Bring the manual and/or guide to class to report the general safety guidelines listed in the front of the publication.
4. Prepare a PowerPoint presentation on how to avoid back problems when lifting objects on the job. Also, students are to locate pictures on exercises to strengthen back muscles. Show the best presentations to the class.
5. Conduct an online search to learn more about OSHA, the federal agency. Research its mission, activities, and enforcement role. Also, find out what an employer must provide to workers, according to OSHA regulations. Summarize your findings in a report to the class.
6. Search *workplace physical disability* online to gather the following statistics: the number of Americans this affects; the percentage of cases related to workplace accidents or injuries, the primary causes of workplace-related disabilities; and the top three jobs/industries in which workplace disabilities occur.

Building Career Knowledge and Skills

1. Read a newspaper story about a work-related accident. Write a paragraph summarizing the accident. Write a second paragraph summarizing what, if anything, could have been done to prevent the accident.
2. Research one aspect of first aid. Present your findings to the class in an oral report.
3. Write a report about the history of the OSHA agency, the workers' compensation program, or the social security program.
4. Demonstrate a safety tip to the class.
5. Invite a firefighter to speak to your class about fire protection. Be prepared to ask questions.
6. Interview a worker regarding safety and sanitation procedures that are in place at his or her place of employment. Describe the rules and regulations that must be followed to ensure workplace safety.

Building Workplace Skills

Participate in a Safety Awareness campaign at school. Working with two or three classmates, examine the school premises and determine what safety tips need to be emphasized to students. Decide as a team how to divide the work. Using a computer software program, create posters highlighting the safety message. Post them in appropriate locations around the school. Research the frequency of accidents—locally, statewide, or nationally—caused by the situation your posters address. Prepare a two-page report and briefly summarize your findings to the class.

What changes can affect my job status?

Chapter 16
Handling Changes in Job Status

Chapter Objectives

After studying this chapter, you will be able to

- **determine** factors to consider when changing from part-time to full-time work.
- **identify** reasons why workers are fired from their jobs.
- **explain** what positive action people should take after losing their jobs.
- **describe** ways to prepare for a promotion.
- **list** reasons why people change jobs.

Key Terms

wages
overtime pay
salary
commission
laid off
fired
letter of resignation

Key Concepts

- Changing from part-time to full-time work brings changes in income, fringe benefits, and lifestyle.
- If you lose a job, try to maintain a positive attitude.
- If you prepare for a promotion, you will be ready if a higher position becomes available.
- When you leave a job, do so in a professional manner.

Activity
Ask three adults how many jobs they have held since graduation from high school or college. How many of these jobs were in the same field? Did these jobs involve relocation?

Resource
Reinforcing Vocabulary, Activity A, WB. Students match terms with the definitions.

Resource
Starting Full-Time Work, Activity B, WB. Students interview a full-time worker to learn what transitions were needed following part-time employment.

Changing from Part-Time to Full-Time Work

Throughout your career, you are likely to experience several changes in job status. One change in job status might occur when you change from part-time to full-time work. See 16-1.

Many people begin working on a part-time basis. Some work part-time because they cannot find full-time jobs. Others choose to work only a certain number of hours each week. Students often have part-time jobs while going to school.

Changing from part-time to full-time work is a big step. It requires some careful thinking. Full-time work brings changes in income, fringe benefits, and lifestyle.

Income

wages
The money earned for doing hourly work.

overtime pay
The wages earned, usually one-and-a-half times the regular wage, for working additional hours beyond the normal 40-hour week.

Income is the money a person receives for doing a job. Most part-time and many full-time workers earn hourly ***wages***. They earn a set amount of money for every hour of work. An example is $8.00 per hour.

A full-time worker may be able to earn ***overtime pay***. This is usually one-and-a-half times the regular wage. It is usually paid for hours worked beyond the normal 40-hour week. For instance, a worker may earn $8.00 per hour for 40 hours and $12.00 for each extra hour of work thereafter. ($8.00 + $4.00 = $12.00)

16-1
Many people get early work experience with a part-time job in food service. Some people go on to full-time food service careers.

A full-time worker may earn an annual ***salary***. This is a set amount of money for a full year of work. The amount is divided into equal payments. As an example, a worker with an annual salary of $36,000 earns $3,000 a month or about $692.31 every week. The same amount is earned each pay period regardless of the number of hours worked. For example, some weeks may require more than 40 hours of work.

Some full-time workers, especially those in sales, earn commissions. A ***commission*** is a percentage of the dollar amount of sales made. Therefore, a salesperson who sells more will earn more. For instance, a 10% commission on sales of $100 is $10. The same rate of commission on sales of $200 is $20.

Some people do not feel secure working for a commission because they do not receive a stable income. A good salesperson can achieve high earnings by working for commission. However, if a salesperson makes very few sales, he or she will not have much income.

When changing to a full-time job, think about the income you want to earn. Do you want a job where you would earn hourly wages? Would you want to receive overtime pay for extra work? Would you enjoy the steady pay of a job with a salary, or would you prefer the flexibility of commissions?

salary
A set amount of money paid to an employee for a full year of work.

Discuss
Discuss the difference between being paid a salary versus a commission.

commission
A percentage of the money received from a sale.

Resource
Forms of Income, reproducible master 16-1, TR. Students list the advantages and disadvantages of earning income in various forms.

Community Connections

Interview people who are paid on commission. Find out the answers to the following questions: How do they feel about being paid on commission versus getting a regular paycheck? Do they budget their money any differently? Does commission work make them view their job differently than if they received a regular paycheck?

Fringe Benefits

Fringe benefits are extra financial rewards beyond regular paychecks. Examples include medical, dental, life, and disability insurance, 16-2. Others are paid holidays, vacations, and sick leave. Some companies also offer bonuses, pension plans, tuition aid, and child care assistance.

Part-time workers receive few, if any, fringe benefits. The fringe benefits offered to full-time workers vary widely from company to company. When you look for a full-time job, consider fringe benefits as well as income.

Lifestyle

Taking a full-time job will affect your lifestyle. A full-time job usually involves at least 8 hours of work a day for a total of 40 hours per week. When you accept such a job, your employer expects you to be there full time. You should not arrive late or leave early. You should show up every day. You should not take time off unless you are truly ill.

16-2
Dental insurance is just one of many fringe benefits companies often provide for full-time employees.

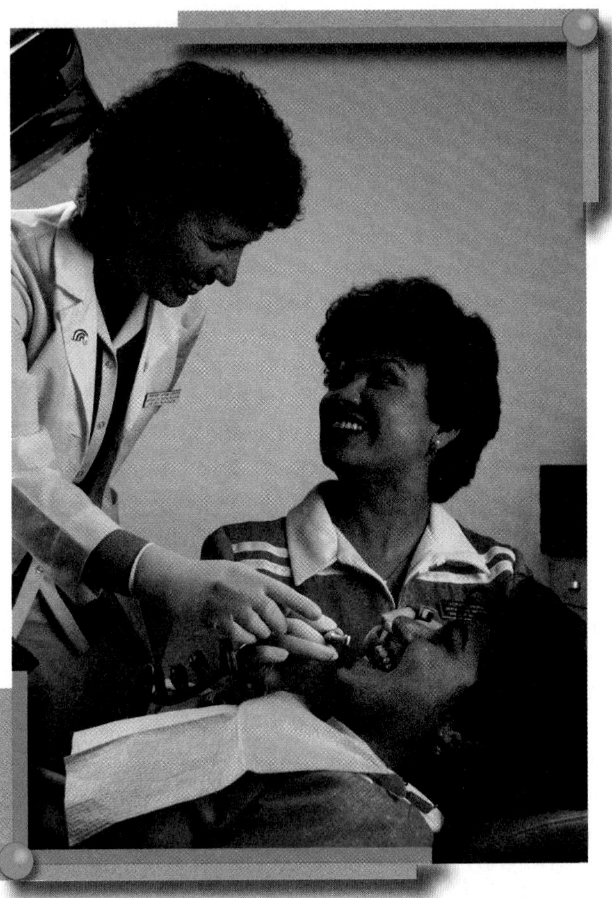

Example

Help students understand how valuable fringe benefits are by using the example of dental benefits. Under many insurance plans, annual dental check-ups do not cost anything. If you had to pay for dental services out of your own pocket, routine cleaning and X-rays could cost $100 or more.

Your Reading

What types of changes might you encounter when changing from part-time to full-time work?

Your time at work should be devoted to your job. You must arrange to take care of personal and family matters after work or on your days off. This means that you will not have as much free time as you did as a student or part-time worker.

Getting accustomed to working 40 hours a week may take some time. You may feel tired at the end of the workday or workweek. After a while, you will adjust to the longer hours. Until you do, you may have to give up some of your activities.

Reflect

If someone in your family got laid off from a job, how would (or did) you feel? What helped them get through that emotional period?

Losing a Job

No one wants to think about losing a job. It is an unpleasant experience. However, the fact remains that people do lose their jobs for various reasons. Some are laid off and others are fired.

laid off
To lose a job because the employer must release the employee for financial reasons.

The reason for being ***laid off*** is beyond a worker's control. A worker may be laid off because the company is failing and short of money. The company may be reorganizing or cutting back on production. In such cases, the last person hired is usually the first one to be laid off. Being laid off is not the worker's fault. It does not mean the person was not a good worker.

Being ***fired*** from a job is different. A worker is usually fired because of poor performance. The person's work may be unsatisfactory. The person may not be able to get along with others. Common reasons why people are fired are listed in 16-3.

fired
To lose a job because of unacceptable work or behavior.

Take Positive Action

If you lose a job, try to maintain a positive attitude. Brooding about a job loss is useless. The sensible thing to do is to take a good, long look at yourself. List your personality traits, interests, aptitudes, and abilities. Think about your values and goals. Decide what kind of work you want to do. Find out if you need more education. If you need retraining to enter another field, get it. When you are ready, go out and seek another job.

If you were fired from your job, learn from the experience. Look at the situation from your employer's point of view. Think about what went wrong. Correct your faults and move ahead. Be determined not to make the same mistakes again. Think positively and begin a new job search.

Vocabulary
Explain the differences between a worker who is *laid off* versus *fired* from a job.

Discuss
Give reasons why a company might lay off workers rather than fire them.

Discuss
Figure 16-3 shows reasons for firing employees. Do any of the reasons listed surprise you? Do you think any other reasons should be added to the list?

Common Reasons for Firing Employees

- Disregarding orders and being disrespectful
- Failing to follow rules and policies
- Abusing drugs or alcohol
- Being dishonest
- Making costly mistakes and failing to do the work properly
- Being lazy
- Often arriving late or being absent
- Failing to get along with supervisors, coworkers, and/or customers
- Causing trouble and acting carelessly
- Behaving rudely and using abusive language
- Always acting dissatisfied
- Making fun of coworkers
- Acting superior and bossing others around

16-3
Employers consider any of these behaviors to be a "just cause" for firing employees.

Your Reading
What are some reasons a person might lose a job?

Making a Difference

Create posters that express positive ways to keep a job. Check various places in the community, such as a local shelter or welfare-to-work programs that would welcome the posters to encourage the clients they are training to become competent workers.

Your Reading

Why might a person seek a promotion?

Resource

Prepare for a Promotion, color transparency CT-16, TR. Students discuss what employees can do to be considered for a promotion.

Reflect

Has a parent or someone close to you changed jobs recently? Is the person happy in the new job?

Being Promoted

At some point, you may feel that you have achieved all the goals you set for yourself in a job. You want new challenges. When this happens, it is time to seek a promotion. A promotion is a move up to a higher position within a company.

You may need to be patient to get a promotion. Generally, a higher position becomes available in two ways. In some cases, an employer creates a new position to be filled. More often, a position becomes available when a worker leaves it. That worker quits, is fired, retires, or is promoted to a different job.

If you want a promotion, start preparing for it early. Do your best to be ready when a higher position becomes available. The following tips will help you prepare:

- Always strive to do your job well.
- Maintain a good attendance record.
- Have a positive attitude about work.
- Get along with everyone.
- Volunteer to do extra work.
- Look for ways to learn on the job.
- Take additional training or further education.
- Be willing to accept more responsibility.
- Express your desire for new challenges.
- Be able to accept change and use it constructively.

Changing Jobs

The average person changes jobs at least eight to ten times during a career. Because employers do not expect workers to stay in the same jobs forever, they try to promote them into new positions. This is not always possible. Therefore, people change companies and sometimes careers. Common reasons for changing jobs are listed in 16-4.

Some people change jobs for a good reason. Others change jobs without thinking through their decisions. Before you make a decision to change jobs, you should ask yourself the following questions and answer them honestly and thoughtfully:

Common Reasons for Changing Jobs

- Problems with supervisors and/or coworkers
- Problems with health that dictate a job or environment change
- Transportation problems
- Desire to have one's own business
- A company closing or relocation
- Elimination of one's job (because of technological changes, company restructuring, or other reasons)
- Desire for better pay and/or fringe benefits
- Desire for more opportunities for advancement
- Desire for better working conditions or hours
- Desire for a job that better uses knowledge, skills, and abilities

16-4
People change jobs for many reasons during their careers.

Resource
Climbing the Career Ladder, reproducible master 16-2, TR. Students examine how promotions can turn a job into a career.

Discuss
Use Figure 16-4 to talk about the reasons for changing jobs. Can you add any more pros or cons to the list?

Resource
Changing Jobs, Activity C, WB. Students identify advantages and disadvantages of changing jobs.

Adapting the Lesson
Have students who are low functioning circle appropriate reasons to change jobs from a list of good and bad reasons that you provide. Discuss the choices with them.

Discuss
Do you think that moving frequently for job reasons would affect you and your family? What are the pros and cons?

Resource
Leaving a Job, Activity D, WB. Students rewrite a poorly written letter of resignation to incorporate more positive language.

- What are my real reasons for leaving this job? Am I leaving to accept something better? (If not, maybe you shouldn't be considering a change at this time.)
- Am I getting along with my boss and my fellow employees? (If not, why not? Is there something you can do to change a bad situation into a good one? Have you discussed your feelings with your employer? Many problems can be solved through employer-employee discussions. Perhaps you just need a change in job assignment or a transfer to a different department.)
- Have I given myself and the job a chance? (Employers do not want an employee who seems to hop from one job to another. Employers don't expect employees to stay with them forever, but they do expect a stay of a year or more.)
- If you aren't sure you want to change jobs, don't rush. Take time to think about both the pros and cons of changing jobs, as listed in 16-5. Close friends or family members can help you explore your reasons for seeking a new job.

Leaving a Job

Once you decide to change jobs, resist the urge to quit your current job right away. Instead, start looking for a new

Pros and Cons of Changing Jobs
Pros
• Chance for a new beginning
• Higher pay scale
• Better fringe benefits
• More room for advancement
• New opportunities for training or learning
• New experiences and challenges
Cons
• Unfamiliar people and surroundings
• Possible loss of some vacation benefits
• Possible loss of accumulated paid sick time
• Possible loss of seniority benefits
• The need to establish a new daily routine
• Being labeled a job-hopper

16-5
Consider the advantages and disadvantages carefully before making a job change.

Community Connections

Talk to a human resources representative from an area employer to learn how companies handle employee resignations. Ask how employee resignation should be handled so no negative feelings result. Ask the representative for tips on how employees should behave during the period of employment following the official notice of resignation.

one while working at your current job. Employment is not always easy to find. Unless you have enough money set aside, consider keeping your current job until you find a better one.

When you are ready to quit your job, do so in a professional manner. Tell your employer before you tell any of your coworkers. Give at least two weeks' notice, preferably three. Your employer needs that time to find a replacement for you.

The most polite and professional way to exit a job is to put your plan to quit or resign in writing. A sample letter of resignation is shown in 16-6. Your ***letter of resignation*** should include the following points:

letter of resignation
A formal letter stating plans to quit or resign from a job.

- your last day of work
- a positive reason for your resignation
- a few nice words about your present employment

It is wise to personally give notice to your employer. You can do this just before you hand in your letter of resignation. Take time to tell your employer about your new job. Also tell your employer how much you have gained from working in your current job. You can also use this time to ask your employer for a letter of recommendation. It could help you the next time you search for a job.

Resource
Job Changes Through a Career, Activity E, WB. Students examine a case study regarding various job changes.

3 Park Avenue
Perth Amboy, NJ 07728
August 10, 20XX

Ms. Arlene Banks
First Bank and Trust Company
33 Main Street
Perth Amboy, NJ 07728

Dear Ms. Banks:

Please accept my resignation from the position of bank teller as of August 24, 20XX.

My decision to resign is based on my desire to further my business education. I recently enrolled as a part-time business student at Taft Community College. Therefore, I have accepted a teller position with the Union Bank, located across the street from the Taft campus. This will allow me more flexibility in scheduling my business classes.

My position with First Bank and Trust Company has been rewarding both personally and professionally. I wish to thank you for providing me with the opportunity to enhance my skills in the banking field.

Sincerely,

Terry Smith
Terry Smith

16-6
Leaving a job in a professional manner involves giving your employer a letter of resignation.

Resources
Report on Changes, Activity F, WB. Students write a report on a magazine article that covers a topic discussed in the chapter.

Activity
Role-play an employee giving an employer notice and a letter of resignation. Show how the employee should act. Demonstrate how body language can also play a part in communicating this information.

Resource
What Happened to Joe's Job? reproducible master 16-3, TR. Use the adapted worksheet to reinforce chapter concepts in students who are low functioning.

Make every effort to be on friendly terms with everyone when you leave. During your last days at work, continue to do your job to the best of your ability. Do not complain about your current job. Do not brag about your new job. Be as pleasant as possible to your supervisor and coworkers. You may need their help sometime in the future. You may need to use their names as references in future job hunts. You may even find your career paths crossing again. It is better to have friends than enemies.

Your Reading

What is the most professional, polite way to exit a job?

Summary

Throughout your career, your job status is likely to change many times. One change may be from part-time to full-time work. Taking that step will create other changes in income, fringe benefits, and lifestyle.

Try to avoid losing a job. If you are laid off or fired, you take positive action to find another job.

A change for the better in job status is a promotion. Start preparing for a promotion early. Then you will be ready if a higher position becomes available.

If you are like the average worker, you will change jobs at least eight to ten times during your career. Think carefully before you decide to change jobs. Consider both the pros and cons. Once you decide to leave, do so in a professional manner. Give your employer at least two weeks' notice. Submit a letter of resignation. Do your best to leave on friendly terms.

Reviewing Key Concepts

1. When a person's income is stated as $30,000 a year, that person is earning _____.
   A. hourly wages
   B. overtime pay
   C. an annual salary
   D. a commission
2. List five examples of fringe benefits.
3. Describe one way in which changing from part-time to full-time work might affect a person's lifestyle.
4. Differentiate between being laid off and being fired.
5. List five reasons why people are fired.
6. What positive action should a fired employee take?
7. Name five ways to prepare for a promotion.
8. List five reasons why people change jobs.
9. Why should workers give their employers at least two weeks' notice when they decide to change jobs?
10. What three points should a letter of resignation contain?

Answers to *Reviewing Key Concepts*

1. C
2. (List five:) medical, dental, life, and disability insurance; paid holidays, vacation pay, and sick leave; bonuses; pension plans; tuition aid; child care assistance
3. (Student response.)
4. The reason for being laid off is beyond a worker's control, but being fired is usually the result of the worker's poor performance.
5. (List five. See Figure 16-3 of text.)
6. (Student response.)
7. (Name five. Student response.)
8. (List five. Student response.)
9. Their employers need that time to find workers to replace them.
10. date of the last workday, positive reason for the resignation, some nice words about the employment

Building Academic Skills

1. **Math.** Use the current minimum wage to estimate your income in a 40-hour week. List what you believe your expenses would be for all necessary items. After all deductions, what will your take-home pay be? Write a paragraph describing the type of lifestyle you would be able to afford on this salary.
2. **Writing.** Write a paragraph describing the career you hope to have. In a second paragraph, describe the lifestyle you plan to maintain. Finally, in a third paragraph, describe the work schedule you will have and the leisure activities you will pursue in your free time.

Building Technology Skills

1. Visit a Web site such as **houseandhome.msn.com** that will allow you to compare the cost of living in various cities. Use the average salary of $38,000 in Dallas, Texas, with five other cities for comparison. What did you learn about the cost of living in various cities?
2. Locate Web sites using **yahoo.com** that address getting along with the boss. Do a second search on getting along with coworkers. Use the information you found to compile a list of do's and don'ts regarding how to relate to coworkers and supervisors. Share your lists with the class.

Building Career Knowledge and Skills

1. Read the want ads in a newspaper. Find two jobs that offer hourly wages, two that offer annual salaries, and two that offer commissions. Identify which jobs mention fringe benefits and what they are.
2. Find a news story about a company that laid off workers. Prepare an oral report about the story. In it, explain why the workers were laid off. If the news story includes interviews with the workers, describe how they felt and what actions they planned to take to find new jobs.
3. Interview someone who has changed jobs. Find out why the person decided to change jobs. Ask what the pros and cons of the decision were. Find out what steps the person took in leaving the old job. Prepare a written report.
4. Write a letter of resignation for a fictitious job.
5. Interview someone who has been laid off. Describe the personal feelings experienced as well as the process involved in finding another job. What lifestyle adjustments were necessary until the person was settled in another job?
6. Interview someone who moved from part-time to full-time employment or vice versa. Describe the lifestyle adjustments experienced and the advice that the person would offer regarding changing status of employment.

Building Workplace Skills

Suppose you own a small flower shop with three full-time employees. All three do the same job; they create floral arrangements for most of the day and interact with customers. You have $7,000 to divide among the three for bonuses and/or pay raises next year, but first you must decide how to determine which worker qualities or accomplishments deserve a bonus or more pay. First, list the outstanding characteristics and/or behaviors that should be considered. Then develop a chart or table to analyze how employees rate in each category.

Part Five

Developing Personal Skills for Job Success

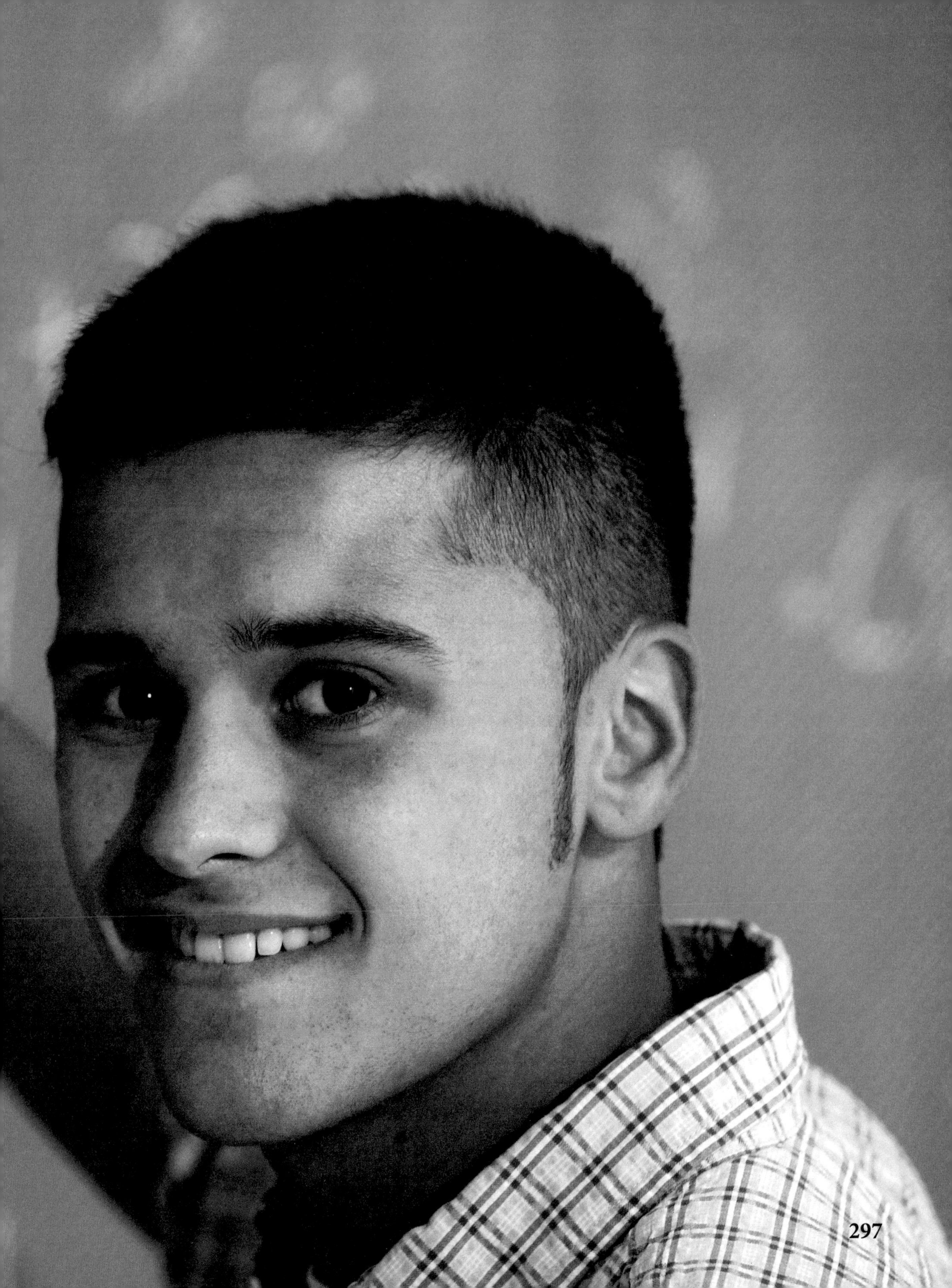

How do reading, writing, and math relate to my success on the job?

Chapter 17
Basic Skills for Job Success

Key Terms

vocabulary
illiterate
proofread
metric system
meter
gram
liter
degrees Celsius (°C)

Chapter Objectives

After studying this chapter, you will be able to

- **state** the importance of the basic skills: reading, writing, and math.
- **count** change correctly.
- **describe** the metric system of measurement.
- **identify** basic computer skills.

Key Concepts

- Reading, writing, and math are essential skills for finding and keeping a job.
- Understanding basic math, counting change, and taking measurements are skills that employers expect.
- Basic computer skills are needed for most jobs today.

The Starting Point—Basic Skills

Basic skills are taught throughout your years in school because they are so important in your life. The three basic skills are reading, writing, and math. Why are these skills called basic? It is not because they are simple. Reading, writing, and math are called basic skills because they are the foundation for the development of more advanced skills. Basic skills also are keys to success.

Why are the three basic skills important?

Reading Skills

As you read this sentence, you are practicing the basic skill of reading. Imagine not being able to read. How would you find your way to a new place if you could not read a map or street signs? How would you know where to apply for a job if you could not read the newspaper want ads?

Most jobs involve reading in some way. At work, you may need to read the following:

- business letters
- customer orders to fill
- directions for operating pieces of equipment
- instructions from your supervisor
- the policies and procedures of your workplace

Once you have learned the basic skill of reading, you will need to continue practicing. The more you read, the better your reading skills will become. Reading for pleasure is a good way to improve your reading skills. *Reading for pleasure* means taking time to read any subject that interests you. You can choose books, magazines, or newspapers. Reading newspapers is also a great way to keep up with events that are occurring around you.

Reading helps you to increase your vocabulary. Your ***vocabulary*** is the group of words you know and use. Likewise, increasing your vocabulary helps to improve reading skills. If you do not understand a word you read, take time to look it up in a dictionary. You will learn a new word, which increases your vocabulary. You will get more enjoyment from what you are reading because you will understand it. Good reading skills are a requirement for the higher-paying jobs in the workplace, 17-1.

Resource

Reinforcing Vocabulary, Activity A, WB. Students match terms with their definitions.

Activity

List everything you did yesterday on paper. Put a star by items that involved reading. What percentage of listed items has stars?

Resource

Strengthening Your Vocabulary, Activity B, WB. Students identify unfamiliar words in a brief article and find their definitions.

vocabulary
The group of words known and used by an individual.

How does reading relate to vocabulary?

17-1
Health professionals need to be able to read instruments and patients' records.

Making a Difference

According to the United Nations Educational, Scientific and Cultural Organization (UNESCO), there are 771 million illiterate adults in the world. Find out how you can help others in your community overcome illiteracy. Visit the ProLiteracy Worldwide Web site at **proliteracy.org** to locate a volunteer organization in your area.

Activity

Select a career that interests you. Write down all the basic tasks you will do in that career. Go back to your list and put a star by those that involve writing. What percentage of items involved writing?

Writing Skills

A number of work tasks involve writing. Your job may require you to write the following:

- e-mails to coworkers
- business letters to customers
- orders from customers
- reports of your job activities
- research reports
- telephone messages, 17-2

Writing skills are closely related to reading skills. People who enjoy reading are likely to be good writers. Good writers use their vocabularies to express themselves on paper.

Your writing skills include your ability to spell and use proper grammar. Writing skills also involve your ability to construct clear sentences and organize paragraphs.

17-2
Workers are expected to have the skills necessary to take complete, accurate messages.

Resource
Building Your Word Power, reproducible master 17-1, TR. Students match terms to their definitions and write sentences using the terms.

Vocabulary
Use the term *illiterate* in a sentence to demonstrate understanding.

Like reading, writing is a basic skill needed to perform most jobs. A person who does not know how to read or write is ***illiterate***. Thousands of people in the United States are illiterate. This often interferes with their ability to get or keep a job and earn a decent wage.

illiterate
Being unable to read or write.

The quality of your writing says a lot about you. Whenever people read something another person has written, they form an impression of that person. If there are many errors, they may assume that person lacks writing skills. On the other hand, they may think the person is too careless or lazy to check what they have written and correct the errors. It is important to be a good writer. You do not want people to think you don't care about your work.

Reflect
How do you think someone feels who cannot read well? Do you think such students will ask for the help they need?

Resource
Proofreading for Accuracy, Activity C, WB. Students proofread sentences and mark all errors they find.

Whenever you write something for someone else to read, be sure to proofread it carefully. To ***proofread*** means to read something and mark any errors. As you read, think carefully about what your words say. Do they make sense? Are your ideas stated in an orderly manner? Use a dictionary to check your spelling. Use a language reference book to check your grammar and punctuation. Be sure to correct your errors as you rewrite or retype what you have written.

proofread
To read something, check for mistakes, and mark any errors found.

Practicing your writing skills can help you to improve. Try to write something every day. Writing can be in the form of a letter to a friend, an essay for school, or an entry in a personal journal or diary. When you are in school, much of

Activity

Survey the class to learn how many students have parents who use computers on their jobs. Did they need to have special training to learn the computer at their workplaces?

Discuss

Why is it important to proofread in addition to using your computer's spell check feature?

Reflect

How well do you type? Can you easily use word processing programs? Do you know how to find the synonym feature on your computer?

your writing is done for homework. On days when you are not in school, try writing a short letter or e-mail message to a friend or family member. If you are creative, try writing a short story. You might want to keep a journal. This is a good way to record your thoughts on paper in a casual style. Whether you are writing for pleasure, for a job, or for school, always try to use good grammar and proper punctuation.

Using the Computer

One way to practice writing is with a computer. Some people write more easily with a computer than with a pen and paper. This requires basic keystroking skills that are perfected with practice. Using the computer for writing will strengthen your writing skills and prepare you for the workplace, 17-3.

The computer software programs that specialize in creating written communications are *word processing* programs. They usually include a feature that checks spelling, grammar, and punctuation. This feature does not, however, help you with *synonyms*, such as *sail* and *sale*. These are words that sound alike but are spelled differently. This is one example of the need for proofreading even when using a computer.

Computers are also used for writing e-mails. Again, proper grammar, capitalization, and punctuation are

17-3
The ability to use a computer to communicate is a requirement for many jobs.

important. Do not get into the habit of using shorthand or abbreviations common in instant and text messaging. Most e-mail programs include a spell-check feature, but it is still important to proofread before sending.

Your Reading

What abilities are needed to write well?

Math Skills

Jobs that require high-level math skills often have special computer programs for workers to use. Most jobs require basic math ability. This involves adding, subtracting, multiplying, and dividing.

Many people use these basic math skills every day in their job. They count money, count items to fill an order, add prices to get totals, and take inventory. Accountants, cashiers, and bank tellers continually work with numbers. Many other workers need a good working knowledge of numbers, too.

- Bakers and chefs measure ingredients, 17-4.
- Nurses must give patients the correct doses of medicine.
- Architects use precise measurements when drawing plans.
- Salespeople add totals and subtract discounts.
- Carpenters take frequent measurements when building houses.

Resource

Math Practice, Activity D, WB. Students use basic math skills to solve various problems.

Activity

Given a list of as many careers as possible, have students name those needing math skills. Discuss the types of math skills needed in the jobs. Discuss math skills needed to manage a household. Make a list of all the everyday activities that require knowledge of numbers and calculations.

Hershey Entertainment and Resort Company

17-4
Determining portion size and ordering the right amount of ingredients are some food service tasks that require good math skills.

Discuss

Discuss the need for math ability in the food service industry. What could go wrong in a restaurant if someone has poor math skills?

Community Connections

Food service workers use math skills on a daily basis. Interview someone you know who works in this industry. Create a list of all the routine tasks accomplished by the employee that require math. Compare the results of your interview with a classmate's interview experience.

Even if a job does not require math ability, employers expect workers to be able to make basic calculations when needed. To prepare yourself for a variety of jobs, you should be able to work with whole numbers and mixed numbers. You should also know how to figure percentages, decimals, and fractions.

You have probably learned and reviewed each of these math skills. Identify the areas that give you trouble and practice solving math problems that address them. If you practice now, you will develop confidence and become better at math. Your efforts now in perfecting these skills may help you avoid job problems in the future.

Counting Change

Many jobs involve accepting money and counting change. Examples are the jobs of bank tellers, store clerks, food servers, and cashiers. People in these jobs must account for every penny of each transaction. Knowing how to count change is an important skill in your personal life, too. If you cannot accurately count money, you may cheat yourself or someone else. Most businesses today use cash registers to calculate the amount of change the customer receives. Workers who handle money usually receive special training and instructions.

Some basic guidelines will help you count change accurately.

- Place the cash from the customer on top of the register until the transaction is complete. This way there can be no mistake about the amount the customer gave you.
- Remove the correct amount of change from the cash drawer, as indicated by the register.
- Next, count the change out loud to the customer.
- Count from largest denomination to smallest. For example, when making change for a $20 bill, count the $10 bill, then any $5 bills, and dollar bills last. Repeat the process for any coins.
- Give the customer the change.
- Place the cash from the top of the register in the drawer.

Discuss

Think about purchasing items at a store. What helps the clerk make the correct change? Describe some of the ways people make change. What is the most accurate way to give a customer change back?

Note

When people do not receive the correct change, they may think you are trying to cheat them.

Do not rush! Take your time and count clearly. This may be difficult when there are 10 people in a cashier's line. Just stay calm and steady. The customer will appreciate your taking the time to assure accuracy. See 17-5.

Vocabulary
What is the metric system of measurement? What terms are used in metric measuring?

Note
The International System is often referred to as *SI*, which is an abbreviation of the French name *Système International d'Unités*.

Measurements

Many jobs involve taking and using measurements. Fashion designers need to take body measurements and measure fabric. Chemists need to measure chemicals. Engineers need to measure distances. If measurements are not made precisely, work may not be completed accurately.

Many countries follow the International System of measurement, also known as the ***metric system***. It is a decimal system of weights and measures. In the metric system, the basic unit of measuring distance is a ***meter***. One meter (m), about 39 inches, is slightly longer than one yard, which is 36 inches.

metric system
A decimal system of weights and measures.

meter
The basic unit of measuring distance in the metric system.

17-5
Businesses require their employees to count change out loud in front of customers.

Activity
Provide groups of students with a meter stick or tape measure. Have the groups rotate around the room, measuring items such as the height of chairs, length of a table, width of classroom doors and windows, size of floor tile, and so forth.

Reflect
Recall your first experience with using metric measurements. Was it in the science or foods lab? What were your feelings at first? Did you eventually find the system easy to use?

Adapting the Lesson

Have students who are high functioning research the metric system to find out who invented it and how it is used in industry. Students are to create a list of pros and cons about the United States converting to the metric system.

In the United States, the basic units for measuring distance are inches, feet, yards, and miles. This measurement system is called the *U.S. customary system*. The terms *conventional* and *traditional* are also used to refer to the U.S. system.

Many products used in the United States are imported from countries that use the metric system. Therefore, being familiar with both systems will help you in many jobs. For instance, mechanics often use tools sized to fit metric parts.

Weight is measured in ounces, pounds, and tons in the United States. In the metric system, the basic unit of measuring weight is a ***gram***. One gram (g) is much smaller than an ounce.

Volume is measured in cups, pints, quarts, and gallons in the U.S. system. In the metric system, the basic unit of measuring volume is a liter. One ***liter*** (l) is somewhat more than a quart.

Meters, grams, and liters are the basic units of measurement in the metric system. The size of the units are increased or decreased in multiples of 10. Six prefixes are added to the basic units to increase or decrease the size of the units. They are *kilo, hecto, deka, deci, centi,* and *milli*. See 17-6.

gram
The basic unit of measuring weight in the metric system.

liter
The basic unit of measuring volume in the metric system.

17-6
The metric system uses these prefixes to increase or decrease the size of meters, grams, and liters by multiples of 10.

Metric Prefixes

Prefix	Meaning	Distance	Weight	Volume
kilo	one thousand	kilometer (km) 1000 meters	kilogram (kg) 1000 grams	kiloliter (kl) 1000 liters
hector	one hundred	hectometer (hm) 100 meters	hectogram (hg) 100 grams	hectoliter (hl) 100 liters
deka	ten	dekameter (dam) 10 meters	dekagram (dag) 10 grams	dekaliter (dal) 10 liters
deci	one-tenth	decimeter (dm) .1 meter	decigram (dg) .1 gram	deciliter (dl) .1 liter
centi	one-hundredth	centimeter (cm) .01 meter	centigram (cg) .01 gram	centiliter (cl) .01 liter
milli	one-thousandth	millimeter (mm) .001 meter	milligram (mg) .001 gram	milliliter (ml) .001 liter

Discuss

Name some beverage containers that use U.S. customary measurements. Name some that use metric measurements.

Activity

Make flash cards using Figure 17-6. Have students work in groups to match prefixes used in metric measures to such categories as *meaning, distance, weight,* and *volume*. Have an answer sheet available for self-correcting.

Temperature in the United States is measured by degrees Fahrenheit (°F). Water freezes at 32°F, and it boils at 212°F. In the metric system, the basic unit of measuring temperature is measured in ***degrees Celsius (°C)***. Water freezes at 0°C and boils at 100°C. One degree Celsius is somewhat more than two degrees Fahrenheit.

degrees Celsius (°C)
The basic unit of measuring temperature in the metric system.

Changing from one unit to another in the U.S. system can be confusing. All the units are in different proportions. For instance, to change inches to feet, you must divide by 12. However, to change feet to yards, you must divide by 3.

Discuss

Do you believe the United States should convert to the metric system? Explain your opinion.

Changing from one unit to another is easier in the metric system. All the units are multiples of 10. To change centimeters to decimeters, you divide by 10. To change decimeters to meters, you also divide by 10. (Simply moving the decimal point left one place is an easy way to divide by 10.)

Formulas can be used to convert between measurement systems. See 17-7. Normally you will work with one system rather than converting between the two. Working with different forms of measurement leads to mistakes if conversions are not made correctly. One example is the Hubble telescope, one of the most important space telescopes. The use of different measurement systems during construction led to errors and problems when first launched.

What does basic math ability include?

Computer Skills

As you read in Chapter 1, the computer revolution has changed the way people live and work. At stores, computers itemize purchases and calculate their cost. Computers permit cell phones to operate without wires. At the gym, computers track membership and even workout results, 17-8.

Activity

Ask students to search their home for items already using the metric system. Check the tools and the garage for items in metric. Make a list of the items found. Share results with the class.

Think about how often you come in contact with computers every day. You might use computers at school to take online tests. You might use computers at home to check e-mail, print digital photos, and write papers. All of these interactions help prepare you for using technology in the workplace. In many careers, workers use computers for several tasks:

- compose business letters and memos
- create reports, brochures, or newsletters
- e-mail business contacts

Resource

Which Jobs Need Basic Skills? reproducible master 17-2, TR. Use the adapted worksheet to reinforce chapter concepts in students who are low functioning.

Resource

Getting Down to Basics, color transparency CT-17, TR. Students describe how the basic skills can be applied to work.

17-7
These equations can help you convert between measurement systems.

Measurement Conversions (approximate)				
Converting to Metric				
Known		**Multiplied by**		**Equals**
Distance				
inches	x	25.4	=	millimeters
inches	x	2.54	=	centimeters
feet	x	0.3	=	meters
yards	x	0.91	=	meters
miles	x	1.61	=	kilometers
Weight				
ounces	x	28.35	=	grams
pounds	x	0.45	=	kilograms
Volume				
fluid ounces	x	29.57	=	milliliters
pints	x	0.47	=	liters
quarts	x	0.95	=	liters
gallons	x	3.79	=	liters
Temperature				
Fahrenheit	x	0.56 (after subtracting 32)	=	Celsius
Converting from Metric				
Known		**Multiplied by**		**Equals**
Distance				
millimeters	x	0.04	=	inches
centimeters	x	0.39	=	inches
meters	x	3.28	=	feet
meters	x	1.09	=	yards
kilometers	x	0.62	=	miles
Weight				
grams	x	0.04	=	ounces
kilograms	x	2.2	=	pounds
Volume				
milliliters	x	0.03	=	fluid ounces
liters	x	2.11	=	pints
liters	x	1.06	=	quarts
liters	x	0.26	=	gallons
Temperature				
Celsius	x	1.80 (then add 32)	=	Fahrenheit

Adapting the Lesson

Have students who are high functioning find out which countries in the world operate on measurement systems other than the metric system, or operate on another system in addition to the metric system. Ask students to list those countries as well as the system of measurements they use. (Students do not need to list countries operating exclusively on the metric system, unless they prepare a separate list.)

Activity

Divide the class into teams of four. Give each team four food packages or labels from empty food containers with the metric measurements concealed or removed. In five minutes, see which team can convert the most items to metric measurements.

Discuss

Do you feel the United States should use one measuring system exclusively rather than convert back and forth between two? Explain your opinion.

17-8
Workers at fitness clubs use computer databases to track member information.

- conduct Internet research
- compile and analyze data in a spreadsheet or database
- prepare slide shows for meetings and presentations

In today's workplace, many jobs require the use of a computer to get work done. As a result, employers expect job applicants to have basic computer skills. These skills include word processing, sending e-mail, accessing the Internet, managing data, and creating slide presentations. Your computer skills will impact your ability to find and keep a job.

Some jobs require advanced computer knowledge. Additional skills can be learned through on-the-job training, continuing education, or independent study. Such skills are also learned through extracurricular activities. For example, if you are interested in filmmaking, you might join an audiovisual club to learn video editing software.

Community Connections

A chamber of commerce is an organization of community business owners. Contact your local chamber of commerce by phone or e-mail. Ask for the names of three companies that employ a large number of people in your area. Visit the company Web sites and look for job announcements. Write a list of the basic and advanced computer skills needed to work at one specific job at each company.

Why is it important to have basic computer skills?

Summary

Basic skills are needed in school, at work, and in your personal life. You should do all you can to develop good reading, writing, and math skills.

Knowing how to write messages correctly is a skill needed by people in all types of careers. Writing well requires expressive language and accurate spelling, grammar, and punctuation. All the writing you do improves your writing skill, even writing for pleasure.

Math skills, like the other basic skills, are needed to succeed both personally and professionally. You should be able to add, subtract, multiply, and divide. These skills will allow you to perform basic job functions like counting change and using measurements.

You will most likely use some sort of computer on your job. Employers will expect you to have basic computer skills. These skills include word processing, sending e-mail, accessing the Internet, using spreadsheets or databases, and preparing slideshow presentations.

Reviewing Key Concepts

1. Identify the three basic skills.
2. Describe two work tasks that involve reading.
3. How can you improve your reading skills?
4. Why is illiteracy an obstacle to finding a job?
5. What impressions might people form about a writer whose material is full of errors?
6. How can you improve your writing skills?
7. Name three careers in which basic math skills are used every day.
8. What are the guidelines for counting change accurately?
9. Why is changing from one unit to another easier in the metric system?
10. Name four computer skills that many employers expect job applicants to have

Answers to *Reviewing Key Concepts*

1. reading, writing, and math
2. (Describe two. Student response.)
3. by reading for pleasure
4. because every job involves reading or writing in some way
5. Perhaps the writer lacks writing skills or is careless, lazy, or disorganized.
6. by reading more, doing some writing every day, and proofreading what you write
7. (Name three. Student response.)
8. place the cash from the customer on top of the register; remove the correct amount from the cash drawer; count change out loud; count from largest denomination to smallest
9. All units are multiples of 10.
10. (List four:) word processing, sending e-mail, accessing the Internet, managing data, creating slide presentations

Building Academic Skills

1. **Writing, speaking.** List ways to improve reading ability and vocabulary. Present your recommendations to the class.
2. **Reading, writing.** Read a book, magazine article, or newspaper story about a topic that interests you. Make a list of any words you do not understand. Use a dictionary to look up the words and write their definitions. Share your new vocabulary words in class.
3. **Writing.** Write a brief report summarizing what you read in the previous activity. Read your report and circle in ink any errors you find. Rewrite the report making any necessary corrections.
4. **History.** Research the role of moneychangers in early societies, particularly in areas where currencies varied. Give an oral report of your findings to the class.

Building Technology Skills

1. Investigate the U.S. rate of literacy using an Internet search. Compare this rate to the literacy rate for your community. Brainstorm ideas to increase student reading in your school.
2. Use a word processing program to write a story about a pet and exchange stories with a classmate via e-mail. Edit the story on the computer using track changes or a different colored font. After editing, e-mail the story to the original creator for a final draft. Discuss with your classmate whether the editing was helpful.
3. Conduct an online search of measurements and measuring systems. Find answers to the following questions: How did systems of measurement originate? Which societies made the greatest impact on the development of such a system? What was the system designed to measure? Is any ancient measuring system still in use?

Building Career Knowledge and Skills

1. Correspond with a pen pal. Share information with each other about yourselves, your families, and your career goals for the future. Remember to use good grammar and proper punctuation.
2. Visit a supermarket and find 20 different items. Develop a chart, and list each item's customary and metric measures.
3. Write a report explaining why a word processing program cannot check all spelling errors. Explain the possible outcomes of work reports with misspelled words.
4. Examine the classified ad section of the newspaper and identify ads that interest you. Describe how the basic skills of reading, writing, and math will be used in the jobs you identified.
5. Using play money, work with a partner and practice counting change.

Building Workplace Skills

Imagine you are in charge of determining work schedules for a small clothing store. Your doors open at 9:00 a.m. and stay open until 9:00 p.m. Your busiest hours are from 4:00 p.m. to 8:00 p.m. on weekdays and all day Saturday. During these busy hours, at least two people are needed on duty. Your store closes at 6:00 p.m. Saturday. You have one full-time employee who works five 8-hour days each week at $10.00 per hour. She knows the store well enough to take care of it when you are gone. You can get part-time helpers who work less than 30 hours per week for $8.00 per hour. Using a computer, develop a chart showing who works when—including yourself—for every hour the store is open. Total the cost of your helpers. Summarize your plan and report it to the class.

What can I do to make the best use of my time and develop good study habits?

Chapter 18
Time Management and Study Skills

Key Terms

time management
time log
IRS time
priorities
procrastination
concentrate

Chapter Objectives

After studying this chapter, you will be able to

- **examine** how you spend your time by keeping a daily time log.
- **list** five suggestions for making the best use of your time.
- **take** notes that will help you review what you study.
- **identify** helpful tips related to preparing for, taking, and learning from tests.
- **compare** good and poor study habits.

Key Concepts

- Creating a time log will help you complete important tasks efficiently.
- Taking good notes improves learning.
- Proper test preparation leads to better test scores.
- Good study habits will help you learn more quickly.

Why Is Time Management Important?

Time management is a skill that is needed throughout life. Adults need to manage the time they spend at work and at home. As a student, you need to manage the time you spend at school as well as studying after school. You need to manage the time you spend with your family and the time you have for other activities, too. This chapter will help you plan and manage your time. It will also help you identify good study habits to help you make the best use of your study time.

Discuss

What is the key to success in time management? Why is it important to manage your time?

Resource

Reinforcing Vocabulary, Activity A, WB. Students match terms with their definitions.

Resource

Time Thief, color transparency CT-18, TR. Students brainstorm a list of the many ways people waste time.

Time Management

Time can be a valuable ally or your worst enemy. Time only moves forward, never backward. You can never recapture misused time or undo what has already happened. Learn to use time as a valuable resource. The way you manage this resource can make the difference between success and failure.

Planning how to use your time is ***time management***. It is a key element in your study habits. No one can plan or manage your time but you. Too many people fail to control their use of time. Some people even allow others to use up their time. The key to success, however, is to make wise use of time.

time management
Planning and carefully using time.

If you are in the habit of wasting time, you can work to break the habit. Managing your time is not a difficult or unpleasant task. Much of your time is planned for you, such as your school and work hours. Your teachers and school officials set the hours you are in school. Your employer determines the time you are assigned to work. It is your job to manage the rest of your time. You might plan for the following activities:

- uninterrupted periods for study
- personal duties and tasks
- relaxation and fun

Most people don't know how they spend their time. They are often surprised to find out how much time they waste. If you are in the habit of wasting time, you should work to break the habit. Do you know how you spend your time? A good way to find out is to keep a daily time log for two weeks. A

Adapting the Lesson

Have students who are low functioning take an assignment they need to complete and break it down into short, manageable steps. Make a chart for them titled "Assignment to Be Done." List *Step 1*, *Step 2*, and so forth down the page, with room under each to add notes. Reuse the chart as needed to help students understand how to complete assignments.

time log
A written record of a person's use of time.

time log is a written record of a person's use of time. A sample time log is shown in 18-1. At the end of two weeks, you may be surprised to see how you spent your time.

18-1
A time log shows the number of hours used for different activities. It can help you see how much time you are wasting.

Sample Time Log

	Sun	Mon	Tues	Wed	Thurs	Fri	Sat	Total
Sleeping	9	8	8	7.5	8.5	7	8	56
Eating	1.5	.75	1	.75	.75	1.25	1.25	7.25
Grooming	1	.5	.75	.75	.75	1	1.25	6
Going to school	0	7	7	7	7	7	0	35
Studying/doing homework	2	1.25	2	1	2.5	0	1	9.75
Working at a job	6	3.5	0	3.5	0	0	6	19
Doing household tasks	.75	.5	0	.25	.25	.25	.75	2.75
Participating in extracurricular activities	0	0	2	0	2	0	0	4
Watching TV/ listening to music	.5	1.25	.5	1	0	2	1.25	6.5
Phoning/ messaging friends	1.25	.5	1.5	.5	.25	.75	.5	5.25
Visiting friends	0	0	.75	0	1.5	3	3	8.25
Reading and relaxing	0	0	0	.25	0	.25	.5	1
Doing other activities	2	.75	.5	1.5	.5	1.5	.5	7.25

Resource
Time Log, Activity B, WB. Students keep a time log for one week.

Resource
Time Log Review, Activity C, WB. Students evaluate their one-week time log.

Discuss
Explain what a time log is. How will a time log help an individual keep track of the amount of time spent on various activities?

Activity
Use Figure 18-1 to discuss the various ways in which an individual can use time. Where do you see time being wasted?

Resource
IRS Time, Activity D, WB. Students create a to-do list and prioritize the items.

The Computer and Time Management

Using a computer can help you save time. Creating a time log using a spreadsheet program is quick and easy. If the spreadsheet is set up to perform calculations, it can automatically total the time spent daily, weekly, or monthly on each activity. Using the data from the spreadsheet, you can create graphs that visually demonstrate how your time is spent. Once the time log is created, it is easy to continue tracking your time on a regular basis.

The computer can also be a source of distraction. Instant messaging, checking and sending e-mail, surfing the Internet, visiting social networking sites, and playing computer games can waste valuable time. When creating a time log, schedule separate times for school, work, and leisure computer activities. Make a commitment to stick to your schedule. When you use the computer for studying, sign out of e-mail and instant messaging services to reduce interruptions.

Making a Difference

It's never too early to start learning time management and study skills. Use a computer to create a booklet that gives helpful advice to students in lower grades. Topics may include managing time, effective studying, and test taking. Ask your teacher to review the booklet before you print a final copy. Contact one of your former teachers who might be interested in providing this information to his or her class.

IRS Time

You know that you cannot create more time. The earth's timetable is fixed at 365 days a year, 24 hours a day, 60 minutes an hour, and 60 seconds a minute. How can you get more time for everything you want to do? The answer is to be a better manager of time. One suggestion is to place yourself on IRS time. ***IRS time*** is defined as Individual Responsibility for Saving time. You take whatever steps are needed to make the best use of your time. The following suggestions may help you:

- Make a to-do list each day. Don't rely on your memory to recall what is important. Get into the habit of writing it down.
- Organize your time according to your priorities. ***Priorities*** are everything you consider highly important. Tasks that are most important have the highest priority. You should do those first. Using your to-do list, rank each of your tasks. Write A beside each task that you must do. Write B next to the tasks you should do. Use C to mark the tasks you want to do if you have time. Then follow your list. After you finish the A-list, do your Bs and, if time permits, work on your Cs.
- Avoid ***procrastination.*** In other words, do not delay or put off decisions or activities. Try to work on them right away. Do a little each day on long-term assignments, too. Suppose you are assigned a paper to be completed by the end of the term. Do not wait until the day before it is due to start.

IRS time (individual responsibility for saving time)
Taking whatever steps are needed to make the best use of time.

priorities
Everything you consider highly important.

procrastination
Delaying decisions or activities.

Reflect

How often are you guilty of putting off jobs that you need to do? How often do you make a list of important jobs and prioritize them?

Resource

Setting Priorities, reproducible master 18-1, TR. Students rank the priorities of various activities.

- Reduce interruptions of your planned study time. If friends call during your study time, exchange a few words, but excuse yourself quickly. Let them know you have something to do. If they are true friends, they will understand. Remember, you cannot recapture lost time. Therefore, get in the habit of telling them you'll call back later. Return immediately to what you were doing before the interruption. Better yet, study in a place where common interruptions cannot occur. Do not let time thieves steal your time, 18-2.
- Focus on one task at a time. It is difficult to focus on your studies while watching television or talking to friends. You can study best when you devote your full attention to it.

What activities should you include in a time log?

Study Skills

Many students can improve their study skills. The most common cause of poor study habits is poor use of time. Study periods or study halls are often used as social periods. That is an unwise use of time unless you are working on a team project. The schoolwork that could be accomplished in a study period must then be done after school. One secret to becoming a better student and getting better grades is to use time wisely.

18-2 Watching TV, daydreaming, and talking on the phone can be "time thieves" that steal your time from more important activities.

Discuss

Do you think the time thieves in Figure 18-2 show the three biggest time wasters? Are there any other activities you would add to the bag of time wasters? What can you do to reduce the amount of wasted time?

Begin your study period with a positive attitude. A good attitude will help you get right into your study assignment. Make up your mind to tackle the hardest part first. Set a time limit for study, perhaps two hours. Let others know this is your time for study, not interruptions. Avoid trying to study in a noisy crowd. Instead, find a comfortable, quiet place at home, at school, or in the library. In this way, you can get the most accomplished in the least amount of time.

Reflect

How would you describe your study area at home? Do you feel it helps you concentrate and remain productive?

Resource

Check Your Study Skills, reproducible master 18-2, TR. Students identify a study habit that needs improvement and explain how they can change it.

Make sure your desk or tabletop is clear of distractions. Don't leave anything on it that will keep you from your assignment. Put away magazines and books not needed for your assignment. Make sure you have everything you will need to complete the assignment. Gather the necessary books, papers, pens, pencils, and other supplies before you start. See 18-3. Don't waste valuable study time looking for these items while trying to get your assignment done.

The hardest part of any job, even studying, is getting started. Once you sit down, make up your mind to begin. Then concentrate right away on your assignment. To ***concentrate*** means to focus your attention and effort. Stay

concentrate
To focus attention and effort on something.

18-3
Good study habits include working in a quiet area with all your supplies at hand.

Adapting the Lesson

Divide students who are low functioning into small teams to develop posters listing helpful hints for studying well. Encourage students to use pictures and make them colorful. Display the posters around the school.

Making a Difference

Some students cannot afford basic school supplies. It can be difficult to develop good study habits without access to books, paper, pens, pencils, and highlighters. Organize a classroom project to donate school supplies. Visit **adoptaclassroom.com** to find a school in need.

involved in what you are doing. Don't waste valuable study time daydreaming or thinking about something else.

Plan to study when you are rested. Being rested is important because a tired person will find it difficult to concentrate. If you can't concentrate, you won't be able to remember what you have read.

Another important study tip is to take a few moments after you study to think about what you have learned. Sometimes you can mentally review the material by just sitting back and recalling the main points. Reflecting on your studies will improve your level of learning.

Taking Notes

Taking notes is an important study skill to develop. Good notes come in handy when it's time to review what you have studied. They help you recall the important points of information.

Taking notes does not mean writing down every word that is said. In fact, people who are too busy writing generally do not hear everything being said. Try to listen carefully to your teacher or study partner and write down only the key points. Teachers often identify key points with phrases that focus attention, like "the cause was," "the result was," or "to sum up."

When taking notes during a slide show presentation, pay attention to how the text is organized on the slide. Slide show presentations often prioritize content by using main points and indented subpoints. Following the slide format can help you create an outline as you take notes.

Resource

Good and Poor Study Habits, Activity E, WB. Students distinguish good study habits from poor habits.

Reflect

What are your biggest time wasters?

Discuss

Share with the class what you do to get ready to study. What important study tips help you learn? What advice can you share with others that would help them study?

Helpful Tips

The following tips may help you learn to take good notes:

- Use one side of a sheet of paper.
- Number each page, especially for a loose-leaf notebook. It is easy for pages to shift out of order.
- Leave a margin at the top of the page. You can use this space to write key information, such as the date an assignment is due. Also use this space to identify the class, topic, date, and teacher.
- Write only the important points.

- Use an outline format.
- Whenever possible, use symbols and abbreviations. Write = for *equals*, ≠ for *does not equal*, and + for *plus*. You may use other symbols, too, as long as you remember what they mean.
- Write notes to yourself in the margins. They may be questions, suggestions, or reminders.
- Highlight key words when you review your notes, 18-4.
- Keystroke handwritten notes on the computer to review what you learned.

Good study skills will help you on the job, too. Your employer may ask you to attend a meeting and report to coworkers what was discussed. Being able to take good notes will help you prepare your report.

Reflect

Do you feel that you have enough time to get everything done that you need to do? Would notes help you make better use of your time?

Discuss

How many of you make to-do lists? What are some methods you use to stay organized? How many of you have a set time to study and do homework?

Note

Emphasize that good note taking and study habits make taking tests easier.

Using a Computer to Study

Some schools make teacher materials available to students online. Such access is helpful to students who miss a class or just want to review the material that was covered on a certain

18-4
Reviewing your notes regularly and highlighting key words will help you remember important concepts.

Discuss

Why is it important to evaluate the credibility of a Web site when doing Internet research? How can you determine the source of the information provided? How can you find out when the Web site was updated?

Discuss

What actions can you take to make it easier to concentrate while using a computer to study?

Adapting the Lesson

Have students who are high functioning research study habits and helpful hints given in online resources. Students are to compare information found online to that given in the textbook. Have students share additional suggestions with the class.

day. A school's online site can provide access to teacher notes, slide shows, handouts, and other class materials.

The computer can be a very effective study tool when a textbook has a companion Web site. Such sites provide quizzes and learning activities for students to complete at their own pace. These exercises help students review chapter concepts and reinforce their learning.

In some cases, students are able to access their entire textbook online or from a CD. These students do not need their books to study, but can read the text on their computer screens. Some programs even provide sound, which lets students hear the lessons as well as correct pronunciations.

Searching the Internet is an easy way to find additional information about topics you are studying. When conducting Internet research, it is important to use reliable Web sites that have a reputation for providing accurate facts. Your teacher can help you learn to recognize such sites. The information you find online can be used to complete homework assignments, do special projects, and gain a deeper understanding of the subject matter, 18-5.

18-5
Using the Internet, you can quickly find additional information about the topic you are studying.

Taking Tests

Tests are given to find out how much you have learned. They provide feedback for both you and your teachers. Tests are not meant to scare you or to make you look bad. Their purpose is to measure how much you know and don't know. Your job is to do your best to show all that you know. To do that, you can't rely on magic or luck. You need to prepare yourself.

Before the Test

Cramming the night before is not the best way to prepare for a test. You need to keep up with what is being taught in your classes. Studying and doing your homework regularly will help you understand information better and remember it longer. However, you may want to give extra effort to your studies the last few nights before a test. The following tips will help you as you give special attention to test material:

- Review the material in the textbook on a regular basis—daily, if possible.
- Pay particular attention to your notes.
- Try to determine what questions will be asked.
- Recall what kinds of questions were asked on the last test in the class.
- Consider studying with a classmate, taking turns to ask each other questions.
- Get a good night's sleep.
- Eat a good breakfast to start the day.

See 18-6 for a summary of good study habits that are wise to develop. The chart also lists some poor study habits to avoid.

Taking the Test

The way you take a test can affect how well you do on it. The following suggestions may help improve your test performance:

- Be relaxed and have a positive mental attitude.
- Look over the entire test before starting it.
- Read and follow directions carefully.
- Read each test question accurately.

Example

Share with the students how you prepare to take tests. Repeat some of the successful strategies you have used.

Reflect

Recall a time when you took a test and immediately felt that the results would be good. How did you prepare for that test? What did you do that made taking the test easy?

Discuss

What are your greatest concerns in taking tests? Is it easier to study with another person in the class? What methods have you used to make studying for tests easier?

Reflect

When you take a test, are you relaxed? Do you look over the entire test before you get started? Do you take a few minutes to look over the test before you turn it in?

Resource

Where Does My Time Go? reproducible master 18-3, TR. Use the adapted worksheet to reinforce chapter concepts in students who are low functioning.

18-6
Using good study habits will help you benefit most from your study time.

Discuss
Figure 18-6 gives good and poor study habits. Read through each to be sure students understand what they mean. Select several of the poor study habits and ask the students what are the consequences of following those choices?

Good Study Habits	Poor Study Habits
• Tackle the hardest parts first when you sit down to study.	• Study the easiest parts first.
• Study in a comfortable place where you will not be disturbed.	• Study in a noisy crowd or another area where you will be easily distracted.
• Clear the desk or tabletop of magazines, books, and other objects you are not going to use.	• Study in a cluttered area.
• Gather the books, papers, pens, pencils, and other supplies you need before you start to study.	• Waste time looking for books, papers, pens, pencils, and other supplies you need.
• When you sit down to study, begin concentrating right away.	• Allow your mind to wander when you sit down to study.
• Study when you are well rested.	• Study when you are tired.
• Take a few moments after you study to think about what you have learned.	• As soon as you finish studying, go on to another activity.
• Write down only the key points when taking notes.	• Try to write down every word that is said when taking notes.
• Get a good night's sleep before taking a test.	• Stay up late studying the night before a test.
• Begin projects and start studying for tests well in advance.	• Try to cram all your studies into the last minute.
• Give your studies your full attention.	• Try to do something else while you study, such as watch television.

Community Connections

Your guidance counselor can be a helpful resource for improving your study skills. Make an appointment to see your guidance counselor. Before the meeting, write a list of questions and concerns that you have about your test-taking skills. At the meeting, discuss the list and ask your counselor to share test-taking hints and stress-relieving techniques.

- Think before you write your answer.
- If you get stuck on a question, skip it and return later after answering the other questions.
- Before handing in your test, review it and make corrections where necessary.

When You Get Your Test Back

Learning does not stop once you turn in your test. When you get the test back, you can use it to prepare for future tests. The following suggestions might help you get more from your tests:

- Congratulate yourself for everything you answered correctly.
- Honestly evaluate your test. Were you really prepared?
- Read the teacher's comments and corrections.
- Ask for help on topics that gave you difficulty.

Start preparing immediately for the next test. Learning from your mistakes and reviewing regularly as you study will help you perform well on future tests, 18-7.

Your Reading

What can you do to improve your concentration when studying?

18-7 Reviewing mistakes can help you identify how to better prepare for your next test.

Reflect

When you get your graded test back do you read the teacher's comments? How often do you ask for help with areas of the test in which you did score well?

Discuss

What do you do with your papers and tests when they are returned to you? Do you ever save them to look over and find out what types of questions the teacher asked? Would this help you in preparing for the next test?

Summary

Time management is a key life skill. Although you can't change the amount of time in a day or week, you can change the way you use it. You can learn to make the best use of your time.

Using a computer can help you save time and can assist you when studying. Scheduling specific times for school, work, or leisure activities on the computer will help you use it to your advantage.

Good study habits help you make the most of your study time. They can also help you learn more and get better grades.

Taking notes is a study skill that improves with practice. The key is to listen carefully while writing only the important points.

By taking tests, you find out how much you have learned. You can improve your performance on tests by following certain steps. The steps can help you prepare for tests, take tests with confidence, and learn from the results of the tests.

Reviewing Key Concepts

1. What is the purpose of a time log?
2. Describe how to avoid wasting time when using the computer.
3. How can you get more time to do everything you want to do?
4. List five suggestions for making the best use of your time.
5. Identify two phrases that teachers often use to highlight key points that should be written down in notes.
6. List three ways to use the information you find online when studying.
7. List five steps to take to prepare for a test.
8. List five tips that can help you perform well during a test.
9. When you get a test back, list three steps to follow for improving your test-taking skills.
10. Rate each of the following study habits *good* or *poor*.
    A. Clear your desk or tabletop of distractions before beginning.
    B. Study when you are well rested and alert.
    C. Start with the easiest part of the task.
    D. When taking notes, write everything the teacher says.
    E. Take a few moments after you study to think about what you have learned.

Answers to *Reviewing Key Concepts*

1. to find out how a person spends time
2. schedule separate times for school and leisure computer activities, stick to your schedule, and sign out of e-mail and instant messaging services when studying
3. by becoming a better manager of time
4. Make a to-do list each day. Set priorities for your time. Do not procrastinate. Reduce interruptions of your planned study time. Concentrate on one task at a time.
5. (Name two:) "The cause was . . .," "The result was . . .," "To sum up . . ."
6. to complete homework assignments, do special projects, and gain a deeper understanding of the subject matter
7. (List five. Student response.)
8. (List five. Student response.)
9. (List three. Student response.)
10. A-good, B-good, C-poor, D-poor, E-good

Building Academic Skills

1. **Math.** Create a time log. Exchange your time log with a classmate. Analyze your classmate's time log to determine what percentage of each day is devoted to various activities.
2. **Writing.** Write a paper about successful habits for studying, note taking, or test taking. Submit it to the school paper.

Building Technology Skills

1. Use a spreadsheet program to create another type of time log—one that reflects unscheduled times in each day. Make a chart with *Hours of the Day* heading the first column, followed by seven columns—one for each day of the week. Make rows for each hour of the day.
2. E-mail five people and survey them for the following information: how they manage their time, save time, and work efficiently. Compile your list and report your findings to the class.
3. Conduct an online search for ways to take good notes. Write three or four of the best suggestions recommended on the sites you search and note the address of each Web site used. Share your recommendations in class.

Building Career Knowledge and Skills

1. Ask several people to tell you their best time management tips. Share your tips with the class.
2. Test your concentration. Go to the library and find two newspaper articles that are about equal in length. Study one article in a quiet place for a certain length of time, perhaps 15 minutes. Then write as much about it as you can remember. Later, go to a noisy place or sit in front of a television. Study the second article for the same amount of time. Then write as much about it as you can remember. Compare the results. Which setting allowed you to concentrate better? In class, discuss how study efforts are affected by a person's surroundings.
3. Practice taking notes during classes. Later, compare your notes with those of a classmate to make sure you included all the key points.
4. Keep a daily time log for at least one week. Graph how the time was spent. Identify time wasters and develop a plan to avoid them.
5. Research how to do more tasks more efficiently. Pick one suggestion to try for one week. Record what was done and the time involved. Write a statement summarizing the experience.

Building Workplace Skills

Do a three-step study to compare how you think you spend your time with how you want to spend it and how you actually spend it. Using a computer, create a time sheet that lists all your activities and allows room for recording times. First, estimate how much time you think you spend with each activity. Then, imagine yourself leading an ideal life and estimate how much time you would like to spend on each activity. Finally, keep a daily log for two weeks to find out how you actually spend your time. Write a brief report about what you learned from this exercise. Include ideas on how you could improve your time management.

What are the best ways to share ideas, feelings, and information?

Chapter 19
Communication Skills

Key Terms

communicate
verbal communication
active listening
feedback
multitasking
nonverbal communication
body language

Chapter Objectives

After studying this chapter, you will be able to

- **identify** ways to send and receive messages.
- **compare and contrast** the three basic communication styles.
- **list** helpful tips for public speaking.
- **explain** the importance of feedback in the communication process.
- **demonstrate** how to make and receive business telephone calls.
- **write** business letters, memos, reports, and e-mails.
- **identify** several forms of nonverbal communication.

Key Concepts

- Business and personal relationships depend on effective communication.
- An assertive communication style expresses ideas and opinions in a positive, respectful way.
- Good speaking, listening, and writing skills are necessary in the workplace.
- How others perceive your nonverbal communication is important.

Methods of Communication

To ***communicate*** is to share ideas, feelings, or information. When people communicate, two things happen—a message is sent and a message is received. Communication can take place between just two people or among millions of people.

People communicate in many different ways. Chart 19-1 lists some of the many ways people send and receive messages. This chart also lists channels through which people communicate. In this chapter, you will read about the common ways that messages are sent and received in the workplace.

communicate
To share ideas, feelings, or information, both verbally and nonverbally.

Resource

Reinforcing Vocabulary, Activity A, WB. Students use vocabulary terms to complete partial sentences.

Resource

Getting Your Message Across, color transparency CT-19, TR. Students discuss various examples of how communication takes place.

Communication Tools

All forms of communication require some type of tool in order for communication to take place. The human voice transmits spoken messages. To communicate without words, people may use pictures, sign language, or facial expressions. A pen and paper is commonly used for written communication.

Communication		
Ways to Send Messages	**Ways to Receive Messages**	**Channels of Communication**
speaking	listening	conversations
writing	reading	meetings
drawing	seeing	speeches
touching	feeling	lectures
singing		newspapers
using gestures or facial expressions		magazines
sending signals		telephones
using sign language		photographs
		e-mail
		art
		music
		letters
		books

19-1
There are many ways to send and receive messages.

Activity

Ask for five volunteers. Have volunteers line up across the front of the room, standing about three feet apart. Have three sentences written on a piece of paper. Whisper the sentences to the first person, who whispers them to the next person, and so on. When it gets to the last person, ask him or her to repeat what was said aloud. How accurate was the message?

How has technology changed communication?

Advances in technology have led to communication tools that can be used in many different ways. The computer is primarily used for composing and sending written messages. However, with a web camera or microphone, the computer can be used to transmit communications. Cellular phones and handheld organizers can be used to make phone calls and send e-mail, text messages, and pictures. As technology changes, communication tools will offer more ways to send and receive messages.

Styles of Communication

Knowing your communication style and how others interpret it will help you to be an effective communicator. It is important to understand three common styles of communication:

- passive
- aggressive
- assertive

Reflect

Think about a time when you used an aggressive or passive communication style. What was the outcome? How would the outcome be different if you used an assertive communication style?

Activity

Role-play how a passive, aggressive, and assertive communicator would act in the following situations: an employee disagrees with a change in workplace procedures, employees are asked to share their opinions during a group meeting, and an employee receives negative feedback during a performance review.

Enrich

Search for an online quiz that determines your communication style. After taking the quiz, write the answers to the following questions: Do you feel the quiz was accurate? In what ways do you need to improve your communication style?

Passive Communication

A person with a passive style tends to avoid conflict at all costs. This person usually has low self-esteem and is afraid to speak up. A passive communicator allows others to choose and make decisions for him or her. Others achieve their goals at this person's expense.

Aggressive Communication

A person with an aggressive style is forceful and makes decisions for others. An aggressive communicator makes others feel humiliated, defensive, resentful, and hurt. This person's goals are achieved at the expense of others. The result is a win-lose situation in which the aggressor wins and everyone else loses. Being aggressive sometimes causes conflict.

Assertive Communication

A person with an assertive style has the ability to honestly express opinions, attitudes, rights, and feelings in a way that respects the comments of others. *Being direct* is another way of saying that a person is using assertive communication. This communication style results in a win-win situation that leaves everyone feeling satisfied. Some techniques to develop an assertive style are shown in 19-2.

Everyone tends to use one communication style most often. However, people use all three styles at one time or another. Becoming assertive may never feel as comfortable as your typical style, but the rewards are worth it. By working to develop an assertive style, you will improve your communication skills and avoid misunderstanding.

Your Reading

Why is it important to develop an assertive communication style?

Speaking

Speaking is the most widely used form of ***verbal communication***, which is communication involving the use of words. People speak to express ideas, give information, or ask questions.

verbal communication
Communication involving the use of words.

Almost all types of work require the proper use of the spoken word. Speaking clearly will help you express ideas to coworkers, 19-3. Failure to communicate clearly can lead to hazardous situations. In some cases, you could lose your job if you do not communicate well.

Resource

Speech Evaluation, Activity B, WB. Students evaluate a classmate's and their own speech.

A clear speaker is more likely to have job success. For example, a salesperson who can tell customers about a product's good features is likely to make more sales. More sales mean more commission and, therefore, higher pay.

Becoming an Assertive Communicator

- Think before you speak. Make sure you are conveying the correct message.
- Listen for feedback from others. Be open to other points of view.
- If negative feedback is valid, accept responsibility.
- Stick to your opinions or ideas when you can make a strong case for their support.
- Learn to say "no" when you mean no.

19-2
Assertive communicators express their opinions and ideas while respecting others.

19-3
Good communication skills are required for most jobs. Your supervisors and coworkers need to understand what you say.

Improving Your Speech

Your speech is part of the image you project. It affects the impressions people form of you. If you speak clearly and use proper grammar, people are likely to form favorable impressions of you.

Keeping in mind some simple guidelines will help you improve your speech in day-to-day conversations. First, think about your message before you speak. Use just enough words to convey your idea clearly. Try not to talk too much. No one likes to listen to a person who can't quickly get to the point.

When you speak, use simple sentences. Use words that both you and your listener will understand. Also, use good grammar. Mispronouncing a word or using poor grammar is very distracting to the listener. Speak clearly and in a normal tone. The following tips will help you improve your speech:

- Always speak slowly and clearly. Rapid, mumbled speech is difficult to understand.
- Practice good grammar at all times. People who use poor grammar are less likely to get good jobs.
- Think about what you are going to say before you say it. Pause before answering a question or making a statement. This gives you a chance to respond in the best possible way.

Reflect
Think of a person who you feel was a dynamic speaker. How would you describe the characteristics of a great speaker?

Activity
Write a three-minute speech to convince your sales department that they should sell a new product—chocolate chip cookies. Have an introduction, discussion, and a closing. Present speeches to the class.

Activity
Have students use the information presented about communication skills on this page to write five true/false questions. Write the questions on a piece of paper. Put all papers in a large container so each student can draw a paper and take the quick quiz. Talk about the results.

- Avoid using slang, such as "cool," "yeah," or " 'ya' know." Most employers think that using slang is unprofessional. They may be less likely to hire or promote an employee who uses slang.
- Do not use profanity. It is unprofessional and it offends others.
- Always pronounce your words clearly and completely. Try not to drop the endings of words. Don't say "singin" instead of "singing."

Note

Emphasize that practice makes it much easier to feel comfortable giving presentations in front of a group. Share with the students that you can practice in front of a mirror, a friend, or a family member.

Discuss

Which form of communication do you think is used most often in the workplace? How accurate do you think verbal communication is?

Adapting the Lesson

Have students who are low functioning practice, then give a short speech. Students can choose topics and use information from this chapter, such as how to: improve a speech, receive phone calls, place a business order, write a business letter, and so forth.

Public Speaking

Public speaking is the act of making speeches in public before audiences. It is much like talking to your friends. There are, however, more receivers of your message and the response is slower.

There are several reasons why you might give a speech. One common reason is to inform people. Another is to convince people to think your way.

While in school, you will be encouraged to make presentations to your classmates. Perhaps you will speak at group meetings, too. These speaking opportunities can help prepare you for the career world. See 19-4.

Being able to speak in front of a group is expected in the work world. Workers speak in front of coworkers and

Photo courtesy of Skills USA

19-4
Taking advantage of speaking opportunities through student organizations will help prepare you for future business presentations.

Reflect

How do you feel about giving speeches in class? What can you do to feel more comfortable with these assignments?

supervisors for many reasons. Members of production teams give progress reports at weekly group meetings. Researchers share their findings with people working to develop new products. Salespeople present product information to groups of customers.

When you prepare a speech, you should make an outline of the points you want to cover.

- Start with the *introduction*—a short statement telling the audience what the topic of your speech is.
- Move into the *discussion*—the main idea or message you want to get across.
- Finish with the *closing*—a short summary of what you have said.

Be sure you know your subject well. Be prepared to discuss the topic briefly and concisely. Don't memorize your speech, but practice it. You may want to tape your speech so you can listen to how you sound.

When you give the speech, speak clearly. Use a normal tone of voice, but be sure to speak loud enough to be heard. Keep eye contact with members of the audience. Show enthusiasm. Use gestures for emphasis, like pointing to steps displayed on a screen. Do not overuse gestures.

Dress neatly and appropriately. Stand straight with good posture. Be friendly and firm in your presentation. Try to enjoy the experience. Remember, it is a chance for you to inform people or to convince them to think your way.

Why are good speaking skills important in the workplace?

Community Connections

Investigate speaker's bureaus and public speaking resources in the community. Recommend an expert in this subject who could share some tips on public speaking with your class.

Listening

Communication involves the sending and receiving of a message. Listening is the most common method of receiving messages. Listening is not the same as hearing. In order to listen, you must pay attention to the message being sent.

The world is full of so many sounds that people automatically block out many of them. They choose to listen only to certain sounds. As an example, think about an air conditioner. It makes noise when it is on. Most people can hear the noise, but they do not listen to it. They do not pay attention to it.

Have you ever missed part of the directions for a school project because you were not listening? You probably heard the teacher talking, but you didn't listen to what he or she was saying.

Often, communication fails because people are poor listeners. Instead of listening, they are daydreaming or thinking about something else. Some people fail to listen because they are not interested in what is being said. Others are too busy trying to guess what the speaker will say next. Several types of poor listeners are described in 19-5.

A good listener tries to thoroughly understand what the other person is saying. This involves active listening. ***Active listening*** is listening and responding to improve mutual understanding. Active listening concentrates on what is being said. Thoughts and ideas are understood. Questions are asked to clarify concepts. You can become an active listener by practicing the following good listening skills.

- Pay close attention to what the speaker is saying.
- Repeat back in your own words what the speaker said.
- Observe the speaker's behavior when key points are emphasized.
- Don't let outside noises distract you.

active listening
Listening and responding to another person to improve mutual understanding.

Poor Listeners	
Detail seekers	Try to memorize all the facts.
	Concentrate on small details while missing important information.
Daydreamers	Are easily distracted.
	Do not concentrate on what the speaker is saying.
Emotional listeners	Become upset over certain words or phrases.
	Concentrate on the speaker's poor choice of words or phrases and not on the actual message.
Critics	Are more concerned with the speaker's personal qualities than the message.
	Spend too much time concentrating on such matters as the speaker's clothes, hairstyle, or accent.
Notetakers	Are too involved in writing everything down.
	Often miss the speaker's main ideas.
Arguers	Begin building their arguments before hearing the speaker's point of view.

19-5
Poor listeners prevent true communication from taking place.

Discuss
If you are sitting in class and not listening, what happens? What do you miss when you are not paying attention? What are the consequences of paying attention to distractions?

Reflect
Refer to Figure 19-5. Do any of these categories fit you? How would you rate your listening skills? How often are you easily distracted during class?

Vocabulary
Define *feedback*. Use the word in a sentence to demonstrate understanding.

Discuss
Give examples of how the listener can provide feedback.

Activity
Have members of the class role-play the body language of communication "senders" and "receivers" who are providing good feedback.

Discuss
Use Figure 19-6 to trace the full cycle of the feedback pattern. What are the benefits of feedback in the workplace?

- Keep an open mind. Don't jump to conclusions. Wait until the speaker's points have been made before you speak.
- Don't try to listen and talk at the same time.
- Don't try to memorize everything the speaker says. Concentrate on the speaker's main points.
- When you take notes, don't try to write everything down. List only the important facts and main ideas.
- Ask questions if you don't understand something or if you feel you have missed a point.

Feedback

feedback
The return of information to a sender by a receiver trying to understand the message.

Good, clear communication involves more than the sending and receiving of a message. It also requires that both the sender and the receiver understand the message in the same way. The link to this understanding is feedback. ***Feedback*** is the return of information to the sender by the receiver trying to understand the message. Good listeners provide feedback. They restate the message in their own words to respond to the speaker. This is a way to be sure both sides understand the message. See 19-6 for an illustration of the following example:

Employer: "Check these orders with our inventory. If there are problems, bring them to me."

Employee: "OK, I'll check to see if we have enough stock to fill all these orders. If there are any orders we can't fill, I'll bring them to you."

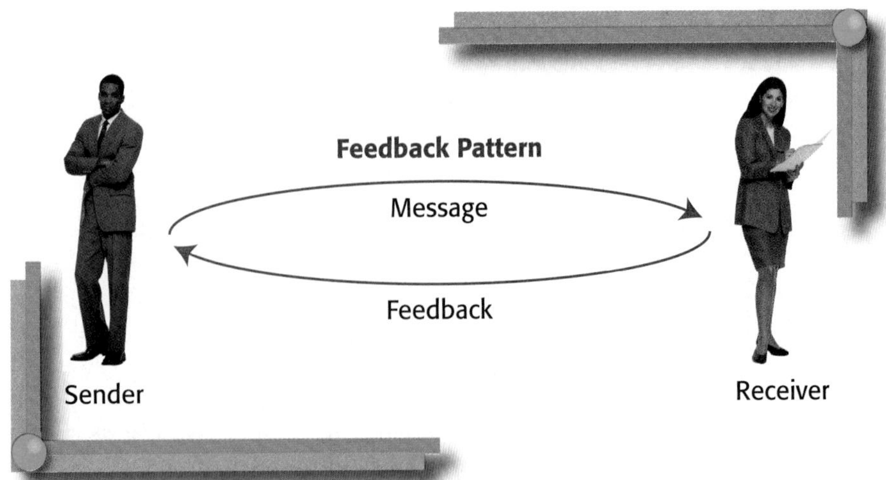

19-6
Feedback from the receiver informs the sender that his or her message has been understood.

Employer: "Good, please start right away."

Recall a time when a teacher asked you to do a task. You did what you thought you were asked to do. Later you realized that your teacher was referring to something else. Who is at fault when a misunderstanding occurs? Many times, it is both the sender and the receiver. If no feedback is requested or given, both parties assume the message is clear. This is a major mistake many people make in the communication process.

You will receive many instructions on the job. Make sure you understand what they mean. Ask questions to clarify the assignment. Repeat in your own words what you understand the assignment to be. Feedback will improve your communication skills. It will help you become a better employee.

Note

It is never possible for the receiver to not communicate because the very act of *not communicating* sends a message, such as "I'm mad at you," "I'm busy," or "I don't understand."

Example

The act of *not communicating* sends one of the following messages: the receiver is angry with the sender, is confused over the meaning of the message, is too busy to respond, or didn't receive the message due to interference.

Discuss

Has anyone here received training on how to multitask while using a headset? Describe the experience. Is it easy to learn this skill?

Multitasking

Employees who wear headsets while working are multitasking. ***Multitasking*** means doing more than one job at a time. Wearing headsets on the job is an increasingly common way to keep coworkers informed.

multitasking
Doing more than one job at a time.

One example is a fast-food worker who takes your order. While talking with you, the order-taker's words are heard through the headset by the kitchen staff. A cook may reply, "It won't be ready for 10 minutes." After the order-taker warns you about the delay, you may decide to change your order. The headset allows coworkers who handle various parts of a job to work smoothly as a team.

Multitasking requires good speaking and listening skills. Headsets allow employees to do their job while hearing the status of related tasks at other locations.

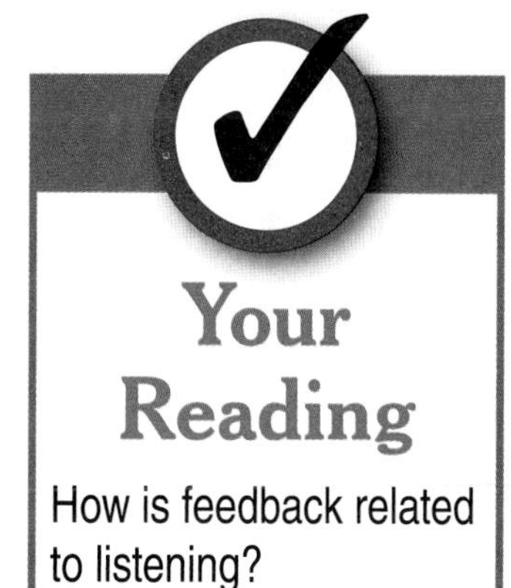

How is feedback related to listening?

Using the Telephone

Many business matters are conducted on the telephone, 19-7. The telephone is a communication tool that requires good listening skills and good speaking skills. Learn to use your employer's telephone wisely.

When using the phone, you must remember that people with whom you talk cannot see you. They cannot see if you are shaking your head to convey a yes or no. Without facial expressions or gestures, your words and tone of voice are

19-7
Many businesses rely on telephone communication.

even more important. Use them carefully to convey the same friendliness, sincerity, and interest you would express in a face-to-face meeting.

Receiving Calls

If you are responsible for receiving calls, answer the telephone promptly. Greet the caller and identify your company. Give the caller your full attention. What the caller has to say is important.

First impressions are lasting. How you sound on the telephone is important in creating a favorable impression. Make an effort to sound pleasant. Smiling as you speak helps relay a cheerful tone. Always be polite. Say, "thank you" and "you're welcome." Make the caller feel comfortable and let him or her know that you want to help. Observe these and the following points when speaking on the telephone:

- Speak slowly and clearly. Don't mumble.
- Never shout.
- Speak directly into the telephone.
- Be patient.
- Be thorough, making sure to give and get all information accurately.

Activity

Poll the class to determine how many students love to talk on the phone. How many students would love a phone sales job? What skills do you think are necessary to be successful in this job?

Resource

The Telephone—It's Everybody's Business, reproducible master 19-1, TR. Students describe how various types of employees might use the telephone.

Activity

Make a small poster of telephone do's and post these by the phones that students use in the school. Use the posters to encourage good telephone manners.

If you direct a call to someone else, be sure the person is available. If the person is not available, take a message. When taking a message, get the following information:

- caller's name (and if mentioned, the caller's title or department)
- name of the caller's company
- caller's telephone number and extension
- reason for the call
- time and date of the call

It is a good idea to repeat information to make sure you have it right. You cannot afford to make mistakes when taking messages. You must spell the caller's name correctly. You must get the company's name right. If the call should be returned, you must write down the correct telephone number. However, if the caller is leaving a confidential message, do not repeat the information out loud.

Resource

Telephone Practice, Activity C, WB. Students think through what they would say on the phone in given situations.

Activity

Role-play several phone calls in which the student must take a business message for their parents. After the class has observed and seen the situation, check for accuracy in the written message taken.

Making Business Calls

Remember, you are representing your company when making calls on the job. To do your best, you need to be prepared and organized. You also need to speak clearly and use a pleasant tone of voice.

All business calls should be brief and to the point. Therefore, you should take time to plan your calls. Ask yourself, "Why am I making this call?" Is it to give information, get information, or place an order?

Before placing a call, have the necessary information in front of you. Outline your main points. Don't trust complex facts to memory.

Placing Orders

If you are calling to place an order, have all the details in writing. Read your notes slowly and clearly. Speak at a normal pace. Give the person a chance to ask questions and repeat information.

Tell the person who you are. State the name of your company and why you are calling. Give all the necessary facts in the correct order. Tell how many parts are needed. A typical business telephone order is illustrated in 19-8.

Making a Difference

Make a list of three community organizations for which you would like to volunteer. Plan questions to ask about available volunteer opportunities. Use the telephone to contact the organizations, making sure to use good speaking and listening techniques. Choose the organization that best fits your interests and start volunteering.

19-8
Always speak clearly and listen carefully when placing a business order by phone.

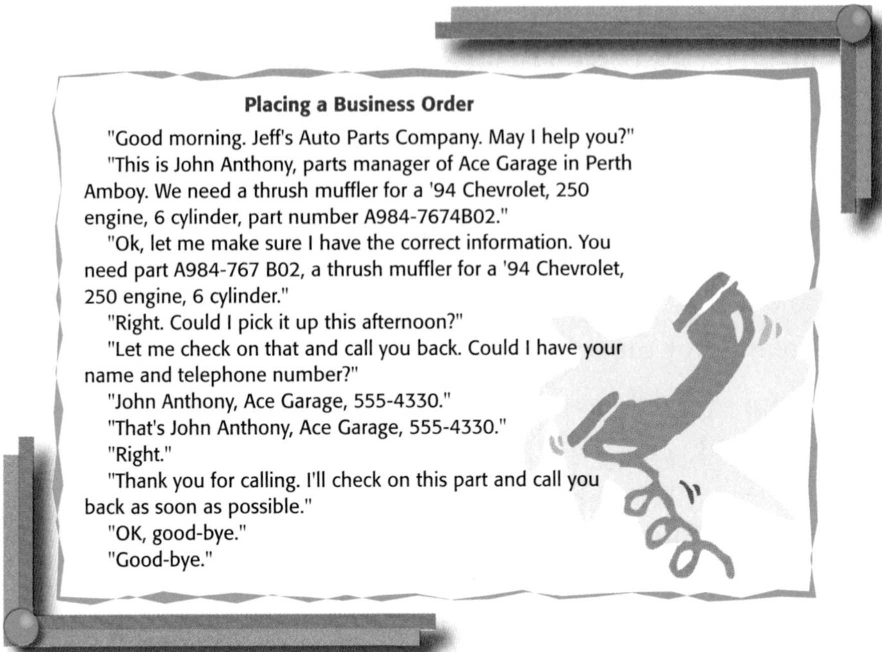
Placing a Business Order

"Good morning. Jeff's Auto Parts Company. May I help you?"

"This is John Anthony, parts manager of Ace Garage in Perth Amboy. We need a thrush muffler for a '94 Chevrolet, 250 engine, 6 cylinder, part number A984-7674B02."

"Ok, let me make sure I have the correct information. You need part A984-767 B02, a thrush muffler for a '94 Chevrolet, 250 engine, 6 cylinder."

"Right. Could I pick it up this afternoon?"

"Let me check on that and call you back. Could I have your name and telephone number?"

"John Anthony, Ace Garage, 555-4330."

"That's John Anthony, Ace Garage, 555-4330."

"Right."

"Thank you for calling. I'll check on this part and call you back as soon as possible."

"OK, good-bye."

"Good-bye."

Activity

Read Figure 19-8 together in class. Point out all the errors in this phone conversation that could happen. Discuss what to do to minimize errors in numbers.

Adapting the Lesson

Have students who are low functioning practice placing phone orders. Give them a prepared list of information they must order. Some phone-ordering examples include: items for class sewing projects, groceries to be delivered to the school, or a catalog order for home delivery. Have another student on the other side of the classroom take the order. Check for accuracy.

Discuss

Do you have emergency numbers by the telephone? Do you have paper and pencil handy? What emergencies might arise in your home?

Making Emergency Calls

In the event of an emergency on the job, you must know what to do. Learn what the company expects of you. Many companies have guidelines to follow during emergencies. Check with your supervisor. Learn where emergency telephone numbers are posted. You may need to call the police, an ambulance, or the fire department. Most towns and cities call *911* to report an emergency. If you don't know what number to call in an emergency, just speak to the operator.

When reporting an emergency, remain calm. Clearly describe the injury or accident. Give your company's address. Stay on the line and do exactly as you are told until help arrives.

What should you do before making a business phone call?

Accepting Personal Calls

Many companies do not allow employees to use work phones for personal calls. Be sure to follow your workplace's policy. Making personal calls at work is unprofessional and may be grounds for dismissal.

Companies often discourage the use of personal cellular phones in the workplace, except during lunch or breaks. Avoid using your cell phone during work hours to text message, make personal calls, check e-mail, or access the Internet. Guidelines on how, when, and where to use cell phones are listed in 19-9.

Cell Phone Etiquette

- Speak in a moderate tone to keep your conversation private.
- Turn off your cell phone or use the silent mode in meetings and at public gatherings. Never take personal calls during business meetings or interviews.
- Carefully select ring tones. Some are not appropriate for business and social environments.
- Avoid talking and driving. It is dangerous and illegal in some states. If you must talk, use a headset. Pull off the road to a safe area before text messaging.
- Don't conduct nonessential calls in public places. Spare others from being forced to listen to your conversation.
- Talk to the person you are with. It is impolite to play games, accept calls, or send text messages in front of someone who expects your attention.
- Don't send inappropriate messages.
- Let callers leave messages on your voice mail. Most calls are not emergencies. If you're not sure, answer the call by saying, "If this is not an emergency, I'll call you back."

19-9
Etiquette is important when using a cell phone in the workplace.

Writing Business Communications

Using clear, concise writing and standard formats will ensure that business messages are understood. Common business communications include letters, memos, reports, and e-mails. Employees in good-paying jobs are expected to communicate well in writing.

Activity
Practice being an employee of a company that handles customer orders over the phone. Have students write both positive and negative situations. Have the class critique the performances.

Writing Letters

Writing letters is a common way to communicate with individuals and groups. Knowing how to write business letters is an important job skill. A sample business letter is shown in 19-10. The essential parts of a business letter are described as follows:

- *Return address.* Use your business address, which is the address of the company or organization for which you are writing. (Usually this is included on the company's letterhead.)

Activity
After reading about how to write a business letter, provide groups of students with copies of business letters that have mistakes. Have the students critique the letters to find the errors.

Resource
Business Letter Format, transparency master 19-2, TR. Students examine the basic parts of a business letter.

19-10
Follow this format when writing business letters.

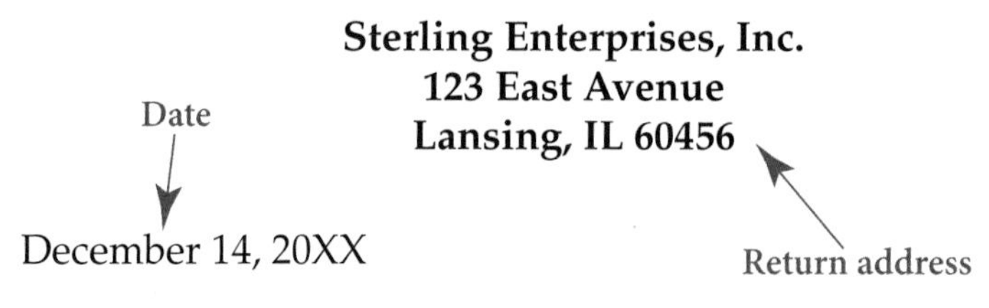

Sterling Enterprises, Inc.
123 East Avenue
Lansing, IL 60456

December 14, 20XX

Ms. Jane Wright, Sales Manager
Greenbaugh Equipment Company
128 South Avenue
Freetown, PA 08956

Dear Ms. Wright:

Please send me your current catalog of commercial food equipment. I would also like to receive information regarding ordering and shipping procedures, warranties, and return policies.

I am planning to expand my operation this coming February. Therefore, I would appreciate receiving these materials at your earliest convenience.

Thank you for your assistance.

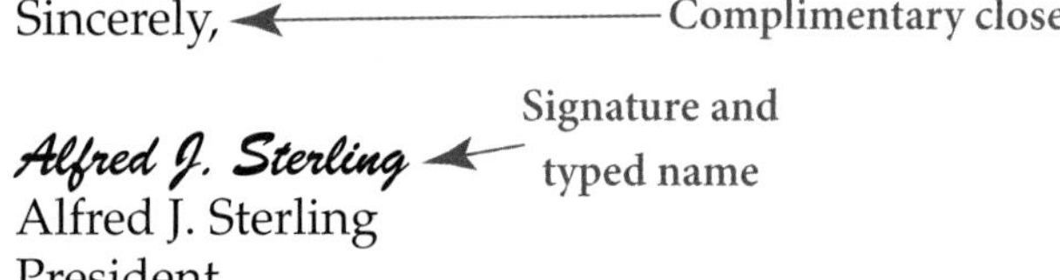

Sincerely,

Alfred J. Sterling
Alfred J. Sterling
President

Resource

Writing Business Letters, Activity D, WB. Students write a business letter.

Activity

Review the business letter format shown in Figure 19-10. Review what information must be included in such a letter.

Note

Even though many computer programs provide templates for writing letters in correct form, plus spell-check and grammar-check functions, letters must still be proofread to catch hidden errors.

- *Date.* Use the date you are writing the letter.
- *Inside address.* Use the complete name and address of the person to whom you are writing. Be sure to include the person's job title, too.
- *Salutation or greeting.* Begin your letter with a greeting. "Mr. Jones:" and "Dear Sir or Miss:" are examples.
- *Body of the letter.* This is the message you want the reader to receive.
- *Complimentary close.* Conclude your letter with "Sincerely," or "Yours truly."

- *Signature with typed name and title.* Always sign your letter.

The most difficult part of writing a letter is starting it. First, make an outline of the important facts or ideas you want to convey. If you are writing about events, list them in the order they occurred or are scheduled. If you are writing about ideas, cover the most important topic first and save the least important for last.

When writing a thank-you letter, state why you are thanking the person. Explain why you appreciate what was done. Send a thank-you letter as soon as possible after receiving the favor or gift.

When writing a letter requesting information, explain in detail what you need. Also indicate when you need the information. Close the letter with a short statement showing your appreciation for the person's help.

When you are providing information in response to a request, open the letter by thanking the person for requesting the information. Then give the information. Close the letter by assuring the person that you were happy to help. Be brief and to the point.

Writing Memos

Memos are usually written to communicate information within a company or organization. They are generally sent to coworkers and colleagues. Memos are used to inform the reader about new or revised policies, training sessions, work schedules, and so forth. Unlike a business letter, you do not need to include a formal salutation or closing remark. Include your initials at the end of the memo. A sample memo is shown in 19-11.

Memos are usually short and concise. The first sentence of the memo should tell your readers why you are writing. Include in the body of the memo only what your reader needs to know, but be sure it is clear. The sender may indicate a due date for responses or recommendations. Include your phone number or e-mail address at the bottom of your message.

Activity

Create an outline for a letter inviting a local business owner to speak to your class about the importance of communication in the workplace. Then write the letter using your outline as a guide.

Reflect

When was the last time you wrote a thank-you letter? Did you send the letter promptly?

Activity

Write a memo informing employees of a training session on using new computer software. Ask employees to RSVP by a certain date and include a phone number or e-mail in the memo.

19-11
Follow this format when writing a memo.

Interoffice Memo

To: All personnel

From: Hugh Li, Human Resources Director

Date: May 7, 20XX

Subject: Summer holiday schedule

The company will be closed on the following holidays:

- Memorial Day
- Independence Day
- Labor Day

To accommodate travel plans and allow employees more time with their families and friends, the offices will close at noon on the workday before each holiday.

If you have any questions, please call me at (867) 563-9800 ext. 1298.

HL

Activity

Review the memo format shown in Figure 19-11. Review what information must be included in such a memo.

Making a Difference

Work with your classmates to assess the recycling and waste management/reduction programs at your school. For instructions on how to conduct a waste assessment, visit **epa.gov** and search for "tools to reduce waste in schools." Prepare a report of your assessment. Use charts and graphs to summarize the data. Include recommendations for reducing the amount of waste produced by your school. Present your report to the class. Consider presenting it to the school board.

Creating Reports

Written reports are an important tool in all types of businesses and professions. The purpose of a report is to distribute information in a clear and concise manner. A report should be easy to read and professional in its presentation. A report should generally include the following sections:

- title page
- introduction
- body
- conclusion

Depending on the length and purpose of the report, it might also include these additional sections:

- letter of transmittal
- table of contents
- executive summary or abstract
- recommendations
- appendix
- bibliography
- list of abbreviations and/or glossary

Before you begin writing, make sure you understand the reason for compiling the report. Then decide what information you will need to gather. The reader will be looking for easy-to-read information, presented in a logical order. Whenever possible, charts and graphs should supplement the data. Any appendix, bibliography, or reference list should be placed at the end of the report.

Sending E-mail

E-mail is a fast and efficient way to communicate over the Internet. Like all business correspondence, you need to be professional at all times. This should be a rule you follow in your personal correspondence as well.

The first step is carefully entering the receiver's e-mail address. In the subject line, include a clear and concise description of the message. When writing e-mails, always use correct grammar and punctuation. Begin with a salutation or greeting, such as those used in a standard business letter. Include your name, telephone number, and fax number at the end of your message. Before sending, run spell check and proofread for clarity and accuracy.

Once you send an e-mail, you have no control over who forwards it, saves it, or makes a printout. Don't send emotional or incomplete messages. Avoid forwarding frivolous messages or chain letters that can carry viruses.

It is a good idea to review your company's electronic mail policy. Remember, the e-mail you send and receive while at work is not private. Your employer can check it at any time. Therefore, give it the same careful treatment you would give to any business message.

Adapting the Lesson

Have students who are high functioning research online information on how to create business reports. Students are to prepare a list of helpful hints to be shared with the class.

Discuss

Do you think that the frequent use of casual e-mail messages, which often do not contain perfect grammar and punctuation, causes people to forget the rules of proper English?

Reflect

Do you think it is appropriate to forward chain e-mails to coworkers?

Discuss

Do you think employees should have separate personal and work e-mail addresses? Do you think it is appropriate for employees to use their work e-mail to communicate with family and friends?

How is a memo different from a letter?

Nonverbal Communication

nonverbal communication
The sending and receiving of messages without the use of words.

Not all messages involve words. ***Nonverbal communication*** is the sending and receiving of messages without the use of words. It is used in sign language, which is communication through hand gestures. It is used by sailors aboard ships who send messages using flags or lights. It is used by mimes, who tell stories using only body movements and facial expressions. Musicians and artists also use it. The saying "a picture is worth a thousand words" refers to the power of this form of communication. See 19-12.

Resource
Understanding Body Language, Activity E, WB. Students interpret various examples of body language.

Activity
Brainstorm a list of various examples of nonverbal communication.

Resource
A Picture Is Worth a Thousand Words, reproducible master 19-3, TR. Students create symbols to convey various messages.

Nonverbal communication is as old as cave drawings, smoke signals, and drumbeats. It is part of modern society, too. Police officers use whistles and hand movements to direct traffic. Politicians smile, wave, and shake hands to express their goodwill. In the game of charades, players use nonverbal communication to help their partners guess the words.

A single body movement or gesture may have several meanings. This is especially true if the gesture is not accompanied by spoken words. Thinking about the situation in which a movement is used will help you determine its meaning.

19-12
Your facial expressions can send messages to others about your feelings and attitude.

Body Language

Your ***body language*** tells others a lot about you. In this form of nonverbal communication, you send a message with your use of body movements. You also speak with your facial expressions and hand gestures.

To learn more about body language, watch people without listening to them. Sit on a bench at a shopping mall and watch the crowd. Also, watch TV with the volume off. Pay attention to the movements, gestures, and expressions you see. What can you learn?

After watching body language, transfer what you have learned into action. Use body language to help you communicate more clearly. Make sure you are sending the signals and messages you want to send.

body language
A form of nonverbal communication in which a person "speaks" with the use of body movements, facial expressions, and hand gestures.

Adapting the Lesson
Have students who are low functioning use magazines to cut pictures of communication using body language. Students are to glue the pictures onto a blank piece of paper below the following headings: Mad, Happy, Intense, Confused, and Serious.

Body Language on the Job

On the job, body language tells others about you. See 19-13. Slouching during an interview may suggest a lack of interest in the job. Even though you answer the questions thoughtfully, the interviewer may think you are lazy and sloppy. Staring into space while at a planning meeting may suggest that you are bored. Even if you contribute ideas, your boss may think you are uninterested.

You must stay aware of your body movements. Know what kind of impression you are making. Then, go a step further. Use body language to make the kind of impression you want to make. Chart 19-14 lists various impressions your body movements might give.

Your Reading
How can you use body language to communicate more clearly?

19-13
Use body language to send a positive message during work meetings by maintaining good posture and making eye contact.

Resource
Good Manners Are Important! reproducible master 19-4, TR. Use the adapted worksheet to reinforce chapter concepts in students who are low functioning.

Discuss
Describe what the speaker in Figure 19-13 is feeling. What is happening in the picture?

19-14
Each body movement, gesture, and facial expression can convey a number of messages.

Interpreting Body Language			
Nonverbal Communication	**Possible Meaning**	**Nonverbal Communication**	**Possible Meaning**
Tears	joy sorrow love pain	Arms folded at chest	reservation displeasure disagreement defiance
A wink	a greeting a shared secret a signal teasing	Handshake	a greeting a farewell an agreement peace sportsmanship
A fist	power defiance a threat	Smile	friendliness humor happiness affection approval ridicule
Crossed fingers	a good wish or hope good luck a lie		

Discuss

Use Figure 19-14 to compare nonverbal forms of communications with possible meanings. Clarify any words not understood by the students.

Summary

Communication is a major factor in all relationships—business and personal. Understanding different communication styles will help you effectively send and receive messages. Keys to success in communication include speaking clearly, being an active listener, and using feedback.

When employees use headsets, telephones, and computers, they are communicating as representatives of their companies. They should be polite, thorough, accurate, and businesslike. In case of an emergency, they should know how to make emergency calls.

Employees are expected to know how to compose business letters, memos, reports, and e-mails. Writing clearly and knowing standard business formats are important job skills.

People are constantly sending messages about themselves without words. They do this through their body language. People should know what message their body language conveys so it is consistent with the one they want to send.

Reviewing Key Concepts

1. Name three ways to send messages, three ways to receive messages, and three channels of communication.
2. Which of the following describes aggressive communications?
   A. Results in a win-win situation for everyone.
   B. Achieves goals at the expense of others.
   C. Honestly expresses opinions without infringing on the rights of others.
   D. Avoids conflict at all costs.
3. List five tips for improved speech.
4. List and describe the three parts of a speech.
5. Why is feedback important in the communication process?
6. What information should you always record when taking a telephone message?
7. True or false. If employees reserve company phones for business use, it's okay to receive personal calls on their own cellular phones during work.
8. What are the seven essential parts of a business letter?
9. How do you speak in body language?
10. Give an example of a message communicated on the job through body language.

Answers to
Reviewing Key Concepts

1. (Name three of each. See Figure 19-1.)
2. B
3. (List five:) Speak slowly and clearly. Use good grammar. Think first before speaking. Avoid slang. Avoid profanity. Pronounce words clearly and completely.
4. The introduction is a short statement telling the audience what the topic of the speech will be. The discussion is the main idea of the speech. The closing is a short summary of what was just said.
5. It ensures that both the sender and the receiver of a message understand it in the same way.
6. name of the caller, name of the company, caller's telephone number and extension, reason for the call, and time and date of call
7. false
8. return address, date, inside address, salutation or greeting, body of the letter, complimentary close, and signature with typed name
9. with the use of body movements, facial expressions, and hand gestures
10. (Student response. See Figure 19-13.)

Building Academic Skills

1. **Speaking.** Conduct a debate on how using slang affects communication. Discuss the following: Can a person sound professional while using slang? Does slang clarify communications or cause confusion?
2. **Speaking.** Work in groups of five to coordinate a team speaking assignment based on a favorite movie. Each person should speak for three minutes on the impact of one factor on the movie's main message. Factors may include lighting, set design, music, special visual effects, unique filming techniques, costumes, and characters.
3. **Writing.** Interview a worker to determine how communication skills are important at a particular work site. What expectations are in place? What forms of communication are required on a daily basis? What advice can he or she provide on effective communication skills?

Building Technology Skills

1. Working with a group of your classmates, create a video that shows each of the communication styles discussed in the chapter. Demonstrate how people with different communication styles would act in a variety of workplace scenarios. Share your video with the class.
2. Write an e-mail message to a family member or friend about what you have learned so far in this course. Before sending the message, share your e-mail with another student to analyze the tone and nonverbal content of the message. Revise your e-mail if needed.
3. Using the Internet, research the nonverbal communication customs in different countries. How do the differences impact international business? Why should companies know the nonverbal communication customs where they do business? Share the results of your research with the class.

Building Career Knowledge and Skills

1. Write a story, factual or fictional, describing a problem created because feedback was not understood correctly.
2. Prepare and give a speech to the class on the importance of delivering speeches well.
3. For at least 24 hours, log the body language you observe, categorizing it as a positive or negative. Write a paper about the experience.

Building Workplace Skills

Write a fictitious letter to a company requesting career information on specific types of jobs available. Using a computer, outline the points to include in the letter. Access the word processing program to view the business letter formats available. Decide on the best format to use, and compose a letter from your outline. Work with a classmate to review each other's letters. Determine if they meet the requirements for a well-written business letter, as described in this chapter.

How can I look my best?

Chapter 20
Your Appearance

Chapter Objectives

After studying this chapter, you will be able to

- **describe** good grooming guidelines related to hair, skin, hands, breath, makeup, and fragrance.
- **plan** a wardrobe for work.
- **judge** the quality of clothing according to fabric, construction, and fit.
- **summarize** the proper care of clothing.

Key Concepts

- Good grooming helps you feel better about yourself and present a professional image.
- With careful planning, you can assemble an attractive, affordable wardrobe for work.
- Caring for your clothes will extend the life of your wardrobe.

Key Terms

grooming
acne
dress code
wardrobe inventory
accessories
fads

Good Grooming

grooming
The way in which people take care of themselves.

Your appearance is an important part of the first impression you make on people. They often form opinions about you based on your personal appearance. Therefore, it is always important to look your best. ***Grooming*** is the term used to describe how people take care of themselves. Good grooming means being clean, neat, and well dressed.

Hair

Resource
Reinforcing Vocabulary, Activity A, WB. Students match vocabulary terms with their definitions and write a paragraph with the terms.

Note
Stress to the students that their appearance can create a great first impression on others, while poor grooming habits create a negative impression.

Discuss
What does good grooming mean in terms of taking care of your hair?

Adapting the Lesson
Have students who are low functioning use magazines to find two pictures of people who have acceptable grooming habits and two pictures of people with unacceptable habits. Students are to mount these pictures on a piece of paper with a description of their appearance below.

The appearance of your hair can add to or detract from your overall appearance. To look your best, keep your hair neatly trimmed and off your face. Whether you choose to keep your hair long or short, be sure to have it cut regularly. It should always look neat and fashionable. Avoid extreme hair colors or styles.

People have different types of hair, so they need to follow different hair care routines to be well groomed. Some people need to wash their hair every day. Others need to wash their hair less often. You should be sure your hair is clean at all times. Ask you hairstylist or barber what type of shampoo and conditioner you should use to keep your hair clean and healthy.

If you choose to have a mustache or beard, keep it clean and neatly trimmed. Having a beard or mustache is acceptable at some jobs but not others. Some employers have rules about hair length and facial hair. Check to see if your employer has such rules.

Skin

To look fresh and healthy, your skin must be kept clean. That means your entire body. Bathe or shower daily. Be sure that you look clean and smell fresh when you go to work. Use deodorant or antiperspirant to help keep you fresh.

acne
A skin disorder caused by the inflammation of the skin glands and hair follicles.

Many people, especially teens, have acne. ***Acne*** is a skin disorder caused by inflammation of the skin glands and hair follicles. It may result in blemishes on the face, neck, scalp, upper chest, or back. If you have acne, take extra care to keep your skin clean, 20-1. If you are worried about your complexion, seek a doctor's advice.

20-1
Good grooming habits include bathing daily and caring for your complexion.

Hands

In the workplace, shaking hands is a common practice. Since this gives people a chance to notice your hands, you should keep your hands clean and well manicured. You should be sure your nails are smooth and clean. Keep them at a reasonable length. Women may choose to polish their nails. Polished nails should always be kept fresh. Chips in the polish should be repaired daily. Nail polish is not allowed in many foodservice jobs. Be sure you know your workplace policy.

Breath

Having fresh breath is important when you work with other people. One factor that affects the freshness of your breath is whether your teeth and gums are clean and healthy. You need to brush and floss your teeth daily to keep them clean. You should visit your dentist regularly to keep your teeth and gums healthy. You may also want to use mouthwash to freshen your breath.

Discuss
What do you need to do to keep your skin fresh and healthy?

Reflect
Why might an employer have rules about the length of hair and having facial hair? How would you feel if an employer said you had to cut your hair to keep your job?

Resource
Check Your Grooming Habits, Activity B, WB. Students evaluate their personal grooming habits.

Discuss
How do you maintain fresh breath? Why is this important on the job? What would you do if you worked closely with someone who has bad breath?

Community Connections

Contact your local department store to invite guest speakers to your class. Invite a consultant from the cosmetics counter to demonstrate the proper way to apply and wear makeup. Also, invite the men's department manager to share how to select dress clothes, tie a tie, and coordinate business casual clothes.

Makeup

If you choose to wear makeup, carefully select the proper type. When you like your appearance, you will be able to turn your attention away from yourself. You will be able to think of others and concentrate on your work.

Makeup is proper for women to wear on most jobs. The key to wearing makeup well is using flattering colors and keeping it light, 20-2. If you are uncertain about what colors and products are right for you, go to a local department store. Ask the skin care consultants to help you choose the makeup that is best for you.

Fragrance

Sometimes individuals wear a fragrance to work. Usually all types of after-shave lotion, cologne, hair spray, and perfume have fragrance. When wearing grooming products, be sure their fragrances are very light and pleasant. Fragrances that are too strong may annoy your coworkers or customers or cause others to have an allergic reaction.

20-2
Proper makeup application can improve women's appearance and confidence.

Your Reading

What does good grooming mean?

Wardrobe

Different types of jobs require different types of clothes. People who work on farms or in construction can wear jeans and T-shirts to work. People in offices must wear more formal clothes to work, such as jackets and dressy shirts. Whatever work you do, remember that your clothes say something important about you. The way you dress has an effect on how people think of you. Your clothes should always be neat and clean, no matter what work you do.

Resource

What's Too Casual for the Workplace? color transparency CT-20, TR. Students discuss the clothing and accessories that are inappropriate for the workplace.

Discuss

Describe the man in Figure 20-3. Point out all of the good-grooming tips you think he follows.

Dress Codes

Practically all workplaces have a dress code. Many schools have dress codes, too. A ***dress code*** is a set of rules that individuals must follow regarding clothing and general appearance. Find out what your place of work requires. For instance, a company may require you to wear a uniform, special footwear, or a lab coat.

dress code
A set of rules that individuals must follow regarding clothing and general appearance.

Some companies have dress codes because they have a certain image they want their employees to maintain. For instance, an accounting company may want its employees to convey a professional image by wearing suits and dressy clothing. Employees may be required to cover visible tattoos or remove body piercings. Other companies have dress codes for safety reasons. A distribution company, for instance, may require its warehouse employees to wear hard hats, 20-3.

20-3
Many company dress codes include policies to keep employees safe.

Community Connections

Many schools have dress codes for students. Organize a debate on having a school dress code. Invite parents, students, and administrators to be a part of the panel. Provide pictures and suggestions for what clothes would be acceptable if a dress code were imposed. Identify the benefits of having a dress code. If your school already has a dress code, organize a debate about what changes are needed.

Resource

What Workers Wear, Activity C, WB. Students identify types of clothing appropriate for various occupations.

wardrobe inventory
A list of all the clothes and accessories found in a person's closet and drawers.

accessories
Items that complement a wardrobe, such as shoes, handbags, belts, neckties, and jewelry.

A trend in workplace is *relaxed dress codes*. This means wearing casual clothes, such as men wearing trousers and knitted shirts with collars, and women wearing informal blouses or sweaters with slacks. Other names for this trend are *corporate casual*, *business casual*, and *workday casual*. Casual dress days were once reserved for Fridays, but more employers are allowing casual clothing on other days as well. However, business dress is usually required for meetings with clients or customers.

A relaxed dress code is not the same as no dress code. Ripped jeans, cut-offs, shorts, halter tops, and clothing you would wear to the beach are not suitable items for the workplace. With suitable casual clothes, workers can feel more comfortable on the job and still convey a professional image.

Jewelry

Company dress codes may apply to jewelry as well as clothing. In some work settings, jewelry can get caught in machinery and become a safety hazard. Employees may not be allowed to wear long chains, earrings, rings, necklaces, bracelets, or watches. Where jewelry is allowed, it should be chosen with care and worn in moderation. Simple pieces that accent an outfit are a better choice than dramatic, overpowering items.

Wardrobe Planning

Before you buy new clothes for work, take time to determine what you need. If you are unsure about what you should wear on the job, look at the clothes that other employees wear. Then, review your wardrobe. Do your clothes seem compatible with that workplace? If not, you will need to do some planning to assemble an appropriate wardrobe.

The first step in wardrobe planning is to know what you already have. A good way to find out is to take a ***wardrobe inventory***. This is a list of all the clothes and accessories you have in your closet and drawers. ***Accessories*** are items, such as shoes, handbags, belts, neckties, and jewelry that are needed to complete outfits. As you make your wardrobe inventory, briefly describe the color and condition of each item. For instance, you may have a white shirt that is in good shape and a blue shirt that needs replacing.

Once you know what you have, you can decide what to add or replace. Make a list of exactly what you want or need to buy. Note the style and color of each item on the list. As you do this, think of what you will wear with each new piece of clothing or accessory. Plan complete outfits. Don't buy items that won't go with anything else in your closet.

If your job requires you to wear a dressy wardrobe, begin by buying a few basic pieces of clothing. You can add to them later when you can afford to do so. If your job does not require a special wardrobe, then you may be able to wear many of the clothes you have now. No matter what you wear to work, always be sure your clothes are clean and neat. See 20-4.

Resource

Wardrobe Planning for Work, Activity D, WB. Students develop a clothing inventory.

Example

Share examples of pictures of workers dressed in different outfits. Describe the jobs they have. Compare the workers' outfits to how you think they would perform on the job.

Avoiding Fads

As you plan your wardrobe, remember that fashions constantly change, but many of the changes are fads. ***Fads*** are items that are popular for a short period of time, perhaps one or two seasons. Pants with flared legs and ankle socks with lace ruffles are examples of fads. Avoid spending a lot of money on fads. Instead, look for classic styles that will always be popular. Oxford shirts, straight-leg pants, and straight skirts are all classic styles.

fads
Clothing items or styles that are popular for a very short period of time.

20-4 Even employees who do not have a dress code should make sure their work clothes are neat and clean.

Adapting the Lesson

Have students who are low functioning use Figure 20-4 to describe the grooming habits of the person pictured. Have students answer these questions: What would an employer think about the grooming habits of this person in a job interview? Why would this person create a good impression during an interview?

Resource

Clothing Care Checklist, reproducible master 20-1, TR. Students evaluate their personal clothing care habits.

Discuss

What do you look for in quality clothes? Have the students list the "quality" flaws they occasionally find when shopping.

Resource

Getting Dressed for Work, reproducible master 20-2, TR. Students "dress" male and female silhouettes for work after deciding their occupations.

Shopping for Quality

Always try to buy clothes of good quality. They may cost more, but they will look nicer and last longer than clothes of less quality. One well-made shirt for $40 may be a better buy than three shirts of less quality totaling $40.

The three signs of clothing quality are good fabric, construction, and fit. Check all three before you buy.

Fabric quality is judged by how the material looks and feels. In general, natural fibers, such as cotton, offer comfort. Synthetic fibers, such as polyester, help prevent wrinkles. The labels in your clothes list the fiber content and provide clothing care directions.

The construction of clothing refers to the way clothes are put together or sewn. In quality clothes, the seams are straight and securely stitched. Zippers and pockets lie flat. Buttons are secure. See 20-5. Stripes, plaids, or other patterns in the fabric match at the seams.

20-5
Good construction is a sign of quality clothing.

Discuss

When you shop for clothes, is it important to select items that you can care for at home rather than dry-clean?

Activity

Find out the cost of dry-cleaning various clothing items for men and women at several local businesses. Do costs vary much?

Activity

Assign students the task of doing their own laundry for a week. Document what was learned. Have parents provide a signature as proof of completion.

Clothes must fit properly to look good. Use the following guidelines to judge fit:

- Movement should be comfortable when the garment is on.
- A garment should lie smoothly across the body without wrinkling, bunching, or sagging.
- Shirt or blouse sleeves should be a little longer than jacket sleeves.
- Men's ties should extend to the belt.
- Dress or skirt hems should not be too short.
- Pants should be long enough to extend to the tops of shoes but not to the floor.

Making a Difference

Dress for Success® is a not-for-profit organization that provides professional clothing and career development resources to disadvantaged women. Visit **dressforsuccess.org** to learn how your school can organize a suit drive. The suits will be given to women who can't afford to purchase a professional wardrobe.

Laundry and Ironing

No matter how expensive your clothes are, they will look cheap if they are dirty or cleaned improperly. You need to make sure your clothes are cleaned appropriately. They will look better and last longer if you do.

Every clothing item must have a firmly attached, readable care label. This label, which may show symbols instead of words, explains how to clean the item. See 20-6. Care labels can be fused, glued, or sewn inside. Many clothing items can be washed in a washing machine. If not, you will need to wash them by hand or have them dry-cleaned.

	International Symbols on Care Labels
	This symbol means it's safe to machine wash: one dot, use cold water; two dots, warm; three dots, hot.
	A triangle means it is safe to use bleach.
	A drying symbol means machine drying is safe: one dot, use low heat; two dots, medium; three dots, high.
	An iron tells how to press: one dot, cool setting; two dots, medium setting; three dots, use a hot iron.
	A circle means that it is safe to dry-clean the garment.
	An X through a symbol means do not use.

20-6 International symbols on care labels tell consumers how to care for their garments.

Resource

Reading Clothing Labels, reproducible master 20-3, TR. Students examine clothing care labels.

Hand-washing means the clothes must be soaked in soapy water and washed by hand. After soaking them a few minutes in a clean sink or tub, gently rub them with your hands. Then rinse them thoroughly in clean water. Dry them on a hanger or flat on a rack, depending on the care instructions. Some hand-washed items can be dried in a dryer on a *gentle* setting with low or no heat.

Your Reading

What aspects of a person's appearance does a dress code cover?

Clothes must be dry-cleaned if their labels say *dry clean only*. The cost of dry cleaning can be expensive. Shop around to find a cleaner that does a nice job at reasonable prices. If you must dry-clean clothing frequently, be sure to include this expense in your monthly budget.

In addition to having clean clothes, be sure your clothes appear ironed. Ironed clothes have no wrinkles. They look smooth and neat. They give you a more professional appearance. See 20-7. Some fabrics need to be ironed more than others. Linen wrinkles easily, while polyester resists wrinkling.

20-7
Wear wrinkle-free clothes to present a professional image in the workplace.

Resource

What Are the Secrets to a Good Look? reproducible master 20-4, TR. Use the adapted worksheet to reinforce chapter concepts in students who are low functioning.

Summary

You should always try to look your best. Your appearance affects the way other people think of you. Looking your best also helps you feel good about yourself.

Good grooming includes keeping your hair, skin, and hands clean and attractive. It includes keeping your breath fresh and using makeup and fragrances wisely. It also includes wearing clothes that are clean, neat, and appropriate.

Different types of work require different wardrobes. When you start a job, find out what the other workers wear. Then make plans to put a similar wardrobe together.

As you shop for clothes, avoid spending a lot of money on fads. Look for signs of quality in clothing. After buying clothes, be sure to care for them properly.

Reviewing Key Concepts

1. Give one good-grooming tip for each of the following:
   A. hair
   B. skin
   C. hands
   D. breath
   E. makeup
   F. fragrance
2. What types of jewelry are safety hazards in some jobs?
3. What are two reasons for a company dress code?
4. What is the first step in wardrobe planning?
5. List five examples of accessories.
6. Why avoid spending a lot of money on fads?
7. What are three signs of quality clothing?
8. Name three guidelines for judging the fit of clothes.
9. Why should clothes be properly maintained?
10. Where can you find washing and drying instructions for your clothes?

Answers to *Reviewing Key Concepts*

1. (Student response.)
2. long dangling items that may get caught in machinery
3. to convey an image, to protect employees from hazardous working conditions
4. identifying what you already have by making a wardrobe inventory
5. (List five:) shoes, hand bags, belts, neckties, and jewelry
6. They are popular for a very short period of time.
7. good fabric, construction, and fit
8. (Name three. Student response.)
9. to help the clothes look better and last longer
10. on the attached labels

Building Academic Skills

1. **Writing.** Write a written response to the following questions: Do current clothing and grooming fads conflict with the good-grooming advice discussed in the text? State your opinion in two or three paragraphs.
2. **History.** Research the historical clothing worn in the United States during a specific era or in a specific region. Share your findings with the class, providing pictures wherever possible.

Building Technology Skills

1. Conduct online research to determine Web sites that provide information on grooming. Make a list of Web sites that offer suggestions on the following: hair care and styling hair, makeup and facial care, oral hygiene, and care for hands and nails. Share your information with the class.
2. Conduct online searches for how to plan a wardrobe. Investigate ways to mix and match outfits and determine appropriate colors and styles. Present your findings to the class.
3. Create a virtual model at **mvm.com**. Dress your model in an outfit for a relaxed dress code. E-mail your model to your classmates and have them evaluate whether you made appropriate choices.

Building Career Knowledge and Skills

1. Develop a weekly grooming chart for yourself. List what you will do daily and weekly to stay well groomed.
2. Visit several stores that sell clothes of various styles, qualities, and prices. Look for both fads and classic styles. Compare the fabric, construction, and fit of different clothes. Give an oral report about what you learned.
3. Take an inventory of your wardrobe. Identify items that are fads. Shop online for accessories that can update and add interest to your wardrobe. Make a list of what you would need to add to your wardrobe to dress appropriately for your chosen career path.
4. Call three dry cleaners in your area. Make a comparison list of their prices for cleaning each of the following: a man's suit, dress, coat, sweater, and pair of slacks.
4. Research ways to create different outfits using a few pieces of clothing. Identify basic pieces you already own or could borrow from family members.
5. Research ways to stretch your clothing dollars. Write a report of your findings.

Building Workplace Skills

Visit one place where you would like to work to observe how people are dressed. Make an appointment with someone in the personnel or human resources department to discuss the organization's dress code. Obtain a copy of the dress code, if one exists. Find out what type of clothing is forbidden and what the penalty is for wearing these to work. Present your findings to the class in an oral report. Create a poster to use during your report that shows the do's and don'ts of dressing for work.

How does my health relate to my job?

Chapter 21 Good Health and Job Success

Chapter Objectives

After studying this chapter, you will be able to

- **incorporate** enough activity in each day to maintain fitness.
- **list** guidelines for choosing foods that will provide a balanced diet.
- **determine** ways to handle stress.
- **explain** why people should avoid smoking.
- **describe** the negative effects of abusing alcohol and drugs.

Key Concepts

- Eating a balanced diet and exercising regularly is the foundation of good health.
- Managing stress prepares you for handling changes in your life.
- Smoking is a risky habit that yields no positive benefits.
- Using drugs illegally harms your body, your relationships, and your work.

Key Terms

physical fitness
balanced diet
nutrient
stress
drug
drug abuse
addiction
drug screening

Reflect

How healthy are you? How would you rate your diet? What are your health habits regarding exercise?

Discuss

List ways you can stay physically fit.

Staying Healthy

Maintaining your health is important to all areas of your life. If you are not in good health, you cannot do your best in school. You may not be able to fulfill your family responsibilities. Poor health can also affect your attendance and performance at work. Start caring about your eating and lifestyle habits while you are young. How you treat your body now will impact your health later. There are many ways to enjoy food and promote good health at the same time.

The *Dietary Guidelines for Americans* is a general guide to promoting good health. The U.S. Department of Agriculture and Department of Health and Human Services developed the plan. The *Guidelines* help children and adults make personal choices to achieve and maintain good health. See 21-1.

Balance Food and Physical Activity

Being healthy isn't just about eating the right foods. It also involves physical activity. Regular physical activity is necessary for your overall health and fitness. It also helps you control your body weight by balancing your calorie intake

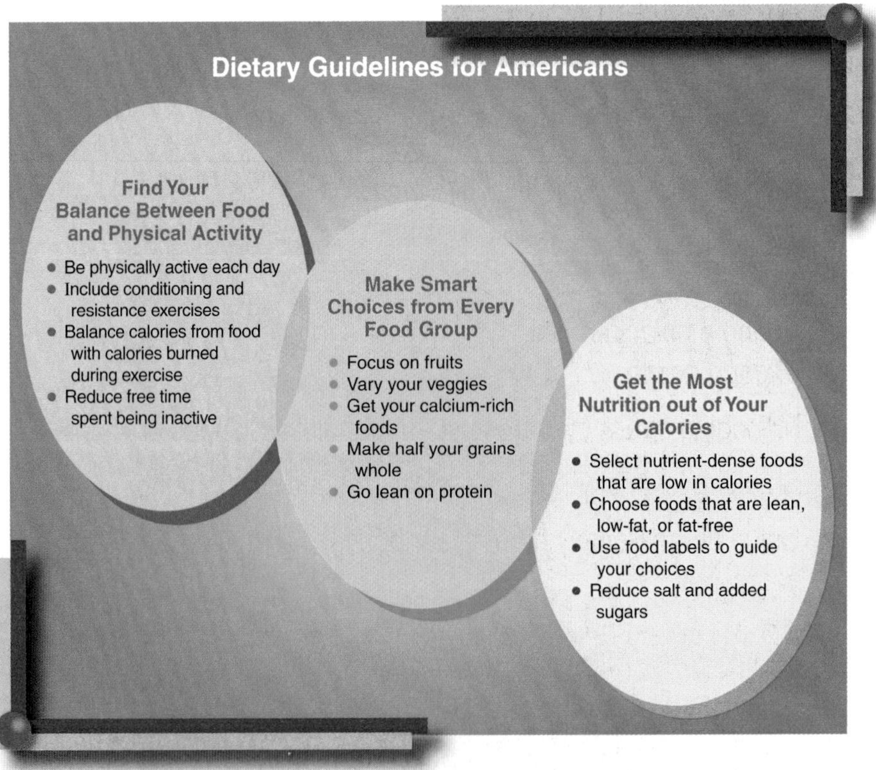

21-1
The Dietary Guidelines for Americans include these basic steps to good health.

Resource

Reinforcing Vocabulary, Activity A, WB. Students use vocabulary terms to complete partial sentences.

with the calories your body uses. Physical fitness is your goal. ***Physical fitness*** is the ability to perform daily tasks easily with enough reserve energy to respond to unexpected demands. Achieve physical fitness by including cardiovascular conditioning, stretching exercises for flexibility, and resistance exercises for muscle strength.

physical fitness
The ability to easily perform daily tasks with enough reserve energy to respond to unexpected demands.

The best way to promote physical fitness is to incorporate activity into each day as much as possible. You don't need to set aside a special block of time to exercise. Simply accumulate at least 60 minutes of moderate activity throughout the day on most days of the week. Longer periods of activity or more-vigorous activities are even better.

If possible, ride a bike to school instead of taking a bus. Use stairs instead of escalators or elevators. These are two easy activities you might be able to do. On the other hand, if you prefer to schedule a specific time of day for an exercise workout, then do that. The objective is to get the activity you need to maintain good health.

Before any vigorous activity, be sure to begin with warm-up exercises to help prevent strains and pulled muscles. A good warm-up prepares your muscles and joints for the strenuous motions to follow. Many coaches and trainers recommend at least 10 minutes of warm-up exercises.

Brisk activity provides good conditioning for your heart and lungs. Walking, running, swimming, rowing, jumping rope, bicycling, playing tennis, and skiing are more-intense forms of exercise. Team sports like basketball, soccer, and hockey are also good. You may want to try several activities.

Joining a health or tennis club, local park district program, the YMCA, or the YWCA are good ways to get exercise. You should start any new exercise program slowly and build it gradually. As the activity becomes easier, you can do a little more. Don't try to do too much on your first or second try. You may overdo it and get sore muscles. Then you might lose your desire to continue. A word of caution: it is wise to consult a physician before beginning a strenuous exercise program.

Activity
Have students work in groups to create lists of common daily activities for students and adults in your community. For each, list a possible way to modify the activity to increase the exercise level for the individual. Do some of the modifications greatly increase the time required to accomplish the activity?

Enrich
Find out how many calories are burned doing various activities. How many calories are burned doing housework, swimming, running, and sitting in class? Create a chart to show the results.

Discuss
Talk about the health benefits of team sports. What are the other benefits besides the health benefits of this activity?

What kinds of physical activity are needed for good health?

Make Smart Food Choices

balanced diet
An intake of food that supplies the body all the necessary nutrients in the needed amounts to maintain good health.

nutrient
A chemical substance in food that nourishes the body.

A good way to maintain a healthy body is to eat a balanced diet. A ***balanced diet*** is an intake of food that supplies all the nutrients in the needed amounts to maintain good health. ***Nutrients*** are chemical substances in foods that nourish the body. To create a balanced diet, you must choose the foods you eat with care. Eating foods that are good for you helps you feel good. That is why some people say, "You are what you eat." A balanced diet also helps you avoid obesity, diabetes, heart disease, and many other health problems.

Resource
MyPyramid, color transparency CT-21, TR. Students discuss the basic principles behind MyPyramid.

Resource
Making Balanced Food Choices, reproducible master 21-1, TR. Students evaluate two menus and judge which is more healthful.

No single food provides all the needed nutrients. Eating a wide variety of foods is the best way to obtain all the nutrients required for good health. Using MyPyramid can help you recognize your food choices. MyPyramid is an individualized food guidance system developed by the U.S. Department of Agriculture. It divides foods into groups according to the nutrients they provide. Simply go to **MyPyramid.gov** and enter your age, gender, and activity level. You can learn how to plan a healthful diet around your food preferences. See 21-2.

Eat plenty of whole grains, vegetables, and fruits. These are high in fiber and nutrients. They also tend to be low in fat and calories. You lose weight if you eat fewer calories than you

21-2
Eating foods from all the groups in MyPyramid in the right amounts gives you the nutrients you need daily.

Resource
What's in Your Pyramid? reproducible master 21-2, TR. Students go to MyPyramid.gov to determine their recommended amounts of each food group.

Resource
A Balanced Diet, Activity B, WB. Students create a one-day meal plan using MyPyramid recommendations for a typical teen.

use. You maintain your weight when the number of calories you eat equals the number of calories you use.

Choose a diet low in saturated fat and cholesterol, and moderate in total fat. No more than 20 to 35 percent of calories in your diet should come from fat. Fried or greasy food, butter, margarine, oils, salad dressing, and lunchmeat are common fat sources. Too much of the wrong kinds of fat in the diet is linked to health problems. Moderate amounts of olive oil and the fats in fish, avocados, nuts, and seeds are needed for good health.

Sugars and other sweets contribute many calories and few nutrients. Use sugars, salt, and sodium in moderation. Too much sodium has been linked to high blood pressure in some people. Many processed foods contain large amounts of salt.

Keep foods safe to eat by cleaning hands and work surfaces often. Always keep hot foods hot and cold foods cold. Keep raw, cooked, and ready-to-eat foods separate while shopping, preparing, and storing. When in doubt, throw it out instead of taking a chance on spoiled food.

A varied diet coupled with regular activity will help you maintain a healthy weight. Try to avoid eating too much of any one item. Bad habits are easy to form and hard to break.

Children and adolescents should not drink alcoholic beverages. Poor nutrition can result if alcohol replaces foods in the diet. Also, alcohol consumption is a major cause of accidents among teens.

Making a Difference

The first step in making smart food choices is having access to healthy foods. Organize a classroom food drive. Collect nonperishable canned and packaged goods, aiming for a wide variety. Organize the food into separate bags, making sure each bag contains a healthful assortment. Deliver the bags to a local shelter or food pantry.

Learn to Handle Stress

You face various types of stress every day. ***Stress*** is a feeling of tension, strain, or pressure. It is usually the result of some change. Stress can affect both the body and the mind. See 21-3.

Both good and bad changes create stress. Getting a new job causes stress; so does losing a job. Making the basketball team causes stress; so does an injury or illness. Dating someone new causes stress; so does ending a relationship.

Both big and little pressures create stress. Big worries, like money problems, drug abuse, divorce, and the death of a loved one, can cause extreme stress. Homework, tests, and deadlines can cause stress, too.

Your Reading

How can MyPyramid help you make smart food choices?

stress
A feeling of tension, strain, or pressure.

21-3
A person's body language can show signs of stress.

Resource

Learning About Stress, Activity C, WB. Students examine their thoughts about stress.

Discuss

What are some sources of stress for students? What are the health concerns of having too much stress in life? In what ways can people relieve stress?

Reflect

Do you know people with considerable stress in their life? Are you aware of resources to help people deal with stress?

Adapting the Lesson

Have students who are low functioning review a list of ways to relax and ask them to circle their five favorite ways. Have students find pictures in magazines of ways to relax and reduce stress. Ask them to glue the pictures to the back of their list.

Some stress is good for you. It makes life interesting and exciting. It keeps you on your toes. It challenges you to react to new situations.

On the other hand, trying to handle too much stress repeatedly can be harmful. Severe stress can affect your behavior. You may not be able to concentrate on your work. You may feel frustrated. You may become rude to people. Too much stress can also harm your health. It can affect the development of ulcers, heart problems, and strokes.

Since you cannot avoid stress in your life, you need to learn how to handle it. The following tips on managing stress often help:

- Practice good eating and sleeping habits. Avoid eating too many high-calorie snacks. Eat balanced meals. Get plenty of rest. Most students your age need eight or nine hours of sleep every night. These habits will help keep you healthy and more able to handle stress.
- Use physical activity to relieve stress. Let off steam by working out, playing a sport, or pursuing other forms of exercise. See 21-4.

21-4
Team sports are a fun way to exercise your body and relax your mind.

- Talk about your problems. Choose to talk to people you trust and respect. They may be able to help you see your problems from a different view. Sometimes professionals, such as psychologists, clergy, and counselors, can offer great help.
- Maintain a positive attitude. Keep away from complainers. Surround yourself with positive-thinking people who feel good about themselves. Develop a "can do" philosophy. Set realistic goals and objectives. Then go after them.
- Manage your time. Control your time by setting priorities. Develop a to-do list for each day and stick to it.
- Keep a balance between work and family responsibilities. When you are with your family, spend quality time together. At work, take advantage of flexible work schedules, if available.
- Develop a positive work ethic and outlook on life. Associate with others who share your beliefs and values. Seek out those who find similar meaning for their lives and encourage their friendship.

Discuss

Describe what you see in Figure 21-4. How would you rate the stress of these players? What are other ways to relieve stress?

Activity

This page talks about managing your time and creating a to-do list. Have the class create a list for today and one for the week.

Reflect

Do you have a favorite hobby or song that helps you relax?

Community Connections

Some jobs cause more stress than others. Research the 10 most-stressful occupations in the United States. Prepare a presentation on why stress levels are higher in these careers. Where in your community do these high-stress occupations exist? Conduct your presentation for the class.

- Learn to manage multiple roles, especially if you are responsible for caring for younger siblings or aging parents and relatives. Avoid overextending yourself by carefully planning how to use your time and energy. Communicate with other family members if you need help.

Ways to Relax

A good way to reduce stress is to relax. When you are relaxed, you feel at peace with yourself and the rest of the world. You feel renewed and regain strength. It is important that you reserve some time for total relaxation.

There are many ways to relax. Like exercise, you have to find the ways that suit you best. Consider the following possibilities:

- Read something inspiring, entertaining, or informative.
- Play a game of chess, checkers, or cards.
- Listen to music.
- Spend time alone to think about your goals and life plans.
- Talk with someone about a topic of mutual interest.
- See a movie, play, concert, or television program.
- Attend a lecture or social function.

The type of work you do may determine the relaxation that's best for you. If you read all day at school and work, you may want to rest your eyes while listening to music. No matter how you choose to relax, do so whenever you feel the need. Give your body and your mind some time to reduce the everyday stresses of life.

Your Reading

What are the causes and possible effects of harmful stress?

Example

Share specific examples of how to deal with stress. Talk about the activities you do as a teacher to relax.

Avoid Tobacco Use

When it comes to tobacco use, there isn't much good to say about it. At best, it is a bad habit. At worst, it is a killer. The Surgeon General has warned that cigarette smoking is dangerous to your health. Smoking causes lung cancer, heart disease, and emphysema, and may complicate pregnancy. See 21-5. Smokeless tobacco—chewing tobacco and snuff—can cause oral cancer, gum disease, and other

Surgeon General's Warning: Cigarette smoke contains carbon monoxide.

Surgeon General's Warning: Quitting smoking now greatly reduces serious risks to your health.

Surgeon General's Warning: Smoking causes lung cancer, heart disease, emphysema, and may complicate pregnancy.

Surgeon General's Warning: Smoking by pregnant women may result in fetal injury, premature birth, and low birth weight.

21-5
All cigarette packages and ads must display warnings that underscore the health hazards associated with smoking.

health problems. Besides the health issues, there are many reasons why tobacco users should quit.

- Smoking is an expensive habit. Heavy smokers spend hundreds of dollars every year on cigarettes.
- Smokers' clothes often carry a smoke odor.
- Tobacco use causes bad breath and discolored teeth.
- Tobacco use dulls the senses of smell and taste.
- Smokers are fire hazards. The National Fire Protection Association reports that smoking is a major cause of fatal residential fires.
- In most states, it is illegal for persons under a certain age to purchase and use tobacco products.

Old views of smoking as something glamorous, worldly, and "cool" have been shattered. Yellowed teeth and diseased lungs are the mental images now linked to smoking.

Smokers are finding it more difficult to comply with the increasing strictness of nonsmoking policies in the workplace. Some employers allow smoking only in a designated smoking room for limited periods. In many workplaces, however, cigarette smoking is banned completely. See 21-6.

Smoke-free workplaces protect all workers from exposure to secondhand smoke. *Secondhand smoke* is a mixture of smoke exhaled by a smoker and emitted from the burning tip

Discuss

In what ways does tobacco use affect the workplace? Suppose the person working next to you is a heavy smoker, how would you feel about that?

Discuss

Figure 21-5 shows several warnings that have appeared on cigarette labels. Read through each and be sure you understand them.

Reflect

Do you feel strong pressure from peers to smoke? Do members of your family smoke?

Discuss

What would you recommend to convince people your age not to smoke? What types of efforts are ineffective?

21-6
Workers tend to be more productive in a tobacco-free environment.

Reflect
How would you feel if your best friend started smoking? How might you help him or her see the potential consequences of this habit?

Community Connections
Many state and local governments require smoke-free workplaces. Research the policies that apply to workplaces in your community. Then, survey area employers to find the answers to these questions: Is smoking allowed anywhere on company premises? If smoking is allowed, does the company have any plans to issue a smoking ban? Does the company pay for tobacco cessation programs for its employees? Share your findings with the class.

of a cigarette, cigar, or pipe. It contains many chemicals that cause cancer, heart disease, and other health problems. When you are exposed to secondhand smoke, your body absorbs these toxic chemicals. There is no safe level of exposure—your body's heart and circulation is affected immediately.

According to the Surgeon General, most cases of secondhand smoke occur in homes and workplaces. Smoke-free workplaces promote the health and productivity of all employees. They usually help smokers to cut back or quit smoking.

How to Quit Smoking

There are many ways to quit smoking. People who smoke must choose the methods that work best for them. The first step is to decide they truly want to quit. Smokers must have the desire and the will to quit. The methods described in the following paragraphs have helped millions of smokers quit. Similar methods can help users of smokeless tobacco, too.

One way to quit smoking is known as *cold turkey.* With this method, smokers make the decision to stop smoking at a specific time. Then they do it. They never again smoke another cigarette. This method takes willpower and determination. It's tough, but it works.

Another way many people quit smoking is by gradually reducing the number of cigarettes they smoke. They may start with 20 cigarettes a day. They may cut down to 15, then 10, then five, then three, then two, then one, and finally none!

People who want to quit smoking may find that chewing gum or candy can help. Whenever they have the urge to smoke, they can replace the cigarette with chewing gum or candy. There also are commercial products available to help those who want to quit smoking.

Individual or group therapy is another option. Therapy can provide the professional support that people need. If you smoke, you may want to talk with your doctor about the best way for you to stop.

Your Reading

What are the dangers of secondhand smoke?

Avoid Drug Use

A ***drug*** is any chemical substance that brings about physical, emotional, or mental changes in people. ***Drug abuse*** is a term used to describe the reckless use of drugs. It means using a drug in a way that can damage a person's health or ability to function. No workplace permits drug use among employees.

drug
A chemical substance that brings about physical, emotional, or mental changes in a person.

drug abuse
The use of a drug in a way that can damage a person's health or ability to function.

Drugs such as marijuana, heroin, cocaine, crack, Ecstasy, PCP, and LSD are illegal. However, drugs do not have to be illegal to be abused. Drug abuse can easily occur with prescription medications and over-the-counter remedies.

Some athletes abuse performance-enhancing drugs. These drugs are *anabolic steroids*. They mimic the male sex hormone, testosterone, and increase muscle mass and athletic performance. Steroids are illegal if used w ithout a doctor's prescription. They can cause acne, stunted growth, increased aggression, and damage to the kidney, liver, and heart. Males that use steroids may experience breast growth and shrunken testicles. Females may develop more-masculine qualities such as decreased breast size, increased body hair, and deepened voices. The side effects of steroids can be irreversible and lead to life-long health problems.

Different drugs affect the body in different ways. Drugs may have harmful effects on the heart, lungs, brain, and reproductive system. Drugs can dull the senses, alter behavior, impede judgment, and impair driving skills. Drugs can cause dizziness, vomiting, convulsions, coma, and death.

Vocabulary
Use the terms *drug* and *drug abuse* in a sentence to demonstrate understanding.

Activity
List the problems a company would have if workers used drugs on the job.

Discuss
What problems might employees and supervisors have if a coworker uses drugs before or during work?

Not only do drugs affect the user's body, they also affect the user's relationships. Drug abusers seldom live successful lives. Those who depend on drugs lose interest in school, family, and jobs. They spend most of their conscious time searching for drugs or stealing money to buy more. They usually develop an addiction. An ***addiction*** is the never-ending obsession to use a drug.

addiction
The never-ending obsession to use a drug.

Typical drug abusers have few friends except other drug abusers. Practically all begin their drug habit by simply experimenting, believing they can stay in control. In the end, drugs take over their lives. Eventually every drug abuser learns—the hard way—that drugs can't bring happiness or solutions to problems. Drugs only cause more problems.

Your Reading

What are the harmful effects of drug abuse?

Enrich

Interview a counselor from a drug treatment facility. Document the ways in which this professional helps people get treatment. Document the career training that a counselor needs.

Discuss

What would your responsibility be as a fellow worker if you suspect someone is under the influence of drugs or alcohol on the job?

Resource

Avoiding Substance Abuse at Work, Activity D, WB. Students examine substance abuse in the workplace from the employer's viewpoint.

Avoid Alcohol Use

Most people do not associate alcohol with drugs. They should. Alcohol is a drug. It can alter your behavior and damage your health. Alcohol abuse can ruin personal relationships. It can lead to health problems such as brain damage, cirrhosis of the liver, and heart failure. It can also cause economic and legal problems. It is illegal for teens to buy alcohol. By avoiding alcohol, you can protect your health and legal status.

Are you aware that alcohol-related car accidents are the number one cause of death among teenagers? Here's why: alcohol moves quickly into the bloodstream and to the brain. When this happens, the person's vision, muscle coordination, and reaction time are impaired. Drinkers usually feel more powerful and in control. In reality, their body functions are slowed down. They have less control.

Just one drink can affect a driver's performance. The message is clear. Drinkers shouldn't drive, and anyone planning to drive shouldn't drink. If you plan on drinking at a party or event, you should also plan to have a designated driver. A designated driver is someone who agrees not to drink and will drive others home safely. Be responsible.

Alcohol and Other Drug Problems at Work

Practically all employers will require you to take a drug test before they hire you. This is called ***drug screening***. Drug screening tests can reveal the presence of drugs in a person's body. During the workday, some employers periodically test their employees *randomly*. This means a small percentage of workers are selected, without warning, to take an immediate drug test.

drug screening
Tests that can reveal the presence of drugs in a person's body.

Drug screening is one way for employers to reduce problems at work. Employee problems due to alcohol and drugs cost businesses billions of dollars each year. Many companies have policies that deal with alcohol and drug abuse on the job. See 21-7. Disciplinary action is taken against employees who are found intoxicated while on duty or who illegally use or possess drugs. In some cases, use of alcohol or drugs on the job is grounds for immediate dismissal.

Activity

Use an online directory to locate treatment facilities in your area. Find out if agencies exist in your community to deal with alcohol and drug abuse.

21-7
Workers who operate tools or machinery can't afford to have their motor skills impaired by alcohol.

Reflect

How can you help a friend who uses alcohol? What might happen to them if they continue to abuse alcohol? What could you do to help them kick the alcohol habit?

Discuss

What are the skills needed in Figure 21-7? What happens if the worker in this picture uses alcohol or drugs?

Note

Emphasize to the students that many agencies and health care givers are willing to help those with alcohol and drug problems.

Community Connections

Your school may provide resources for students with alcohol and drug abuse problems. Invite a counselor to your classroom to discuss substance abuse treatment programs. Ask the counselor to explain how to refer a classmate to a treatment program. Talk about ways to show support to a friend in treatment.

Your Reading

What resources are available for people with substance abuse problems?

Alcohol and drug abuse on the job contribute to the following problems:

- poor quality control
- more safety risks
- increased absenteeism and lateness
- more health risks
- poor relationships among coworkers
- increased risk of internal theft (to pay for drug or alcohol addiction)

Abusing drugs or alcohol outside work can also jeopardize your employment status. Workers are closely regulated if they drive company cars or work in the transportation industry, including trucking, aviation, railroad, and shipping. If an off-duty worker gets a *driving under the influence (DUI)* or *driving while intoxicated (DWI)* ticket, the employer can require more testing. Employers may prevent such a worker from returning to the job until a clean drug test is achieved. If you are charged with a DUI or DWI, it appears on a criminal record, which may affect your future employment opportunities.

Where to Get Help

Many organizations are available to help people who have alcohol or drug problems. These organizations can provide information, counseling, and treatment. If you or someone you know needs assistance, contact help immediately. Turn to the yellow pages of your phone book. Look under *Alcoholism Information* and *Treatment Centers*. Help may also be listed under *Drug Abuse and Addiction–Information and Treatment*.

People who need information or help can also turn to family members and friends. School nurses, counselors, teachers, coaches, and religious leaders may be able to suggest sources of help. Employee assistance programs are often available in workplaces. Also, community agencies, religious organizations, and hospitals may offer helpful programs. Remember this important point: when someone with a problem is ready to face it, immediate action should be taken. See 21-8.

Substance Abuse Treatment Programs

Assessment

Upon admission to a treatment facility, this process evaluates the patient's addiction and recommends an appropriate treatment program.

Detoxification

This process is designed to safely withdraw patients from addictive substances as an initial step in breaking their dependence on the substances.

Inpatient Care

In this program, patients become residents of the treatment facility to help them begin their recovery in a protected environment. Food, lodging, and 24-hour nursing care are provided in addition to the treatments included in outpatient programs. This program is often recommended for patients who are unable to abstain from substance use without constant supervision or whose health has been weakened by their addiction.

Outpatient Care

In this program, patients visit the treatment facility for group therapy, individual counseling, and education exercises. Friends and family members may be encouraged to participate in some activities with patients. This program is often recommended for patients able to abstain from the use of substances without constant supervision. Patients who begin treatment on an inpatient basis may continue on an outpatient basis once their condition has stabilized.

Family Support Programs

These programs educate family members of addicted persons about addiction and its impact on the family. The programs allow family members to share experiences with other families in the same situation.

Aftercare

Aftercare programs provide continued support through group therapy and individual counseling sessions to help patients remain free of addiction. Programs also provide support for friends and family members.

21-8

Many types of treatment programs are available to help individuals and families affected by drug addiction.

Reflect

How would you handle a family member with a drug or alcohol problem? Do you know whom to contact for help and support?

Discuss

Figure 21-8 describes a substance abuse treatment program. Explain the process to students and check for their understanding by asking questions.

Reflect

How would you go about finding help for a friend? Do you know where to begin?

Resource

How Do You Practice Good Health? reproducible master 21-3, TR. Use the adapted worksheet to reinforce chapter concepts in students who are low functioning.

Summary

Health is an important factor in all aspects of your life. Feeling well allows you to live your life to its fullest. When you are physically fit, you can perform well at school and work. You also have enough energy to enjoy your leisure time.

Regular activity and a balanced diet are two keys to good health. They give your body what it needs to function well.

Stress is a part of life. To maintain good health, you must learn to handle stress. Finding ways to relax will help.

Good health depends on what you do as well as what you don't do. It is important to avoid smoke and using alcohol and other drugs. If you have any problems in these areas, make an effort to solve them. Many sources of help are available.

Answers to *Reviewing Key Concepts*

1. at least 60 minutes of moderate activity accumulated per day for most days of the week
2. A good warm-up prepares your muscles and joints for more strenuous activity and helps prevent sport injuries, like pulled muscles and strains.
3. Eating a wide variety of foods is the best way to get all the nutrients you need since different foods contain different nutrients.
4. false
5. A, B, C
6. (List five:) Use physical activity; practice good eating and sleeping habits; talk about your problems; maintain a positive attitude; manage your time; develop a spiritual and ethical outlook; balance work and family responsibilities; learn to manage multiple roles; find ways to relax.
7. Cigarette smoking causes lung cancer, heart disease, emphysema, and may complicate pregnancy.
8. Smokers decide to quit smoking at a specific time and never smoke again.
9. Alcohol impairs a drinker's vision, muscle coordination, and reaction time. He or she has less control, so is more likely to be involved in an accident.
10. (List five:) poor quality control, more safety risks, increased rates of absenteeism and lateness, more health risks, poor relationships between coworkers, increased risks of internal theft to pay for the drug or alcohol addiction

Reviewing Key Concepts

1. How much physical activity is recommended for good health?
2. Why should you warm up before vigorous exercise?
3. Why is it important to eat a variety of foods?
4. True or false. You lose weight if you eat more calories than you use.
5. Which of the following statements is true?
   A. Stress can affect both the body and the mind.
   B. Both good and bad changes create stress.
   C. Some stress is good for you.
   D. No stress is good for you.
6. List five ways to handle stress.
7. According to the Surgeon General, how is cigarette smoking dangerous to your health?
8. Describe the *cold turkey* method of quitting smoking.
9. Why should someone who has been drinking avoid driving?
10. List five problems caused by alcohol and drug abuse on the job.

Building Academic Skills

1. **Health.** Ask your health/physical education teacher for material that explains the exercise abilities and fitness levels appropriate for your age group. Practice the exercises and note any areas where you need improvement. Develop a plan to achieve your optimal fitness level.
2. **Math.** Calculate the cost of smoking for one year and 20 years. Also, calculate the cost of a lifetime of smoking. Determine how many packs of cigarettes the average smoker smokes during these periods. Identify some items you could buy with the money saved from not buying cigarettes.
3. **Science.** Find out how drug-screening tests work. What is the science behind the tests? Are there different types of tests or is one type uniformly used? What is examined and how is the presence of drugs determined? For what drugs are workers tested? Share your findings with the class.
4. **Health.** Invite guest speakers on the topic of how to quit smoking. Speakers can include health experts as well as ex-smokers who can talk about what they did to kick the habit. Consider including visuals of what happens to the lungs of smokers.

Building Technology Skills

1. Research the number of calories in some of your favorite snack foods. Also research the number of calories burned when walking, biking, climbing stairs, swimming, playing tennis, and so forth. Create a spreadsheet that shows how many minutes of exercise are needed to burn off the calories in your favorite snack foods. Show figures for moderate versus vigorous activity. Based on this analysis, what foods and exercise options would you choose?
2. Conduct online research to determine the adult obesity rate in your state. Create a graph that shows the rise or fall of the obesity rate over the last 10 years. Also, research current trends in health and wellness programs offered by employers. Prepare a slide show presentation on how employers can help fight obesity and promote good health.
3. Conduct online research to determine how companies try to prevent drug and alcohol problems in the workplace. Examine various companies regarding their drug and alcohol policy, the use of drug-screening tests, and the related services provided to employees in need. Compile your findings in a written report.

Building Career Knowledge and Skills

1. Do further research and write a report on one of the following topics about stress: the causes, the effects, or ways to handle it.
2. Read current news stories about the problems businesses face because employees use alcohol and other drugs. Present your findings in an oral report to the class.
3. Ask a dietitian to talk to your class about choosing foods for a balanced diet. Be prepared to ask questions.
4. For one week, keep a time log that lists periods of moderate and vigorous activity. Determine if you are meeting the recommendations for physical fitness. If not, develop a plan of action to incorporate more activity in your daily routine.
5. Pick a situation or challenge that adds regular or constant stress to your life, such as getting to school on time. Develop a plan to deal with the stress and implement the plan for one week, recording the experiences you encounter. Summarize the steps you could take to limit the stress in your life.
6. Research quick and healthy snack and lunch ideas. Try out at least one new idea and report your experience to the class.
7. Research what employee assistance programs can do for employees. What is the process involved in getting the help needed?

Building Workplace Skills

Working with your classmates, organize a reference file of community resources to help people who want to quit smoking or stop using alcohol or other drugs. Include the names, addresses, hours, and key contact people of the area organizations with a brief description of their services. Determine the most useful way to organize and distribute the information. Before actually beginning work, report what you understand your part of the assignment to be.

How can I become a leader?

Chapter 22
Developing Leadership Skills

Chapter Objectives

After studying this chapter, you will be able to

- **identify** leadership traits.
- **discuss** how leadership traits and skills can be applied to work situations.
- **name** and describe the nationally recognized career/technical student organizations.
- **explain** the purpose of parliamentary procedure.

Key Concepts

- With practice, you can develop effective leadership skills.
- Participating in a career/technical student organization helps you explore future careers and build leadership skills.
- Knowing parliamentary procedure allows you to be an active meeting participant.

Key Terms

leadership
leader
career/technical student organization (CTSO)
agenda
parliamentary procedure
Robert's Rules of Order

Leadership

leadership
The ability to lead or direct others on a course or in a direction.

leader
A person who influences the actions of others.

Leadership is the ability to direct others on a course or down a path. When thinking of people who have that quality, you tend to think of famous people. Many famous people are leaders, but many ordinary people are leaders, too.

A ***leader*** is a person who influences the actions of others. The captain of a sports team is a leader. However, the teammate who encourages the team to do its best is a leader, too. Many people are leaders because they inspire those around them to perform well, 22-1.

Discuss
Give examples of leaders in your community.

Discuss
Talk about Figure 22-1. In what ways are leadership skills being used in this situation? Why are leaders important in the workplace?

Resource
Reinforcing Vocabulary, Activity A, WB. Students match vocabulary terms with their definitions.

In the workplace, leadership is not reserved just for the head of the department or the company. A workplace that values teamwork encourages the development of many leaders. Sometimes a work team has *shared leadership* responsibilities. In this case, no single individual holds the position of leader. Instead, different members come to the forefront to lead a project when it involves their area of expertise. After the phase is complete, another team member leads the next phase.

Few people will become company presidents. However, all of us will need to be leaders on many occasions in our lives. The success of schools, businesses, cities, and nations depends on effective leaders.

22-1
Leaders challenge other members of a group to do their best, no matter what the activity is.

Resource
Being a Good Leader, Activity B, WB. Students write descriptions of how good leaders can demonstrate leadership traits.

Activity
Take each of the leadership traits listed in italic on the next page and explain them in your own words. Give examples of how people demonstrate these traits.

Leadership Traits

Effective leaders have certain traits. These traits can be practiced and acquired. Having leadership traits is helpful in all aspects of everyday life.

- *Leaders respect the rights and dignity of others.* They are willing to accept responsibility and work within the group. They are able to get along with people in a friendly and peaceful manner.
- *Leaders are straightforward.* They give praise where praise is due. They communicate their thoughts and feelings in a clear and understandable manner.
- *Leaders are well informed on matters that concern the group.* They are confident and honest. They trust their fellow group members.
- *Leaders are positive and excited about the group's work.* They are open-minded.
- *Leaders inspire accomplishments.* They can help a group set goals. They also know how to get a group started and keep it on track.

Community Connections

Contact volunteer organizations in your community, such as the Rotary club or American Cancer Society. Ask for job descriptions of the available volunteer opportunities. What leadership skills are required? Why would it be important for volunteers to demonstrate leadership traits? Are volunteers expected to run meetings? Report your findings to the class.

Effective Leadership at School and at Work

You may be surprised to learn that the traits and skills used by effective leaders in the workplace are the same as those used by effective students. Refer to the chart in 22-2. There you'll find common steps individuals can take to become leaders at school and at work.

Your Reading

Why is it important to have leaders?

School Organizations Create Leaders

The best way to develop leadership skills and prepare for the world of work exists right in your own school. A variety of student organizations, clubs, and extracurricular activities are available to help you explore new interests and develop leadership skills.

22-2
If you have accomplished some of these steps, you are well on your way to becoming a leader.

Steps to Becoming a Leader

- Arrive early for meetings and appointments.
- Act and speak in a way that will leave a favorable impression.
- Develop good conversational skills. This includes being a good listener and an interesting speaker.
- Make a special effort to remember the names of everyone you meet.
- Stay out of arguments. No one ever wins an argument.
- Avoid complaining and being critical of others.
- Make an effort to find something good to say in all situations.
- Try to make challenges a win-win situation for everyone.
- Always appear interested, friendly, and pleasant.
- Say “please” and “thank you” often.
- Demonstrate your best effort at all times.
- Always try to make the best use of resources.

Note
Having leadership traits is helpful in every aspect of everyday life. Emphasize that employers will look for employees who can be leaders at their company.

Discuss
How important is it for a leader to do the following: say “please” and “thank you” often? act in a way that leaves a good impression on others? give the best effort at all times?

Consider joining a ***career/technical student organization (CTSO)***. These are school groups that help students learn more about certain occupational areas. You could join an existing organization, or you could ask a teacher to help you start a chapter of a student organization at your school. A teacher-advisor offers help when needed. In these organizations, students run the activities. They make the decisions.

career/technical student organization (CTSO)
School groups that help students learn more about certain occupational areas.

As a member of a career/technical student organization, you share interests and career goals with other students. By working with them, you also share many benefits of an active club. You can learn about careers in your field of interest, 22-3. You can enjoy social activities and participate in civic activities. You can develop leadership skills and participate in organization meetings and annual conferences. All career/technical student organizations sponsor local and national competitions, too. Meanwhile, you will be building your self-confidence, self-esteem, and motivation.

Resource
Learning About Career/Technical Organizations, Activity C, WB. Students link the classes offered at school with the particular student career/technical organizations.

Photo courtesy of SkillsUSA

22-3 Participating in SkillsUSA events will help you explore different careers.

Discuss
What organization is pictured in Figure 22-3? What happens at state or national organization meetings? How can you get more information about this group?

Activity
In groups of four, list all school organizations and extracurricular activities that are available in your school. Compare lists. How many activities does your school offer?

Enrich
Select a student organization that interests you. Interview members of that organization to learn more about its activities.

Resource
Your Career-Related CTSO, Activity D, WB. Students research the career/technical student organization of their choice.

The career/technical student organization to join should be the one that best matches your career goals. It should be related to your school program. The following career/technical student organizations are nationally recognized:

Business Professionals of America (BPA) is for students enrolled in business and information technology programs. The group's purpose is to help students learn job-related skills for careers in business management, office administration, and information technology. Activities focus on promoting job skills, leadership traits, and social awareness. Students who join BPA learn about jobs as office coordinators, paralegals, computer support specialists, and government administrators, among others.

DECA–An Association of Marketing Students is for students who are interested in the broad business of marketing. Programs focus on career development, economic understanding, leadership, and civic duties. Members learn about marketing, management, entrepreneurship, sales, hospitality, finance, and related careers. Through DECA, members can explore job opportunities such as store managers, travel agents, meeting and convention planners, international distribution managers, and company sales representatives, among others.

Discuss

What activities and clubs have a direct connection to a future career you are considering?

Family, Career, and Community Leaders of America (FCCLA) is open to students through grade 12 who have taken or will take courses in family and consumer sciences. This organization encourages personal growth and fosters family and community involvement and leadership. Students participate in community service projects, financial education programs, and leadership activities, 22-4. Members prepare for careers in early childhood education, food production and services, hospitality and tourism, housing and interiors, textiles and apparel, and family and consumer sciences education. Students who join FCCLA gain experience for jobs such as interior designers, social workers, executive housekeepers, child care teachers, chefs, and many other positions.

Reflect

When you read about these clubs, which one appeals most to you? In which do you feel you would best "fit in"? About which clubs did you want more information?

22-4
FCCLA members learn how to foster positive relationships and build teams.

Photo courtesy of FCCLA

Activity

Using the information about the career/technical clubs in this chapter, create two fill-in-the-blank sentences about each. Trade yours with another student to see if you can answer the questions. This will help you get to know the clubs and learn more about them.

Future Business Leaders of America–Phi Beta Lambda (FBLA-PBL) is for students interested in business careers. The group helps students understand American business enterprise and set career goals. It also helps them develop character and self-confidence. Other goals of the group are to promote sound financial management and competent business leadership. Activities focus on civic and community service, career development, social awareness, and economic education. Students explore careers as human resources managers, investment analysts, city managers, sports/entertainment managers, actuaries, and other business-related occupations.

Reflect

In what activities would you like to participate? How would you feel about having a leadership role in one of these clubs?

Health Occupations Students of America (HOSA) is for students interested in health occupations. The group helps students develop leadership skills, civic responsibilities, and occupational skills. Students become aware of health care issues and concerns. They participate in group discussions, conferences, and educational projects. HOSA members gain experience for such future careers as registered nurses, radiologists, speech and language pathologists, dentists, paramedics, and laboratory technicians.

National FFA Organization (FFA) is for students preparing to enter careers in agriculture, agribusiness, and agriscience. Conferences and award programs operate on local, state, and national levels. They give students practical experience in applying the agricultural knowledge and skills gained in the classroom. The group works to promote leadership, personal growth, and career success through agricultural education. See 22-5. Students explore job opportunities such as ranch managers, wastewater managers, forensic scientists, marine biologists, or county extension agents.

SkillsUSA provides education experiences that help students develop leadership, teamwork, citizenship, and character development. Programs offer training and employment opportunities as well as exposure to members of the workforce. The organization stresses high ethical standards, superior work skills, life-long education, and pride in the dignity of work. SkillsUSA prepares students to enter trade, industrial, technical, and skilled service occupations including health careers.

22-5
National FFA Organization projects and events give student members a chance to apply their knowledge of plants and soils.

Photo courtesy of National FFA Organization

Activity
Imagine your school does not have an FFA Organization. Use Figure 22-5 as a basis for brainstorming ideas offered by this club that could benefit the school. What skills would students learn from this club?

Reflect
How would you want your favorite student club to be run? What rules would you like to see established?

Technology Student Association (TSA) is open to any student who is taking or has taken technology courses. Activities include individual and group projects and school and community services. Students gain insight into careers and learn skills for jobs such as drafters, chemists, information technology service technicians, multimedia artists/animators, software designers, and mechanical engineers. Members also develop the leadership, personal, and social skills needed for living in a modern, technical world.

Your Reading
How do career/technical student organizations prepare students for the workplace?

How Student Groups Operate

Student groups have various names, such as clubs, organizations, and associations. They allow people with a common interest to meet and exchange information. When you join a school group, you will find its organizational pattern is similar to other groups.

All student groups have officers, who generally lead the group. The members elect the officers—usually president, vice president, secretary, and treasurer. Student groups also have one or more committees. Each committee focuses on one aspect of the group's work. Groups often use committees to handle events, publicity, and membership. See 22-6.

Monmouth County Vocational School District

22-6 This project committee is preparing for a competition.

Meetings are usually held on a regular basis. They may be scheduled weekly, monthly, or quarterly. The highlight of most meetings is an informational program. A part of each meeting is devoted to conducting the business of the student group.

Good meetings require advance planning. Usually the officers or members of a program committee plan the meetings. The president of the group conducts the meetings.

An ***agenda*** is a list of activities that will occur during a meeting. An agenda is also known as an order of business. An agenda should be presented to the membership a few days before each meeting. That allows people to plan for the meeting. It helps them prepare to intelligently discuss the business of the group.

The success of a group depends primarily on the quality of its meetings. Good meetings are described in the following statements:

- The meeting agenda is carefully planned in advance.
- The meeting follows the agenda, and starts and ends on time.
- The meeting room has good lighting and comfortable seating.
- Officers use parliamentary procedure to run the meeting.

Making a Difference

Determine what projects could be done for your community by the various career/technical organizations active in the school. Brainstorm a list of project options. Compile a list of helpful projects these organizations could do and submit them to the club presidents for consideration.

agenda
An order of business that lists activities that will occur during a meeting.

Your Reading

How are student groups organized?

parliamentary procedure
An orderly way of conducting a meeting and discussing group business.

Discuss
Have you ever attended an important meeting that had no agenda? Was the meeting organized or confused? If it was organized, what helped to make it so?

Resource
Parliamentary Procedure, color transparency CT-22, TR. Students are introduced to parliamentary procedure and the parts of an agenda.

Robert's Rules of Order
The most common reference book used to describe the parliamentary procedure used at business meetings.

Parliamentary Procedure

Persons who attend meetings of various organizations find that the meetings usually follow the same pattern. Most groups conduct their gatherings according to ***parliamentary procedure***. This is an orderly way of conducting a meeting and discussing group business. Its purpose is to help groups run their meetings fairly and efficiently.

Parliamentary procedure provides an orderly way to propose, discuss, and act on items of business. It provides a chance for fair discussion and action by the group. Both the majority and minority sides of an issue are handled fairly. Finally, parliamentary procedure provides rules for conducting group business quickly and according to the will of the majority. See 22-7.

Robert's Rules of Order is the most common reference used in parliamentary law. There are other references on parliamentary procedure that you may find easier to read. As an officer or member of a group, you should be familiar with parliamentary law so you can find the answers to problems that arise during club meetings. You should also know the terms in 22-8 so you can easily participate in meetings.

22-7
Career/technical student organizations often use parliamentary procedure to run meetings and elect officers.

Photo courtesy of FBLA

Your Reading

Why is it important to use parliamentary procedure in meetings?

Terms Used in Parliamentary Procedure

Adjourn—To end a meeting
Agenda—A list of things to be done and discussed at a meeting
Amend the motion—To change the wording of a motion that has been made
Aye—The formal term for *yes* (pronounced *eye*)
Bylaws—The rules and regulations that govern the organization
Chair—The presiding officer at a meeting, such as the president or chairperson
Debate—To speak *for* or *against* a motion. Every member has a right to debate an issue
Majority—At least one more than half of the members present at the meeting
Minutes—A written record of the business covered at a meeting
Motion—A recommendation by a member that certain action be taken by the group
Nay—The formal term for *no*
Quorum—The number of members who must be present to legally conduct business at a meeting
Second the motion—The approval of a motion by another member
Table the motion—To delay making a decision on a motion
The floor—The right to speak in a meeting without interruption from others

22-8 The terms used in parliamentary procedure date back to medieval England.

Resource
Defining Parliamentary Procedure, reproducible master 22-1, TR. Students define terms used with parliamentary procedure.

Resource
What Makes a Good Leader? reproducible master 22-2, TR. Use the adapted worksheet to reinforce chapter concepts in students who are low functioning.

Summary

Leadership traits can be practiced and acquired. They can help you be successful in many different settings. They are helpful in clubs, at work, and in everyday group situations.

Career/technical student organizations bring students with common career goals together. Eight career/technical student organizations are nationally recognized. Each focuses on a certain career field.

As a member of such a group, you will learn how meetings are run. You will be able to practice parliamentary procedure. You may have the chance to serve as an officer or committee member. Participating in career/technical student organizations has other benefits, too. You can learn more about careers. You can take part in many activities and competitions. You can learn new skills and build self-confidence.

Answers to *Reviewing Key Concepts*

1. (List four:) respects the rights and dignity of others, is straightforward, is well informed on matters that concern the group, is positive, inspires accomplishments
2. (List six. See Figure 22-2.)
3. help students develop leadership skills and get prepared for working in certain occupational areas
4. (List three:) learn about careers in a field of interest, enjoy social activities, develop decision-making and leadership skills, participate in conferences and competitions
5. Future Business Leaders of America, Business Professionals of America
6. B
7. false
8. (List four:) are carefully planned, start and end on time, follow the agenda, have good lighting, have comfortable seating, are run by capable officers, are conducted with parliamentary procedure
9. to run a meeting fairly and efficiently
10. Robert's Rules of Order

Reviewing Key Concepts

1. List four leadership traits.
2. Name six steps for a student to take at school or work to become a leader.
3. What is the function of career/technical student organizations?
4. Name three benefits of being involved in a career/technical student organization.
5. Name two career/technical student organizations for students who are interested in business occupations.
6. A career/technical student organization for students who are interested in marketing is ______.
   A. TSA
   B. DECA
   C. BPA
   D. HOSA
7. True or false. FCCLA is for students who are preparing to enter careers in agriculture, agribusiness, and horticulture.
8. List four characteristics of a good meeting.
9. What is the purpose of parliamentary procedure?
10. What book is commonly used as a reference on parliamentary procedure?

Building Academic Skills

1. **Art.** Prepare a poster that illustrates one of the five traits of effective leaders. Use color, graphics, or photos to make the poster attractive and interesting. Display your poster with those prepared by your classmates.
2. **Writing.** Imagine that you are leading a committee to organize a book drive for your library. Outline an agenda for the first meeting of your committee. The meeting is expected to last one hour.
3. **Listening, writing.** Attend a meeting in your school or community. Take notes on the use of parliamentary procedure. Write a brief report of your findings.

Building Technology Skills

1. Conduct online research on the topic of *leadership skills.* Report back to class on the leadership skills taught by youth organizations such as the Boy Scouts and Girl Scouts.
2. Use the Internet to investigate the "Planning Process" used by Family, Career, and Community Leaders of America (FCCLA). Make a poster showing the symbols for this planning process. Discuss how they can be used in planning service projects for your class.
3. Visit the Web sites for each of the career/technical student organizations listed in this chapter. Create a spreadsheet to compare the following features of each organization: number of members, mission/purpose, career areas served, major activities, competitions held, and membership requirements. Also, identify the organizations that are available at your school.

Building Career Knowledge and Skills

1. Interview members of one of the career/technical student organizations in your school. Ask them about their participation in the group. What have they gained from belonging to the group? Also ask them how the organization has affected their career goals. Present your findings to the class in an oral report.
2. Contribute to a class discussion about the traits of effective leaders. Discuss how these same traits can be applied to situations at work and in everyday life.
3. Ask a member of a career/technical student organization in your school to talk to your class about the benefits of belonging to the group.
4. Look for examples of everyday leaders in action. Observations can take place at home, work, school, or in the community. Log your observations. Summarize the characteristics of effective leaders.
5. Interview a worker regarding the leadership at his or her place of employment. Write a report on what you learned about leadership in the workplace.

Building Workplace Skills

Working with several classmates, research one aspect of parliamentary procedure. Possible topics include: order of business and programs, making a motion, committees and their reports, secretary's and treasurer's reports, nominating committee and elections, and officers and their duties. Help your group decide how to divide the tasks. Using a computer, create an informational handout to teach other members of the class about your topic. Make a brief presentation to the class using the brochure. After all groups have made their presentations, participate in a mock meeting to elect officers.

Part Six

Managing Your Money

How can I make sense of my paychecks and taxes?

Chapter 23 Paychecks and Taxes

Key Terms

pay period
gross pay
net pay
Form W-4
dependent
Form W-2
Internal Revenue Service (IRS)
income tax
Federal Insurance Contributions Act (FICA)

Chapter Objectives

After studying this chapter, you will be able to

- **explain** the difference between gross pay and net pay.
- **discuss** the use of Form W-4 and Form W-2.
- **list** considerations when filing tax returns.

Key Concepts

- Understanding the difference between gross pay and net pay will help you to understand the paycheck you earn.
- Form W-4 determines how much of your pay should be withheld for taxes.
- Form W-2 states how much you were paid and how much of your income was withheld for taxes.
- Your tax money pays for government services.
- As a wage earner, you have a responsibility to prepare and file a tax return on time.

Payday

Payday is usually a happy day. It is the day you are paid for the work you have done. Your paycheck, however, may be smaller than you expected. In this chapter, you will learn what goes into your paycheck—and what comes out of it.

Companies pay their employees for the work they did during a ***pay period***. Most companies have weekly, biweekly (every two weeks), semimonthly (twice a month), or monthly pay periods. In many companies, payday is not the last day of the pay period. Many companies delay pay for a week or a full pay period. For instance, suppose a company pays its employees every Friday. Each check covers the pay period that ends the previous Saturday. See 23-1. This delay allows the company to accurately pay employees for all the time they worked during the period.

When you start working for a company, there may a delay in payment. Wages earned during the delay time may be held back. Suppose you start a job on Monday with the company described earlier. You will not receive a paycheck on your first Friday on the job. The wages you earn during this period will be paid to you on the following scheduled payday.

Suppose you decide to quit your job, and your last day of work is Friday. The company will owe you a paycheck on the

pay period
A length of time for which an employee's wages are calculated. Most businesses have weekly, biweekly, semimonthly, or monthly pay periods.

Community Connections

Ask a parent or guardian the following questions: What is the pay period at your place of employment? Would you prefer a different pay schedule? What potential problems do you see with being paid once a month? Share your results with the class.

FEBRUARY

Sunday	Monday	Tuesday	Wednesday	Thursday	Friday	Saturday
					1	2
3 ←	4	5 Pay	6 Period	7	8 →	9
10	11	12	13	14	15 Payday	16
17	18	19	20	21	22	23
24	25	26	27	28		

23-1 Many companies delay payday for a week or more to do proper record keeping.

Discuss
Give examples of common pay periods among companies.

Resource
Reinforcing Vocabulary, Activity A, WB. Students match vocabulary terms with their definitions.

next payday. It will include the wages earned since the last pay period. If you are terminated, some state laws require that you must be paid on your last day of work.

Your Reading

What is a pay period?

Paychecks and Paycheck Deductions

Most companies pay their employees by check. Using checks helps companies keep records of what was paid and when it was paid.

gross pay
The total amount of money earned during a pay period.

A typical paycheck has a stub attached to it. A *paycheck stub* provides detailed information. It states your ***gross pay***. This is the total amount of money you earned during the pay period. It is figured by multiplying the number of hours you worked by your hourly wage. Suppose you worked 17.5 hours at a wage of $12.50 per hour. Your gross pay would be $218.75 (17.5 x $12.50 = $218.75).

Discuss
Why do companies delay paying new employees for usually a week of actual time worked?

Resource
The Shrinking Paycheck, color transparency CT-23, TR. Students review the common deductions taken from paychecks.

Discuss
Your paycheck stub will have deductions listed on it. What types of deductions can be taken from your gross pay? Which are mandatory? voluntary?

Discuss
Explain how net pay is calculated.

A paycheck stub lists all paycheck deductions. These are amounts of money subtracted from your gross pay. Examples of deductions include the following:

- federal and state income taxes
- social security taxes
- medicare tax
- health and dental insurance
- union dues
- life insurance
- long term care insurance
- saving plans
- pensions
- uniforms
- loans
- charity contributions

net pay
The amount of money left after all deductions have been taken from the gross pay.

The amount of money left after all deductions are taken from your gross pay is called your ***net pay***. Your net pay is your take-home pay. In this example, the total deductions are $55.86 ($32.15 + $14.01 + $6.54 + $3.16 = $55.86). Your net pay is $162.89 ($218.75 – $55.86 = $162.89). See 23-2 for how the following deductions are shown on a typical paycheck stub.

- $32.15 for federal income tax
- $14.01 for social security tax (FICA)
- $6.54 for state income tax
- $3.16 for medicare tax

Your Reading

What information is typically provided on a paycheck stub?

The W-4 Form

Each time you begin work with a new employer, you must fill out a ***Form W-4***. This form is also called an *Employee's Withholding Allowance Certificate*. It determines how much of your pay should be withheld for taxes.

The government allows taxpayers to claim certain allowances. Each allowance that you claim results in less tax taken from your pay. You may claim a personal allowance for yourself only if no one else can claim you as a dependent. Some taxpayers may claim additional allowances for age, blindness, and dependents. A ***dependent*** is a person who relies on the taxpayer for financial support, such as a child or nonworking adult.

A Form W-4 is a two-part form. See 23-3. To fill it out, you generally follow these simple directions:

- Print or type your name in block 1 with your address directly below.

Form W-4
Employee's withholding allowance certificate, a form filled out by an employee when beginning a new job. It determines how much of the employee's pay should be withheld for taxes.

dependent
A person, such as a child or nonworking adult, who relies on a taxpayer for financial support.

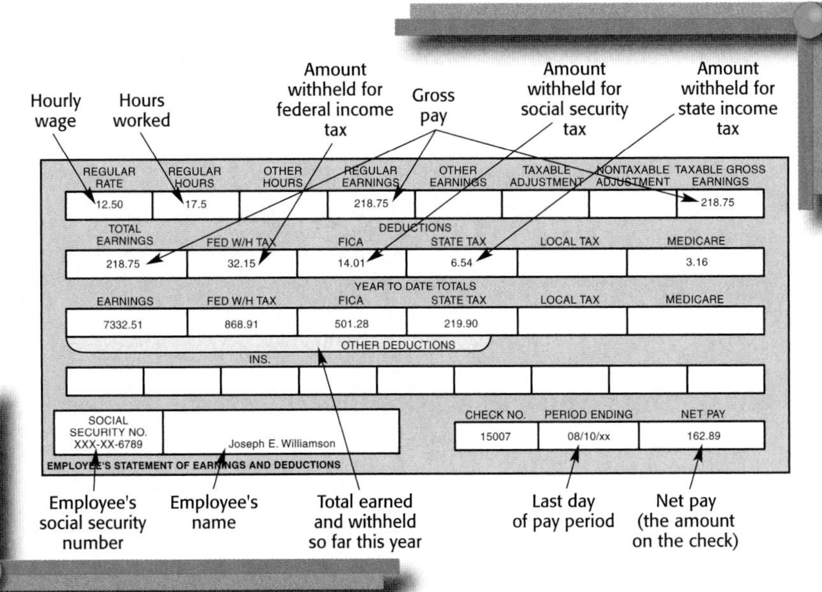

REGULAR RATE	REGULAR HOURS	OTHER HOURS	REGULAR EARNINGS	OTHER EARNINGS	TAXABLE ADJUSTMENT	NONTAXABLE ADJUSTMENT	TAXABLE GROSS EARNINGS
12.50	17.5		218.75				218.75

TOTAL EARNINGS	FED W/H TAX	FICA	STATE TAX	LOCAL TAX	MEDICARE
218.75	32.15	14.01	6.54		3.16

YEAR TO DATE TOTALS

EARNINGS	FED W/H TAX	FICA	STATE TAX	LOCAL TAX	MEDICARE
7332.51	868.91	501.28	219.90		

OTHER DEDUCTIONS
INS.

SOCIAL SECURITY NO.	
XXX-XX-6789	Joseph E. Williamson

CHECK NO.	PERIOD ENDING	NET PAY
15007	08/10/xx	162.89

EMPLOYEE'S STATEMENT OF EARNINGS AND DEDUCTIONS

23-2
This important paperwork shows total earnings, deductions, and reasons for the deductions.

Resource
Reading a Paycheck Stub, Activity B, WB. Students analyze the parts of a paycheck stub.

Resource
Form W-4, reproducible/transparency master 23-1, TR. Students assume they are new employees as they complete a Form W-4.

23-3

A Form W-4 tells an employer the correct amount of federal income tax to withhold from an employee's pay.

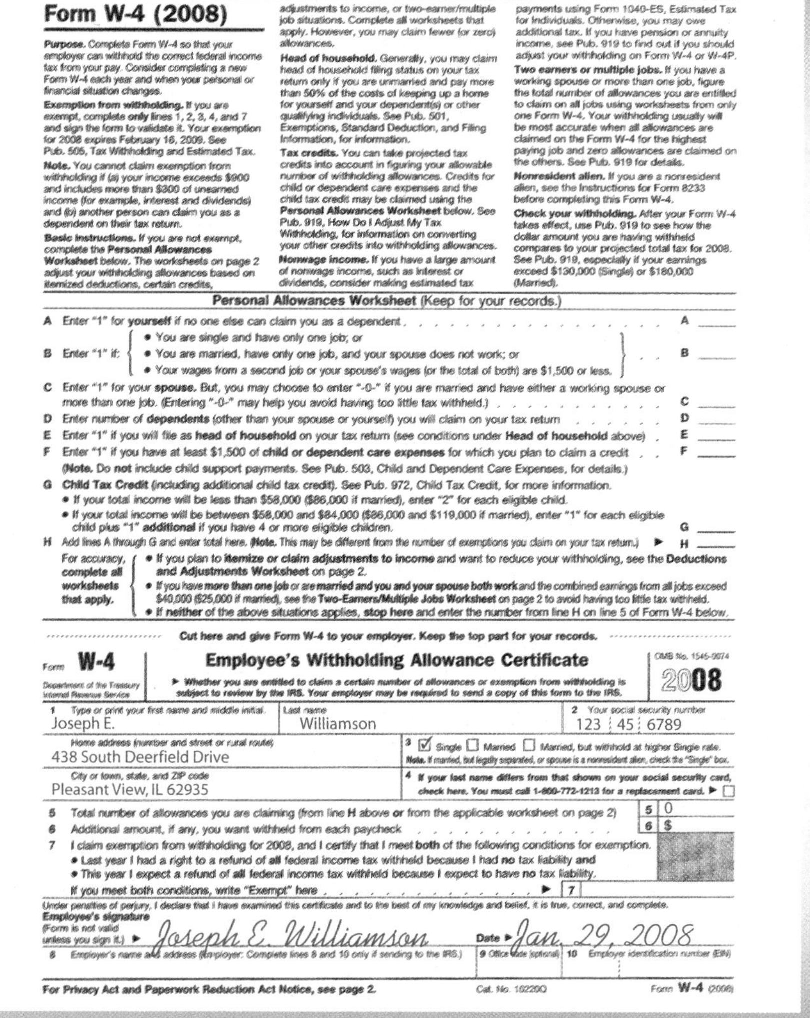

Form W-4 (2008)

Purpose. Complete Form W-4 so that your employer can withhold the correct federal income tax from your pay. Consider completing a new Form W-4 each year and when your personal or financial situation changes.

Exemption from withholding. If you are exempt, complete **only** lines 1, 2, 3, 4, and 7 and sign the form to validate it. Your exemption for 2008 expires February 16, 2009. See Pub. 505, Tax Withholding and Estimated Tax.

Note. You cannot claim exemption from withholding if (a) your income exceeds $900 and includes more than $300 of unearned income (for example, interest and dividends) and (b) another person can claim you as a dependent on their tax return.

Basic instructions. If you are not exempt, complete the **Personal Allowances Worksheet** below. The worksheets on page 2 adjust your withholding allowances based on itemized deductions, certain credits, adjustments to income, or two-earner/multiple job situations. Complete all worksheets that apply. However, you may claim fewer (or zero) allowances.

Head of household. Generally, you may claim head of household filing status on your tax return only if you are unmarried and pay more than 50% of the costs of keeping up a home for yourself and your dependent(s) or other qualifying individuals. See Pub. 501, Exemptions, Standard Deduction, and Filing Information, for information.

Tax credits. You can take projected tax credits into account in figuring your allowable number of withholding allowances. Credits for child or dependent care expenses and the child tax credit may be claimed using the **Personal Allowances Worksheet** below. See Pub. 919, How Do I Adjust My Tax Withholding, for information on converting your other credits into withholding allowances.

Nonwage income. If you have a large amount of nonwage income, such as interest or dividends, consider making estimated tax payments using Form 1040-ES, Estimated Tax for Individuals. Otherwise, you may owe additional tax. If you have pension or annuity income, see Pub. 919 to find out if you should adjust your withholding on Form W-4 or W-4P.

Two earners or multiple jobs. If you have a working spouse or more than one job, figure the total number of allowances you are entitled to claim on all jobs using worksheets from only one Form W-4. Your withholding usually will be most accurate when all allowances are claimed on the Form W-4 for the highest paying job and zero allowances are claimed on the others. See Pub. 919 for details.

Nonresident alien. If you are a nonresident alien, see the Instructions for Form 8233 before completing this Form W-4.

Check your withholding. After your Form W-4 takes effect, use Pub. 919 to see how the dollar amount you are having withheld compares to your projected total tax for 2008. See Pub. 919, especially if your earnings exceed $130,000 (Single) or $180,000 (Married).

Personal Allowances Worksheet (Keep for your records.)

A Enter "1" for **yourself** if no one else can claim you as a dependent . . . A ____

B Enter "1" if:
- You are single and have only one job; or
- You are married, have only one job, and your spouse does not work; or
- Your wages from a second job or your spouse's wages (or the total of both) are $1,500 or less. . . . B ____

C Enter "1" for your **spouse.** But, you may choose to enter "-0-" if you are married and have either a working spouse or more than one job. (Entering "-0-" may help you avoid having too little tax withheld.) . . . C ____

D Enter number of **dependents** (other than your spouse or yourself) you will claim on your tax return . . . D ____

E Enter "1" if you will file as **head of household** on your tax return (see conditions under **Head of household** above) . E ____

F Enter "1" if you have at least $1,500 of **child or dependent care expenses** for which you plan to claim a credit . . F ____
(**Note.** Do **not** include child support payments. See Pub. 503, Child and Dependent Care Expenses, for details.)

G **Child Tax Credit** (including additional child tax credit). See Pub. 972, Child Tax Credit, for more information.
- If your total income will be less than $58,000 ($86,000 if married), enter "2" for each eligible child.
- If your total income will be between $58,000 and $84,000 ($86,000 and $119,000 if married), enter "1" for each eligible child plus "1" **additional** if you have 4 or more eligible children. G ____

H Add lines A through G and enter total here. (**Note.** This may be different from the number of exemptions you claim on your tax return.) ▶ H ____

For accuracy, complete all worksheets that apply.
- If you plan to **itemize or claim adjustments to income** and want to reduce your withholding, see the **Deductions and Adjustments Worksheet** on page 2.
- If you have **more than one job** or are **married and you and your spouse both work** and the combined earnings from all jobs exceed $40,000 ($25,000 if married), see the **Two-Earners/Multiple Jobs Worksheet** on page 2 to avoid having too little tax withheld.
- If **neither** of the above situations applies, **stop here** and enter the number from line H on line 5 of Form W-4 below.

Cut here and give Form W-4 to your employer. Keep the top part for your records.

Form **W-4** Department of the Treasury Internal Revenue Service

Employee's Withholding Allowance Certificate

▶ *Whether you are entitled to claim a certain number of allowances or exemption from withholding is subject to review by the IRS. Your employer may be required to send a copy of this form to the IRS.*

OMB No. 1545-0074 **2008**

1 Type or print your first name and middle initial. Joseph E. | Last name Williamson | 2 Your social security number 123 45 6789

Home address (number and street or rural route) 438 South Deerfield Drive

3 ☑ Single ☐ Married ☐ Married, but withhold at higher Single rate.
Note. If married, but legally separated, or spouse is a nonresident alien, check the "Single" box.

City or town, state, and ZIP code Pleasant View, IL 62935

4 **If your last name differs from that shown on your social security card, check here. You must call 1-800-772-1213 for a replacement card.** ▶ ☐

5 Total number of allowances you are claiming (from line **H** above **or** from the applicable worksheet on page 2) 5 0

6 Additional amount, if any, you want withheld from each paycheck . . . 6 $

7 I claim exemption from withholding for 2008, and I certify that I meet **both** of the following conditions for exemption.
- Last year I had a right to a refund of **all** federal income tax withheld because I had **no** tax liability **and**
- This year I expect a refund of **all** federal income tax withheld because I expect to have **no** tax liability.

If you meet both conditions, write "Exempt" here . . . ▶ 7

Under penalties of perjury, I declare that I have examined this certificate and to the best of my knowledge and belief, it is true, correct, and complete.

Employee's signature (Form is not valid unless you sign it.) ▶ *Joseph E. Williamson* Date ▶ *Jan. 29, 2008*

8 Employer's name and address (Employer: Complete lines 8 and 10 only if sending to the IRS.) | 9 Office code (optional) | 10 Employer identification number (EIN)

For Privacy Act and Paperwork Reduction Act Notice, see page 2. Cat. No. 10220Q Form **W-4** (2008)

Discuss

Has anyone in the class filled out a Form W-4 yet? Describe the experience.

Note

The name of the Form W-4 is the *Employee's Withholding Allowance Certificate*, while the name of the Form W-2 is the Wage and Tax Statement.

Activity

Use Figure 23-3 to explain the information on a Form W-4. Have students take turns reading the information aloud on this form. Provide students with a blank copy of the form and have them complete the form for practice.

- Write your social security number in block 2.
- Check *single* in block 3.
- Enter a zero in block 5 to indicate that you are not claiming any allowances. (You cannot claim an allowance for yourself if a parent or guardian is claiming you as a dependent.)
- Sign your name and write the date on the appropriate line.

If you think you will owe taxes at the end of the year, you can enter an amount in block 6. Paying a little more each pay period is easier than paying a lot when your tax bill is due.

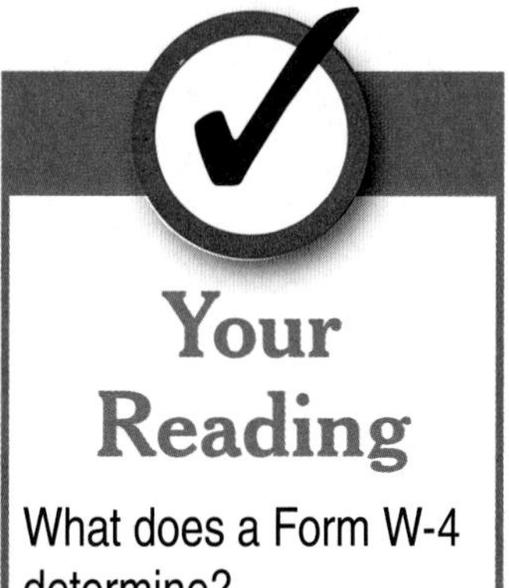

Your Reading

What does a Form W-4 determine?

If you are married, have dependents, or have other sources of income, these directions may not apply to you. In these cases, complete a Form W-4 worksheet before filling out the form. (Brief worksheets also appear on other tax forms. Always be sure to fill them out to obtain the correct data.)

Your employer will compare your Form W-4 to withholding tables prepared by the government. Based on your income, your employer will determine how much money to withhold from each paycheck for income tax. The total amount withheld during the year should come close to your total tax bill for the year.

Discuss
Explain the difference between a Form W-4 and Form W-2.

Form W-2
Wage and tax statement, a form showing how much a worker was paid and how much income was withheld for taxes in a given year.

The W-2 Form

Every January, you should receive a ***Form W-2*** from each employer that paid you wages in the previous year. The Form W-2 is also known as a *Wage and Tax Statement.* It states how much you were paid and how much of your income was withheld for taxes. An example is shown in 23-4.

When you receive your Form W-2s, look at them carefully. You may want to compare them to your paycheck stubs. The information should be the same.

Keep your Form W-2s in a safe place. You will need them to fill out your income tax return.

Your Reading
How does the information provided on a Form W-2 help you to fill out your income tax return?

22222 | a Employee's social security number XXX-XX-6789 | OMB No. 1545-0008

b Employer identification number (EIN) 98-7654321

c Employer's name, address, and ZIP code
Fill-It-Up Service Station
273 South Main Street
Pleasant View, IL 62935

d Control number

e Employee's first name and initial Last name Suff.
Joseph E. Williamson
438 South Deerfield Drive
Pleasant View, IL 62935

f Employee's address and ZIP code

1 Wages, tips, other compensation	2 Federal income tax withheld
16321.14	1958.52
3 Social security wages	4 Social security tax withheld
16321.14	1011.90
5 Medicare wages and tips	6 Medicare tax withheld
16321.14	236.65
7 Social security tips	8 Allocated tips
9 Advance EIC payment	10 Dependent care benefits
11 Nonqualified plans	12a
13 Statutory employee / Retirement plan / Third-party sick pay	12b
14 Other	12c
	12d

15 State Employer's state ID number	16 State wages, tips, etc.	17 State income tax	18 Local wages, tips, etc.	19 Local income tax	20 Locality name
IL 987654321	16321.14	489.63			

Form **W-2** Wage and Tax Statement 2007 Department of the Treasury—Internal Revenue Service
Copy 1—For State, City, or Local Tax Department

23-4
A Form W-2 states an employee's earnings and tax withholdings for a year.

Community Connections

Invite a representative of the Small Business Administration to talk to the class about the tax responsibilities of businesses. Prepare questions in advance, including the following: When are business income taxes due? What is the penalty for nonpayment of taxes? Where can businesses turn for help in filing tax returns?

Taxes

One of the responsibilities you have as a wage earner is to pay taxes. The government gets money needed to run the country through taxes. Your tax money pays for government services. Tax money supports public education. It pays for government-assistance programs and certain health services. It pays for social security and veterans' benefits. Tax money also supports the nation's armed forces and police and fire departments.

The U.S. Congress passes federal tax laws. The ***Internal Revenue Service (IRS)*** is the agency that enforces the tax laws and collects taxes.

State and local governments work in similar ways. Legislatures pass tax laws. Revenue agencies enforce the laws and collect the taxes.

There are many different types of taxes. Two types of taxes that are deducted from your paycheck are income tax and social security tax.

Internal Revenue Service (IRS)
The agency that enforces federal tax laws and collects taxes.

income tax
A tax on all forms of earnings.

Income Tax

As a wage earner, you have to pay income tax. ***Income tax*** is a tax on all forms of earnings. The federal government, most states, and many cities place a tax on income. It is figured as a percentage of the money you earn each year from wages, interest, and investments.

Your employer withholds tax from your paychecks. It is sent to the government. By April 15 of each year, you must file a tax return for the previous year. As you complete your income tax return, you may find that you have more tax to pay. On the other hand, you may find that too much was withheld during the year. In that case, you would receive a refund from the government.

Vocabulary
To what does *IRS* refer? What does this agency do?

Activity
What services do you receive because taxes are collected?

Social Security Tax

Social security taxes are federal taxes based on income. Almost all workers in the United States pay them. People pay social security taxes while they work so they can collect monthly payments after they stop working.

Your employer deducts social security taxes from your

paychecks. The deductions appear on your paycheck stubs under the heading ***FICA***, which means ***Federal Insurance Contributions Act.***

Social security taxes are figured as a percentage of your earnings. Whatever you pay, your employer makes a matching payment. For instance, suppose $14.01 is deducted from your paycheck for FICA. Your employer would also pay $14.01. Your employer would send a total of $28.02 to the IRS as your FICA contribution.

As you work and make contributions, you earn work credits. Later, if you become disabled or retire, you will receive benefits in the form of monthly payments. If you die, your survivors will receive monthly payments. *Medicare* is another kind of social security benefit. It is a form of hospital and medical insurance.

Federal Insurance Contributions Act (FICA)
An act that allows the federal government to reserve a percentage of a paycheck for social security tax.

What are two types of taxes deducted from your paycheck?

Filing an Income Tax Return

Your federal tax return for the previous year ending December 31 must be filed by April 15 each year. This gives you enough time to prepare your return and file it by the deadline. See 23-5.

When filing your first tax return, you will need to obtain a form online or from a local library, bank, post office, or IRS office. There are three common federal tax return forms.

Reflect

How do you feel about paying taxes? Do you think the government has any other options for funding programs?

Vocabulary

What does *FICA* mean? Locate this deduction on a pay stub.

23-5
Filing taxes can be a hassle if a person waits until the last minute or misplaces important papers.

Discuss

If $22 is deducted from your paycheck for FICA, how much does your employer pay toward your FICA account? ($22)

Community Connections

Use the Yellow Pages to locate tax preparers in your community. Compile a reference list with names, addresses, and phone numbers. Find out what it costs to have tax forms prepared by one of these professionals.

These include Form 1040EZ, Form 1040A, and Form 1040. Which tax form you choose will depend on your income level and whether you itemize deductions. Other restrictions, which often change from year to year as new tax laws are passed, affect the use of these forms.

You should use the simplest tax form for your needs. This will save you time in preparing your return and will also enable the IRS to process your tax return more quickly. *Form 1040EZ* is the easiest federal tax form. *Form 1040A* is often called the "short form." This form allows you to claim the most common adjustments to income. *Form 1040*, often referred to as the "long form," requires more information and time to prepare.

Failing to obtain or receive a form is no excuse for not filing a return. As a wage earner, it is your responsibility to prepare and file a tax return on time. See 23-6 for income tax filing tips.

Enrich

Research the tax penalties. Find out what happens during a government audit of your taxes. Write a report and share what you learned.

State Income Tax

If your state collects income tax, that return is due at the same time as the federal income tax return. Since each state's form is different, you must obtain one from your own state. Follow the directions provided.

Tax Penalties

The IRS has established certain penalties for filing late without permission, failure to file, lying, and cheating. Take the time to do your taxes correctly and on time. If you need assistance, ask a family member or tax preparer to help you.

Don't panic if you are audited. An *audit* is simply the government's way of checking your return. The auditor may find that your return is correct. On the other hand, the auditor may find a mistake. You may have made a math error, or perhaps you forgot to include interest earned on a savings account. Honest mistakes like these could be settled easily. You would have to pay any tax you owe and perhaps a penalty for late payment. For intentional errors and fraud, major penalties can be applied.

What are the three most common federal income tax forms?

Helpful Suggestions for Filing Tax Returns

- Keep all your financial records together. For tax purposes, you may need the following:
  - records of income including wages, tips, and taxable benefits
  - records of interest earned and dividends received
  - canceled checks for expenses entered on tax returns as deductions
  - interest payment records for a home mortgage
  - past tax returns
- Read all the instructions carefully before beginning.
- Prepare a copy of the form in pencil first so any errors can be erased easily.
- Get additional help when needed by using one or more of the following:
  - IRS Web site **(irs.gov)**. Learn how to get answers to tax-filing questions either online or by talking to a representative.
  - tax-preparation software program
  - one of the many self-help guides printed annually and available in bookstores
  - a reputable accountant or tax-preparation service
- Check the math carefully or have someone check it for you before writing a final copy of the form in ink.
- Make a copy of the completed form, and keep it with other important papers.

23-6
These suggestions can help you complete tax forms.

Resource
Your Tax Dollars at Work, Activity C, WB. Students interview officials about how tax dollars are spent and write an article about it.

Resource
Test Your Tax Knowledge, reproducible master 23-2, TR. Students answer questions about information provided in the chapter.

Discuss
Do you feel U.S. citizens should willingly fulfill their obligation to pay taxes, or should try to avoid paying taxes in whatever legal way is possible?

Discuss
Are you aware of tax preparers who, for an additional fee, lend taxpayers money equivalent to the expected tax return as part of the tax preparation process? What are cautions regarding these transactions?

Resource
How Do I Read My Paycheck? reproducible master 23-3, TR. Use the adapted worksheet to reinforce chapter concepts in students who are low functioning.

Summary

When you accept a job and start working, you need to understand your paycheck. Some of the money you earn cannot be taken home. The stub attached to your paycheck will list deductions from your earnings for taxes and other expenses.

When you start a new job, you should fill out a Form W-4. It will determine how much of your pay should be withheld for taxes. Each January, you should receive Form W-2s from each of the places you worked during the previous year. The forms tell how much you were paid and how much of your income was withheld for taxes.

One of the responsibilities of wage earners is to file income tax returns. Whatever form you use, you must file your return on time. If your state has an income tax, that return is due at the same time. There are penalties for failing to file, filing late without permission, and filing a false return.

Answers to *Reviewing Key Concepts*

1. to allow time for accurate bookkeeping
2. Gross pay is the total amount of money earned during a pay period. Net pay is the take-home pay left after all paycheck deductions have been made.
3. (List five:) federal income tax, state income tax, social security tax, medicare, health insurance contributions, union dues, savings plans, pensions, uniforms, loans, charity contributions
4. Employee's Withholding Allowance Certificate; to determine how much pay should be withheld for taxes
5. Wage and Tax Statement; total annual income and the portion withheld for taxes in a given year
6. (Name five:) public education, government-assistance programs, certain health services, social security, veterans' benefits, the armed forces, police and fire departments, postal service
7. U.S. Congress; IRS
8. D
9. April 15
10. Obtain a form online or pick up a form at a local library, bank, post office, or IRS office.

Reviewing Key Concepts

1. In many companies, why is payday not the last day of the pay period?
2. Explain the difference between gross pay and net pay.
3. List five types of paycheck deductions.
4. What is another name for the Form W-4? What is its purpose?
5. What is another name for the Form W-2? In general, what information does it give?
6. Name five ways tax money is used.
7. Who passes federal tax laws? Who enforces them?
8. Which of the following statements is true?
   A. Social security taxes are federal taxes based on income.
   B. On paycheck stubs, deductions for social security taxes appear under the heading FICA.
   C. Whatever employees pay in social security taxes, their employers pay matching amounts.
   D. All of the above.
9. What is the deadline for filing a federal income tax return?
10. Where can you obtain a tax return form?

Building Academic Skills

1. **Social Studies.** Examine the social security system in greater detail and find answers to these questions: What role does the government play in FICA deductions? What controversies have been in the news lately about the health of the social security system? What are your parents' views of social security? your grandparents' views?
2. **History.** Research the history of the U.S. tax system. Find answers to the following questions: How did the federal tax system originate? In what year was the first federal tax returns filed? In what year was (were) the first state tax return(s) filed? for which state(s)?

Building Technology Skills

1. Conduct Internet research on Form W-2. Write a report on the additional information you learned about this form and the obligation on employers to complete them. Share information with the class.
2. Obtain a copy of the latest Form W-4 from the IRS Web site: **irs.gov**. Examine whether the form differs from the one shown in Figure 23-3. Share your findings with the class.
3. Conduct an online search to determine the differences in the rates of income tax levied on individuals in five states in various parts of the country. Use the search term *state income tax* on the following Web site: **houseandhome.msn.com**. Identify the tax rate (or rate range) on individuals' income in each state selected.

Building Career Knowledge and Skills

1. Poll several businesses to find out when their paydays occur. (Inform them that you are requesting the information for a class project.) Share your findings in class.
2. Ask parents and friends about the different types of deductions made from their paychecks. Discuss their answers in class.
3. Research how tax money is collected and spent by your state or local government. Design posters to illustrate your findings. Display the posters throughout your school in April.
4. Ask an IRS auditor to talk to your class. Be prepared to ask questions about tax forms and audits.
5. Find media examples that cover how tax money is spent. Share your findings with the class.

Building Workplace Skills

Research the social security system using the Internet to find out as much information as possible. Work with two or three of your classmates. Together decide who will do which tasks. Find out when social security began and why. Who is eligible for social security payments today? Why do a growing number of people believe that the system should have an overhaul? Present your findings to the class in charts and/or posters.

How do I make my income cover my expenses?

Chapter 24 Budgets

Key Terms

budget
fixed expense
flexible expense

Chapter Objectives

After studying this chapter, you will be able to

- **identify** sources of income.
- **list** fixed and flexible expenses that may be included in a budget.
- **develop** and evaluate a spending calendar.
- **prepare** a want list with both short-range and long-range goals.
- **plan** a budget.

Key Concepts

- Managing your money wisely will help you live within your income.
- Identifying your income and expenses can help you in making a budget.
- A spending calendar can help you to know where your money goes.
- Preparing a "want" list can help you to reach your goals.
- An effective budget can guide your spending and saving.

The Need for Money Management

You need money to buy the things you need and want. The amount of money you earn affects what you are able to buy. However, how you spend your money can have just as much effect as how much you earn.

In Chapter 1, you learned that people work to fulfill their needs and wants. *Needs* are what you must have to survive. Examples of needs include food, clothing, and shelter. *Wants* are what you would like to have but do not need to survive. Examples of wants might be designer clothes, a luxury apartment, or vacations.

No matter how much money they earn, some people find it difficult to live on what they make. The more they earn, the more they spend. On the other hand, others seem to have few money problems. They usually have enough money for what they need. They are even able to save money.

You must learn to manage your money wisely in order to live on what you earn. If you do not, you will probably have money problems. Wise planning will help you live within your income. Planning will help you buy what you really need and still have money left to get the things you want. See 24-1.

Reflect

Are you good at handling money? Would you be able to take out a loan and faithfully make the payments? Are you good at keeping track of your spending habits now?

Note

Emphasize that students must learn to manage money wisely and live on their income or they will have money problems.

Resource

Reinforcing Vocabulary, Activity A, WB. Students complete a crossword puzzle with the chapter's key terms.

Activity

List source of income for middle school students on the board. Find out how many students have held these part-time jobs?

24-1 People need money to buy food and other basic daily needs.

Your Reading

How can a budget help you to manage your money?

budget
A plan for the use or management of money.

A plan for the use or management of money is called a ***budget***. An effective budget helps you maximize your earnings and manage your spending. Now is a good time to start following a budget. Learn to manage the money you earn now. As your income grows, you will be able to adjust your money management decisions.

Community Connections

Search the classified section of the local newspaper to locate a part-time job that interests you. Find a job that states a wage. Calculate your income if you held that job for an entire year, working 15 hours per week.

Sources of Income

The first step in making a budget is to identify your sources of income. You need to know how much money you can expect to receive within an average week, month, and year. Knowing your expected income will help you plan how to manage your money.

Start identifying your sources of income by listing the money you are sure to receive. If you work, you should list your average monthly take-home pay. Include tips you receive on a regular basis in your budget plan. Since no two days or weeks are exactly alike, you cannot always accurately estimate an exact figure on tips. Use a conservative average and plan on a minimum amount.

Some additional sources of income are bonuses, commissions, and overtime pay, which are offered by some jobs. Interest on savings and dividends from investments are also sources of income. Cash gifts for birthdays and special occasions count as income, too. Such sources of income generally vary from month to month. Including them in a budget may be risky. It is safer to base a budget on sure and steady sources of income.

How does knowing your expected income help you in making a budget?

Types of Expenses

The next step in making a budget is to list your expenses. Expenses are usually described in terms relating to how often they are paid. If you pay bus fare every day, it is a daily expense. Many expenses are paid weekly or monthly. See 24-2. Quarterly expenses are paid four times a year. *Semiannual* expenses are paid twice a year. *Annual* expenses are paid once a year.

fixed expense
Something for which a set amount of money must be paid regularly, such as rent, insurance, or tuition.

Fixed and flexible are other terms used to describe expenses. A ***fixed expense*** is a set amount of money due on a set date. Examples of fixed expenses include the following:

- rent or mortgage payments
- insurance premiums

24-2
Paying back the loan for a new or used car usually involves several years of monthly payments.

Adapting the Lesson

Give students who are low functioning a list of sources of income for teenagers. Include on the list babysitting, yard work, allowance, birthday money, pool jobs, chores, and so forth. Have students circle the ways they currently "earn" money. Have them draw squares around the words that indicate the new ways in which they plan to earn money in the future.

Resource

Fixed and Flexible Expenses, Activity B, WB. Students identify the category into which common items fall.

Resource

The Budget Balancing Act, color transparency CT-24, TR. Students discuss the relationship of income and expenses to a budget.

Discuss

Make a list of all your expenses that fit the *flexible expenses* category.

- tuition
- membership dues
- property taxes
- installment payments (for a car loan, major purchase, or credit card balance)

As a rule, fixed expenses must be paid when due. They cannot be changed, delayed, or reduced. Therefore, they are considered first when making a budget. (To encourage saving, some people include savings as a fixed expense. However, since amounts you may be able to save can vary from month to month, savings is listed under flexible expenses.) ***Flexible expenses*** are expenses that vary in amount. The most common flexible expenses include the following:

- food
- clothing
- home furnishings

flexible expense
An expense that varies in amount and does not occur on a regular basis, such as food, transportation, or entertainment.

Your Reading

What is the difference between a fixed expense and a flexible expense?

- utilities
- transportation
- medical needs
- savings
- recreation and entertainment

You have more control over flexible expenses than fixed expenses. Some flexible expenses vary with your wants. You can often adjust how much money you spend for these expenses. For instance, suppose you want to eat in nice restaurants. This will make your food expense higher than eating at home. However, if you adjust this expense by eating more meals at home, you can save money. This money might be used for another flexible expense, such as clothing or recreation.

As you manage your money, try to keep your fixed expenses to a minimum. Plan ahead and save for major purchases instead of making installment payments. This will keep your money available for flexible expenses. As a result, you will have more control over the use of your money.

Reflect

Do you feel people spend too much money on recreational activities? Do you consider going out to eat a recreational activity? How much do you think an average family could spend on flexible expenses?

Activity

Use the telephone directory to investigate how many businesses in your community rely on recreational activities to make money? Are some recreational activities not found in your area that you feel people would use?

Adapting the Lesson

Have students who are high functioning research Web sites that sell food and clothing online. Have them select five food items and five clothing items, determine their online prices, then find out their costs in local stores. Are delivery fees also charged for online purchases (which would increase the price of the items)? Have students show the cost difference in a chart.

How Do You Spend Your Money?

Do you know where your money goes? How much of your income goes toward fixed expenses? How much goes toward flexible expenses? In order to use your money wisely, you must know how you spend it.

A Spending Calendar

Use a spending calendar like the one shown in 24-3 to find out how you spend your money. Start the calendar when you receive your next paycheck. Record all your expenses for each day on your calendar. Total your expenses for each week. Use the column at the far right to record your weekly totals.

How you spend your money will vary from week to week. No two weeks of spending are exactly alike. Using a spending calendar for a full month will help you get a pattern of your spending habits. At the end of the month, you will have a

Spending Calendar							
Sunday	Monday	Tuesday	Wednesday	Thursday	Friday	Saturday	Weekly Totals
1 Charity $5.00	2 Lunch $4.50	3 Lunch $5.45 Stamps $8.20	4 Lunch $4.95	5 Lunch $4.50	6 Lunch $5.50 Movie $9.00 Pizza $11.00	7 Hamburger, fries, drink $6.75	$64.85
8 Charity $5.00	9 Lunch $4.25	10 Lunch $5.35 Birthday Card $4.25	11 Lunch $4.25	12 Lunch $3.95 Computer Repair $65.90	13 Lunch $4.75 Ball Game $10.00	14 New shirt $18.00	$125.70
15 Charity $7.00 Movie $9.00	16 Lunch $4.65	17 Lunch $4.75	18 Lunch $4.25 Greeting Card $4.50	19 Lunch $5.15	20 Lunch $5.45	21 CD $12.00	$56.75
22 Charity $5.00	23 Lunch $4.25	24 Lunch $4.95	25 Lunch $5.15 DVD $19.00	26 Lunch $4.95	27 Lunch $4.25 Hair-cut $18.00	28 Pizza $9.50 Movie $9.00	$84.05
29 Charity $8.00 Ice Cream $3.50	30 Lunch $4.25						$15.75

24-3
A spending calendar can help you keep track of what you do with your money.

What is the purpose of a spending calendar?

good idea of where your money was spent. You will have taken a big step toward controlling your money. This is how to make your money work for you.

How Do You Want to Spend Your Money?

A good money management system helps you use your money to get what you want. Do you know what you want? Are you putting your money to work for you? Are you using it to reach your goals?

Reflect
Do you know how much money you spend in one month? Do you think you are good at managing the money you have?

Discuss
Using Figure 24-3 talk about how much money this student spends each week. Do you think the amounts spent are reasonable? Do you think any money was wasted?

Resource
Spending Calendar, reproducible master 24-1, TR. Students fill in a spending calendar to map their purchases for one month.

Discuss
How would you describe the spending habits of your friends? When you go shopping together, does anyone check for sales?

Community Connections

Collect sales brochures from local stores and use them to cut items for a pictorial "want list." Record the prices shown in the ads as you "shop" and make lists of items you want now and want later. Total the costs of items on the lists and write goals, indicating how you plan to acquire the money.

A "Want" List

As you prepare to plan a budget, develop a list of things you want. Make two columns on your "want" list. Label one *now* and the other *later.* Estimate the cost of each item you list to help you plan your savings goals.

Your *now* column is for those things you want quickly. You should be able to obtain these items in a year or less. Such items might include new clothing, membership at a sports club, and a DVD player.

Your *later* column is for your long-range goals. This column is for items you want that may take more than a year to get. This list might include continuing your education, buying a car or a home, and taking a trip to Europe. See 24-4.

Look at your completed "want" list. Remember that you can't afford to buy everything at once. You will need to set priorities for your spending. What is most important to you now and in the future? What can you afford to buy with the money you have now or will earn? What can you do without? What don't you need? How can you trim expenses to get what you want? Could you delay some purchases? Are you beginning to think about opening a savings account?

By asking yourself these questions, you are developing money management skills. You are learning how to make your money work for you.

Your Reading

How does a "want" list help you set priorities?

Planning a Budget

A budget helps you make wise money decisions. It is your personal guide to spending and saving. You develop it and make it work.

24-4

Deciding what things are important to you now and in the future will help you set goals for budget planning.

"Want" List			
Now	**Cost**	**Later**	**Cost**
jacket	$ 85	laptop computer	$ 2,000
digital camera	$125	trip to Europe	$ 5,000
cell phone	$150	car	$11,000

A review of your spending calendar can help you plan a budget. It shows how you are spending your money. It helps you see your options for flexible expenses. Your spending calendar helps you identify areas where you can make changes in your use of money.

A review of your "want" list can also help you plan a budget. It gives you direction. It helps you focus on your goals.

You don't need to account for every penny in your budget. Instead, work with estimates and follow this guide:

1. Estimate your income.
2. List your fixed expenses.
3. Review your short-range and long-range goals.
4. Estimate your flexible expenses.
5. Set aside a portion of each paycheck for savings and miscellaneous expenses.

Different people plan for different time periods in their budgets. Some plan weekly budgets. Some who are paid every two weeks set up two-week budgets. Others prefer monthly budgets because most of their fixed expenses are paid monthly.

How you set up your budget is up to you. Just be sure to be consistent. If you set up a monthly budget, convert all income and expenses to monthly figures. The following formulas may help you:

- Weekly income ÷ 52 weeks = yearly income.
- Yearly income ÷ 12 = monthly income.
- Quarterly expense ÷ 3 = monthly expense.
- Semiannual expense ÷ 6 = monthly expense.
- Annual expense ÷ 12 = monthly expense.

Once you set up a budget, make a sincere effort to follow it. Review your budget often. Make adjustments for changes in income or expenses.

A monthly budgeting guide for a young person just entering the workforce is shown in 24-5. You can use a budget-planning guide, such as this one, as you design your own budget. Remember, this is your money-management plan. Your budget should help you reach your goals. It should

Vocabulary

What is the meaning of the term *impulse buying*? What implications does it have on budgeting?

Resource

Making Your Money Work for You, Activity C, WB. Students evaluate their purchasing goals in order to plan a budget.

Discuss

How do you set priorities for getting the items on your "wish lists"? What suggestions do you think adults would give you for making a major purchase?

24-5
This could be a typical budget for a young person beginning a career. To have a workable budget, the total estimated income must be equal to, or greater than, the total estimated expenses.

Resource

Planning a Budget, Activity D, WB. Students plan a monthly budget for themselves.

Activity

Interview your parents for advice on planning a budget. Ask for three to four helpful hints on setting up a budget. Interview your grandparents and compare their suggestions to those provided by your parents. Report your findings to class.

Resource

Buying a Car, reproducible master 24-2, TR. Students examine many of the important considerations involved in buying a car.

Discuss

Use Figure 24-5 to discuss how a monthly budget guide is used. How many of the categories shown would apply to you? Do you think the amounts listed in the budget categories are accurate?

Monthly Budgeting Guide

Estimated Income		**Estimated Flexible Expenses**	
Net income (wages)	$2765	**Food**	
Tips		At home	$140
Other		Away from home	$80
Total	$2765	**Clothing and Accessories**	
Estimated Fixed Expenses		New clothes	$70
Housing		Cleaning and laundry	20
Rent or mortgage payments	$650	Accessories	20
Maintenance fees		Grooming aids	30
Other *Garage Rental*	45	**Household**	
Insurance Premiums		Home furnishings	35
Life	35	Maintenance and repair	
Health/medical	75	Gas	45
Automobile	95	Electricity	60
Home		Water	
Other		Telephone	65
Debts and Obligations		**Transportation**	
Automobile loan payments	220	Gasoline	120
Other installment loan payments	45	Automobile maintenance	30
Contributions	45	Public transportation	
Tuition		**Medical Needs**	
Membership dues	20	Doctor	50
Other		Dentist	50
Taxes and Licenses		Other	
Property taxes	120		
Automobile registration/ plates	5	**Savings**	
Other		Savings account	100
Total	$1355	Other *IRA*	100
		Recreation and Entertainment	
		Movies	36
		Vacation	90
		Sport events	25
		Books and magazines	
		Other	
		Total	$1166

Summary

Total estimated income	$2765.00
Total estimated expenses ($1355 fixed + $1166 flexible)	–$2521.00
Balance (income minus expenses)	$244.00

not force you to live by strict rules that do not work for you. Be patient. Learning to use a budget takes time, but it is worth the effort. A workable budget will help you manage your money. The main goal of a budget is to help you get the greatest satisfaction from your money.

Using Personal Finance Software

Using personal finance software is another way to prepare a budget. The programs feature budget forms that can provide reports and graphs, giving you a clear illustration of where your money is and where it is going. It allows you to plan financial goals and provides financial calculators to help you estimate costs and plan for expenses and savings.

Many personal finance software programs allow you to manage your finances by allowing transactions to be downloaded from your online bank account. You may also be able to use the software to view current account balances, pay bills, and transfer funds.

Resource

Where Does My Money Go? reproducible master 24-3, TR. Use the adapted worksheet to reinforce chapter concepts in students who are low functioning.

Activity

Demonstrate how personal finance software can be used to prepare a budget. If possible, compare two or three different programs.

Summary

Learning to manage money is an important skill. No matter how much money you earn, it may not be enough if you don't use it wisely.

A plan for the use of money is called a budget. Its purpose is to help you manage your money so you can reach your goals. To design a budget, you must know your total income and total expenses. To have a workable budget, your income must be equal to or greater than your expenses.

A spending calendar and a want list will help you design a budget that will work for you. They will help you see your options and focus on your goals.

Reviewing Key Concepts

1. Name five sources of income.
2. List five fixed expenses.
3. List five flexible expenses.
4. True or false. You have more control over fixed expenses than flexible expenses.
5. Why should you try to keep fixed expenses to a minimum?
6. What is the benefit of developing and using a spending calendar?
7. How can a "want" list help you plan a budget?
8. List five steps to use as a guide for setting up a budget.
9. Convert each of the following amounts to monthly figures:
   A. weekly income of $150
   B. quarterly expense of $120
   C. semiannual expense of $60
   D. annual expense of $72
10. What is the purpose of planning and using a budget?

Answers to *Reviewing Key Concepts*

1. (Name five:) take-home pay, tips, bonuses, commissions, overtime pay, interest on savings, dividends from investments, cash gifts
2. (List five:) rent or mortgage payments, insurance premiums, installment payments, tuition, membership dues, property taxes
3. (List five:) food, clothing, home furnishings, utilities, transportation, medical needs, savings, recreation and entertainment
4. false
5. to have more money available for flexible expenses, which permits greater control over its use
6. It shows you where your money is going and helps you see your options for flexible expenses.
7. It gives direction as you plan a budget and helps you focus on your goals.
8. Estimate your income. List your fixed expenses. Review your short-range and long-range goals. Estimate your flexible expenses. Set aside a portion of each paycheck for savings and miscellaneous expenses.
9. A-$600, B-$40, C-$10, D-$6
10. A budget should help a person manage money and reach his or her goals.

Building Academic Skills

1. **Speaking, listening.** Prepare interview questions for your parents or other adults. Ask them to give you tips on managing money and budgeting. What works for them? What doesn't work? Share the responses with the class.
2. **Math.** Describe your desired income and goals. Prepare a budget, estimating your fixed and flexible expenses. Does your budget balance? What adjustments were necessary?

Building Technology Skills

1. Go to the Web site **about.com** to search *budgets*. Read several of the articles available, summarize how to set up a budget, and list the top five tips you found most helpful for following budgets.
2. Use a software program to develop a survey to find out how much money the average student spends in one month. (Make the surveys voluntary and the findings private, but report the average monthly dollar total.) Document the types of jobs held to earn money.
3. Conduct an online search using the term *car buying*. Develop a list of helpful hints for buying a first car and create a list of Web sites helpful for comparing car features, prices, and performance ratings.
4. Use the Internet to research different brands of personal finance software. Create a spreadsheet to compare the different features of each program, including the ability to create budgets, pay bills electronically, balance checkbooks, create financial reports, and access online bank accounts. Also evaluate the cost and operating system requirements. Based on your research, decide which program would be best for you and share your decision with the class.

Building Career Knowledge and Skills

1. Write a fictional story about money management skills. If the character has money problems, explain why and suggest solutions. If the character has no money problems, describe the management techniques he or she uses to achieve money-management success.
2. Ask a financial counselor to talk to your class about money management and budgets. Be prepared to ask questions.
3. Collect several printed budget forms. Discuss their usefulness in class.
4. Discuss options that are generally available for handling the flexible expenses of a budget.
5. Identify ways that you or others waste or mismanage money. List your observations and determine solutions for change.
6. Research strategies to manage your money wisely. Record your findings and identify the strategies you believe will work for you. Try out one or more of the strategies and summarize your experience.

Building Workplace Skills

Following the examples in this chapter, develop a spending calendar, "want" list, and monthly budgeting guide. Begin by creating a spending calendar that describes and itemizes everything you buy for one month. Include short-term and long-term goals in your "want" list. With that information, prepare a monthly budgeting guide that addresses your income, expenses, and selected "wants" for which you plan to begin saving. Use a calculator to total and check your figures. Also estimate when you believe you will achieve each of the short-term and long-term goals in your "want" list. Describe in a one-page report what you learned from this exercise.

How can a checking account help me to manage my money?

Chapter 25
Checking Accounts

Key Terms

check
debit card
overdraw
deposit slip
endorse
bank statement
certified check
cashier's check
money order
traveler's check

Chapter Objectives

After studying this chapter, you will be able to

- **demonstrate** how to write checks and use debit cards.
- **list** factors to consider when selecting a financial institution.
- **explain** how to open a checking account and make a deposit.
- **show** how to record transactions and balance a checkbook.
- **describe** four special types of checks.

Key Concepts

- With a checking account, you can pay bills and make purchases by writing checks or using a debit card.
- Recording all transactions in a check register prevents the costly mistake of overdrawing.
- Special types of checks are often used for making expensive purchases, sending money in the mail, and carrying money when traveling.

The Convenience of Checking

Resource

Reinforcing Vocabulary, Activity A, WB. Students match vocabulary terms with their definitions.

Resource

Identifying Parts of a Check, Activity B, WB. Students identify parts of a check.

A checking account is a safe place to keep your money. A checking account is also a money management tool that helps you keep a record of your expenses. Money that you earn, such as an allowance or a paycheck, is deposited into the checking account. Deposited funds can be used to pay bills or make purchases with a check or debit card.

Checks

A ***check*** is a written order to pay someone. It instructs a bank to take money from the checking account of the person writing the check. The amount specified on the check is paid to the party named on the check. See 25-1. Checks should be written in ink. This will prevent others from trying to use it by changing the amount or name on the check. The bank will return checks unpaid when information has been erased, crossed out, or changed in any way.

check
A written order instructing a bank to take a specified amount of money out of the account on which the check is drawn and give it to the person whose name appears on the check.

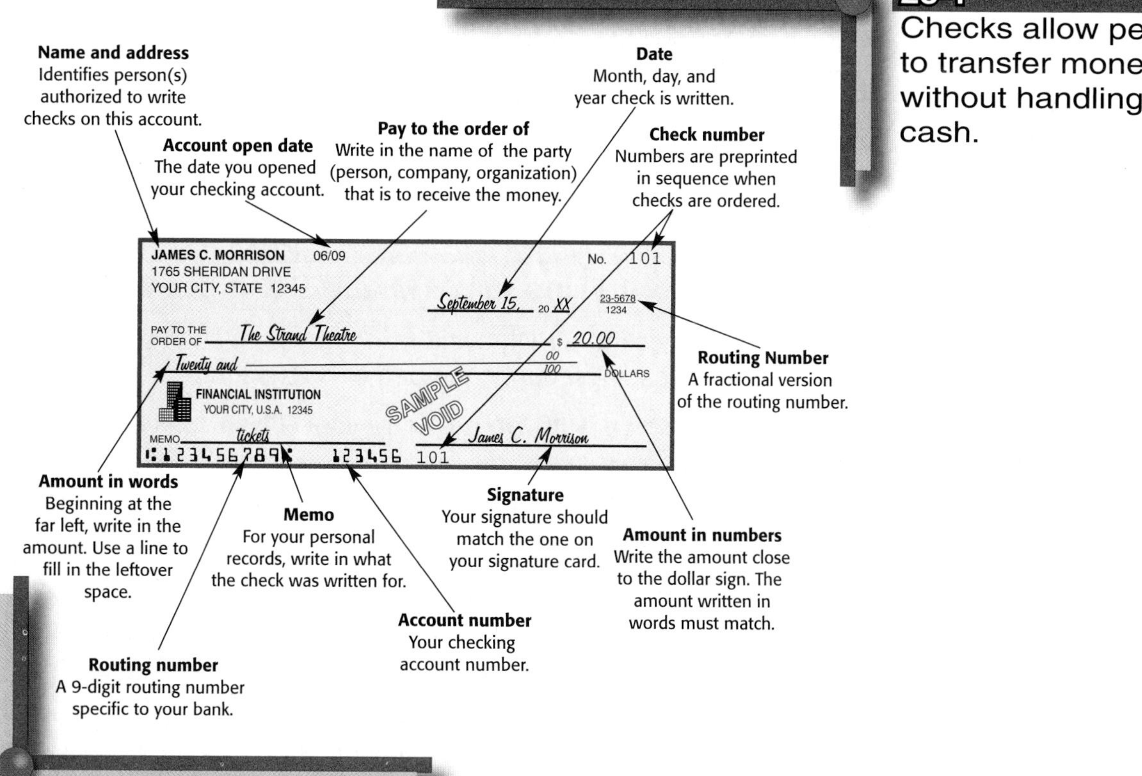

25-1
Checks allow people to transfer money without handling cash.

Reflect

When you are shopping, do you see many people paying for purchases by debit card?

Note

Receipts from debit card purchases and ATM withdrawals may contain your personal information. Be sure to take your receipt with you.

Activity

Create five multiple choice or true/false questions about ATM and debit cards. Exchange papers and take your neighbor's test.

If a check is lost or stolen, you can stop payment on it. To stop payment on a check, you should contact your bank and fill out a form. You will need to pay a fee, which may be $25 or more.

You can pay your bills through the mail by check. Never send cash through the mail. If cash is lost or stolen, the money is gone.

ATM Cards

ATM cards are used at *automated teller machines* (ATMs) to withdraw cash from your checking account. You will need to enter a security code called a *PIN* (personal identification number) when using an ATM card. A service fee may be charged if you use an ATM card at a machine that is not operated by your bank.

Debit Cards

debit card
A card used to immediately deduct a purchase amount or cash withdrawal from a checking account.

Debit cards, also called *check cards*, combine the functions of checks and ATM cards. Debit cards can be used to make purchases, pay bills, and withdraw cash from ATMs—all without writing a check. The funds are immediately withdrawn from the account. Debit cards bear the logo of a credit card company, such as Visa or MasterCard. Usually, you will need to enter a PIN when using a debit card in stores or at ATMs. Chart 25-2 lists guidelines for using a debit card safely.

Debit cards offer a great deal of convenience. However, these cards also make it easy for some people to overspend. You

25-2
Following these tips will help you use your ATM or debit card wisely.

Security Tips for ATM and Debit Cards

- When selecting a PIN, avoid using numbers such as your birthday, social security number, or home address.
- Memorize your PIN. Do not carry your PIN in your wallet or write it on your card.
- Keep a written record of your account number and expiration date, and the telephone number of the card issuer. File the record in a safe place.
- Review ATM or debit card transactions carefully before entering your PIN or signing a receipt. Upon approval, funds are immediately withdrawn from your account.
- Report a lost or stolen card immediately.

must have enough money in your account to cover all checks, debit card purchases, and cash withdrawals. If you ***overdraw*** your account, you spend more than is in your account. When you overdraw, your check will *bounce*. You will be charged a high fee for each bounced check and overdrawn debit or ATM card transaction. Avoid overdrawing your account by recording every check and debit or ATM card transaction.

overdraw
To spend more money than what is in the account.

Where to Open an Account

The first step in opening a checking account is to select a financial institution. *Commercial banks* offer a full range of services to both individuals and corporations. *Savings banks* also offer a variety of services to individuals. *Credit unions* offer services to certain groups of people, such as employee groups.

When choosing a financial institution, consider the following factors:

- convenience
- services
- types of accounts
- fees

Shopping for a financial institution is much like shopping for a car. You would want to compare the features of several before making a choice.

Reflect
Do you know at which bank(s) your parents have accounts? Ask them what factors persuaded them to keep accounts there.

Resource
Checking a Financial Institution, color transparency CT-25, TR. Students review factors to consider when choosing a bank or similar institution.

Reflect
Do any of your friends have their own checking accounts? Would you like to have one?

Convenience

A convenient financial institution is one that is near your home or workplace. This would allow you to bank on your lunch hour or on your way to or from work. If the institution has branch offices, it provides even more convenience. You can deposit or withdraw money at any branch office. Therefore, you might find it convenient to have a branch where you shop or spend leisure time. To avoid ATM service charges, choose a financial institution with bank-operated ATMs near where you work, live, and shop. See 25-3.

Another aspect of convenience is its hours. It should be open at times when you can get there. It may have early, late, or extended weekend hours.

25-3
An automated teller machine is one of the many services offered by most financial institutions.

Discuss
Do your parents use any online banking services? What do you think the advantages of using online banking services are?

Making a Difference

Invite a representative from a local banking institution to class to discuss procedures for first-time checking account customers. Have the guest discuss helpful hints for managing your first checking account. Find out what population groups in the area tend to avoid checking accounts, but could benefit from using them. Ask the guest what services are available to make checking accounts more accessible to different population groups.

Services

Financial institutions offer a variety of checking and savings accounts as well as other services. If certain services are important to you, find out which institutions offer them. Compare services before making your choice. Service might include the following:

- automated teller machines (ATMs)
- drive-up banking
- online banking
- debit cards
- overdraft protection
- credit card services
- safe-deposit boxes
- certified checks
- money orders
- cashier's checks
- traveler's checks
- loans

Types of Accounts

As a single person, you will probably open an *individual account*. Only your signature can be used to authorize a check. You may also open a *joint account* with another person, which permits either of the owners to sign a check. Both owners may have separate debit cards that withdraw funds from the shared account.

Some checking accounts pay interest. An *interest-paying account* works much like a savings account. Interest is paid according to how much money is in the account.

Discuss

Does your family use ATMs or drive-up banking? What do you think are the advantages of these services?

Discuss

What are the differences between an *individual*, *joint*, or *interest-paying* account? Which type of account do you think you are most likely to open as your first account?

Fees

A checking account usually costs money, but fees differ among financial institutions. Some charge a fee for each check you write. Others offer free checking if you keep a savings account there. Others provide free checking if you maintain a minimum balance in either your checking or savings account.

You usually pay a fee to order checks. That fee varies depending on the design you choose. When ordering, people may have checks mailed to their bank instead of their home to protect against theft.

Consider all the various fees when choosing a bank. Fees vary among banks. Check large and small banks to determine the right one for your needs.

Opening a Checking Account

Once you select a financial institution, you are ready to open your checking account. The process is an easy one. Ask to see the person in charge of new accounts. That person will have you fill out an application form. This form includes spaces for your name, address, telephone number, and if you work, your business address.

You will be asked to sign a *signature card*, which will be used to check the signatures on your checks. See 25-4. This helps prevent the crime of *forgery*. Falsely imitating someone else's signature on a check is forgery. You will also be asked to show some identification, such as a driver's license or passport. Remember to bring your social security number. Banks must have your social security number on file for tax purposes.

25-4
This is a combined application form and signature card for opening a checking account. Some institutions use two separate forms.

Checking Account Application

OUR TOWN BANK
ANY ONE AUTHORIZED SIGNATURE WILL BE SUFFICIENT FOR EACH WITHDRAWAL, CHECK OR OTHER ORDER.

ACCOUNT NUMBER

TITLE

THIS ACCOUNT WILL BE SUBJECT TO THE RULES AND REGULATIONS OF THE BANK, ALL LAWS, REGULATIONS AND RULES OF THE UNITED STATES, AND OF THE STATE OF NEW JERSEY, AND ALL CHANGES IN THOSE RULES, REGULATIONS, AND LAWS THAT MAY IN THE FUTURE BECOME EFFECTIVE. I FURTHER AGREE BY MY SIGNATURE BELOW THAT I HAVE RECEIVED A COPY OF--

- ☐ BASIC CHECKING AGREEMENT
- ☐ SAVINGS AGREEMENT
- ☐ TIME DEPOSIT OPEN ACCOUNT AGREEMENT
- ☐ JOINT ACCOUNT SUPPLEMENTAL AGREEMENT
- ☐ NOW ACCOUNT AGREEMENT
- ☐ STATEMENT SAVINGS AGREEMENT
- ☐ TRUST ACCOUNT SUPPLEMENTAL AGREEMENT

DEPOSITOR'S SIGNATURE DEPOSITOR'S SIGNATURE

TYPE ☐ NOW ☐ CHECKING ☐ SAVINGS
SPECIFY TYPE OF ACCOUNT

FOLD

ADDRESS WRITE ZIP CODE AFTER STATE

SOCIAL SECURITY NO.	BIRTH DATE	SOCIAL SECURITY NO.	BIRTH DATE
HOME PHONE NO.	BUSINESS PHONE NO.	HOME PHONE NO.	BUSINESS PHONE NO.
EMPLOYER		EMPLOYER	
JOB TITLE		JOB TITLE	

DATE OPENED	DATE CLOSED	RELATED ACCOUNT NUMBERS	
IDENTIFICATION SOURCE	BRANCH NO.	OFFICER NO.	OPENED BY:

SIGNATURE CARD

Discuss
Use Figure 25-4 to talk about the information on this signature card/application form. Talk about how this signature card is used by the bank.

Discuss
Do you think students should have checking accounts? Explain your view.

Resource
Making Checking Deposits, reproducible master 25-1, TR. Students practice filling out deposit slips.

Making a Deposit

deposit slip
A form filled out before depositing money into a bank account.

You must put money into your checking account before you can write checks. The teller will ask you to complete a deposit slip. Use the ***deposit slip*** to record how much money you are going to put into your checking account. Space is provided for you to list cash and/or checks.

Give the completed deposit slip and your money to a teller. The teller will record your deposit and give you a receipt. You will be given temporary checks and deposit slips to use. Later, you will receive your own personalized checks and deposit slips in the mail. See 25-5.

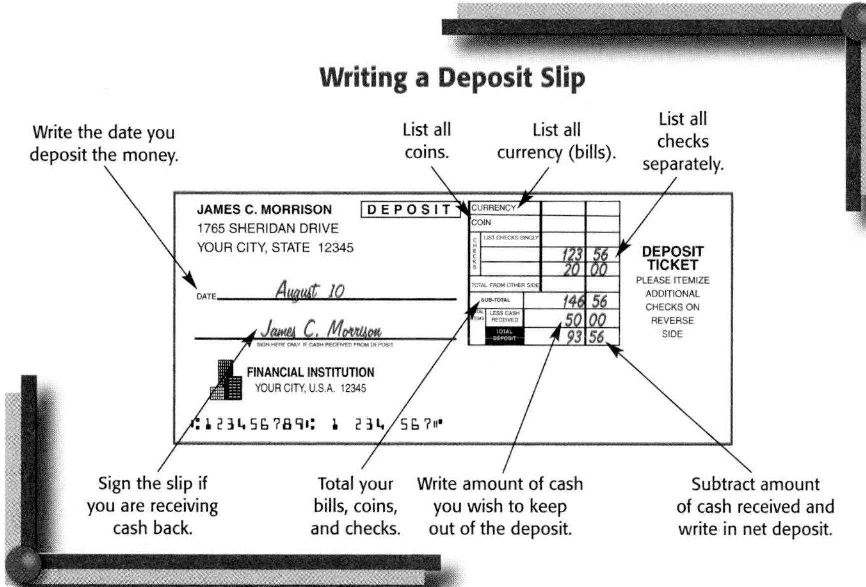

25-5
Personalized deposit slips come with checks to make it easy to add money to a checking account.

Reflect

Are you ready to handle the responsibilities of a checking account? Do you feel confident in knowing how to fill out a deposit slip?

Activity

If your parents have personalized checks, ask to see a copy of their personalized deposit slips. Does it resemble Figure 25-5?

Resource

Writing Dollar Amounts Correctly, reproducible master 25-2, TR. Students practice writing dollar amounts as they should appear on checks.

You can deposit money electronically. You can transfer money from your other existing accounts or between accounts. If you transfer money electronically, you will not have a deposit slip. It is important that you keep accurate records if you wish to use this method.

Endorsing a Check

When depositing a check made out to you into your account, you must first endorse it. To ***endorse*** a check, you sign your name on the back of its left edge. Your signature must go in the area provided. Many checks will indicate "do not write, stamp, or sign below this line." Sign your name exactly as it is written on the front of the check. See 25-6.

endorse
To sign the back of a check in order to deposit or cash the amount specified.

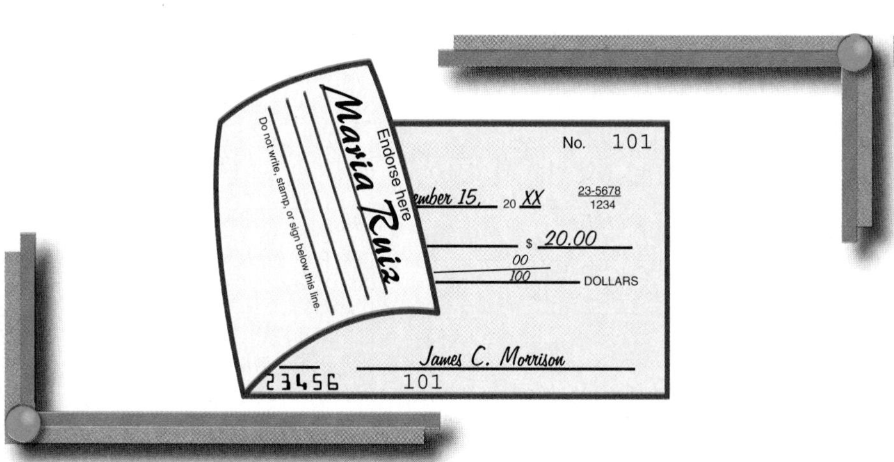

25-6
A check endorsement must be written on the back of the left edge of the check within the space provided.

Your Reading

How do you open a checking account?

Activity

Suppose you receive a birthday gift in the form of a check. List the sequence of steps needed to put this money into your bank account.

Resource

Using a Checking Account, Activity C, WB. Given the information provided, students fill out checks, a deposit slip, and a check register, accordingly.

Endorsed checks can be cashed as well as deposited. Do not endorse a check until just before you cash or deposit it. Once your check is endorsed, anyone can cash it. If an endorsed check is lost or stolen, the money is gone.

Recording Transactions

Most checks come with check registers. A *register* is simply a place to record all the deposits and credits that affect your account. Keeping your register up-to-date will help you keep track of how much money you have in your checking account.

You should complete the register before you write a check or use your ATM or debit card. Record each check, electronic transaction, and deposit on the register. Deposits and interest are added to your balance. Checks, electronic transactions, and service fees are subtracted from your balance. See 25-7.

Instead of a register, some checks come with stubs or duplicates. Both serve as written records of the check numbers, dates, amounts, and parties to whom checks are written. If you have check stubs, you must write this information on the stub for each check. If you have duplicates,

25-7
Recording each deposit and withdrawal in a check register helps checking account holders keep track of their account balances.

AD-Automatic Deposit AP-Automatic Payment DC-Debit Card

NUMBER or Code	DATE	DESCRIPTION OF TRANSACTION	PAYMENT/DEBIT (-)	√ T	FEE (IF ANY) (-)	DEPOSIT/CREDIT (+)	BALANCE
							$ 169 23
164	5-6	FIRST UNITED METHODIST	$ 25 00		$	$	25 00
							144 23
DC	5-12	TURNING HEADS SALON	23 00				23 00
							121 23
165	5-16	ILLINOIS BELL	33 17				33 17
							88 06
AD	5-18	DEPOSIT				173 32	173 32
							261 38
AP	5-21	COMMONWEALTH ELECTRIC	23 65				23 65
							237 73
166	5-24	B & B TIRE & AUTO	20 28				20 28
							217 45
AD	6-1	DEPOSIT				192 82	192 82
							410 27
167	6-1	DORCHESTER REALTY	210 00				210 00
							200 27
DC	6-2	AMERICAN CANCER SOCIETY	10 00				10 00
							190 27

Discuss

Do you think most check registers look as neat and organized as Figure 25-7? Can you see how simple it is to maintain a check register when it resembles Figure 25-7?

the information is automatically recorded as a "carbon" copy of the check written.

You should always know how much money is in your account. That way you can avoid overdrawing your account.

Reflect

Have your parents given you a check to write out and trusted you with the responsibility of filling in the amount? Do you think you would do a good job of keeping your check register accurate?

Online Banking

Most banks offer online access to your checking account. You will need to register a user name and password with your bank to access the online account. Online banking allows you to pay bills using your computer. You can also transfer funds between accounts. In addition, you can view your account statement and monitor transactions.

Enrich

Interview two adults and find out if they use online banking to manage their checking account. Find out how often they use online services to pay bills, transfer funds, and monitor transactions. Report the results to the class.

Bills can automatically be paid at the end of a billing cycle with an automatic debit to your account. This is just like writing a check. Automatic payment is usually applied to a bill that occurs every month for the same amount. For example, it can be used to pay your automobile insurance monthly or quarterly. If you use an automatic payment method, be sure your account balance will cover the payment. Also, deduct the amount from your account when the payment comes due.

Using this form of payment requires careful bookkeeping on your part. If you don't make proper deductions on time, your account won't balance. You may cause an overdraft. Checking your online statement regularly can help you keep up-to-date records.

Why is it important to record every transaction?

Balancing Your Checkbook

You should receive a monthly or quarterly statement from the bank. The ***bank statement*** lists all your deposits, cash withdrawals, check withdrawals, electronic transactions, service charges, and interest payments. It also lists your beginning and ending balances. See 25-8. You may receive your bank statement in the mail or access it through online banking.

bank statement
A balance sheet listing deposits, withdrawals, service charges, and interest payments on an account with a financial institution.

Instructions for balancing your checkbook are given on the back of most bank statements. Balancing your checkbook is also called *reconciling* your account. When you review your statement, check off the processed checks and electronic transactions in your checkbook register. It is up to you to make sure your checkbook balance agrees with the bank statement.

Resource

Balancing a Checkbook, Activity D, WB. Students balance a checking account, using the information given.

25-8
A bank statement provides a periodic summary of checking account activity.

FI
Financial Institution

Statement for
James C. Morrison
1765 Sheridan Drive
Your City, State 12345

This statement covers
5/01/XX through 5/31/XX

Checking Account 123456		
	Previous Statement Balance On 4/30/XX	169.23
	Total of 1 **Deposits For**	173.32+
	Total of 5 **Withdrawals For**	125.10-
	Total Interest Earned	.99+
	Total Service Charges	0
	New Balance	218.44

Checks and Other Debits	**Check**	**Date Paid**	**Amount**
	164	5/10	25.00
	165	5/20	33.17
	166	5/28	20.28
	Debit Card Withdrawal #00967 Turning Heads Salon	5/12	23.00
	Automatic Payment Withdrawal #02653 Commonwealth Electric	5/21	23.65

Deposits and Other Credits		**Date Posted**	**Amount**
	Direct Deposit from #09876 on 5/18	5/18	173.32
	Interest	5/31	.99

Thank you for banking with your Financial Institution

Community Connections

Interview three adults in the community who have checking accounts to find answers to the following questions: Do you immediately record each written check or cash withdrawal? Do you always keep your check register up-to-date so you know your current account balance? Do you routinely check the bank's monthly statement against your record for any discrepancies? Do you never, sometimes, or frequently overdraw your account? Keep the identity of the adults confidential as you report your findings to the class.

Resource

Correcting an Imbalance, Activity E, WB. Students reconcile a bank statement with a check register.

Some retailers and credit card companies process checks as electronic payments, called *electronic check conversion*. Even though you wrote a check, the payment is deducted from your checking account as if you used a debit card. These transactions appear on your statement as electronic payments.

Also check off all the deposits listed on your statement. Add any interest shown on your statement to the balance in your checkbook. Subtract any service charges from your checkbook balance.

As you go over your statement, you may notice that several of your checks have not cleared your bank. Checks clear the bank at different times. People and companies often hold checks for a while before cashing them. Checks that have not cleared are called *outstanding checks*. When balancing your checkbook, list outstanding checks and subtract them from the bank's statement. You may also have used your debit or ATM card since the statement was issued. Be sure to list and subtract any outstanding debit card purchases or cash withdrawals. See 25-9.

When you have balanced your checkbook, the bank's statement should match your records. If you find the bank has made an error (such as incorrectly recording a deposit), call the bank and explain the problem. Before you call, however, make sure the error isn't yours.

Where can you find instructions for balancing your checkbook?

Special Types of Checks

In addition to personal checks, there are several other types of checks:

- certified checks
- cashier's checks
- money orders
- traveler's checks

Enrich

Interview your parents to find out how they balance their checkbooks. Find out if they do any electronic banking. What advice do they have for you about your future banking?

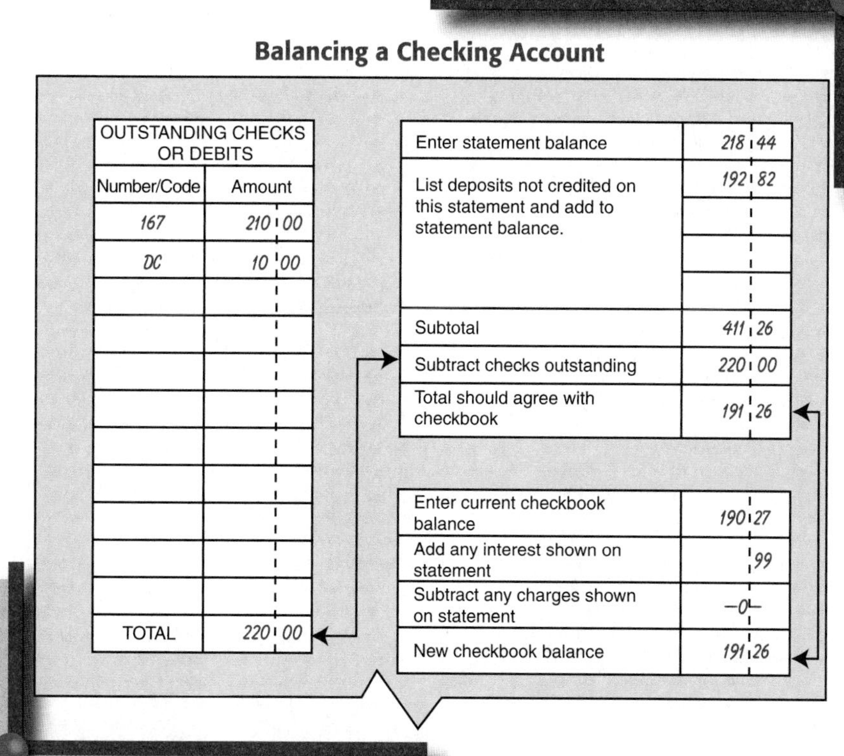

Balancing a Checking Account

OUTSTANDING CHECKS OR DEBITS	
Number/Code	Amount
167	210 00
DC	10 00
TOTAL	220 00

Enter statement balance	218 44
List deposits not credited on this statement and add to statement balance.	192 82
Subtotal	411 26
Subtract checks outstanding	220 00
Total should agree with checkbook	191 26

Enter current checkbook balance	190 27
Add any interest shown on statement	99
Subtract any charges shown on statement	–0–
New checkbook balance	191 26

25-9 Most bank statements have a form similar to this on the back to help customers balance their checkbooks.

Adapting the Lesson

Provide students who are low functioning with a copy of a bank statement to color code the information it contains. Ask them to use these colors: red for the account number, green for the service charge, orange for the account balance, yellow for the checks listed, electronic payments, and ATM withdrawals, and blue for the deposits.

The use of these checks is explained in the following sections.

Certified Checks

certified check
A check for which a bank guarantees payment.

Sellers of very expensive items often require payment by certified check. A ***certified check*** is one for which the bank guarantees payment. The bank withdraws the requested amount from your checking account. The bank teller stamps your check "certified." A bank official signs the check, guaranteeing the bank has set aside your money for payment. A small fee is charged for this service. See 25-10.

Vocabulary
Define the term *certified check.* Explain how it differs from a personal check.

Cashier's Checks

cashier's check
A check drawn on a bank's own funds and signed by an officer of the bank.

A ***cashier's check*** is drawn by a bank on its own funds. A cashier's check may also be referred to as a bank check. A bank officer, usually the cashier, signs it. People who don't know you may feel safer accepting a cashier's check than a personal check.

You don't need a checking account to get a cashier's check. You can go to any bank and buy a cashier's check. You pay the amount of the check plus a service fee. Some banks will waive the fee if you have an account with the bank. A bank representative will help you fill out the check.

Discuss
What are the advantages of a certified check? Give examples of situations that might require you to pay with a certified check.

25-10
Certified checks are often used for expensive items, such as paying for closing costs when buying a home.

Activity
Draw two columns on a sheet of paper. Title one column Cashier's Check; the other, Money Order. First, describe each. Then, list the advantages and disadvantages of each.

Resource
How Would I Handle a Checking Account? reproducible master 25-3, TR. Use the adapted worksheet to reinforce chapter concepts in students who are low functioning.

Money Orders

A ***money order*** is an order to pay a certain amount of money to a certain party. As with checks, money orders can be used to pay bills safely by mail. You don't need a checking account to get money orders.

You can purchase money orders from several places:

- financial institutions
- U.S. post offices
- American Express agencies
- Railway Express agencies
- Western Union offices

To buy a money order, you pay the amount of the money order plus a service fee. The agent prepares the money order and fills in the amount. You fill in the name of the person or company to be paid. If you have a checking account, you normally don't need this service.

Traveler's Checks

Traveler's checks are checks purchased in common denominations that are replaceable if lost or stolen. You can buy traveler's checks from banks and credit card companies. You do not need an account at the institution to buy traveler's checks.

There may be a service fee for buying traveler's checks. Organizations like the American Automobile Association (AAA) offer their members no-fee traveler's checks. Traveler's checks can be issued in foreign denominations and easily cashed.

You will be required to sign your name on each traveler's check at the time of purchase. Later, when you cash the checks, you will have to sign them a second time. The person receiving a check compares the second signature with the first one. If the signatures match, the person knows the check is really yours. You may find fewer businesses willing to accept traveler's checks.

Community Connections

Work with a group of your classmates to draw a simplified map of the business district in the community, marking the main business streets in all directions. From memory, have students plot and label the banks or financial institutions and ATMs in the area. Ask students to walk or drive around that area within the next week to check the accuracy of their map.

money order
Used like a check, this is an order purchased for a specific amount to be paid to a certain party.

traveler's checks
Checks purchased in common denominations that are replaceable if lost or stolen.

Your Reading

When would you use a certified check?

Summary

A checking account provides both convenience and safety. Before you open a checking account, shop for the best financial institution for you. Compare the features of several before you make your choice.

Once you have a checking account, use it responsibly. If you have an ATM or debit card, know your PIN number and keep track of all transactions. Learn the correct way to fill out deposit slips, endorse checks, and write checks. Know how to use check stubs or a check register. Access your online banking account, if available, to monitor transactions and make electronic payments. Understand how to balance a checkbook. Then be sure you put your knowledge to good use. A checking account can be a helpful money management tool. However, if you misuse and overdraw it often, you will have problems.

At times, you may want to use certified checks, cashier's checks, money orders, or traveler's checks. All these services are for your convenience. Become familiar with them now so you will know how to use them when you choose to do so.

Reviewing Key Concepts

1. Name two advantages of having a checking account.
2. Why should a check be written in ink?
3. What is the difference between a debit card and an ATM card?
4. What four factors should be considered when choosing a financial institution?
5. When you open a checking account, why are you asked to sign a signature card?
6. What form do you fill out when you want to put money into an existing checking account?
7. What is the purpose of using check stubs or a check register?
8. What items should be recorded in a check register?
9. You need a checking account to write a ______.
   A. certified check
   B. cashier's check
   C. money order
   D. traveler's check
10. What is the primary reason for buying traveler's checks?

Answers to *Reviewing Key Concepts*

1. (Name two:) helps to keep a record of your expenses, is a safe place to keep money, is a place to deposit an allowance or paycheck, allows a person to make purchases or pay bills with a check or debit card
2. to prevent others from changing the amount or the name on the check
3. Debit cards can be used for purchases or withdrawing cash. ATM cards can only be used at automated teller machines to withdraw cash.
4. convenience, types of accounts, fees, services
5. Your signature card will be used to check the signatures on your checks in order to help prevent forgery.
6. deposit slip
7. to keep track of how much money you have in the account
8. checks, deposits, withdrawals, electronic transactions, service fees, and interest payments
9. A
10. to easily replace any money that may become lost or stolen

Building Academic Skills

1. **Math.** Your bank statement last month showed you had a balance of $1,723.34. You had three checks outstanding, totaling $67.89. This month you deposited $487.53. You wrote checks totaling $134.80. Your bank charges were $4.50. What is the total in your bank account?
2. **Writing, speaking.** Working with a group of classmates, write a short skit that advertises the use of traveler's checks. Include information about where to buy them, how to use them, and their advantages over other forms of money. Perform your skit for the class.
3. **History.** Analyze how money transactions were handled before the use of credit cards and checking accounts. Did something equivalent to "time payments" exist? Where did the average person store money? Besides coins and paper currency, what other forms of money were accepted? Were women or children able to have money or use it?

Building Technology Skills

1. Conduct an online search to determine if the utility companies in your area offer automatic payment options. What is required to set up an automatic payment plan? In your opinion, what are the advantages and disadvantages of paying utility bills automatically instead of sending a check? Report your findings.
2. Conduct an online search to determine what is needed to open an online checking account. Find out what the system requirements are and what fees may be charged for this service. Report this information to the class.
3. Design a Web page that a full-service financial institution could use to advertise its many products and services. Include information that customers would need to know.

Building Career Knowledge and Skills

1. Write a short paper on the advantages and disadvantages of using a debit card.
2. Invite a representative of a financial institution to visit your class. Ask questions about various services, fees, and types of accounts.
3. Investigate the consequences of having a check bounce. Talk to store managers and bank officials to get both sides of the story. Discuss your findings in class.
4. Design posters to illustrate the topics discussed in this chapter. Display them throughout your school.

Building Workplace Skills

Visit three financial institutions in your area and compare them for convenience, services, fees, and types of accounts available. Work as a team with two or three of your classmates and assume you are old enough to open a joint account. When you visit each institution, speak to a bank representative and explain that your visit is a class project. Be sure to obtain relevant brochures. What are the costs and requirements of a joint checking account at each institution? Using a computer, create a report that compares the facts you gathered. Decide which institution you would choose to open the new account. Make a brief presentation to the class explaining your team's decision.

Why should I get into the habit of saving money?

Chapter 26 Savings

Key Terms

interest
principal
compound interest
annual percentage yield (APY)
direct deposit
savings club
certificate of deposit (CD)
money market account
U.S. savings bond
mutual fund
annuity

Chapter Objectives

After studying this chapter, you will be able to

- **determine** reasons for saving.
- **list** the types of financial institutions that offer savings accounts and the agencies that insure them.
- **compare** the various ways to save.
- **identify** ways to protect yourself against investment fraud.

Key Concepts

- Saving money allows you to meet future financial goals.
- Savings accounts differ in terms of safety, yield, fees, convenience, and account requirements.
- Saving for the long term, especially retirement, requires an understanding of how money can grow over time.
- Savers must stay alert to fraud schemes because they can destroy a lifetime of savings.

Reasons for Saving

Saving money is sound personal money management. You should save a portion of each paycheck based on your take-home pay and personal needs. The more you make, the more you should save.

A general rule to help make saving a priority is to pay yourself first. This means setting aside a fixed amount of your income every pay period. Treating your savings as a fixed expense and avoiding excuses will help you achieve future goals. See 26-1.

There are many reasons for saving for the future. These reasons are as varied as each person's wants and needs. The following events are common reasons for saving:

- emergencies
- possible job loss
- travel and recreation
- advanced education
- major purchases such as a car or home
- retirement

Resource

Reinforcing Vocabulary, Activity A, WB. Students complete partial sentences with vocabulary terms.

Discuss

What are some reasons for saving money? What percentage of an allowance do you feel students should save?

Your Reading

What does it mean to *pay yourself first*?

Excuses for Not Saving Money	
Excuse	**Rebuttal**
I can't afford it.	The first check you write every month should be to yourself, even if it's for a small amount. Carefully tracking your finances can help identify ways to eliminate unnecessary spending and save more money.
I'll start saving when I'm older.	Time is a valuable resource when saving money. Interest-earning savings increase over time, so the earlier you start saving, the more your money will grow.
Someone else will take care of it.	You are responsible for your own financial future. It is up to you to make saving a priority.
I deserve to get what I want.	Buying expensive items can bring immediate gratification, but it doesn't outweigh the long-term satisfaction of financial independence.

26-1
Overcoming these common excuses is an important step in developing the habit of saving.

Resource

Save for a Rainy Day, color transparency CT-26, TR. Students discuss reasons for saving.

Resource

Financial Institutions, Activity B, WB. Students compare similarities and differences among local savings institutions.

Community Connections

Compare the savings rates of various types of accounts offered by banks and financial institutions in the area. Create a chart that lists the banking institutions alphabetically down the left side, with the names of the various methods of saving money across the top. Identify specific requirements for each account.

Where to Save

You have several options for saving your money. Become familiar with the types of financial institutions that offer savings accounts. Find out how much interest each pays on the accounts. Then decide where you want to deposit your money.

- **Commercial banks** are known as the department stores of finance. They offer a full variety of banking services. They make loans and transfer funds. They also provide financial advice and offer savings accounts.
- **Savings banks** are primarily known for lending money to homebuyers. Their primary customers are small businesses and individuals.
- **Internet banks** provide banking services online and have no physical branch offices. With minimal operating expenses, Internet banks are able to offer higher interest rates for savings accounts, CDs, and money market accounts. Internet banks can be either commercial or savings banks.
- **Credit unions** are nonprofit financial institutions. They are owned by and operated for their members. Most credit unions serve people in a particular community, group, company, or organization. Credit unions make loans to their members at low interest rates. Also, they usually pay higher interest rates than banks do on savings accounts.

Why is it important for savings to be FDIC insured?

Will Your Savings Be Safe?

Financial institutions that are insured are safe places to keep your money. You get more protection from them than you would if you kept your money at home. Each account is insured up to $100,000. If the bank suffers a fire, bankruptcy, or any other disaster, your money stays safe. Before you open a savings account, check to see that it would be insured.

Two agencies are responsible for insuring most of the money in savings accounts. The *Federal Deposit Insurance Corporation (FDIC)* protects deposits in most commercial and savings banks. The *National Credit Union Association (NCUA)* protects deposits in credit unions.

Ways to Save

There are many ways to save. You should discuss your options with customer service representatives in local financial institutions. They will be happy to describe the various savings plans offered. Savings accounts, savings clubs, certificates of deposit, and U.S. savings bonds are some of the more common ways to save.

Resource

Understanding Your Savings Account Statement, reproducible master 26-1, TR. Students identify common elements of bank statements for savings accounts.

Reflect

Do you have friends who seem to always need to borrow money? What is your opinion of this practice?

Vocabulary

What does *interest* mean? Explain how it differs from *compound interest*.

Example

Since accounts are insured up to $100,000, to have $200,000 completely insured, the owner should split the total and hold the money in separate $100,000 accounts.

Savings Accounts

After opening a *regular savings account*, you can make deposits and withdrawals at any time. You receive a monthly or quarterly statement in the mail or online. All deposits and withdrawals are recorded in the statements. Be sure to double-check your account activity when you receive your statement. See 26-2.

Your savings account will earn interest. ***Interest*** is money paid to you for allowing a financial institution to have and use your money. The longer you leave your money in a savings account, the more interest you will earn. Many savings accounts calculate interest daily, but some use the average of all daily balances. Some accounts pay higher interest rates for higher balances. If a withdrawal reduces the balance below the required minimum, you receive no interest for the period and are charged a penalty.

interest
The money paid to customers for allowing a financial institution to have and use their money.

Financial Institution
Your City, U.S.A. 12345

ACCOUNT #29-3689865

DATE	MEMO	INTEREST	WITHDRAWALS	DEPOSITS	BALANCE	TELLER
06-15	--			200.00	200.00	04
06-22	--			50.00	250.00	07
06-26	CW		15.00		235.00	02
06-29	--			50.00	285.00	04
06-30		.51			285.51	05
07-06	--			52.00	337.51	01
07-13	--			50.00	387.51	04
07-21	CW		150.00		237.51	04

26-2
Savings account deposits and withdrawals are recorded in a statement.

principal
The original investment, such as a savings account deposit.

compound interest
Interest figured on the principal plus the earned interest of a financial account.

annual percentage yield (APY)
The rate (or percent) of yearly earnings from an account; also called *annual yield, interest rate,* and *rate of return.*

As interest is added to a savings account, it too begins to earn interest. Both the deposit, known as ***principal***, and the earned interest continue to earn interest. This is known as ***compound interest***.

When comparing savings accounts, look for the annual percentage yield (APY). ***Annual percentage yield*** is the rate (or percent) of yearly earnings from an account. Other names for the APY are *annual yield, interest rate,* and *rate of return*. The higher the APY, the more your savings will grow. See 26-3.

Reflect
Do you know anyone who maintains a savings account in one bank and a checking account in another? What might cause some people to do this?

Opening a Savings Account

Convenience is important when deciding where to open a savings account. Focus on financial institutions close to your home or workplace with hours that meet your needs. Compare Internet banks if you prefer to do your banking online. Next, find out which financial institution pays the highest interest rates for the type of savings account that interests you. Different institutions pay different rates of interest.

26-3
You can find the APY of most savings accounts by visiting financial institution Web sites.

Note
Sometimes to lure new accounts, a financial institution will offer a very high savings rate for just a few months, and then drop it below the average offered by many banks. Always examine special promotions to make sure you don't end up a loser in the long run.

Discuss
Why do you think some banks require you to maintain a minimum balance on your accounts? Do you think it is a good idea for banks to have special accounts for minors?

Finally, keep in mind that you do not need to choose the same institution for all your financial needs. For convenience, you may wish to have your checking account and your savings account in the same place. However, you can have your checking account in one place and your savings account in another. Shop around for the service that best meets your needs.

Comparing Fees

Most banks require you to maintain a minimum balance in your account. If you do not maintain that balance, you may be charged a service fee. Some banks have student accounts that may not require a minimum balance. When you open an account, it is important that you know what fees will be charged.

Often banks will have special programs for minors. Usually these are offered to children of parents or guardians who already have an account at the bank. The programs allow you to keep an account with a small balance without a bank charge.

Making a Deposit

To deposit money in your savings account, you need to fill out a savings deposit form, 26-4. It is important to fill out the form correctly by following certain steps:

- Write your name, the date, and your account number. (Personalized forms that are printed with your checks already contain your account number.)
- On the *currency line*, list the total amount of paper money you are depositing.

Reflect

Do you worry about saving money? Do you feel confident that you know what options you have for saving? Do you think you will be able to save much of your earnings?

Activity

Divide the class into teams of four students. Have each team summarize in their own words the steps necessary to make a deposit. Ask students to write the steps on paper, without writing numbers such as *1*, *2*, and *3*. Have students cut the steps apart and exchange pieces of paper with another team. Finally, the teams are to put the steps in correct order, number them, and provide feedback on the accuracy of the written steps.

Adapting the Lesson

Have students who are low functioning role-play the process of opening a savings account. Students are to prepare questions in advance that they will want answered. Have another teacher or student in the class play the role of the bank employee. Evaluate results.

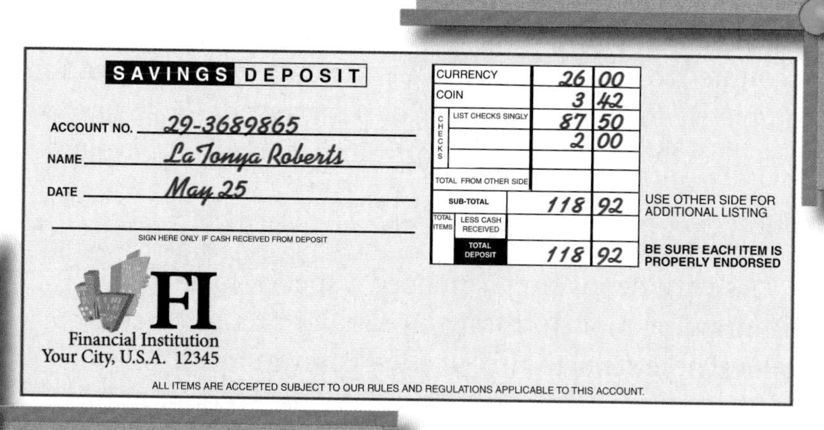
SAVINGS DEPOSIT

ACCOUNT NO. 29-3689865

NAME La Tonya Roberts

DATE May 25

SIGN HERE ONLY IF CASH RECEIVED FROM DEPOSIT

CURRENCY	26	00
COIN	3	42
CHECKS — LIST CHECKS SINGLY	87	50
	2	00
TOTAL FROM OTHER SIDE		
SUB-TOTAL	118	92
TOTAL ITEMS — LESS CASH RECEIVED		
TOTAL DEPOSIT	118	92

USE OTHER SIDE FOR ADDITIONAL LISTING

BE SURE EACH ITEM IS PROPERLY ENDORSED

FI
Financial Institution
Your City, U.S.A. 12345

ALL ITEMS ARE ACCEPTED SUBJECT TO OUR RULES AND REGULATIONS APPLICABLE TO THIS ACCOUNT.

26-4
Savings account customers must complete deposit slips to add money to their accounts.

Resource

Savings Deposits and Withdrawals, Activity C, WB. Students practice filling out savings account deposit and withdrawal forms.

Resource

Savings Survey, Activity E, WB. Students interview a savings account holder about his or her reasons for saving money.

Activity

Have students ask their parents and another adult if their employers offer a direct deposit option and if they use it. What are some reasons people do not use the direct deposit option? Have students report their findings to the class.

- On the *coin line*, list the total amount of pennies, nickels, dimes, and other coins you are depositing. (Currency and coin may be combined on a single *cash* line.)
- List each check separately on the lines provided.
- Add all the money you have listed and write the total on the line provided.
- Indicate the amount of cash, if any, you would like to receive.
- Subtract the amount of cash to be received from the total of the coins, currency, and checks. Write the amount of the net deposit.
- Present your money and the completed deposit form to the teller. The teller will record your deposit in your account. Any interest earned on your savings will be figured into your account at the end of each interest period.

Transferring Funds Electronically

You can also make deposits into your savings account electronically. An *electronic funds transfer (EFT)* is the deposit or withdrawal of funds using a computer instead of paper forms. If you have access to online banking, you may be able to transfer funds between accounts using your personal computer.

Using Direct Deposit

direct deposit
Program that allows an employer to deposit a paycheck directly into an employee's account.

Most employers offer direct deposit of paychecks, which is a type of electronic funds transfer. In a ***direct deposit*** program, you can split your deposit into one or more existing accounts. To take advantage of a direct deposit plan, you must complete a form provided by your employer. Then, your pay goes directly to one or more of your accounts on paydays.

Withdrawing Money

As with depositing, you need a special form for withdrawing money from your savings account. See 26-5. Follow these steps to fill out a withdrawal form:

- Write your name, the date, and your account number.
- Write the amount of money you wish to withdraw.

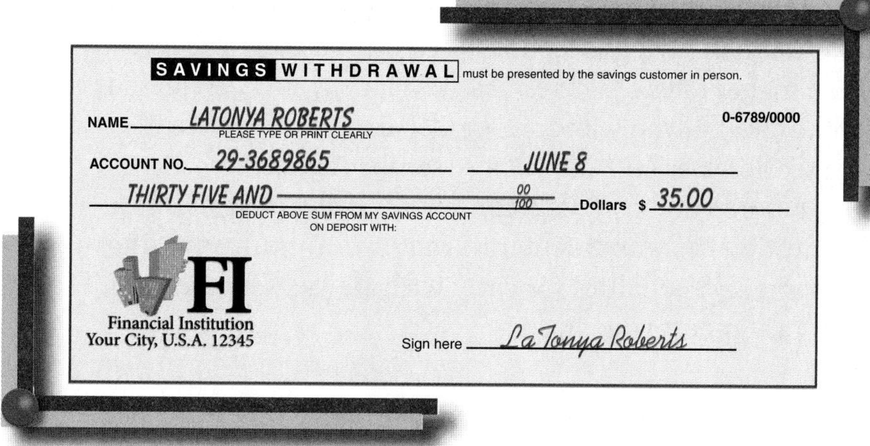
SAVINGS WITHDRAWAL must be presented by the savings customer in person.

NAME LATONYA ROBERTS
PLEASE TYPE OR PRINT CLEARLY
0-6789/0000

ACCOUNT NO. 29-3689865 JUNE 8

THIRTY FIVE AND 00/100 Dollars $ 35.00

DEDUCT ABOVE SUM FROM MY SAVINGS ACCOUNT ON DEPOSIT WITH:

FI
Financial Institution
Your City, U.S.A. 12345

Sign here LaTonya Roberts

26-5
Completing withdrawal slips allows bank customers to take money from their savings accounts.

- Sign your name on the withdrawal form.
- Present your completed withdrawal form to the teller. The teller will deduct your withdrawal from your account, update your balance, and give you your money.

Activity

Have students develop a survey to ask other students in the school about their knowledge of savings options. Each student should then use this master survey when talking to 10 other students. Have students compile results and report back to the class.

Discuss

Name a common reason for participating in a savings club. (*saving money for holiday gifts*)

Discuss

Why might savers join a savings club plan rather than use a regular savings account to save money?

Savings Clubs

A ***savings club*** encourages you to form a habit of saving money. When you open a savings club account, you set up a savings plan. You decide to deposit a set amount of money every week or every month. You are given a savings club book with an account number on it.

Every time you make a deposit, you use a deposit slip from your savings club book. At the end of your savings period, you receive a check for the amount you saved plus the interest you earned. You can then use the money you saved to reach a goal you set for yourself. Some people use savings clubs to save money for holiday gifts or vacations.

savings club
A savings plan into which a set amount of money is deposited regularly until a savings goal is reached.

Certificates of Deposit

As your earnings and savings increase, you should consider expanding your savings. You may wish to invest in a ***certificate of deposit***, known as a ***CD***. You can buy them at a bank or credit union.

At the time of purchase, you must decide how much you want to deposit and for how long. CDs are usually sold in amounts of $500 or more. The money is held for a set period of time. The time period may be as short as 31 days or as long as several years.

certificate of deposit (CD)
A savings certificate earning a fixed rate of interest that is purchased for a specific amount of money and held for a set period of time.

Community Connections

Interview three adults in the community to find out their opinions on saving money and maintaining a savings account. Ask the adults what advice they feel is important on the subject of saving money. Find out how long the savers have had their accounts. Report your findings to the class.

Interest rates for CDs vary. Overall, CDs earn higher rates of interest than savings accounts or clubs. Also, larger CDs usually earn higher rates of interest. However, there are penalties for early withdrawal. If you withdraw money from a CD before the end of the set time period, you will lose some interest.

Before you buy a CD, contact several financial institutions. Compare interest rates, minimum amounts of deposit, and penalties for early withdrawal. Choose the CD that best meets your needs.

Money Market Accounts

money market account
A type of savings account that is similar to a CD, but has no time restrictions.

Your banking institution also offers money market accounts. A ***money market account*** is similar to a CD, but has no time period restrictions. Money can be withdrawn or added at any time with this type of savings account.

Money market savings accounts usually have a rate of interest that is higher than a regular savings account, but lower than a CD. The rate may vary monthly. This type of account also permits limited check-writing privileges. Most money market accounts require a minimum balance of $1,000 to $2,500.

U.S. Savings Bonds

U.S. savings bond
A certificate of debt issued by the federal government that serves as a safe way to save money.

Many people choose to save money by buying a ***U.S. savings bond***. This is a certificate of debt issued by the federal government. There are two types of U.S. savings bonds available.

- **EE bonds** earn a fixed interest rate for up to 30 years.
- **I bonds** earn a fixed interest rate plus a variable rate to protect against inflation. I Bonds earn interest for up to 30 years.

People purchase U.S. savings bonds for several reasons:

- *Safety*—If the bonds are lost, stolen, or destroyed, they can be replaced. The U.S. government issues them.
- *Convenience*—They are available online at the U.S. Treasury Web site for as little as $25 and at financial institutions for $50. Also, many companies offer payroll savings plans. In such plans, an amount determined by the employee is deducted from paychecks for the purchase of the bonds.

Activity

Use the Internet to create a list of area banks and their rates on money market accounts. Determine which bank offers the best option.

- *Higher interest rate*—U.S. savings bonds earn a higher rate than regular savings accounts and savings clubs. Also, the interest earned is not taxed until the bonds are cashed.
- *Patriotism*—Buying U.S. savings bonds is a way to support the government. The money used to buy them goes to the government treasury. See 26-6.

Once you buy a U.S. savings bond, you must keep it for at least twelve months. If you cash a bond before it is five years old, you will lose three months of interest. The longer you keep a bond, the more interest it earns.

Reflect

What would you do if you had money to invest? Do you have enough information about CD's, money market accounts, or savings bonds to make a good decision?

Activity

Find out if your parents have any of the investments mentioned in this chapter. Ask them how they learned about investing.

Mutual Funds

A ***mutual fund*** is a long-term investment that provides a way to invest in stocks and bonds. Over time, it generally provides a greater return than other forms of savings accounts. Many banks offer access to mutual funds as a service to their depositors, but extra fees may be involved.

mutual fund
A long-term investment that provides a way to invest in stocks and bonds.

When you purchase a mutual fund, your money is pooled with many other investors. The money is then invested by a fund manager in various stocks, bonds, or other money instruments. Investing in a mutual fund gives you professional assistance with your investment. You own a share of many different stocks and bonds.

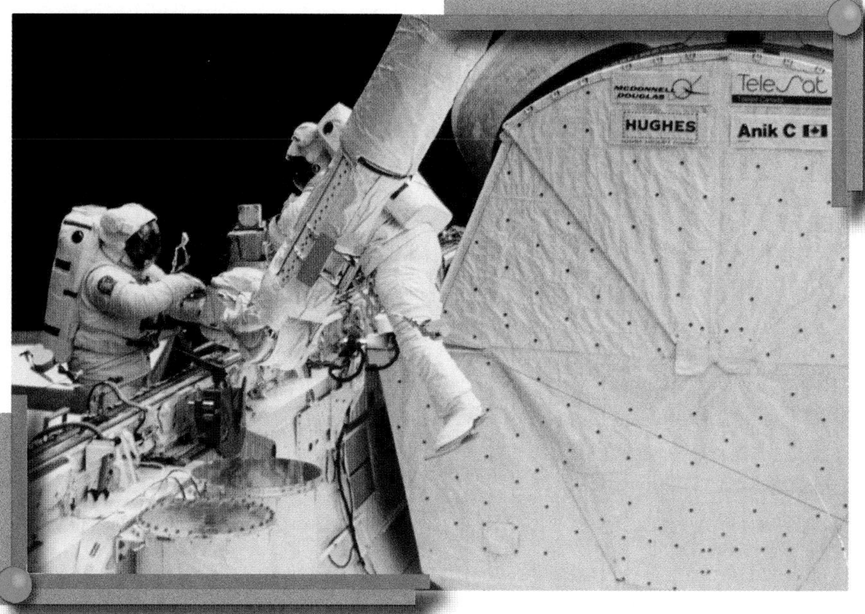

26-6
The government treasury, which includes money from U.S. savings bonds, is used to fund projects such as space exploration.

Adapting the Lesson

Have students who are high functioning conduct online research to identify a stock index fund, a stock growth fund, and a corporate bond fund by searching one of these mutual fund companies: Fidelity or Vanguard. Students are to identify a fund by name for each category and search its rate of return for last week, last quarter, last year, and year-to-date.

Mutual funds are listed in a daily newspaper's business section or on its Web site. Most mutual funds require an initial investment of $2,500, but follow-up deposits can be as little as $100. Initial deposits may be *waived*, or dismissed, if you set up the account for fixed monthly deposits.

It is important to research mutual funds before you invest. By law, the investment firm that manages the fund must provide a prospectus. A *prospectus* is a description of the fund's purpose, past performance, types of investments, and related fees. Read the prospectus carefully. If you don't understand something, ask for an explanation before you invest.

The value of a mutual fund rises and falls with the value of the stocks and bonds they contain. Unlike a checking account or savings account, the government does not insure a mutual fund.

annuity
A form of investment that lasts 10 or 15 years and provides insurance as well as savings.

Annuities

Another form of long-term savings is an ***annuity***. An annuity provides both insurance and savings. Annuities are usually invested for 10 or 15 years. They may be issued longer or the term can be extended. In the event of the owner's death, benefits of an annuity are often paid like life insurance. An annuity is often purchased for retirement or future security. Annuities earnings grow tax deferred. *Tax deferred* means that you don't pay tax on the earnings until you withdraw the money. The government does not insure annuities, but the issuing insurance company may guarantee your initial investment.

Making a Difference

Research Individual Development Accounts (IDAs). How does this type of savings account assist low-income families? What services are offered as part of an IDA? Where can people open an IDA in your community? Design an informational brochure to distribute in your community.

Retirement Accounts

Retirement may be many years away, but saving for it should begin early. While earning an income, you will need to save money to live on later in life. Start saving regularly when you begin working, and your money will benefit from the power of compounding, 26-7. An initial deposit invested over several decades in a taxfree account can generate big earnings.

Some retirement savings plans, such as a 401(k) or 403(b), are offered through employers. It is important to understand how your workplace retirement plan operates, how to make contributions, and where your money will be invested.

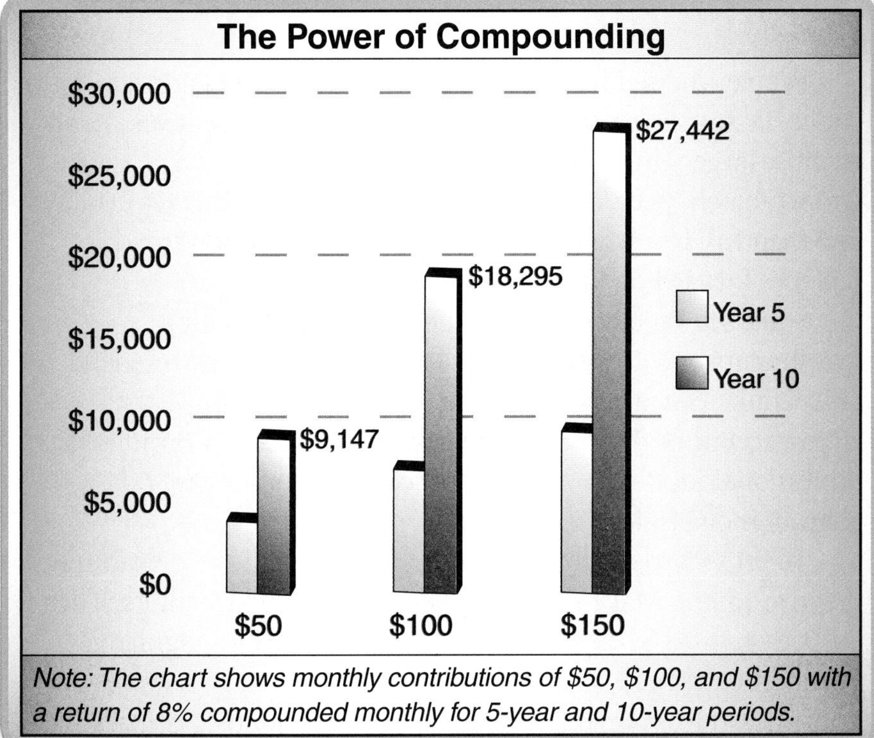

Source: The Ohio Tuition Trust Authority

26-7
Saving for retirement while working will allow your money to grow over time.

Reflect

Do you ever think about retirement? Do your parents discuss retirement options? What can you do now to prepare for retirement?

Resource

How Your Money Grows, Activity D, WB. Students interpret a chart and answer questions about how money grows over time.

Enrich

Use the Internet to research three financial institutions in your area that offer IRAs. Write the answers to the following questions: What is the initial deposit required to open an account? What investment options are available? What are the steps involved in opening an IRA?

Companies may match employee contributions. A plan with matching contributions is a valuable benefit and helps your savings grow more quickly. Many financial experts consider an employer-sponsored "matching" plan to be the best way to save for retirement.

You can also save for retirement by opening an Individual Retirement Account (IRA). An IRA is an investment account that offers tax breaks as an incentive to save for retirement. You will need to choose what type of IRA to open, Roth or traditional, and how to invest the funds. IRA accounts may consist of CDs, stocks, bonds, mutual funds, other investments, and any combination of these. IRA accounts are opened by individuals and closely monitored by the Internal Revenue Service (IRS).

Before investing money in a retirement plan, be sure you fully understand it. The more complex the plan, the more you should seek advice from a certified financial planner or similar expert. Depending on your investment choices, your savings may or may not be insured. Insured savings tend to grow at slower rates.

What factors should you consider when deciding to open a savings account?

Activity

Visit the following Web sites: **ftc.gov**, **nasaa.org**, and **sec.gov**. Review the information available on avoiding investment fraud. Create a brochure that summarizes the information. Distribute the brochure to family and friends.

Resource

Why Save Money? reproducible master 26-2, TR. Use the adapted worksheet to reinforce chapter concepts in students who are low functioning.

Avoiding Investment Fraud

People who sell fraudulent investments use lies and trickery to entice consumers to hand over money. Usually these investments promise large returns and claim to have little or no risk. Unfortunately, people who put money into these schemes usually lose their full investment. See 26-8 for some common fraud schemes focused on investments.

Some selling tactics that signal fraud include selling investments only through social groups or clubs frequented by older adults. Since people nearing retirement often have the largest accounts, they are the biggest targets. Keep in mind that professional-looking brochures, offices, or Web sites are no guarantee of a legitimate company.

To protect yourself from fraud, always take time to examine the investment. Make sure the seller and the investment itself are properly registered/licensed with the state securities regulator. Become acquainted with the many ways to invest by reviewing information from regulatory agencies. The foremost agencies are the Federal Trade Commission (FTC), the North American Securities Administration Association (NASAA), and the U.S. Securities and Exchange Commission (SEC). If you don't understand how a certain investment plan works, don't invest in it. Finally, seek advice from a certified financial expert or similar expert whenever you need it.

Your Reading

What are some clues that an investment may be a fraud?

26-8
Recongnizing and avoiding fraudulent investments will protect your money.

Common Investment Scams

- Chain letters, brochures, or e-mails promising big rewards
- Foreign exchange trading
- "Great" investments that must be purchased immediately
- Internet services
- Investments available only over the phone
- Investments requiring checks made out to the salesperson
- No-risk business opportunities
- Offshore accounts
- Penny stocks
- Phone numbers with 900 codes
- Rare coins

Summary

Saving money is an important part of a personal money management plan. However, the reasons people save vary widely. The ways people save also vary.

Before you choose a financial institution, make sure its deposits are insured. Also check its interest rates and services. A savings account is a common way to save.

You need to plan carefully before buying a certificate of deposit. It will earn a fixed rate of interest and your money will be tied up for a set period of time. A money market account is an alternative to a certificate of deposit. The rate of interest may go up or down. Money market accounts can have deposits at any time and a limited number of withdrawals.

Buying U.S. savings bonds is a safe and easy way to save. The bonds earn good rates of interest and help support the government. Other forms of savings for the long-term are mutual funds and annuities. Long-term savings should be part of your planned saving strategy.

It is important to start saving for retirement early in your career. Retirement savings grow by earning interest over long periods of time.

Staying informed and researching investment opportunities will protect you from becoming a victim of investment fraud.

Reviewing Key Concepts

1. List five reasons for saving.
2. Which financial institutions are known as the department stores of finance?
3. Which financial institutions are primarily known for lending money to homebuyers?
4. Which financial institutions are owned by and operated for their members?
5. Which types of financial institutions are protected by FDIC? Which are protected by NCUA?
6. When both the principal and the earned interest continue to earn interest, that interest is known as ______.
7. True or false. Different financial institutions pay different rates of interest on savings accounts.
8. When you have a savings club account, what happens at the end of your savings period?
9. Why are U.S. savings bonds a safe way to save?
10. Which form of savings is linked to insurance?

Answers to *Reviewing Key Concepts*

1. (List five:) emergencies, possible job loss, travel and recreation, advanced education, major purchases, retirement
2. commercial banks
3. savings banks
4. credit unions
5. Commercial and savings banks are protected by FDIC. Credit unions are protected by NCUA.
6. compound
7. true
8. You receive a check for the amount you saved plus the interest you earned.
9. They are issued by the U.S. government and can be replaced if lost, stolen, or destroyed.
10. annuity

Building Academic Skills

1. **Art.** Design posters to illustrate reasons for saving. Display them throughout your school.
2. **Math.** If you deposit $135 in your bank account and receive five percent interest per year, how much interest will you receive in three months if interest is accumulated quarterly? What will your investment be worth in one year?
3. **Speaking.** Ask a representative of a financial institution to talk to your class about ways to save.
4. **Speaking.** Research U.S. savings bonds to find out how they originated. Share your findings with the class in a brief oral report.
5. **Speaking, writing.** Visit or call two financial institutions in your area. Request information on their current interest rates for a one-year, $1,000 CD. Also ask about the penalties for early withdrawal. Explain where you would buy the CD in a brief written report.

Building Technology Skills

1. Play a money game by going to one of the following Web sites: **moneytalks.ucr.edu**, **younginvestor.com/teens**, or **practicalmoneyskills.com/english/resources/games**. After playing, write a paragraph about what you learned.
2. Visit one of the following Web sites: **kidsbank.com**, **yacenter.org**, or **smithbarney.com/yin/home.htm**. Review the resources available on budgeting, saving, or investing. Calculate a savings plan for money you earn, such as an allowance. Adjust it for inflation, and determine its total in five years.
3. Use a software program to create a flyer on how to fill out a deposit slip for a savings account. Make the flyers colorful and post them around the school in an effort to encourage students to save money.
4. Conduct an Internet search to see how many savings clubs, such as holiday or vacation savings clubs, are available at local financial institutions. List the names of the savings clubs and write a one-sentence summary about each type of plan. Share your findings with the class.

Building Career Knowledge and Skills

1. Research the career opportunities available at financial institutions. What job skills are needed? Summarize your findings in one or two paragraphs.
2. Develop a slide show presentation on certificates of deposit, money market accounts, and U.S. savings bonds. Imagine you represent the financial institution offering these options to consumers. In a presentation, summarize the advantages of these investment options.

Building Workplace Skills

Visit two financial institutions in your area, checking the types of accounts that are available for students your age. Work with two or three classmates on this activity. Check the requirements, penalties, fees, and other obligations for each account. Also check the convenience, location, and banking hours of each institution. In which account would your money grow fastest? After finding answers to all the questions, determine where your team would prefer to bank. Explain why in a brief report to the class.

How can I use credit responsibly?

Chapter 27 Credit

Chapter Objectives

After studying this chapter, you will be able to

- **discuss** the advantages and disadvantages of using credit.
- **describe** four major types of credit.
- **list** ways to begin building a credit history.
- **describe** a person whom creditors would view as a good credit risk.
- **explain** the importance of a good credit rating.
- **list** ways to protect yourself from identity theft.

Key Terms

credit line
collateral
assets
cosigner
credit bureau
credit rating
credit agreement
identity theft

Key Concepts

- There are both advantages and disadvantages to using credit.
- There are four major types of credit.
- People with good credit ratings are viewed as good credit risks.
- You can protect yourself from identity theft.

Resource

Reinforcing Vocabulary, Activity A, WB. Students complete an activity using key terms from the chapter.

Discuss

Do you think people do a better job of keeping track of their money if they spend cash rather than use credit? Do you know families who do not use credit cards?

Resource

Credit Advantages and Disadvantages, Activity B, WB. Students apply their knowledge of credit advantages and disadvantages to their observations and personal decisions.

Making a Difference

Investigate how you can use a credit card to make a microloan. *Microloans* are small loans that help people in need start businesses and end the cycle of poverty. Visit **www.kiva.org** for more information. Write a report about the steps involved in the process of lending and repaying these kinds of loans.

Common Uses of Credit

Billboards and store windows are covered with signs that say, "Buy now, pay later!" Newspaper ads read, "Easy credit terms with no down payment!" Radio and TV commercials advertise offers for "one-day credit approval." These are familiar slogans. They encourage people to buy on credit. They make buying easy—sometimes too easy. They don't mention the fact that credit ends up making items cost more.

Credit can be good. It can help people buy homes, cars, and furniture. It can help people live more comfortably.

Credit, however, can be dangerous. It becomes dangerous when it is overused or abused. It can cause financial problems when people can't make the payments they owe. In some cases, financial problems may lead to other problems. They may cause family arguments. They may also cause stress, which can affect health.

Credit used wisely can enrich your lifestyle. Credit used poorly can create major problems. You need to know when and how to use credit.

Advantages of Credit

When used properly, credit has the following advantages:

- Credit is a convenience. You can shop and travel without the worry of carrying large amounts of cash, 27-1.
- Credit allows you to use goods and services while paying for them. Saving enough money to buy expensive items can be difficult. Credit helps you buy such items and pay for them over a period of time.
- Credit helps you meet financial emergencies. Unexpected costs due to sicknesses, accidents, and repairs can be handled through credit.

Disadvantages of Credit

Credit has some drawbacks, especially if it is overused. The following disadvantages of credit can become problems if credit is used unwisely:

- Credit encourages impulse buying. You might buy more than you need. You may overspend and have trouble repaying.

27-1
People often use credit cards while traveling to avoid the need to carry a lot of cash.

Resource

Don't Get Caught in the Credit Trap, color transparency CT-27, TR. Students discuss examples of consumers who get involved in credit misuse.

Activity

Create a billboard poster that advertises the advantages and disadvantages of credit. Display the posters in class.

Reflect

Would you rather carry cash or a credit card? Would you spend more if you carried only a credit card?

Discuss

Explain what this means: credit ties up future income.

- Credit can get you into serious debt. Many people lose items purchased with credit if they can't make the payments. The items are repossessed or taken back by the sellers.
- Credit makes the cost of goods and services higher. It is usually cheaper to pay cash than to use credit.
- Credit ties up your future income. Any raises you get may need to be used to pay off past credit charges.

When to Use Credit

You should always think carefully before using credit to make a purchase. Ask yourself the following questions: Can you do without the item now? Will you have problems paying back the debt? Are you already spending more than 20 percent of your take-home pay on installment debt? If you answer "yes" to these questions, try to avoid more credit at this time. It is likely that you cannot handle any more payments. Credit should work for you, not against you.

How can credit affect your lifestyle?

Discuss

How many different types of credit cards exist, to your knowledge?

Resource

Four Kinds of Credit, reproducible master 27-1, TR. Students compare and contrast the four types of credit discussed in the text.

Resource

The Cost of Credit, Activity C, WB. Students figure the costs of using various forms of credit.

Types of Credit

As a consumer, you should be aware of the following types of credit available to you:

- charge accounts
- credit cards
- installment credit
- loans

Charge Accounts

A charge account is the oldest type of credit offered by business to consumers. Usually no down payment is required nor is any interest charged. The consumer agrees to pay at a later date. If the consumer does not pay by the assigned date, a fee is usually added to the amount owed. An example of a business offering this type of credit is a utility company that provides natural gas or electricity.

Credit Cards

credit line
The maximum amount that can be charged on a credit card.

Banks, stores, and many other types of companies issue credit cards. See 27-2. When you apply for one, the issuer sets a maximum amount you can charge, called a ***credit line***. This amount is based on how much you earn and your ability to repay. For example, your maximum credit line may be $2,000. You can make any number of purchases as long as the total does not exceed $2,000.

Once a month, you receive a bill. You can pay the entire bill by the due date, which involves no added interest. The other option is to make monthly installment payments. You then have to pay interest on the unpaid balance.

Example

If a credit line is $1,000, and $900 worth of purchases were made during the month, the credit card company will not approve transactions that increase the account beyond $1,000. If this customer tries to buy a $200 TV set using the card, the salesperson will not be able to complete the transaction.

Activity

Make a list of the department stores in your area where students might shop. Find out if these stores also have their own credit cards.

Installment Credit

Many expensive household items, such as computers and refrigerators, are purchased with installment credit plans. In such a plan, you agree to make set payments over a given period of time. For this convenience, you pay the going interest rate plus any service charges. If you fail to make payments, the company can repossess the goods.

27-2
Department stores issue credit cards for consumers to use when buying clothing and household purchases.

Community Connections

Find out the cost of a home and a car you would like to own. Refer to homes from local real estate brochures and the local newspaper. Cut out pictures or descriptions of your "dream" purchases and write a paragraph explaining how you plan to pay for the items.

collateral
Something of value held by a lending institution in case a loan is not repaid.

Loans

Banks and other lending institutions offer credit in the form of loans. People take out loans to borrow money to pay for the following types of expenses:

- cars
- homes
- further education
- outstanding bills
- home improvements
- start-up expenses for a business
- vacations

The important point to remember about loans is that you have to pay back what you borrow plus interest. You can get a signature loan, which is a loan backed by your signature or promise to repay. Many loans, however, require you to put up collateral before you get the money. ***Collateral*** is something of value held by a lending institution in case you fail to repay. For instance, a bank may hold the title for your car until you have repaid your car loan. See 27-3.

When you need a loan, find out more about the different types of loans available to you. The interest charged and the repayment terms can vary considerably.

Your Reading

What are the four types of credit?

27-3
Any car you purchase does not legally belong to you until you have paid for it completely. The creditor keeps the title as collateral.

How to Obtain Credit

If you have never used credit, you have no credit history. If this is the case, you need to begin building a credit history. The following suggestions may help you:

- Establish a steady work record.
- Pay all bills promptly.
- Open a savings account and a checking account, and use them. This shows creditors that you can handle money.
- If your place of employment has a credit union, join it. Credit unions make loans available to their members at lower interest rates than some sources of credit.
- If you drive, apply for a gasoline credit card. Make occasional gas purchases on the card. Make sure you pay the total due on time.
- Purchase an item in a local department store using a lay-away plan. Make payments on time to develop a good credit record.
- Apply for a local department store credit card. Use the card for items you need. Stay within your budget plan.

Reflect
Would you prefer a used car that is more affordable or a new car that is more expensive and would require much bigger or longer credit payments? What are your reasons for your decision?

Discuss
Do you own anything that could be used as collateral? What are examples of items that are used as collateral?

Discuss
What do you think would happen to the economy if credit cards did not exist? How would this change lives? What impact would it have on the economy?

Creditors Look for Good Credit Risks

Creditors want to issue credit to people whom they feel are good credit risks. These are people who repay their debt. Therefore, creditors look for certain traits in people, 27-4. From a creditor's point of view, a good credit risk is a person who has the following traits:

- is honest
- has a job with a steady income
- made regular payments on past loan or credit purchases
- lived in the same community for a few years
- has assets

Assets are valuable possessions you own, such as a house or a car. Assets also include money you have in bank accounts and the value of stocks and bonds you own.

Discuss
Why do you think steady employment is an important consideration when creditors decide who may have one of their credit cards? What happens if you take a job transfer? If the company moves you to another location, is that considered steady employment?

assets
The valuable possessions a person owns, such as a house or a car.

Getting a First Loan

As a minor, it is difficult to borrow money. Generally, a person must be at least 18 years old. Even then, it may be difficult to borrow without a cosigner. A ***cosigner*** signs the loan agreement with the person who is borrowing the money. The cosigner must have a good credit history and guarantee

cosigner
A person who signs a loan with a borrower and is held responsible if the borrower does not pay back the loan.

27-4
Most creditors consider steady employment a requirement for someone who wants to obtain credit.

Reflect
How many people do you know who would be willing to be a cosigner for you?

Enrich
Investigate the number of loans taken out in the United States in a year. Find out how many loans are not repaid. Do you think lenders need to have tougher standards for people who apply for loans?

Discuss
When you lend another student money, is this a form of credit?

Activity
Divide the class into three groups: borrowers, lenders, and credit bureau employees. Have each group select a spokesperson to explain the responsibilities of each person in the credit system.

Discuss
How many students have received credit card applications in their name? How do you think someone under age 18 got on the lists to receive these applications?

Activity
Research credit bureaus. Find out what they do. Find out how they can help consumers. Write about what you learned.

Discuss
What information is asked on a credit application? Do you know all of the answers to the questions on the application? Could you fill out the application on your own right now?

Enrich
Credit bureaus keep records of negative credit ratings for many years. Find out exactly how long they keep these records on file.

credit bureau
An organization that gathers financial information on individuals for businesses to use as a credit reference.

repayment of the loan. In the event the borrower does not make the payments, the cosigner must make them.

You might need to ask a relative or friend to cosign your first loan. Be sure you make your payments. Before you sign for a loan, figure out whether you can afford to pay it back. It would be unfair to the cosigner if you failed to live up to your responsibility. It could also damage your ability to obtain credit in the future.

Credit Applications

Before credit is granted to anyone, the person's job history, credit history, and ability to repay are checked. When you apply for a credit card or loan, you must fill out a credit application. You will be asked to give the following information:

- name, address, and previous addresses
- current and former employers, including their addresses
- current job title (or military rank), salary, and number of years employed
- sources of additional income
- name of a close relative who is not living at your address
- existing sources of credit, including credit card accounts and loans
- all financial accounts, their account numbers, and the names and addresses of the financial institutions

Credit Bureaus and Credit Ratings

Complete all credit applications honestly. The information on your applications will be checked by ***credit bureaus***. Businesses depend on credit bureaus to gather financial information on individuals. Businesses make their decisions to grant or deny credit based on information in reports from credit bureaus.

Don't lie or try to hide information. If you give false information, you run the risk of being denied credit. Credit bureaus keep track of all your loans and lines of credit. They not only know how much credit you already have, they also know if you repay your debts on time.

A credit bureau reports your credit rating. Your ***credit rating*** is an estimate of how likely you are to pay your bills on time. The rating is based on past records of your credit behavior. Your credit rating reflects your level of risk. The more credit cards you have, the lower your credit rating will be. This is because creditors view the cards as potential debts.

If you handle credit well and pay your bills on time, you will have a good credit rating. However, if you abuse credit and fail to repay your debts, you will have a bad credit rating. If you have a bad credit rating, you may have trouble getting credit in the future. Creditors often do not lend money to people who have a history of not paying their bills. If they do lend money, it is at a higher rate. Credit ratings are also used to determine car insurance rates and car and home loan interest rates. If you have a poor credit rating, you will pay more. Work hard to protect your credit rating. Use credit wisely. Don't abuse it.

There may be times when you may not be able to make loan payments. If that happens, call your creditors and tell them the facts. Be honest. You may have lost your job. You may be very ill. Special arrangements could be made until your situation improves. When it does improve, make every effort to meet your obligations.

It is wise to check your credit report periodically to ensure that all the information is accurate. The FACT Act (Fair and Accurate Credit Transaction Act) entitles each U.S. resident to one free copy of his or her credit report from each credit-reporting agency once every 12 months.

credit rating
An estimate of how likely a person is to pay bills on time based on past records.

Community Connections

Invite a representative from the credit department of a local retailer to talk to the class about how to fill out a credit form, establish credit, and develop a good credit history. Ask the guest how his or her company judges a person as a "good credit risk." Prepare in advance the questions you want answered.

Resource

The Credit Game, Activity D, WB. Students review factors that review credit ratings.

Examine All Credit Agreements

Always read a credit agreement before you sign it. A ***credit agreement*** is a contract. It legally binds the lender and the borrower to the credit terms defined. It is important for you to read and understand what you are signing. Some common credit terms you might encounter on credit agreements are listed in 27-5.

Don't be rushed into signing a credit agreement. Study the agreement before you sign it. Never sign a credit agreement that has blanks. Make sure that all numbers are correct. Don't overlook the finance charges.

credit agreement
A written contract that legally binds a lender and a borrower to specific credit terms.

Activity

Make a list of ways a student can establish a credit rating. Put a star by the items on your list that would be easy for you to do.

27-5
Before you sign a credit agreement, know what these terms mean.

Credit Terms

- **Annual fee:** A flat, yearly charge similar to a membership fee. (Many companies offer "no annual fee" cards, and lenders who do charge annual fees are often willing to waive them to keep your business.)
- **Finance charge:** The dollar amount you pay to use credit. (In addition to interest costs, this may include other charges such as cash advance fees, which are charged against your card when you borrow cash from the lender. You generally pay higher interest on cash advances than on purchases.)
- **Annual percentage rate (APR):** The yearly percentage rate of the finance charge.
- **Grace period:** A time period, usually about 25 days, during which you can pay your credit card bill without paying a finance charge. (Under most credit card plans, the grace period only applies if you pay your balance in full each month. It does not apply if you carry a balance forward. Also, the grace period does not apply to cash advances.)
- **Fixed rate:** A fixed annual percentage rate of the finance charge.
- **Variable rate:** Prime rate (which varies) plus an added percentage. (For instance, your rate may be the prime rate plus 5.9 percent.)
- **Introductory rate:** A temporary, lower APR that usually lasts for about six months before converting to the normal fixed or variable rate.

Activity
Collect various credit agreement forms and make an informative poster. Have students evaluate the information presented.

Resource
What Does It Take to Get a Credit Card? reproducible master 27-2, TR. Use the adapted worksheet to reinforce chapter concepts in students who are low functioning.

Your Reading
Why is a good credit rating important?

Ask questions if you are not sure of something in the agreement. You could also seek advice from someone knowledgeable in money matters. If you are in doubt, you should write *no.* When you are satisfied with the contract, sign it. Then be sure to live up to the agreement.

Identity Theft

identity theft
Theft that occurs when someone uses your personal information, such as your name, social security number, or credit card number without your permission to commit fraud or other crimes.

Protecting your credit may be more important than establishing credit. ***Identity theft*** occurs when someone uses your personal information, such as your name, social security number, or credit card number, without your permission to commit fraud or other crimes. An identity thief may rent an apartment, obtain a credit card, or establish a telephone account in your name. You may not find out about the theft until you review your credit report or a credit card statement and notice charges you didn't make—or until you are contacted by a debt collector. Some identity theft victims can resolve their problems quickly, while others spend a great deal of time and money trying to repair damage to their name and credit records. Some people who are victims of identity theft may lose out on job opportunities, or be denied loans for education, housing, or cars because of negative information on their credit reports. In some cases, they may even be arrested for crimes they did not commit.

Tips for protecting yourself from identity theft are listed in 27-6. If your identity is stolen or compromised, file a police report, notify creditors, and monitor financial records.

Your Reading

What is identity theft and how can it affect you?

Protect Yourself from Identity Theft

- Be aware if someone is looking over your shoulder when you are using an ATM or making store purchases.
- Don't leave your receipt behind at the ATM. This could make you vulnerable to fraud.
- Never give your credit card number over the phone unless you initiated the call. Avoid giving your card number out over a cordless phone. Radio scanners can eavesdrop on conversations on cordless phones.
- Make certain you get your card back after you make a purchase. A good way to do this is to leave your wallet open in your hand until you have the card back.
- Always keep a list of your credit cards, credit card numbers, and credit card company numbers in case your card is lost or stolen.
- Shred bank and credit statements and credit card offers before throwing them away. Don't mail checks from your home mailbox. Drop them off at the post office. Also, have new checks delivered to your bank, not your home.
- Obtain your credit reports and scores. Make sure you recognize all the account information listed.
- Close out unused credit cards. Cutting them up is not enough.
- Avoid giving out your social security number. It is the prime target of identity thieves. Never put your social security number on your checks or your credit receipts.
- Install a firewall and buy virus-protection software. If you dispose of a computer, remove data with a disk wipe utility program.
- Don't use the same password for all your accounts. Avoid using easily identifiable words or numbers.

27-6
These tips can help to protect you from being a victim of identity theft.

Discuss

Have you or has anyone you know been a victim of identity theft?

Adapting the Lesson

Have students who are high functioning conduct an online search using the term *credit card fraud*. Ask them to write a one-page summary of their findings. Students are to list ways people can protect themselves from credit card fraud.

Summary

Credit is easily available in today's society. Used wisely, it can be helpful. If abused, it can be dangerous. Always think carefully before using credit. Be sure you will be able to pay for it later.

Four major types of credit are charge accounts, credit cards, installment credit, and loans. Before using them, you should understand how they work. Know what costs and responsibilities are involved.

Although you may not need credit now, you should start thinking about building a credit history. Learn about credit applications, ratings, and agreements. Become familiar with the different types of credit and credit terms.

Avoid becoming a victim of identity theft. An identity thief can steal information to obtain credit in your name. There are ways to protect yourself from identity theft.

Reviewing Key Concepts

1. List three advantages of credit.
2. List four disadvantages of credit.
3. True or false. A charge account usually involves a large down payment and a high interest rate.
4. When you receive a monthly credit card bill, what are your two options?
5. True or false. To buy something using an installment credit plan, a person agrees to make set payments over a given period of time.
6. Why might a lending institution ask for collateral before making a loan?
7. Name three ways to begin building a credit history.
8. Describe five traits of a person who is a good credit risk.
9. What risk does the cosigner of a loan take?
10. What should you do if your identity has been stolen or compromised?

Answers to *Reviewing Key Concepts*

1. (List three: Student response.)
2. (List four: Student response.)
3. false
4. pay the entire bill by the due date or make monthly payments that include paying interest on the unpaid balance
5. true
6. to hold the rights to an item of value in case a person fails to repay the loan
7. (Name three:) Open a savings account and a checking account. Join a credit union. Apply for a gasoline credit card and pay the balance each month. Make a lay-away purchase. Apply for a local department store's credit card and pay the balance.
8. (List five: Student response.)
9. If the borrower does not make the payments, the cosigner must make the payments.
10. You should file a police report, notify creditors, and monitor financial records.

Building Academic Skills

1. **Speaking, Listening.** Debate whether credit causes impulse buying.
2. **Speaking.** Imagine you are a loan officer at a bank in charge of writing a description of the type of borrowers to whom you would lend money. Describe the assets and qualifications you would expect of potential borrowers before you would recommend that the bank would grant them a loan.
3. **Writing.** Thomas Jefferson has been quoted as saying, "Never spend your money before you have it." Write a paragraph about what you think this means and a second paragraph on what you think would be in Thomas Jefferson's wallet today if he were living.

Building Career Knowledge and Skills

1. Investigate the costs and interest rates of three different credit cards. Use the information to prepare a comparison chart.
2. Agree or disagree with this statement: Credit companies should not issue credit cards to students. Prepare a report that explains your position.
3. Research what is involved in using an installment credit plan to buy a computer. What steps do you need to take? How much interest would you pay? What is the final cost of the computer with the added cost of the interest?
4. Research what types of information are used to calculate a person's credit rating/score.

Building Technology Skills

1. Use the following Web sites to investigate how high of a credit line you would be allowed: **calcbuilder.com/cgi-bin/calcs/HEL1.cgi/financenter**, **federalreserve.gov/pubs/HomeLine**, and **compassweb.com/personal/calculators**. Share examples you used on the Web site and what you learned about credit lines.
2. Use a spreadsheet program to document the results of a credit survey you conduct with five adults living in different households. Find out what form of payment people used to make the following five purchases: the primary car of the household, clothes washer, refrigerator, television set, and CD player. Eliminate actual names from the survey.
3. Conduct online research on the topic of good credit risks. Report your findings in a report. Share three sentences to summarize what you learned.

Building Workplace Skills

Working with three or four of your classmates, find the least expensive way to buy a new car, financing it for four years. (As a class, choose one category to explore, such as a two-door compact or a sports utility vehicle.) Check the cost of the car through local dealers versus sources available on the Internet. Check at least five different credit sources. Prepare a written report indicating where your team would buy the car, at what cost, and with what type of financing. What are the monthly payments? What is the cost of financing? Are there any special costs involved? What is the total cost of the new car with all the related costs added? Present your conclusions to the class.

What can insurance do for me?

Chapter 28 Insurance

Key Terms

policy
premium
deductible
health maintenance organization (HMO)
preferred provider organization (PPO)
life insurance
dividend
disability insurance
property insurance
insurance claim

Chapter Objectives

After studying this chapter, you will be able to

- **describe** types of automobile insurance coverage.
- **explain** the importance of health insurance as a fringe benefit of a job.
- **compare** and **contrast** the three forms of life insurance.
- **list** reasons for buying property insurance.
- **explain** how to file an insurance claim.

Key Concepts

- Automobile, health, life, disability, and property insurance provide financial protection.
- An insurance claim must be filed to recover losses.

Financial Protection

Determining your insurance needs should be part of your money management plan. Insurance provides you with financial protection. It is important to shop for insurance just as you would shop for a car. Compare the policies of many insurance companies. Then choose one that is right for you.

Insurance is purchased in the form of a policy. A ***policy*** is a legal contract. It describes your rights and responsibilities as well as those of the insurance company. As you read an insurance policy, you will see the terms *insured* and *insurer.* When you purchase insurance, you are the insured. The insurance company is the insurer. The amount of money you pay for insurance is called a ***premium.***

To purchase insurance, you must complete a written application. Read the application carefully. Be sure you understand the questions before you complete and sign the form. If there is something you do not understand, ask questions. Get help by talking to an insurance agent, a person familiar with insurance, or a lawyer. Understand the policy's benefits. Don't wait until you need to file a claim. (Filing a claim is discussed later in this chapter.)

Automobile Insurance

Several types of coverage should be considered when purchasing automobile insurance. One type is liability insurance. *Liability insurance* protects you against the claims of other people. It also protects you if you give someone else permission to drive your car and that person has an accident. Liability insurance is required in most states, and it is very important to have.

Liability insurance is divided into two categories: bodily injury and property damage. *Bodily injury insurance* protects you against court actions or claims for injuries to other people. It protects you against lawsuits for accidents for which you are responsible.

Property damage insurance protects other people's property against damage that you cause. It covers the cost of repairs to the other driver's car if you are at fault in an accident. It also covers the cost of repairing telephone poles, traffic lights, and guardrails if you damage them in an accident. Property damage does not cover the costs of repairing your own car. See 28-1.

Resource

Reinforcing Vocabulary, Activity A, WB. Students match vocabulary terms with their definitions.

policy
A legal contract describing the rights and responsibilities of a person purchasing insurance and those of the company offering it.

premium
The amount of money paid for insurance.

Reflect

How much do you know about insurance right now? How many different types of insurance do your family members have?

Discuss

Do you know the company through which your parents have car insurance? health, life, and property insurance?

Vocabulary

What does *premium* mean as it relates to insurance? Use it in a sentence to demonstrate understanding.

Reflect

What is your reaction to learning about the responsibility of having car insurance? How do you feel about the cost of insurance?

Resource

Types of Car Insurance, color transparency CT-28, TR. Students are introduced to the various types of car insurance available and the importance of each.

28-1
An insurance agent can help people decide what type of insurance coverage they need.

Activity
Create a poster to identify and describe the various types of car insurance. Include information that would be helpful to other students. Display the posters around the school.

Collision insurance pays for repairs to your car even if you are at fault, 28-2. Collision insurance is often required if you finance a car. It protects the lien holder if the car is damaged. Usually, you must pay a certain amount of money for the repairs. The insurance company pays the rest. The amount you pay is called the ***deductible***. It is usually $200, $500, $1,000, or a percentage of the total cost. If your car is several years old, you may not need to purchase collision insurance. The car may not be worth the cost of the premiums and the deductible.

deductible
The amount a policyholder must pay before an insurance company will pay a claim.

Community Connections

Search the Web site of a automobile insurance company to find out what information the site provides to entice new customers. Report your findings to the class. Explain whether it will be important in your future decisions for the automobile insurance company you choose to maintain a helpful Web site.

Uninsured/underinsured motorist insurance provides for recovery of damages for any injury received from an uninsured/underinsured driver. In the event of an accident involving an uninsured/underinsured driver, the insurance company pays the difference between what the uninsured/underinsured driver can pay and what the injured driver is entitled to receive. This coverage also protects you in a hit-and-run situation if a driver flees the scene of an accident without leaving sufficient identification information. This type of insurance is required in some states.

Car insurance premiums vary a great deal. They are determined by a rating system used by insurance companies. The rating system includes the following factors:

- driving record of the owner(s)
- age of the driver(s)
- home address

28-2
In many states, it is unlawful to drive without having insurance coverage.

- type of car driven
- whether the car is used for business or personal use
- number of miles traveled each year
- whether the car is kept in a garage or outdoors
- satisfactory completion of a driver education course (for new drivers)
- academic record and grades

The amount of deductible a driver is willing to pay also affects the cost of car insurance. The most important factor is probably your driving record. People with good driving records pay lower insurance premiums.

Health Insurance

Health insurance helps people pay the costs of medical care. Some health insurance plans pay for all the costs. Most plans only provide for partial payments.

Health insurance usually covers hospital stays and examinations by physicians. Some also pay for prescription drugs, eyeglasses, and dental work. See 28-3.

Many employers usually provide a group insurance plan for full-time employees and pay a portion of it. Some

Resource

Car Insurance Costs, Activity B, WB. Students contact a local insurance company to obtain policy prices for the car of their choice.

Resource

The Cost of a Broken Leg, reproducible master 28-1, TR. Students attempt to estimate all costs involved with repairing a broken leg.

Adapting the Lesson

Have students who are high functioning research what percentage of the U.S. population has no health insurance of any type. Ask students to provide a brief description of the people who fall into this category. Have students find out what the leading proposal is to provide a form of universal health care to cover uninsured citizens. What is the proposed cost of the plan and possible impact on taxes?

28-3
Members of a health insurance plan often have the option to buy dental and eye-care coverage for an extra fee.

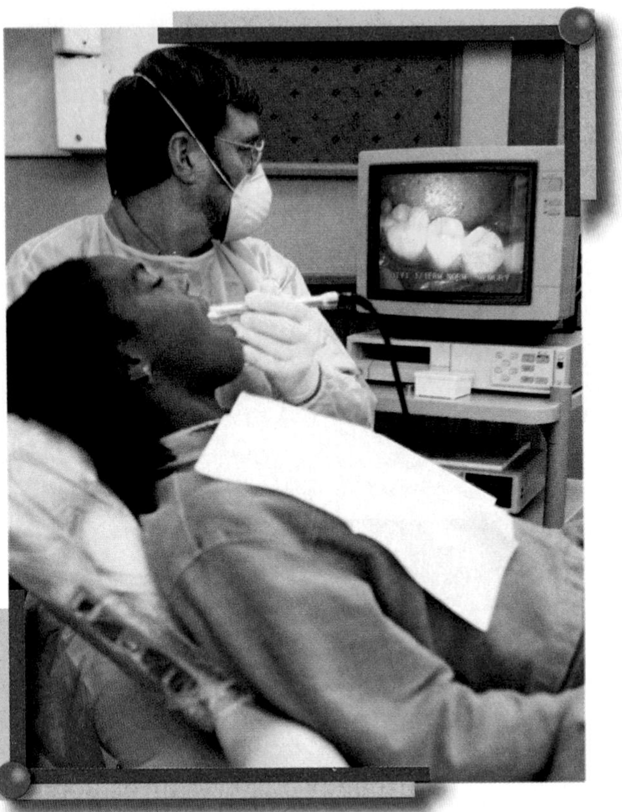

Activity
Research HMOs to write a paragraph about the role they play in the nation's health care system.

Discuss
When you have a doctor who you completely trust, do you feel it is worthwhile to switch to another doctor if you can receive comparable service for less cost?

Enrich
Find out how much a visit to the doctor costs. How much is a dental exam and routine cleaning? How many hours would you have to work at minimum wage to pay for these out of your pocket?

employers allow employees to pay for coverage of family members. Getting group insurance through a company usually costs less than buying health insurance on your own. Company-sponsored health insurance is a valuable fringe benefit. When you begin a job, study the health care plan your employer offers. Find out what it covers.

Even if you have health insurance, some doctors require payment when you receive treatment. Other doctors will wait until the insurance company pays them. Then they will send you a bill for the balance due.

Some employers offer their employees membership in *managed health care plans*. Since managed care plans vary greatly in benefits and out-of-pocket expenses, it is important to review your health insurance choices wisely and try to find the best policy to fit your needs. HMOs and PPOs are examples of managed health care plans.

A ***health maintenance organization (HMO)*** covers most health care services. Set fees are paid in advance. Then when you need medical attention, you go to a doctor or hospital associated with the HMO. Depending on your policy, you receive care often with a *co-pay* (an additional charge).

health maintenance organization (HMO)
A managed health care plan insurance for which members pay a set fee and receive medical care, as needed, from a participating doctor or hospital.

Another form of health insurance is offered by a ***preferred provider organization (PPO)***. A PPO is an organization of doctors or hospitals. They contract with an insurance company to provide health services. Like an HMO, if you use doctors in the PPO, a co-pay is often required. You can choose other doctors and hospitals, but the fees are higher and you will be responsible for paying the difference.

preferred provider organization (PPO)
A managed health care plan in which an organization of doctors or hospitals contract with an insurance company to provide health services.

Life Insurance

Life insurance is designed to provide financial security to the family of the insured, if that person dies. To purchase life insurance, a person may have to take a physical examination. If a physical is not required, the insured may have a waiting period before a policy will go into full effect. Like health insurance, life insurance may be provided to full-time employees as a fringe benefit.

life insurance
Insurance designed to provide financial security to the family of the insured, if that person dies.

After the death of the insured, the face value of the policy is paid to the beneficiary. The policy owner names the beneficiary when he or she buys the policy. In most cases, the beneficiary is a spouse or family member.

Whole life insurance provides the insured with permanent coverage. The policy is in effect until the insured dies or the policy is cashed in. Premiums for most of these policies do not increase over the life of the policy.

Whole life insurance gains cash value over a period of years. This is because a portion of what you pay in premiums earns interest like the money in your savings account. Some whole life policies pay dividends. A ***dividend*** is a payout on money earned. Dividends are usually paid on an annual basis. The dividends can be left in the policy and accumulate interest, or they can be applied toward the purchase of additional insurance. As long as you keep the policy, the cash value grows. After a period of time, you can turn in your policy for its cash value. However, once you cash in your policy, you are no longer insured under that policy.

dividend
A payout, usually annual, on money earned on whole life insurance.

Reflect
Are you aware of the benefits of life insurance? Do you know any widows or widowers who live on the proceeds of life insurance?

Vocabulary
What is the meaning of dividend as it pertains to insurance? Use the word in a sentence to demonstrate understanding.

Discuss
Do you think average, healthy, 18-year-olds living on their own need life insurance? health insurance?

Term life insurance is purchased for a limited period of time, such as five or 10 years. At the end of this time, the policy may be renewed. The premiums for term life insurance are less than the premiums for whole life insurance. However, the premiums increase with each renewal. Term life policies do not gain cash value.

Discuss
Why do insurance companies set limits on the amounts they will pay over a lifetime? Why are some diseases or disabilities not covered by ordinary insurance?

Variable-rate life insurance is another form. In many respects, a variable-rate insurance contract is similar to whole life insurance. The policy provides a guaranteed life benefit. This form of insurance is also an investment tool. You contribute a part of your premiums to investment options. The cash surrender value of this type of policy can greatly increase if your investments are successful. It can also decrease if your choices are unsuccessful. This form of policy is not for everyone. However, they do offer both the single and married person an option. The policy offers a guaranteed life benefit. It also builds cash that can later be withdrawn, similar to an annuity (discussed in Chapter 26).

Deciding how much life insurance to buy is not easy, 28-4. Each person has different financial needs. Generally, a single person has few financial responsibilities. Thus, he or she needs less life insurance than a married person with children.

disability insurance
Insurance that provides for people who become unable to work due to serious illness or injury. It allows disabled employees to receive a percentage of their incomes for an extended period of time.

Disability Insurance

For many young workers, disability insurance is even more important than life insurance. ***Disability insurance*** provides for people who become unable to work due to serious illness or injury. It allows disabled employees to receive a percentage of their incomes for an extended period of time.

28-4
Deciding which type and how much life insurance to buy depends on your financial responsibilities.

Employers often provide this type of coverage as part of their fringe benefit packages. However, policies vary greatly. If you have disability coverage through your employer, read the policy carefully. Evaluate the specific benefits and terms of the policy. Then decide whether you need to purchase additional coverage.

Property Insurance

Whether you rent or own a home, you should insure your property. ***Property insurance*** protects your possessions against fire, theft, or other types of loss. Property insurance also provides liability coverage in the event that someone is injured in your home.

property insurance
Insurance that protects your possessions against fire, theft, or other types of loss. Property insurance also provides liability coverage in the event that someone is injured in your home.

A home fire occurs at least once a minute. Home fires account for billions of dollars in property damage each year. Much more than that is lost each year in thefts and burglaries. Property insurance is a way to protect yourself against such losses.

Be certain the policy you purchase has the type of coverage you need. A renter's insurance policy should cover personal belongings, furniture, appliances, and some jewelry. A homeowner's insurance policy should cover all that and the building itself.

Needs for property insurance may be dictated by various situations. For instance, homeowners or renters may own very expensive jewelry or electronics. They may need an insurance rider to cover those items. An *insurance rider* is a separate mini-policy or clause that extends your homeowners policy to cover the extra value of items that may be excluded under contents insurance or may limit reimbursement to an amount far below the actual value of those items. People who live in areas prone to hurricanes may need hurricane insurance, while those in areas that may flood, may want flood insurance.

Resource
Personal Property Inventory, Activity C, WB. Students take an inventory of their property.

Activity
List the assets you currently possess that should be included in your personal property inventory for insurance purposes.

Standard property insurance covers your belongings for what they are worth at the time you file a claim. For instance, suppose your four-year-old television is stolen. Your insurance company may only give you about 60 percent of what you paid for it four years ago.

An option in property insurance that pays the full cost of new items is called *replacement value coverage*. This type of coverage costs more. However, you may find the extra cost worthwhile if you ever need to make a claim.

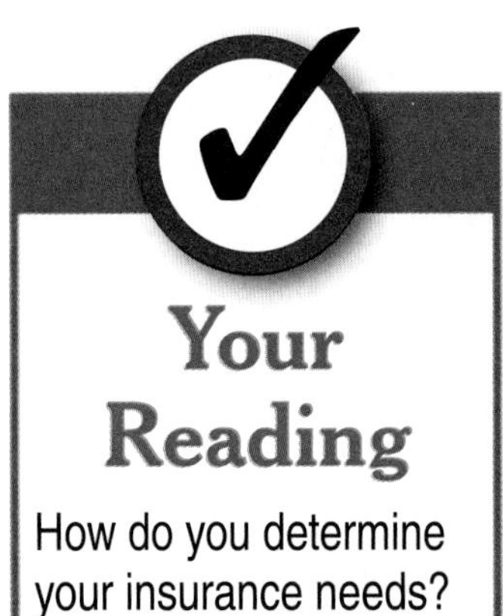

How do you determine your insurance needs?

An inventory, or list, of all of your possessions can help you decide how much property insurance to buy. An inventory also provides a record of your valuables. Such a record would help you file a claim if your valuables were stolen or destroyed in a fire. See 28-5. Photographs or a video of your possessions will help verify the condition and type of item lost if you have a claim. Update photos and/or videos and store them in a safe place other than your home.

Filing a Claim

insurance claim
Requesting payment from your insurance company for a covered loss.

Filing an ***insurance claim*** means requesting payment from your insurance company for a covered loss. For instance, you would file a claim on your car insurance after an accident. You would file a claim on your property insurance after a fire.

28-5
A personal property inventory can help determine the amount of coverage needed.

Inventory of LIVING ROOM Item Description (Include brand name, model #, and/or serial # when possible)	Date of Purchase	Purchase Price and Tax	Place of Purchase
1. SOFA THOMASVILLE, SINWP	5-2-07	$1,159.17	THE FURNITURE PLACE
2. COFFEE TABLE BRASS/GLASS, 141F	11-26-07	$368.45	HOME DECORATORS
3. CEILING FAN W/LIGHT FIXTURE OAK/BRASS, C781153	1-7-08	$297.65	FAN-TASIC
4. BOOKCASE O'SULLIVAN, 121LLY	2-1-08	$425.00	FURNITURE MART
5. FLOOR RUG HANDMADE, INDIAN, 5'7" X 8'4"	6-11-08	$856.93	RUGS TO RICHES
6. SONY 42" FLAT SCREEN LCD HD TV MODEL UC 765489	10-2-08	$1,378.45	BIG J'S ELECTRONICS

Activity
List the TV commercials you have seen about filing an insurance claim. What insurance company commercials have you seen?

Each insurance company may want you to file your claim a bit differently. You will need to provide a list of the valuables that were damaged or destroyed. Other types of information may be required. You may need to describe the details of the accident. Talk with your agent to find out what action you should take.

Make insurance claims wisely. If you file frequent claims or many small claims, your insurance rate may increase or your policy may be cancelled. If you file a false claim, you may be arrested and fined or imprisoned.

Your Reading

What does it mean to file an insurance claim?

Community Connections

Invite an insurance company representative to class to discuss the process for filing car insurance and property insurance claims. Ask the guest to highlight what you need to know to be able to file your first claim properly. In advance, prepare a list of questions to ask.

Resource

Understanding Insurance, Activity D, WB. Students answer questions about insurance concepts covered in the chapter.

Resource

What Do I Need to Know About Insurance? reproducible master 28-2, TR. Use the adapted worksheet to reinforce chapter concepts in students who are low functioning.

Summary

You should shop for insurance to be sure you get the kind of financial protection you need. Read the policies. Know what they cover. Understand the benefits they offer.

Liability insurance is an important part of automobile insurance. It includes both bodily injury insurance and property damage insurance. You may also want to buy collision insurance to pay for repairs to your own car. Uninsured/underinsured motorist insurance is another type of automobile insurance that can protect you.

Health insurance helps pay the costs of medical care. Many employers provide some form of health insurance to full-time employees. It is a valuable fringe benefit.

Life insurance provides financial security to survivors after the death of the insured. Whole life insurance stays in effect until the insured dies or until the policy is turned in for its cash value. Term life insurance is for a limited period of time. When the time period is over, the insured is no longer protected. Variable-rate insurance provides you with an opportunity to determine your own rate of dividend return.

Property insurance protects personal possessions. It also protects the policyholder against liability. A renter's policy covers the contents of a home. A homeowner's policy protects the building as well as its contents.

When you need to file an insurance claim, contact your agent. Follow the steps necessary to receive benefits from your insurance policy.

Reviewing Key Concepts

1. What is the name of the money a person pays for insurance?
2. What legal contract describes the rights and responsibilities of a person buying insurance and the insurance company?
3. What type of insurance would protect you if you caused a car accident that dented someone else's car and a guardrail?
4. What type of insurance would protect you if you caused a car accident in which people were hurt?
5. What type of insurance pays for repairs to a car you own?
6. What term identifies the amount paid to cover loss or damage before the insurance company pays the remainder?
7. What is paid to the beneficiary of a life insurance policy when the insured dies?
8. What is paid to the insured when a whole life policy is turned in before death?
9. What is permanent life insurance called?
10. What must you do to receive payment from an insurance company for a covered loss?

Answers to *Reviewing Key Concepts*

1. premium
2. policy
3. property damage insurance
4. bodily injury insurance
5. collision insurance
6. deductible
7. face value
8. cash value
9. whole life insurance
10. file a claim

Building Academic Skills

History. Examine the development of life insurance by answering the following questions: When and where were the first policies offered? Before life insurance companies existed, what generally provided financial security to the families of people who met untimely deaths? Provide a written or oral summary of your findings.

Building Technology Skills

1. Conduct an online search using the term *financial protection*. List the categories of Web site hits found and the insurance companies listed. Report your findings to the class.
2. Research the work done by the Insurance Institute for Highway Safety by searching the Institute's Web site at **hwysafety.org**. Examine the types of crash tests conducted by the Institute's Vehicle Research Center and summarize them in a brief report to share with the class.
3. Use a computer program to design a personal property inventory form similar to Figure 28-5. Try filling out the form by focusing just on the items in your bedroom. Share information regarding how far you progressed with the project and what lessons you learned. Were you able to complete the form and total the original purchase prices of items?

Building Career Knowledge and Skills

1. Investigate the difference between buying a health insurance policy and becoming a member of an HMO. Which would you prefer? Why? Explain your answers in a written report.
2. Study several life insurance policies. Make a comparison chart of their costs and benefits.
3. Make an inventory of your possessions. Decide how much property insurance you would need to cover them in case of loss. Call an insurance company to find out how much the premium would cost.
4. Research the different needs for insurance as a homeowner and as a renter. Prepare a chart showing the differences between the two. Discuss this difference with your class.
5. Find out what you should do to file a claim when you are in a car accident.

Building Workplace Skills

Talk to an automobile insurance agent about the cost of automobile coverage and the factors that affect premiums. Find out specific premium costs for the car of your choice for a person with a new driver's license and no driving experience. What can be done to reduce the premiums? Obtain information about premium costs from two other car insurers either via phone or the Internet. Use the same make and model of car throughout this exercise. Using a computer, create a chart comparing premiums. Where would you buy insurance for your imaginary car? Make a brief presentation to the class.

Part Seven

Growing Toward Independence

29 A Place to Live
30 Transportation
31 Being a Responsible Citizen

Where will I be able to live?

Chapter 29 A Place to Live

Key Terms

real estate agency
rental agency
verbal agreement
lease
security deposit

Chapter Objectives

After studying this chapter, you will be able to

- **weigh** the advantages and disadvantages of living at home, with a roommate, and on your own.
- **list** ways to look for a place to live.
- **evaluate** housing options according to a person's needs and budget.
- **describe** ideas for furnishing an apartment on a limited budget.
- **explain** the legal responsibilities involved in signing a lease.

Key Concepts

- Before deciding where to live, it is wise to consider the advantages and disadvantages of each option you have.
- When looking for a place to live, consider housing needs and costs.
- Furnishing an apartment can be expensive.
- You take on legal responsibilities when you sign a lease.

Where Will You Live?

As you mature and grow toward independence, you will face many decisions. One may be where to live. You may be able to choose whether to live at home, with a roommate, or on your own. Before deciding where to live, consider the advantages and disadvantages of each option you have. See 29-1.

Living at Home

Many people look forward to leaving home once they enter the workplace. They want the change of pace and new challenges that living away from home offers. On the other hand, some people feel comfortable with their home lives. They are in no hurry to move out.

Living at home has many advantages for young workers. One big advantage is cost. Even if you pay room and board, living at home usually costs less than renting an apartment.

Another advantage is having the company of your family. Not only do family members provide companionship, they also provide assistance. Household chores, such as cooking, cleaning, and laundry, can be shared with others.

However, living at home can have some disadvantages. For instance, you may not be able to be as independent as you want. Your family's social activities may be different from yours. Your family's routines may be different from yours, too.

Making a Difference

Contact a local Habitat for Humanity office. If possible, interview people who volunteer for the organization. What is its purpose? How does it make a difference in communities? Ask about volunteer opportunities in which you could participate.

29-1
When young people begin earning full-time incomes, they often consider new living arrangements.

Resource

Reinforcing Vocabulary, Activity A, WB. Students match vocabulary terms with their definitions.

Activity

Write a contract that would be fair to both you and your parents if you decided to live at home after graduating from high school. Include the chores and responsibilities that you would handle and identify how you would satisfy your financial responsibilities.

Resource

Roommate Wanted, reproducible master 29-1, TR. Students are questioned about the type of roommate they would prefer.

Living with a Roommate

Choosing to live away from home is a big decision. If you want to live with a roommate, try to find someone with a lifestyle similar to yours. A roommate can become a lifelong friend or a terrible enemy. See 29-2.

Living with a roommate has some of the same advantages of living with family members. You can share expenses with a roommate. You have companionship and may meet new friends. You also have someone with whom to share household work.

Living with a roommate may also have some disadvantages. You may not get along with each other or with each other's friends. You may have different tastes in food and decorating. Your roommate may be sloppier or neater than you are. Your roommate may not understand your way of life. Also, your roommate may not pay his or her portion of the bills or rent on time, which could affect your credit rating.

29-2
Friends who share common interests usually make compatible roommates.

Discuss

What reasons would you list for wanting a roommate? What reasons would you list for wanting to live at home? Do the same advantages and disadvantages listed in the text apply to you?

Reflect

How will you handle conflicts with your roommate? What are your options if you have a hard-to-get-along-with roommate at college?

Living on Your Own

Only you can decide if you are ready to live alone. This new experience may be a big change from the environment you know best.

The chief advantage of living alone is that you are totally independent. You decide when, where, and how you are going to do things. You can choose your own furnishings, food, TV programs, and music.

As a disadvantage, living alone can be lonely sometimes. Also, you are responsible for all the household expenses. In addition, you must do all the cleaning, cooking, and laundry.

Reflect

If you could choose to live anywhere in the United States, where would you choose? Do you feel it is important to live near your family?

Looking for a Place to Live

You can start to look for a place to live by asking your family and friends if they know of anything available. Another good place to start looking for a place to live is on the Internet. See 29-3. You can search for thousands of apartments, rooms, or houses for rent all over the country. You can also look in the newspaper, under the

Your Reading

What are three options to consider when deciding where to live?

29-3
The Internet or the classified ads in the newspaper are good places to start a search for an apartment.

Resource

A Place to Live, color transparency CT-29, TR. Students are introduced to the types of housing options available.

Activity

Using apartment rental and real estate brochures available in a grocery store, cut out three ads for each of the following two categories: *apartments for rent* and *houses to rent* that express your housing preferences. Make a chart to compare features and costs.

classified ads in the real estate section of the newspaper. Look under the heading *Rental Properties* or *Apartments for Rent.*

Other sources of information are ***real estate agencies.*** They deal primarily with the buying and selling of houses. However, some real estate agents can help you find places to rent. Look online or in the Yellow Pages of the phone book to find real estate agencies that handle rental apartments and houses.

real estate agency
A business that assists customers with buying and selling houses.

A ***rental agency*** can also help you find an apartment. It is a business that assists customers in the renting of apartments for a fee.

rental agency
A business that, for a fee, assists customers with renting apartments.

A rental agency is different from a real estate agency. The apartment owner pays the real estate agency a commission after the property is rented. You pay a fee to a rental agency before you find an apartment. After you pay the fee, the rental agency will refer you to apartments or houses available to rent. However, paying the fee is no guarantee that you will find a place to live.

What are good sources of information when looking for a place to live?

Housing Needs and Costs

As you look at places to live, think about your housing needs. Also think about the costs related to housing. The following questions may help you:

- Do you need a single room, apartment, or house?
- How much rent can you afford to pay? Some guidelines say to allow one-fourth of your salary for housing costs. Others suggest that you limit rent and utilities to one-third of your take-home pay. You must decide what you can afford based on your income and other expenses.
- How much should you expect to pay for utilities? Check to see which utilities are included in your rental payments, if any. Utilities may include electricity, gas, water, telephone, and waste disposal. Most utility bills must be paid monthly. Many companies require deposits from new utility users until they have proved they pay their bills on time.
- What furnishings and utensils do you need to buy? A bed, sofa, table, and chairs come to mind right away. Have you thought about sheets, towels, dishes, pots, and pans? Cleansers, buckets, and brooms cost money, too. Setting up a household can be expensive.

Resource
Move It! reproducible master 29-2, TR. Students examine the advantages and disadvantages of using professional movers.

Adapting the Lesson
Have students who are low functioning make a list in words or pictures of all of the tasks they would have to handle when living on their own. Have them create another list of responsibilities that could be shared with a roommate.

Resource
Housing Costs, Activity D, WB. Students estimate the cost of moving into an apartment.

- If you need to use public transportation, is it available nearby?
- If you have a car, is safe parking available nearby?
- Are there enough electrical outlets?
- Is there enough storage for your belongings? See 29-4.
- Is the place reasonably close to your work?
- Is the neighborhood safe and clean?

When you look for a place to live, don't think only about the rent. Running a household costs more than just paying the rent. Having a home means more than having a roof over your head. Look for a place where you can feel safe and comfortable.

Your Reading

Why should you consider housing needs and costs when looking for a place to live?

Furnishing Your New Home

Most apartments include a refrigerator and range. If you rent an *unfurnished* apartment, you will need to supply your own furniture. If you rent a *furnished* apartment, the rent will be considerably higher because it will have furniture.

If you shop for furniture, you will see that it costs much more than you expect. You may not be able to afford many new items. Used furniture may be more in keeping with your budget. Family members may have items they are willing to give to you. Look for affordable furniture and household items in newspaper classified ads. Also check garage and yard sales, auctions, and store clearances. See 29-5.

29-4
Storage space in an apartment is an important consideration.

Resource

Apartment Search, Activity B, WB. Students investigate furnished and unfurnished apartments for rent.

Resource

Furnishing an Apartment, Activity C, WB. Students identify everything they would need to furnish an apartment.

29-5
Clearance sales are a good source of bargains for someone furnishing an apartment on a budget.

Activity

Make a list of the "hand-me-downs" and used items that people would be willing to give away to help you furnish your first apartment. If you had to buy these items, list how much they would cost.

Community Connections

Invite apartment renters to class. Ask the guests to identify their views of the advantages and disadvantages of living in an apartment. Prepare questions to ask the guests about the rules and lease agreements that apply to their respective buildings.

verbal agreement
The simplest form of an agreement in which certain terms are specified but not written down.

lease
A written rental agreement, which defines the rights and responsibilities of the tenant and the owner of a rental property.

Your Legal Responsibilities

When you rent housing, both you, the *tenant*, and the owner, the *lessor*, have legal responsibilities. State and city laws regulate what the owner must provide for the tenant, known as the *renter*. The owner is responsible for maintaining the building, hallways, and grounds. In return, you, the tenant, must remember the building is not your property. You are simply paying to use it for a period of time. Therefore, you must take good care of it.

When you rent a place to live, you and the owner agree to certain terms. The simplest form of agreement is a ***verbal agreement***. This is an agreement in which certain terms are specified but not written down. As a general practice, you should avoid verbal agreements.

A written rental agreement is called a ***lease***. It is a legal contract. A lease explains the rights and responsibilities of the tenant and the owner.

Before signing a lease, be sure you understand all its conditions. A lease contains the following information:

- the length of the lease, usually six months or one year
- what the rent is
- when the rent is due
- responsibilities of the renter regarding the condition of the apartment
- what must be done before moving out of the apartment

The lease will also describe the terms concerning the security deposit. See the example in 29-6. A security deposit is usually equal to a month's rent. Most owners require a ***security deposit*** from a new tenant. If you damage the apartment, the owner will use the money to make the necessary repairs. If no damage is done, your deposit will be returned to you when you move away.

security deposit
An amount of money, usually equal to a month's rent, paid to the owner of rental property by new tenants when the lease is signed.

English Manor Apartments
I N C O R P O R A T E D
203 WINDSOR ROAD • LAKE SHORE, N.C. 28401

THIS AGREEMENT OF LEASE, MADE THIS 1st DAY OF May ____________ BETWEEN ENGLISH MANOR APARTMENTS, INC., HEREINAFTER CALLED LESSOR: AND ____________ ____________ HEREINAFTER CALLED TENANT, WHETHER ONE OR MORE.

WITNESSETH, That the Lessor leases and lets unto the Tenant, premises known as ____________ Lake Shore, N.C. 28401, for a term of not less than thirty (30) days from this date at the rental of $ 800.00 per month, to be paid in advance at the office of English Manor Apartments on the first day of each month without formal demand. This lease shall be renewed automatically for successive terms of one month each so long as the terms hereof are complied with at the same rental as hereinabove set forth payable in advance on the first day of each said renewed term, which renewed term shall expire of its own limitation at midnight on the last day of said term.

This will acknowledge the receipt of $ 800.00 as a deposit to cover any indebtedness to the Lessor for charges made for breakage or damage to the property. Any or all of deposit to be returned to the Tenant upon proper termination of the lease providing (1) THE TENANT HAS REMAINED IN POSSESSION AND PAID RENT ON ABOVE PROPERTY FOR AT LEAST SIX (6) MONTHS: (2) KEYS TO THE ABOVE PROPERTY HAVE BEEN RETURNED (3) THE PREMISES ARE LEFT IN A CLEAN CONDITION, AND ALL OTHER CONDITIONS OF THIS AGREEMENT HAVE BEEN MET TO THE SATISFACTION OF THE LESSOR. IT IS FURTHER UNDERSTOOD AND AGREED THAT THE TENANT SHALL GIVE A FIFTEEN (15) DAYS WRITTEN NOTICE BEFORE VACATING PREMISES. IF SAID NOTICE IS NOT GIVEN, TENANT WILL BE CHARGED FOR SAME.

TENANT will pay for any damage other than normal deterioration, wear and tear to the premises of Lessors property and will be responsible for the stoppage of sewer and drainage facilities chargeable to his use of the premises. Tenant will pay all utility bills as they come due. TENANT AGREES TO PAY A $25.00 GAS SERVICE CHARGE UPON VACATING.

LESSOR and its agents reserve the right to cancel this lease for any reason at any time by mailing a written notice to Tenant specifying a day of termination of the lease, which date shall be seven (7) days from the date of mailing the notice of cancellation. The mailing of such written notice by first class mail will constitute the giving of this notice. Any unearned portion of the rent will be refunded to the Tenant.

Should Tenant fail to make payment of the rental herein specified in advance by the first day of the month, this lease shall terminate at midnight of the last day of the preceding month without the necessity of any written notice; and Tenant agrees upon such termination to immediately vacate the premises. Should Tenant fail to vacate the premises, Lessor shall have the absolute right to lock the premises and forbid the use thereof by the Tenant.

The Lessor and its agents shall have the right to enter upon the premises at any reasonable time to assure that this agreement is being complied with and not being violated.

Time shall be of the essence of this agreement. It is agreed that no failure of the Lessor to insist on the strict terms hereof shall constitute a waiver of its rights to insist on such terms on any later occasion. Tenant will comply with the general rules and regulations promulgated by the Lessor for the operation of the apartment of which the subject premises are a part.

I/We accept the foregoing conditions. ENGLISH MANOR APTS.

____________ Tenant ____________ Agent

____________ Tenant

29-6 Tenants are usually required to sign a written lease when they rent an apartment.

What are the legal responsibilities of tenants and lessors?

Adapting the Lesson

Have students who are high functioning conduct online research to learn more about apartment leases. Ask students to find out what advice is given to college students about leasing apartments. Have students create a small brochure on advice for the college student about apartment leases.

Resource

What Do I Need to Live on My Own? reproducible master 29-3, TR. Use the adapted worksheet to reinforce chapter concepts in students who are low functioning.

Summary

As you grow toward independence, you may need to decide where to live. Before making a decision, be sure to think about the advantages and disadvantages of each option. Ask your family and friends for leads. Read the classified ads in the newspaper. You may want to contact a real estate or rental agency.

Think about both housing needs and costs as you look for a place to live. The home you choose should be one that you can afford. It should also be one where you can feel safe and comfortable.

Furnishing a new home can be expensive. Look for ways to buy what you need while staying within your budget.

If you choose to rent a place to live, you will probably be offered a lease. Read it carefully. Understand the legal responsibilities it involves. Once you sign it, you are bound to fulfill your responsibilities.

Answers to *Reviewing Key Concepts*

1. (Student response.)
2. (Student response.)
3. (Student response.)
4. Real estate agencies deal primarily with buying and selling homes. A rental agency deals only with rentals of property.
5. (Student response.)
6. (Name three:) newspaper classified ads, yard or garage sales, auctions, clearance sales, flea markets
7. true
8. D
9. (Student response.)
10. D

Reviewing Key Concepts

1. Name two advantages and two disadvantages of living at home.
2. Name two advantages and two disadvantages of living with a roommate.
3. Name two advantages and two disadvantages of living alone.
4. What is the difference between a real estate agency and a rental agency?
5. List five questions related to housing needs and costs you should consider when choosing a place to live.
6. Name three places where you might find affordable furnishings for a home.
7. True or false. In a verbal agreement, no contract details are in writing.
8. A lease ______.
   A. is a written rental agreement
   B. is a legal contract
   C. explains the rights and responsibilities of the tenant and the owner
   D. All of the above.
9. List five pieces of information included in a lease.
10. A security deposit is ______.
    A. usually equal to a month's rent
    B. used by the owner to repair damages to the property caused by the tenant
    C. returned to the tenant when he or she moves away if the property has not been damaged
    D. All of the above.

Building Academic Skills

Math. Calculate how much you can afford to spend on rent, based on the average beginning wage/salary of your chosen career. Find one-fourth of the annual income—the amount experts recommend for spending on housing—and divide by 12 to figure the monthly rent allowance. Perform the same calculations using the minimum wage. Switch papers with a classmate to double-check the math. Report what you learned.

Building Technology Skills

1. Conduct an online search for *places to live.* Web sites will appear advertising the best places to live in the United States. Read the articles and summarize what you learned.
2. Conduct an online search for apartments to rent. Begin your search with these Web sites: **forrent.com**, **homestore.com**, **apartments.com**, and **findanest.com**. Design a chart to compare apartment features as you conduct two searches: one for apartments in the area, and the other for apartments in another place where you would consider living. Share results with the class.
3. Use a spreadsheet program to create individualized check sheets for apartment searches. Your check sheet should list your preferences, such as pets allowed, off-street parking, indoor pool, and apartment security. Compare sheets to determine if all possible categories have been covered.

Building Career Knowledge and Skills

1. From an Internet search or from a local newspaper, find ads for five places to rent. Find out the location and the rent for each place. Also find out how much space and what facilities each apartment has to offer. In a written report, explain why some cost more than others.
2. Obtain a lease from an apartment complex. Discuss the aspects of the lease in class. What parts of the lease seem to favor the tenant? Which parts seem to favor the owner?
3. Watch for rentals that are open for public inspection. Visit a few and jot down observations. Note which ones best meet your needs, wants, and budget. Which ones give you the best value for your money?
4. Interview people regarding the advantages and disadvantages of living at home, with a roommate, or on your own. Decide which living option seems best for a young person holding his or her first full-time job: living at home, with a roommate, or alone. List four or five reasons for your opinion and share them with the class.
5. Visit several types of places that sell furniture, such as furniture stores, department or discount stores, rummage sales, thrift shops, etc. Note details regarding pieces you find, such as availability, warranty, price, selection, durability, etc. Share your findings with the class.

Building Workplace Skills

Find an unfurnished apartment for rent in your area and investigate sources of affordable furnishings for it. Working with two or three classmates, decide who will do which tasks. Obtain a floor plan of the rental unit or create one. The floor plan should show the room dimensions and locations of doors and windows. Find items to furnish the apartment to suit the needs and tastes of an 18-year-old on a tight budget. Record each item's cost, size, color, and condition (if used). Make an inventory list of the furnishings and their total cost using a computer. List the items in the order of importance, since all items cannot be purchased right away. Present your ideas to the class using fabric swatches, illustrations, product brochures, or photographs wherever possible.

How will I get to where I'm going?

Chapter 30 Transportation

Chapter Objectives

After studying this chapter, you will be able to

- **identify** two forms of self-powered transportation.
- **determine** the pros and cons of driving to work.
- **describe** three types of mass transportation.
- **rephrase** the information in a mass transportation schedule.

Key Terms

car pool
mass transportation
schedule
carrier
transfer

Key Concepts

- Walking or riding a bicycle are two forms of self-powered transportation.
- Driving to work has advantages and disadvantages.
- Buses, trains, and airplanes are used for mass transportation.

Self-Powered Transportation

Choosing where you work is sometimes as important as choosing what you do. When you are looking for a job, you must consider transportation. You must think about how you will get to and from work.

Two forms of self-powered transportation are walking and riding a bicycle. If you live close to your workplace, you can walk. In that case, changes in your work schedule won't create any transportation problems for you. You are completely independent and can come and go as you please without waiting for a ride. Walking is good exercise, and it is free. As long as the area is safe and the weather is suitable, walking is a good form of transportation. See 30-1.

Community Connections

Interview five adults to find out how they generally get to work. Document how much time these people spend traveling back and forth each day. Estimate how much it costs to use their respective modes of transportation.

30-1
Walking to work is a good way to get exercise and save transportation costs.

Resource

Reinforcing Vocabulary, Activity A, WB. Students match vocabulary terms with their definitions.

Reflect

How would you feel about walking to work every day? What would be your limit on the distance you would be willing to walk?

Activity

Estimate how much money you could save if you walked to work.

Riding a bicycle is another option. It is best in areas with good weather, light traffic, and short distances to work. In areas with heavy traffic, it may be too dangerous.

Your Reading

What are examples of self-powered transportation?

Automobile Transportation

Many people choose to drive to work in their own cars. This option provides great flexibility. Drivers who have their own vehicles can travel whenever and wherever they want.

Driving has some drawbacks, too. If you choose to drive to work, you must have a driver's license. You must also have a car. Many new workers cannot afford to buy a new car. Even used cars are very expensive.

Buying a car is not the only expense involved. You must also consider insurance. Car insurance premiums vary. In general, premiums are usually higher for younger drivers, new cars, and urban areas. The cost of gasoline should also be considered. How much you spend will depend on the type of car you drive and how far you travel.

Be careful not to overlook maintenance and repair costs. Even new cars require some maintenance, such as oil changes. The maintenance and repair bills for older cars can be expensive and unpredictable.

If you own a car, you must also think about where you will park it. A garage is the best place to keep a car to protect it from accidents, theft, and bad weather. However, some apartments do not have garages or parking lots. If parking is not available where you live, you may have to park on the street. Renting garage space may be another option, but this would add to the cost of owning a car.

Driving a car gives you flexibility and independence, but it is expensive. See 30-2. Before you accept a job that would require you to drive, think carefully. Decide if you can afford to drive a car. Decide if you want to pay the costs related to driving. Also decide if you want the responsibility of driving.

Resource

Annual Car Costs, color transparency CT-30, TR. Students discuss the annual costs of owning and operating an automobile.

Resource

Car Leasing: Is It Right for You? reproducible master 30-1, TR. Students compare leasing a car to buying one.

Discuss

What are the advantages of using a car pool? Are there any disadvantages?

Activity

List other reasons for which people could use car pools besides work.

Car Pools

One way to cut driving costs is to join a car pool. A ***car pool*** is a group of people who take turns driving, usually to work. In this arrangement, you drive your car less. You still have the costs involved in owning a car. However, you can save money on fuel, maintenance, and repairs.

car pool
A group of people who take turns driving, usually to work.

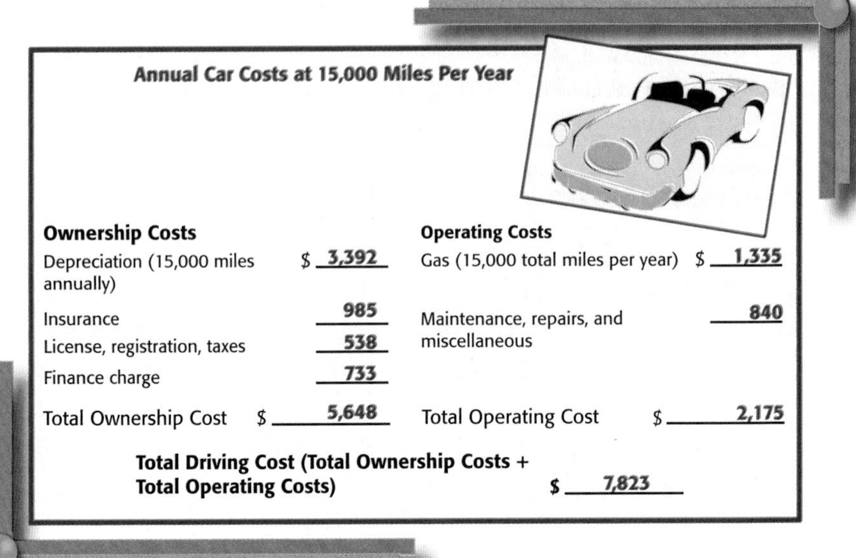

Annual Car Costs at 15,000 Miles Per Year

Ownership Costs		**Operating Costs**	
Depreciation (15,000 miles annually)	$ 3,392	Gas (15,000 total miles per year)	$ 1,335
Insurance	985	Maintenance, repairs, and miscellaneous	840
License, registration, taxes	538		
Finance charge	733		
Total Ownership Cost	$ 5,648	Total Operating Cost	$ 2,175

Total Driving Cost (Total Ownership Costs + Total Operating Costs) $ 7,823

30-2 All the costs of owning and operating a car must be counted when considering the option of driving to work.

Car pools are as reliable as the people who form them. Members of a car pool must cooperate with each other. Each member must do his or her fair share to get everyone safely to work on time.

If you join a car pool, remember that members of a car pool can get sick. They can have appointments, meetings, and other responsibilities. Be sure to have a backup transportation plan ready in case your car pool arrangements change suddenly.

As a new employee, find out if your coworkers have car pools. You can usually get information about car pools from the company's human resources office.

When you join a car pool, you give up some of the flexibility and independence you have when you drive your own car. On the other hand, you gain companionship and reduce transportation costs.

Mass Transportation

Mass transportation is transportation used routinely by the general public. Buses, trains, and airplanes are used for mass transportation. One or more of these types of transportation are available in almost all large towns and cities.

Discuss

What is mass transportation? Is this an option for you to use in commuting to work?

Adapting the Lesson

Have students who are high functioning conduct an online search using the term *mass transportation*. Ask students to write a brief report comparing the mass transportation options available in two cities and the average number of people who use each option.

Before you accept a job that would require driving to work, what factors should you consider?

mass transportation
Transportation used routinely by the general public.

Some mass transportation systems are privately owned and operated. Others are publicly owned. The government supports public mass transportation systems from tax money. There are two major advantages to using mass transportation. Parking problems are eliminated and fuel costs are kept to a minimum.

Schedules

When using public transportation, plan your travel carefully. Check mass transportation schedules. A ***schedule*** lists the expected arrival and departure times for buses, trains, and airplanes. By reading a schedule, you can decide which ride will allow you to arrive at work on time. Schedules also list where stops are located. This allows you to find the stops that are closest to your home and your job. See 30-3.

When you use a schedule, remember that posted times are approximate. Drivers try to stay on schedule, but they can't always control delays. Choose a ride that will get you to work early. This will allow for any delays that may arise along the way.

Printed schedules are available from all carriers. A ***carrier*** is an organization that operates a transportation system. Carriers also provide more detailed information about schedules online or by phone.

Buses

When you take a bus, remember that drivers can't control traffic and road conditions. If traffic is heavy or the weather is bad, your bus may be late. You, in turn, may arrive late for work. Listening to traffic and weather reports will help you foresee problems. If you hear warnings of storms or traffic delays, adjust your schedule accordingly.

Buses follow specific routes. In other words, they do not go down every street and stop at every corner. You are unlikely to find a bus that will drop you off right at your home or job. You may need to walk a few blocks to get to and from the bus stop. See 30-4.

If you work in a large city, you may need to take several routes and transfer between them. To ***transfer*** is to change from one bus or train route to another. Usually a transfer costs nothing extra or a small fee. You should find out if you must transfer when scheduling your transportation.

Community Connections

Interview local officials regarding public transportation in your community. What transportation issues have they recently addressed? What long-range transportation plans are being considered? Report your findings to the class.

schedule
A list of the expected arrival and departure times and locations for buses, trains, and airplanes.

carrier
An organization that operates a transportation system.

Reflect
How do you feel about the safety of mass transportation? Do you think mass transportation is safer than using your own car?

Resource
Reading a Bus Schedule, Activity B, WB. Students interpret a mass transportation schedule.

transfer
To change from one bus or train route to another.

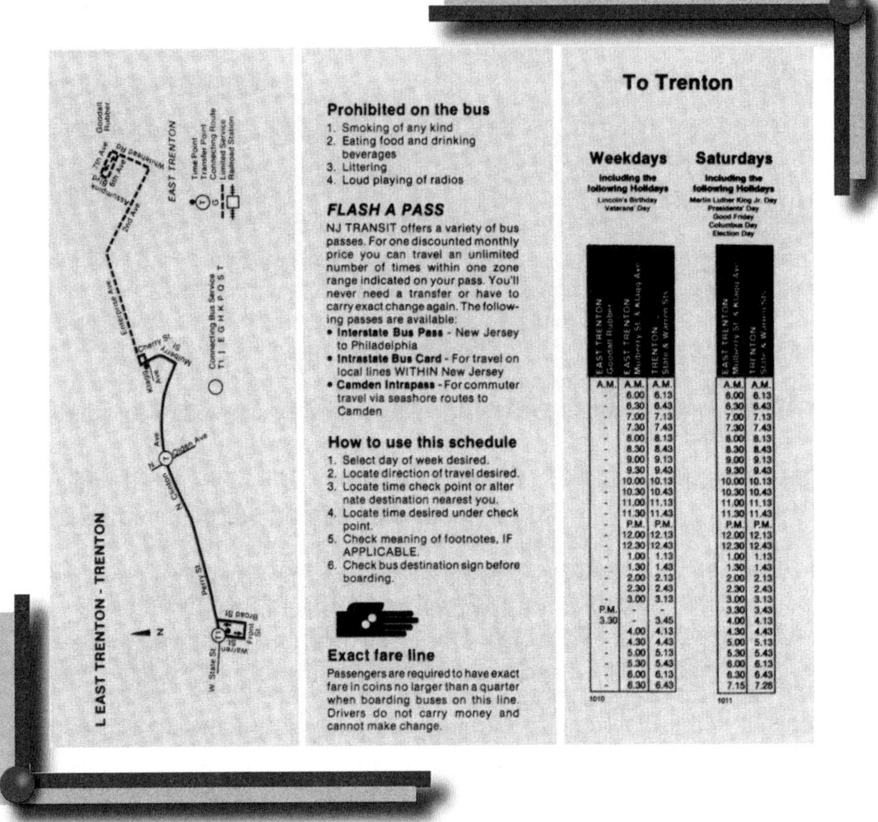

Prohibited on the bus

1. Smoking of any kind
2. Eating food and drinking beverages
3. Littering
4. Loud playing of radios

FLASH A PASS

NJ TRANSIT offers a variety of bus passes. For one discounted monthly price you can travel an unlimited number of times within one zone range indicated on your pass. You'll never need a transfer or have to carry exact change again. The following passes are available:

- **Interstate Bus Pass** - New Jersey to Philadelphia
- **Intrastate Bus Card** - For travel on local lines WITHIN New Jersey
- **Camden Intrapass** - For commuter travel via seashore routes to Camden

How to use this schedule

1. Select day of week desired.
2. Locate direction of travel desired.
3. Locate time check point or alter nate destination nearest you.
4. Locate time desired under check point.
5. Check meaning of footnotes, IF APPLICABLE.
6. Check bus destination sign before boarding.

Exact fare line

Passengers are required to have exact fare in coins no larger than a quarter when boarding buses on this line. Drivers do not carry money and cannot make change.

To Trenton

Weekdays

Including the following Holidays
Lincoln's Birthday
Veterans' Day

EAST TRENTON Goodall Rubber	EAST TRENTON Mulberry St. & Klagg Ave	TRENTON State & Warren Sts
A.M.	A.M.	A.M.
-	6.00	6.13
-	6.30	6.43
-	7.00	7.13
-	7.30	7.43
-	8.00	8.13
-	8.30	8.43
-	9.00	9.13
-	9.30	9.43
-	10.00	10.13
-	10.30	10.43
-	11.00	11.13
-	11.30	11.43
-	P.M.	P.M.
-	12.00	12.13
-	12.30	12.43
-	1.00	1.13
-	1.30	1.43
-	2.00	2.13
-	2.30	2.43
-	3.00	3.13
P.M.	-	-
3.30	-	3.45
-	4.00	4.13
-	4.30	4.43
-	5.00	5.13
-	5.30	5.43
-	6.00	6.13
-	6.30	6.43

1010

Saturdays

Including the following Holidays
Martin Luther King Jr. Day
Presidents' Day
Good Friday
Columbus Day
Election Day

EAST TRENTON Mulberry St. & Klagg Ave	TRENTON State & Warren Sts
A.M.	A.M.
6.00	6.13
6.30	6.43
7.00	7.13
7.30	7.43
8.00	8.13
8.30	8.43
9.00	9.13
9.30	9.43
10.00	10.13
10.30	10.43
11.00	11.13
11.30	11.43
P.M.	P.M.
12.00	12.13
12.30	12.43
1.00	1.13
1.30	1.43
2.00	2.13
2.30	2.43
3.00	3.13
3.30	3.43
4.00	4.13
4.30	4.43
5.00	5.13
5.30	5.43
6.00	6.13
6.30	6.43
7.15	7.28

1011

30-3
Bus and train schedules give passengers the information they need to use the system.

Discuss

Is the bus schedule in Figure 30-3 the same on weekdays and on Saturdays? Can you use a credit card to pay for bus fare? Can you eat and drink on the bus?

Activity

Imagine you are a bus driver. If children were your passengers, what special rules would you enforce on the bus? If you ride a bus to school now, what rules pertain to it?

30-4
Bus stops are located every few blocks along most city routes.

Most bus lines require a ticket purchase in advance. Many bus companies offer reduced fares if you purchase a monthly pass or a quantity of rides. A monthly pass may also save you money by allowing you to make unlimited transfers at no extra cost. In some cities, monthly passes can save you as much as 25 percent. A 25 percent savings means that you get one free ride after three rides. Usually a ticket expires on a certain date.

You can call the bus company for information about using the bus system. You can get information about schedules, routes, and transfer locations. You can also find out about fares and possible discounts.

Vocabulary

In transportation terms, what is a carrier? Use the word in a sentence to demonstrate understanding.

Discuss

Who are the carriers of the bus companies that serve your area?

Discuss

How many people do you know who use mass transportation? What do they like about the service? What disadvantages do they mention?

Reflect

How many choices of transportation do you have in your community? Would you want to live in a community that offered several options of transportation?

Trains and Subways

Large cities often have high-speed transportation systems. Subways and trains are not subject to traffic jams and other delays that slow buses. See 30-5. As a worker in a large city, you may be able to choose among different types of transportation. Plan your route just as you would if you took a bus. People who live in the suburbs and commute to large cities often find trains to be the best way to get to work.

30-5 Many large cities run trains as well as buses for mass transportation.

Activity

Make a list of eight points air travelers would need to do or remember when making a business trip.

Resource

What Transportation Options Do I Have? reproducible master 30-2, TR. Use the adapted worksheet to reinforce chapter concepts for students who are low functioning.

Airplanes

People on business trips often travel by airplane. Airplane schedules are like other mass transportation schedules. They give approximate arrival and departure times. However, airplanes are subject to many delays. It is a good idea to call and check on your flight before going to the airport.

Plan to arrive at the airport at least two hours before your flight is scheduled to depart (earlier for international flights). This will allow you time to check in, go through security, and arrive at your departure gate. See 30-6. Airport security has been tightened due to terrorist threats. All passengers are subject to baggage restrictions and security screening. When traveling by air, you should be aware of security regulations and be prepared to get through airport security with the least amount of difficulty. Regulations and restrictions change. The Transportation Security Administration (TSA) Web site at **www.tsa.gov** will provide you with up-to-date information. You may also check the Web site of the airline you will be flying, as airlines may have additional regulations and restrictions.

Airline passengers must also plan how they will get to and from the airport. Perhaps they drive to the airport or a friend drops them off. In addition to these options, various forms of ground transportation exist. These include buses, trains, limousines, taxis, and rental cars.

Your Reading

What are some examples of mass transportation?

30-6
Airplanes provide fast transportation for people traveling long distances for work.

Resource

Transportation Comparison, Activity C, WB. Students compare the advantages and disadvantages of various forms of transportation.

Discuss

What common modes of transportation get air travelers to and from the airport?

Summary

As an employee, you must be able to get to work on time. You should plan your transportation when you plan your job search. You must find a reliable form of transportation to and from your workplace.

You may be able to walk or ride a bicycle. You may choose to drive your own car or to join a car pool. Depending on where you live, mass transportation may be an option for you. In that case, you would need to read the schedules and plan your routes.

Reviewing Key Concepts

1. Name two advantages of walking to work.
2. When would riding a bicycle be a good option for getting to work?
3. List three expenses related to driving a car to work.
4. How can joining a car pool reduce transportation costs?
5. True or false. The government uses tax money to support public mass transportation systems.
6. What can a traveler learn by reading a mass transportation schedule?
7. Changing from one bus, train, or subway to another to take a different route is a ______.
8. If you ride a bus every day, what is the benefit of buying a ticket for the month or a quantity of rides?
9. Why are subways and trains often much faster than buses?
10. Why should a traveler plan to arrive at the airport at least two hours before scheduled departure time?

Answers to *Reviewing Key Concepts*

1. (Name two:) good exercise, free mode of transportation, does not depend on others
2. in areas with good weather, light traffic, and short distances to work
3. (List three:) purchase of a car, car insurance, gas, maintenance, repair costs
4. You drive your own car less, which saves money on fuel, maintenance, and repairs.
5. true
6. arrival and departure times, length of trips, and location of stops
7. transfer
8. reduced fares
9. are not subject to traffic jams and other delays that slow buses
10. to allow enough time to check in, go through security, and get to the departure gate

Building Academic Skills

1. **Writing.** Write a paper in favor of using mass transportation. Include all the options a person could use to get to work and the advantages of each method.
2. **Speaking.** Hold a debate on the topic of driving versus flying to a business meeting, using the following assumption: The location of the meeting is four hours away by car. You could drive this distance, but flying would save you some time. Based on the costs in terms of time and money, which option is the best?

Building Technology Skills

1. Investigate buying a car online using the following Web sites: **autoweb.com**, **carsmart.com**, and **vehix.com**. Document helpful hints you learn about buying a car. Give specific examples of used cars available online.
2. Research the most popular methods of transportation in other countries. Find out what methods of transportation are used in China, Russia, or some other country of your choice. Write a short report on your findings.
3. Investigate high-speed methods of mass transportation currently being planned or considered. What technologies are involved? What special features will these "people movers" have? Write a report on your findings. Include pictures, if possible.

Building Career Knowledge and Skills

1. Identify a place where you would like to work. Prepare a written comparison of three different ways of getting there and back. Consider the following factors: time, cost, convenience, and reliability. State which method of transportation you think would be best for you.
2. Talk to someone who is in a car pool. What are the pros and cons of this method of transportation? Share your findings with the class.
3. Using your home as the starting point, plan a bus (and/or train) route to the nearest shopping mall. Assume that you are scheduled to begin working as a salesclerk at 9 a.m. Where and when would you catch the bus? What time would the bus arrive at the stop nearest the shopping mall?
4. Plan how you would travel to an interview at your dream job. In an oral report, describe the trip from your home to the job site. List all forms of transportation you would use. Estimate how long the trip would take and how much it would cost.
5. Interview people who travel by air regarding their experiences of going through airport security. Visit the TSA Web site at **tsa.gov** for a current list of regulations and restrictions. Share your findings with the class.
6. Brainstorm lifestyle changes you would experience if you were to change to a different mode of transportation other than what you rely on now. Note advantages, disadvantages, and personal thoughts regarding the change.

Building Workplace Skills

Prepare a budget that lists the complete costs of owning a car. Find out all other costs of owning the car. These may include the sales and/or state tax, license cost, registration fees, and city sticker fee. Also figure the operating costs by interviewing parents and others about gas and maintenance costs and service fees. Present your findings to the class.

What are my responsibilities as a citizen?

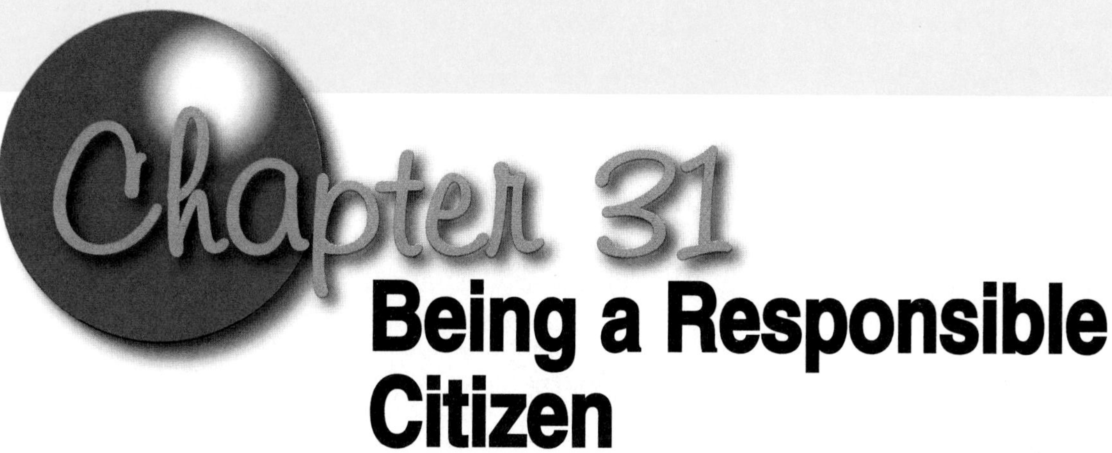

Being a Responsible Citizen

Chapter Objectives

After studying this chapter, you will be able to

- **recognize** the importance of voting in elections.
- **explain** how laws are made.
- **name** the two categories of laws in the United States.
- **determine** situations that might require the services of a lawyer.
- **state** the rights and responsibilities of consumers.

Key Terms

citizen
register
bill
civil laws
public laws
monopoly
competition
recourse

Key Concepts

- Citizens express themselves on public issues by voting.
- Laws protect the rights of citizens.
- A lawyer helps you to interpret laws that affect you as a citizen.
- You have both rights and responsibilities as a consumer.

citizen
A person who owes allegiance to a government.

Being an Active Citizen

A ***citizen*** is a person who owes allegiance to a government. As a citizen of the United States, you have many rights and responsibilities. Your rights are protected by the laws of the government. You are responsible for obeying those laws.

As a citizen you have an opportunity to be an active citizen. You can do this by trying to make your community better by participating in civic organizations. By volunteering your time and talents, you can help to improve life for yourself as well as other citizens.

Making a Difference

Consider participating in youth civic groups and community service projects. These are excellent ways to develop leadership skills and civic responsibility. There are many local, state, national, and international civic and community service organizations that are geared to youth participation. Some of these groups include Boy Scouts of America, Girl Scouts of the USA, 4-H, Police Explorers, Boys and Girls Clubs of America, and the Civil Air Patrol Cadet Program.

The Right to Vote

One of the most important rights of U.S. citizens is the right to vote. The law does not force citizens to vote. It simply gives them the opportunity to do so. See 31-1.

In general, any citizen of the United States who is at least 18 years old has the right to vote. It is the responsibility of each citizen to exercise that right. Voting is one way to express yourself on public issues. If you are eligible, you should vote in national, state, and local elections.

The people who are elected to office make and enforce the laws. As a responsible citizen, you should vote to elect people who will support the kinds of laws you support. When you vote for someone, you are saying, "I want this person to represent me in government." You are also saying, "I think this person will do the best job for the town (or state or nation)."

In order to vote, you must register. When you ***register***, you add your name to the official list of citizens eligible to vote in elections. To be eligible, you must be at least 18 years old. You must be a citizen of the United States. You must have lived in the state and county where you are registering for at least 30 days prior to the election. When you go to vote, election officials check to see if your name is on the list of registered voters. If it is, you can vote.

register
To submit one's name to the official list of citizens eligible to vote in elections.

Resource
Reinforcing Vocabulary, Activity A, WB. Students complete an activity using chapter key terms.

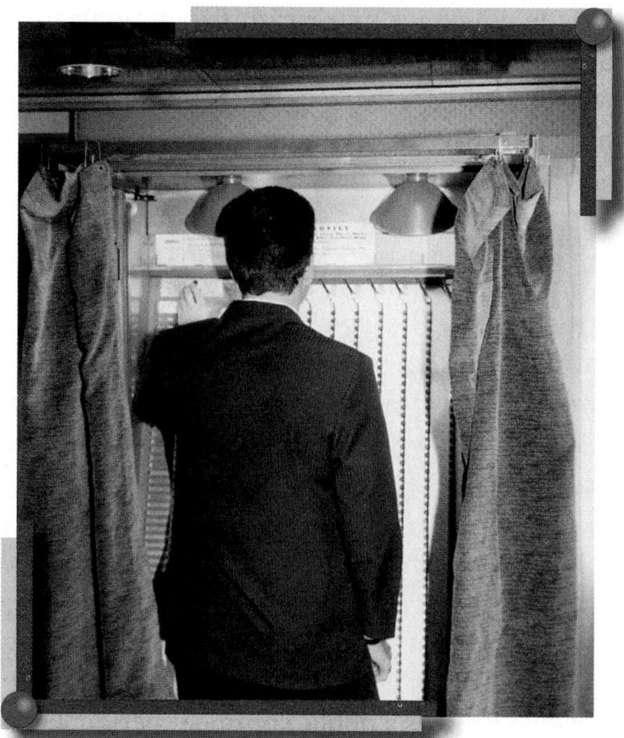

31-1
Exercising the right to vote gives citizens a chance to participate in their government.

Discuss
What does it mean to register to vote? How is this done?

Resource
Be a Responsible Citizen, color transparency CT-31, TR. Students discuss the importance of voting.

Resource
Voters' Survey, Activity B, WB. Students survey voters about their voting habits and opinions.

Resource
Evaluating a Candidate, reproducible master 31-1, TR. Students research a political leader's campaign.

You can register to vote at the office of the county commissioner, the election supervisor, or the municipal clerk. Just before a major election, mobile units for voter registration may visit your neighborhood. They are run by representatives of political parties. They want all eligible citizens to be registered so they can vote in the upcoming election.

Sometimes situations arise that may prevent a registered voter from being able to vote on the day of the election. The voter may be hospitalized, on vacation, a member of the military, a student away from home, or unable to vote on election day for reasons of employment. *Absentee voting* allows registered voters to vote by absentee ballot in any election in which they are qualified to vote. If you have a question about whether you qualify to vote absentee or how to apply, contact your local election office.

Why is it important to vote?

The Laws of the Land

Laws are rules by which people live. A society could not function if people did whatever they desired. Living in a society without laws results in total confusion and turmoil.

Activity

State in your own words what you think the rights and responsibilities of a citizen are.

Discuss

Can anyone describe how the state legislature operates when it is in session? Has anyone visited the local city/town council meetings?

As a citizen, you have many rights that are protected by laws. If your rights are violated, the laws outline what course of action you may take to correct the situation. As a citizen, you also have a responsibility to obey laws. If you fail to do so, the laws define what penalties you will face.

How Laws Are Made

Laws are made by the legislative branches of the various levels of government. Lawmakers at every level are elected to public office. Federal laws are made by the United States Congress, 31-2. State laws are made by state legislatures. Local laws are made by town or city councils.

bill
A proposed law.

To make a new state law, a state legislator introduces a bill to the members of the legislature. A ***bill*** is a proposed law. The members of the legislature discuss the proposed law. They discuss the reasons for having the law and the reasons for not having the law. This discussion is called a *debate*. During the debate period or before the vote, there is a public comment period. During this period, you, as a citizen, have the right to have your opinion heard. You can do this either in person or in writing. The members of the legislature vote on the bill. If it passes, it is sent to the governor. Once the governor signs it, it becomes a law.

Discuss

If the *Bill of Rights* were written today, would the same things be included? How do you think the country's founders would view the government if they came back to visit today?

Federal laws are made in a similar way. A bill is introduced. If it is passed by both the Senate and the House of Representatives, it is sent to the president. Once the president signs a bill, it becomes a law.

31-2
The U.S. Congress is responsible for making laws at the national level.

Sometimes a proposed law is presented directly to citizens as a question. These questions appear on voting ballots as *propositions* or *public questions*. When citizens go to the polls to vote for public officials, they may also vote on one or more public questions. If the majority of voters accept a public question, it becomes law. If people vote down a public question, it does not become law.

Another method of making laws is sometimes used on the local level. A town council member may introduce a bill by reading it at a public meeting. The bill is then printed in the local newspaper. The bill is read again at a second public meeting. Citizens are given time to make comments and express their opinions about the bill. After the discussion period, the council members vote on the bill. If passed, it becomes a law.

Resource

Classroom Council, Activity C, WB. Students work together to write a law.

Discuss

What is the difference between civil and public laws? Give examples of the various types of laws.

Adapting the Lesson

Have students who are high functioning research and write about the political structure at the local and state level where you live. As part of the report, have students draw a chart to show the reporting relationship of the offices.

Reflect

How do you feel about being involved in political issues? What discussions have you heard about political issues?

Types of Laws

The laws in the United States are divided into two categories—civil laws and public laws. ***Civil laws*** define a person's rights in relation to other people. Civil laws relate to cases involving such issues as contracts, inheritances, and the business of corporations. ***Public laws*** define a person's rights in relation to government. Public laws are divided into four groups.

- *Criminal law* relates to punishments for failure to obey the law.
- *Constitutional law* refers to the basic laws of the nation.
- *Administrative law* pertains to the duties and powers of the executive branch of government. The executive branch includes the highest office at each level of government. Presidents, governors, and mayors are members of the executive branches of federal, state, and local governments, respectively.
- *International law* relates to the relationships among nations.

civil laws
Laws that define a person's rights in relation to other people.

public laws
Laws that define a person's rights in relation to government.

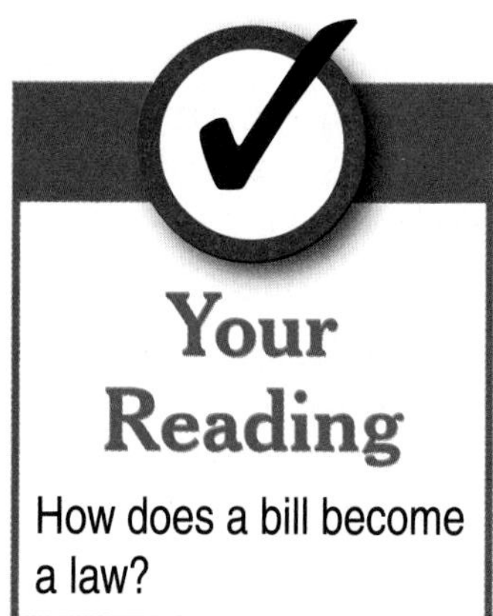

Community Connections

Conduct research to determine the legal costs of the following: buying or selling a house, getting a divorce, defending yourself in a court case, and writing a will. (Some fee ranges for these services may be given in online sources, too.) Share your results with the class.

When You May Need a Lawyer

At some point, you may need a lawyer to help you interpret the laws that affect you as a citizen. If you need help finding a lawyer, you might ask friends and family members. They may be able to recommend lawyers they have used. You could also look in the Yellow Pages of the phone book for a listing of attorneys in your area. When looking in the phone book, you may find a number for a state legal association. Such an association is another source of help for finding a lawyer to meet your specific legal needs.

Lawyers specialize in the types of legal services they offer. Some lawyers specialize in defending criminal cases. Some deal primarily with tax laws or corporate lawsuits. Others primarily handle divorce cases. When choosing a lawyer, it is important to look for one who is qualified to deal with your particular type of problem. See 31-3.

Legal advice can be quite costly. Ask about fees before you hire an attorney. If you are unable to afford a lawyer, you may be able to get free legal help from a public service agency.

31-3 Lawyers generally specialize in a specific legal area, such as real estate transactions, divorces, or personal injury.

Resource

Legal Advice, Activity D, WB. Students examine occasions for which they should hire a lawyer.

Discuss

What movies have you seen about how the legal system works? What questions did it present?

Enrich

Interview your parents to find out if they have consulted a lawyer in real estate matters. Find out if they used a lawyer to buy or sell a house or to review an apartment lease. What types of real estate matters does a lawyer handle?

You might want to seek the advice of a lawyer if you are involved in any of the following situations:

- If you buy or sell a house, a lawyer will review all the legal documents involved. He or she can make sure that your best interests are being served.
- If you get a divorce, a lawyer can help you arrive at a fair settlement.
- If you rent an apartment and wish to break the lease, a lawyer can help you understand your options.
- If you buy a service or product and fail to receive it, a lawyer can help you resolve the problem.
- If you receive a summons or subpoena to appear in court, you may need the services of a lawyer to protect your rights.
- If you are arrested, you may need a lawyer to defend you and represent you in court.
- If you wish to make out a will, a lawyer can help make sure it is a valid document.
- If a loved one dies, you may need a lawyer to help settle the estate.

Activity
Make a list of the situations for which people need legal advice. Divide the list into categories of needs.

Discuss
What qualities do you think a person must have in order to be a lawyer? Why do you think young children often say they want to be a lawyer?

Activity
Have students create a poster on "Consumer Rights and Responsibilities." Display the posters around the school.

Consumer Rights and Responsibilities

As a citizen of the United States, you are entitled to participate in the economy. You do this by working to produce goods and services. You also participate by consuming goods and services produced by others.

The economy of the United States is based on free enterprise. To make this economic system work, both businesses and consumers must be treated fairly. Many laws have been passed to protect the free enterprise system. As a result, you have both rights and responsibilities as a consumer.

Activity

Role-play a customer returning what is believed to be a defective product to the place of purchase. Discuss the rights and responsibilities of each party in this situation.

Discuss

What do you think about your right as a consumer to choose from a variety of products? Have you ever been shopping and had so many choices that you could not choose?

The Right to Information

As a consumer, you have the right to accurate information. Product labels, claims, and advertisements must be truthful. Instructions for the use and care of products must be clear and understandable, 31-4.

Along with this right to information comes the responsibility to use it. You should read product labels and service contracts. You should compare items carefully. Know what to expect from a product or service before you pay for it. Once you buy a product, follow the instructions for its use and care.

The Right to Choose

You and other consumers have the right to choose from a variety of products and services. The government protects that right with laws against monopolies. A ***monopoly*** is total control over a product or service.

monopoly
The exclusive possession and control of a product or service.

31-4
Consumers have the right to expect clear and accurate directions on product packages.

Suppose Company AZ held a monopoly on cars in the United States. In that case, the company would be the sole U.S. manufacturer and seller. Company AZ might decide to make only two-door, compact cars to save money. Meanwhile, the company would charge whatever price it desired. If you wanted a car, you would have to buy an AZ car at a fixed price.

The government has laws against monopolies to encourage a variety of products and services to exist. When monopolies are outlawed, competition reigns. ***Competition*** is the effort of two or more parties acting independently to offer the most favorable product or terms at the fairest price.

competition
Two or more parties acting independently to offer the most favorable product or terms.

Variety is a sign of a free enterprise economy. You and other consumers have the responsibility to select wisely. You should compare different features, qualities, and prices. Then make choices that best meet your needs. See 31-5.

Vocabulary
Show your understanding of the term *monopoly* by using it in a sentence. Why does the government have laws against monopolies?

The Right to Safety

Consumers have the right to be protected from unsafe products. You can expect foods, drugs, toys, appliances, and tools to be safe.

You also have the responsibility to use products safely. Use them as they are meant to be used. Do not share prescription drugs. Do not use items past their expiration dates. Follow directions for the safe use of products that are potentially

Adapting the Lesson
Have students who are high functioning conduct research on business monopolies. Ask students to read three articles on the subject and write a reaction paper on what they read. Have students share their findings with the class.

31-5
Consumers have the right to choose from a variety of products.

Activity
Make a list of the stores where students in your class frequently shop. Find out what their return policies are. Make a chart to compare the information learned.

dangerous. You also have the responsibility to report products that you find to be unsafe. Notify the store where you bought the product. Notify the product's manufacturer. You may also want to notify an appropriate government office.

The Right to Be Heard

recourse
The right to complain and receive an appropriate response.

If you buy a product or service, and it does not meet your expectations, you have the right to recourse. ***Recourse*** is the right to complain and receive an appropriate response.

If you purchase an item that is defective, you should return it to the store where you purchased it. Bring the merchandise and the sales receipt. It is a good practice to save the receipts from all your purchases.

Most stores have a customer service representative. You should explain to that person the problem you have with the merchandise. He or she will follow the store's policy for defective merchandise. Most stores will exchange the item for another. Some stores will issue a store credit for the returned item. You can use that credit to buy something else from the store. Many stores will refund your money. It is a good practice to inquire about a store's return policy before you make a purchase.

Activity
Role-play a situation in which the customer is not satisfied with how the store clerk wants to settle a matter involving a defective product. Have the "customer" ask to speak to the manager of the store. Have students discuss a proper procedure for handling this type of situation.

Resource
Writing a Complaint Letter, Activity E, WB. Students compose a complaint letter for a given problem.

If you are not satisfied with the response of the customer service representative, ask to speak to the supervisor. If after talking to the supervisor, you are still not satisfied, ask to see the store manager. You should be prepared to go as far as necessary to reach satisfaction.

If your problem is not resolved by the store manager, write a detailed letter to the main office of the company. In your letter, explain in detail the facts pertaining to the problem. List the names of all the people to whom you spoke, and describe their responses to your problem. Also state in your letter what you expect from them to bring the matter to a satisfactory close. See 31-6. If you still do not get satisfaction, consider contacting the area's Better Business Bureau (BBB).

For matters that may involve unlawful behavior, contact the consumer protection bureau in your city or state. This department is usually located within the office of the attorney general. The name of the protection group can be found in the telephone book.

323 W. Taft Drive
South Holland, IL 60473
May 18, 20XX

Nancy Milan
Consumer Services
Contemporary Communications, Inc.
2121 West Main Street
Mesa, AZ 85201

Dear Ms. Milan:

One month ago, I purchased a Smart Talk Cordless Telephone from your Contemporary Communications Collection, Model #012988. This purchase was made at the Phone Connections store in South Holland, Illinois.

To my disappointment, the quality of the newly purchased telephone did not live up to its reputation. After only one month of use, the signal is weak and there is static on the line.

To solve my problem, I ask that you please replace my Smart Talk Cordless telephone. It would be greatly appreciated. Please find a copy of my purchase receipt and warranty enclosed.

I hope to hear from you soon with a resolution to my problem. I will wait another month for your response before I return the phone to the Phone Connections store for full reimbursement. You may contact me at the above address or by phone at 708-555-7200. Thank you.

Sincerely,

Jennifer Sims

Jennifer Sims

enc.

31-6
A complaint letter written to the manufacturer will often resolve a consumer's problem with a faulty product.

Discuss

In Figure 31-6, what information do you learn from the letter? What is the tone of the letter? What information do you think should be stated in a letter of complaint?

Resource

Citizen Awareness, Activity F, WB. Students identify true and false statements about chapter topics.

Resource

How Do I Help My Community? reproducible master 31-2, TR. Use the adapted worksheet to reinforce chapter concepts in students who are low functioning.

Generally, the BBB and a government agency will not handle the same complaint at the same time. If you do not get satisfaction through one channel, you may contact the other. Send copies of all your correspondence and ask for their review of the matter. If you still do not get satisfaction, you may need to retain the services of a lawyer to help resolve your problem.

Your Reading

How do laws designed to protect the free enterprise system help consumers and businesses?

Summary

Citizenship involves both rights and responsibilities. One of the most important rights of U.S. citizens is the right to vote. To exercise this right, you must register first.

Laws are rules by which people live. They are made by the people elected to public office. The two categories of laws in the United States are civil laws and public laws. At various times in your life, you may need the services of a lawyer to help you interpret laws.

Another part of being a responsible citizen involves being a responsible consumer. Consumers have rights and responsibilities related to product information, selection, safety, and recourse. If you buy an item that is defective, there are certain steps to follow to solve the problem.

Answers to *Reviewing Key Concepts*

1. false
2. true
3. true
4. Civil laws define a person's rights in relation to other people's rights. Public laws define a person's rights in relation to government.
5. (List three:) friends, family members, Yellow Pages, state legal association
6. (Student response.)
7. (Student response.)
8. through laws against monopolies
9. (Student response.)
10. C

Reviewing Key Concepts

1. True or false. The law requires every eligible U.S. citizen to vote in all elections.
2. True or false. To register to vote, a person must be a citizen of the United States and at least 18 years old.
3. True or false. Federal laws are made by the United States Congress.
4. Name and define the two categories of laws in the United States.
5. List three sources of help for finding a lawyer.
6. List four situations that may require the services of a lawyer.
7. Describe consumers' rights and responsibilities related to product information.
8. Explain how the government protects the rights of consumers to choose from a variety of goods and services.
9. List three responsibilities consumers have concerning product safety.
10. If you have a problem with an item you purchased, you should first contact ______.
    A. the Better Business Bureau
    B. the store's manager
    C. the store's customer service representative
    D. a lawyer

Building Academic Skills

Social Studies. Obtain a copy of the Bill of Rights. Read it and write a paragraph summary about what these rights mean to you. List any questions you still have regarding your rights as a U.S. citizen.

Building Technology Skills

1. Research how laws are made online. Use presentation software to explain the process of how an idea becomes a law. Show the presentation to the class.
2. Conduct online research to determine the latest product safety recalls by using the following Web sites: **cpsc.gov**, **fda.gov/opacom/7alerts.html**, and **fsis.usda.gov/Fsis-Recalls/index.asp**. Write a report on five products or safety issues being addressed in the Web sites.
3. Conduct online research on the Better Business Bureau to find out if there is a local branch in the community. Report the services they provide and the process for obtaining those services.

Building Career Knowledge and Skills

1. Research the right to vote in a country other than the United States. Find out what percentage of eligible voters voted in the last U.S. presidential election. Include this information in a written report along with your own ideas about the right to vote.
2. Prepare a pamphlet describing why, how, and where a person should register to vote. Distribute copies of the pamphlet throughout your school and community.
3. Contact a local election office and ask for information on who may vote using an absentee ballot. How do you apply for an absentee ballot? Discuss your findings in class.
4. Design a bulletin board showing the steps involved in making a federal law.
5. Describe a situation that might require the services of a lawyer. Make a list of the kinds of information a person in this situation would need to bring to the lawyer.
6. Ask class members to play the parts of customer service representatives, store managers, presidents of companies, and customers. Create different situations for making and resolving complaints.
7. Interview someone who has faced a consumer problem and has taken steps to correct it. Describe the problem, the steps taken to correct the problem, and the final outcome. Share your findings with the class.

Building Workplace Skills

Working with three or four classmates, write a skit that demonstrates a store's reluctance to grant a consumer's right to be heard. Include actions a consumer can take at all levels of a store's management until a consumer is satisfied. Incorporate characters into the skit so that each member of your team also performs in the skit. Have the class evaluate whether the consumer problem demonstrated in the skit was appropriately handled in the end.

A

abilities. The skills a person has developed. (7)

accessories. Items that complement a wardrobe, such as shoes, handbags, belts, neckties, and jewelry. (20)

acne. A skin disorder caused by the inflammation of the skin glands and hair follicles. (20)

active listening. Listening and responding to another person to improve mutual understanding. (19)

addiction. The never-ending obsession to use a drug. (21)

advanced training. Special skills and training required for a specific job. (4)

Age Discrimination Act. Law that prohibits employers from not hiring people simply because they are older. (3)

agenda. An order of business that lists activities that will occur during a meeting. (22)

alternatives. Options a person has when making a decision. (8)

Americans with Disabilities Act. Law that prohibits employers from discriminating against people with physical disabilities. (3)

annual percentage yield (APY). The rate (or percent) of yearly earnings from an account; also called *annual yield, interest rate,* and *rate of return.* (26)

annuity. A form of investment that lasts 10 or 15 years and provides insurance as well as savings. (26)

apprenticeship. Occupational training involving learning a trade by working under the direction and guidance of a skilled worker and receiving related classroom instruction and theory. (9)

aptitudes. The natural talents a person has or the potential to learn certain skills easily and quickly. (7)

argumentative. Easily creating arguments. (14)

assets. The valuable possessions a person owns, such as a house or a car. (27)

associate degree. The award granted after completing a two-year college program. (9)

attitude. How you react to a situation. (7)

B

bachelor's degree. The award granted after completing a four-year college or university program. (9)

balanced diet. An intake of food that supplies the body all the necessary nutrients in the needed amounts to maintain good health. (21)

bank statement. A balance sheet listing deposits, withdrawals, service charges, and interest payments on an account with a financial institution. (25)

bill. A proposed law. (31)

body language. A form of nonverbal communication in which a person "speaks" with the use of body movements, facial expressions, and hand gestures. (19)

brainstorming. A way to come up with many ideas in a short time by listing everyone's ideas, no matter how ridiculous the ideas may seem, and then discussing and evaluating them. (14)

budget. A plan for the use or management of money. (24)

C

car pool. A group of people who take turns driving, usually to work. (30)

career. A series of occupations, usually in same or related fields, that help you advance in a chosen field of work. (1)

career clusters. The 16 broad groups of occupational and career specialties. (1)

career ladder. An illustration that shows a sequence of work in a career field, from entry to advanced levels. (1)

career plan. A list of steps a person takes to reach his or her career goals. (10)

career/technical program. A program that teaches students skills necessary for entry-level employment. (9)

career/technical student organization (CTSO). School groups that help students learn more about certain occupational areas. (22)

carrier. An organization that operates a transportation system. (30)

cashier's check. A check drawn on a bank's own funds and signed by an officer of the bank. (25)

certificate of deposit (CD). A savings certificate earning a fixed rate of interest that is purchased for a specific amount of money and held for a set period of time. (26)

certified check. A check for which a bank guarantees payment. (25)

check. A written order instructing a bank to take a specified amount of money out of the account on which the check is drawn and give it to the person whose name appears on the check. (25)

citizen. A person who owes allegiance to a government. (31)

civil laws. Laws that define a person's rights in relation to other people. (31)

closed ad. A classified ad giving general information about a job. (11)

collateral. Something of value held by a lending institution in case a loan is not repaid. (27)

commission. A percentage of the money received from a sale. (16)

communicate. To share ideas, feelings, or information, both verbally and nonverbally. (19)

competition. Two or more parties acting independently to offer the most favorable product or terms. (31)

compound interest. Interest figured on the principal plus the earned interest of a financial account. (26)

compromise. Giving something up to resolve a conflict. (14)

computer revolution. The total change in the way people live and work caused by computers. (2)

concentrate. To focus attention and effort on something. (18)

conflict. Hostile situation resulting from opposing views. (14)

constructive criticism. The process of offering judgmental remarks about you or your work. (14)

cooperative education. A program between schools and places of employment that allows students to receive on-the-job training through part-time work. (4)

corporation. A business that can legally act as a single person, but may be owned by many people. (6)

cosigner. A person who signs a loan with a borrower and is held responsible if the borrower does not pay back the loan. (27)

cost of living. Amount of money needed for rent, food, travel, and other everyday expenses. (4)

credit agreement. A written contract that legally binds a lender and a borrower to specific credit terms. (27)

credit bureau. An organization that gathers financial information on individuals for businesses to use as a credit reference. (27)

credit line. The maximum amount that can be charged on a credit card. (27)

credit rating. An estimate of how likely a person is to pay bills on time based on past records. (27)

D

debit card. A card used to immediately deduct a purchase amount or cash withdrawal from a checking account. (25)

decision. A choice or a judgment. (8)

decision-making process. A seven-step guide for making decisions based on careful thought and planning. (8)

deductible. The amount a policyholder must pay before an insurance company will pay a claim. (28)

degrees Celsius (°C). The basic unit of measuring temperature in the metric system. (17)

demographics. The characteristics or makeup of a population. (2)

dependable. Being reliable. (13)

dependent. A person, such as a child or nonworking adult, who relies on a taxpayer for financial support. (23)

deposit slip. A form filled out before depositing money into a bank account. (25)

direct deposit. Program that allows an employer to deposit a paycheck directly into an employee's account. (26)

disability. A temporary or permanent physical or mental condition that prevents an employee from working. (15)

disability insurance. Insurance that provides for people who become unable to work due to serious illness or injury. It allows disabled employees to receive a percentage of their incomes for an extended period of time. (28)

discrimination. Unfairly treating a person or group of people differently. (3)

dismissal. Another term for being fired. (15)

diversity. The positive result of people of different racial, ethnic, and cultural backgrounds working together. (2)

dividend. A payout, usually annual, on money earned on whole life insurance. (28)

doctoral degree. The most advanced degree, often requiring three years of study beyond a bachelor's degree; also called a doctorate. (9)

dress code. A set of rules that individuals must follow regarding clothing and general appearance. (20)

drug. A chemical substance that brings about physical, emotional, or mental changes in a person. (21)

drug abuse. The use of a drug in a way that can damage a person's health or ability to function. (21)

drug screening. Tests that can reveal the presence of drugs in a person's body. (21)

E

e-commerce. Electronic commerce. (2)

economy. The way goods and services are produced, distributed, and consumed in a society. (1)

education. Gaining knowledge to live and work in today's society. (4)

electronic bulletin boards. These allow you to post and read messages on the computer, acting as a media for the exchange of information among large groups of people, combining the features of electronic mail with private computer conferencing. (11)

e-marketing. Computer technologies combined with marketing and sales of goods and services. (5)

endorse. To sign the back of a check in order to deposit or cash the amount specified. (25)

entrepreneurship. The starting and owning of a person's own business. (6)

entry-level jobs. Jobs that require no previous training. (4)

EOE. Equal Opportunity Employer. (3)

Equal Employment Opportunity Act. A law that makes it illegal for an employer to discriminate because of race, color, religion, sex, or national origin. More recent laws make it illegal to discriminate against people for other reasons, such as disabilities, age, and marital status. (3)

Equal Pay Act. Law that prohibits unequal pay for men and women who are doing essentially the same work for the same employer. (3)

e-tailing. Electronic retailing. (2)

evacuate. To empty or vacate a place in an organized manner for protection. (15)

F

fads. Clothing items or styles that are popular for a very short period of time. (20)

family-friendly programs. Work programs that help employees to balance the demand of work and family. (2)

Family and Medical Leave Act. A law that allows 12 weeks off without pay per year in certain cases to handle special family matters. (3)

Federal Insurance Contributions Act (FICA). An act that allows the federal government to reserve a percentage of a paycheck for social security tax. (23)

feedback. The return of information to a sender by a receiver trying to understand the message. (19)

fire triangle. A symbol representing the three elements that provide the necessary condition for a fire: oxygen, fuel, and heat. (15)

fired. To lose a job because of unacceptable work or behavior. (16)

first aid. Immediate, temporary treatment given in the event of an accident or illness before proper medical help arrives. (15)

fixed expense. Something for which a set amount of money must be paid regularly, such as rent, insurance, or tuition. (24)

flammable liquid. A liquid that can easily ignite and burn rapidly. (15)

flexible expense. An expense that varies in amount and does not occur on a regular basis, such as food, transportation, or entertainment. (24)

flextime. A work schedule that permits flexibility in work hours. (2)

FLSA. The Fair Labor Standards Act is designed to protect the educational opportunities of youth and prohibits their employment in jobs that could endanger their health and safety. (15)

follow-up letter. A brief letter written in business form to thank an interviewer for an interview. (12)

Form W-2. Wage and tax statement, a form showing how much a worker was paid and how much income was withheld for taxes in a given year. (23)

Form W-4. Employee's withholding allowance certificate; a form filled out by an employee when beginning a new job. It determines how much of the employee's pay should be withheld for taxes. (23)

franchise. The right to sell a company's products in specified areas. (6)

free enterprise system. An economy in which individuals and businesses play a major role in making decisions. (2)

fringe benefits. Extra rewards given to workers in addition to salary or wages, such as insurance coverage and paid vacation time. (4)

G

global economy. Goods and services created by companies in one country are sold to customers in other countries. (2)

goals. The aims a person tries to achieve. (10)

gossip. To tell personal information about someone. (14)

graduate degree. An advanced degree requiring education beyond a bachelor's degree. (9)

gram. The basic unit of measuring weight in the metric system. (17)

grapevine. An informal and unofficial flow of information. (14)

grooming. The way in which people take care of themselves. (20)

gross pay. The total amount of money earned during a pay period. (23)

grounded. Connected to the earth to avoid electrical shock. (15)

H

harassment. Doing or saying things that make people feel different or uncomfortable. (14)

health maintenance organization (HMO). A managed health care plan insurance for which members pay a set fee and receive medical care, as needed, from a participating doctor or hospital. (28)

human resources. The resources that people have within themselves. (10)

I

identity. The sum of traits that distinguishes a person as an individual. (1)

identity theft. Theft that occurs when someone uses your personal information, such as your name, social security number, or credit card number without your permission to commit fraud or other crimes. (27)

illiterate. Being unable to read or write. (17)

implement. To put a plan into action. (8)

impulse decision. A decision made quickly, without much thought. (8)

income. The amount of money a person receives for doing a job. (1)

income tax. A tax on all forms of earnings. (23)

insurance claim. Requesting payment from your insurance company for a covered loss. (28)

interest. The money paid to customers for allowing a financial institution to have and use their money. (26)

interests. The ideas, subjects, or activities a person enjoys. (7)

Internet. The global computer linkup of individuals, groups, and organizations in government, business, and education. (2)

intern. A student, seeking skills for a career, who works in a temporary position with an emphasis on on-the-job training rather than employment. (9)

internship. An occupational training program during which a person works at a job, learning from a more experienced person. It can be paid or unpaid, lasting for several weeks, months, or for a year. (4)

interview. A talk between an employer and a job applicant. (12)

interviewee. A job applicant who receives an interview. (12)

interviewer. An employer who talks with a job applicant. (12)

Internal Revenue Service (IRS). The agency that enforces federal tax laws and collects taxes. (23)

IRS time (individual responsibility for saving time). Taking whatever steps are needed to make the best use of time. (18)

J

job. Work a person does, usually to earn money. (1)

job application form. A form completed by a job applicant to provide an employer with information about the applicant's background. (11)

job description. An explanation of tasks to be performed by an employee in a specified position. (12)

job shadowing. Accompanying a person to his or her job to learn about that person's job. (4)

L

laid off. To lose a job because the employer must release the employee for financial reasons. (16)

leader. A person who influences the actions of others. (22)

leadership. The ability to lead or direct others on a course or in a direction. (22)

lease. A written rental agreement, which defines the rights and responsibilities of the tenant and the owner of a rental property. (29)

letter of resignation. A formal letter stating plans to quit or resign from a job. (16)

life insurance. Insurance designed to provide financial security to the family of the insured, if that person dies. (28)

lifelong learning. Continually updating your knowledge and skills. (2)

lifestyle. A person's typical way of life. (1)

liter. The basic unit of measuring volume in the metric system. (17)

logistics. The process of managing, controlling, and moving goods, energy, information, services, or people from a point of origin to a destination in the most timely and cost-efficient manner possible. (5)

M

mass transportation. Transportation, such as buses or trains, used routinely by the general public. (30)

master's degree. An advanced degree involving one to two years of study beyond a bachelor's degree. (9)

mentor. A more experienced person who provides his or her expertise in order to help less-experienced workers advance in their careers, enhance their education, and build networks. (13)

meter. The basic unit of measuring distance in the metric system. (17)

metric system. A decimal system of weights and measures. (17)

money market account. A type of savings account that is similar to a CD, but has no time restrictions. (26)

money order. Used like a check, this is an order purchased for a specific amount to be paid to a certain party. (25)

monopoly. The exclusive possession and control of a product or service. (31)

multitasking. Doing more than one job at a time. (19)

mutual fund. A long-term investment that provides a way to invest in stocks and bonds. (26)

N

needs. The basics a person must have in order to live. (1)

net pay. The amount of money left after all deductions have been taken from the gross pay. (23)

networking. Checking with family, friends, and other people you know to find out about job openings. (11)

nonhuman resources. Time and all the material resources around you. (10)

nonverbal communication. The sending and receiving of messages without the use of words. (19)

nutrient. A chemical substance in food that nourishes the body. (21)

O

occupation. Employment that requires related skills and experiences. (1)

open ad. A classified ad providing specific information about a job. (11)

OSHA. A government agency and a federal law that calls for safe and healthy working conditions. The Occupational Safety and Health Administration is the agency, while the Occupational Safety and Health Act is the law. (15)

outsourcing. The practice of one company contracting with another to handle work more efficiently and keep costs in line. (2)

overdraw. To spend more money than what is in the account. (25)

overtime pay. The wages earned, usually one-and-a-half times the regular wage, for working additional hours beyond the normal 40-hour week. (16)

P

paraprofessional. A trained aid with one to three years of advanced training who assists professionals. (5)

parliamentary procedure. An orderly way of conducting a meeting and discussing group business. (22)

partnership. A business owned by two or more people. (6)

pay period. A length of time for which an employee's wages are calculated. Most businesses have weekly, biweekly, semimonthly, or monthly pay periods. (23)

penalty. A loss or hardship due to some action, such as breaking company rules or policies. (13)

personal interview. A face-to-face meeting between an employer and a job applicant. (12)

personality. The group of traits that makes each person unique. (7)

physical fitness. The ability to easily perform daily tasks with enough reserve energy to respond to unexpected demands. (21)

piecework. A job in which something is produced by an individual that can easily be counted. (3)

policy. A legal contract describing the rights and responsibilities of a person purchasing insurance and those of the company offering it. (28)

portfolio. A selection of materials that you can use to document your accomplishments over a period of time. (11)

preferred provider organization (PPO). A managed health care plan in which an organization of doctors or hospitals contract with an insurance company to provide health services. (28)

premium. The amount of money paid for insurance. (28)

principal. The original investment, such as a savings account deposit. (26)

priorities. Everything you consider highly important. (18)

private employment agency. A business that helps people find jobs for a fee. (11)

privilege. A right that is given as a benefit or favor. (13)

procrastination. Delaying decisions or activities. (18)

profit. The money left in a business after all expenses are paid. (2)

promotion. A move up to a higher position that has increased job responsibilities and requires increased skills and knowledge. (4)

proofread. To read something, check for mistakes, and mark any errors found. (17)

property insurance. Insurance that protects your possessions against fire, theft, or other types of loss. Property insurance also provides liability coverage in the event that someone is injured in your home. (28)

public employment service. A government-supported group that helps people find jobs for free. (11)

public laws. Laws that define a person's rights in relation to government. (31)

punctual. On time. (13)

R

real estate agency. A business that assists customers in the buying and selling, and less often renting, of apartments or houses. (29)

recourse. The right to complain and receive appropriate response. (31)

references. People who can speak about a person's character and skills. (11)

register. To submit one's name to the official list of citizens eligible to vote in elections. (31)

rental agency. A business that assists customers in the renting of apartments for a fee. (29)

reprimand. A severe expression of disapproval. (13)

resource. Anything a person can use to help reach his or her goals. (7)

résumé. A formal written summary of a person's education, work experience, and other qualifications for a job. (11)

retail business. A business that sells products, such as clothing or cars, to consumers. (6)

ridicule. To tease or belittle. (14)

Robert's Rules of Order. The most common reference book used to describe the parliamentary procedure used at business meetings. (22)

routine decision. A decision made often. (8)

rumor. Information passed from one person to another without proof of accuracy. (14)

S

salary. A set amount of money paid to an employee for a full year of work. (16)

sarcasm. The use of cutting remarks. (14)

savings club. A savings plan into which a set amount of money is deposited regularly until a savings goal is reached. (26)

schedule. A list of the expected arrival and departure times and locations for buses, trains, and airplanes. (30)

security deposit. An amount of money usually equal to a month's rent initially paid to the owner of rental property by new tenants. It is used to cover the costs of any damages that may occur during the renter's stay. (29)

self-concept. Recognition of both your strengths and weaknesses. Accepting and feeling good about yourself. (7)

self-esteem. The confidence a person has in himself or herself. (1)

self-sufficient. Individuals who can take care of themselves; who can earn a salary that will support their needs and wants as well as those of their future families. (2)

service business. A business that performs tasks for its customers. (6)

services. Nonmaterial assistance for which people are willing to pay. (2)

sexual harassment. Unwelcome sexual advances, requests for sexual favors, and other verbal or physical conduct of a sexual nature when it is made a condition of employment or of a person's work performance or environment. (3)

skills. Abilities that result from education and training. (4)

sole proprietorship. A business owned by one person. (6)

stockholder. A person who owns a share or shares of stock in a corporation. (6)

stress. A feeling of tension, strain, or pressure. (21)

T

teamwork. Two or more people working toward a common goal. (14)

technology. The application of scientific principles. (2)

telecommuting. Working at home through an electronic linkup with the central office. (2)

telephone interview. A telephone conversation between a company representative and a job applicant. (12)

termination. The end of employment or the loss of a job. (13)

time log. A written record of a person's use of time. (18)

time management. Planning and carefully using time. (18)

trade-off. The giving up of one thing for another. (8)

training. Applying knowledge through practice. (4)

traits. Noteworthy characteristics. (4)

transfer. To change from one bus or train route to another. (30)

transferable skills. Skills used in one career that can be used in another. (1)

traveler's checks. Checks purchased in common denominations that are replaceable if lost or stolen. (25)

U

U.S. savings bond. A certificate of debt issued by the federal government that serves as a safe way to save money. (26)

V

values. All the beliefs, ideas, and objects that are important to an individual. (7)

verbal agreement. The simplest form of an agreement in which certain terms are specified but not written down. (29)

verbal communication. Communication involving the use of words. (19)

vocabulary. The group of words known and used by an individual. (17)

W

wages. The money earned for doing hourly work. (16)

want ad. A source of information about available jobs, found in the classified section of the newspaper. (11)

wants. Items a person would like to have, but are not needed to survive. (1)

wardrobe inventory. A list of all the clothes and accessories found in a person's closet and drawers. (20)

wholesale. A large quantity of items packaged in bulk with a per-item cost below the retail price. (6)

work. An activity done to produce or accomplish something. (1)

workers' compensation. An insurance against loss of income from work-related accidents. (15)

work ethic. A standard of conduct and values for job performance. (13)

working capital. Money needed to start and maintain a business. (6)

A

B

C

D

E

K

L

M

N

O

P

Q

R

S

T

U

V